Help Boxes

The Brief New Century Handbook

Second Edition

CHRISTINE A. HULT
Utah State University

THOMAS N. HUCKIN
University of Utah

PEARSON
Longman

New York   Boston   San Francisco
London Toronto Sydney Tokyo Singapore Madrid
Mexico City Munich Paris Cape Town Hong Kong Montreal

Senior Vice President, Publisher, and Acquisitions Editor: *Joseph Opiela*
Senior Development Editor: *Judith Fifer*
Senior Supplements Editor: *Donna Campion*
Media Supplements Editor: *Nancy Garcia*
Executive Marketing Manager: *Ann Stypuloski*
Senior Production Manager: *Bob Ginsberg*
Project Coordination, Text Design, and Electronic Page Makeup:
    Nesbitt Graphics, Inc.
Cover Design Manager: *Wendy Ann Fredericks*
Cover Designer: *Kay Petronio*
Cover Photo: *Harvey Lloyd/FPG*
Manufacturing Manager: *Dennis J. Para*
Printer and Binder: *Quebecor World Taunton*
Cover Printer: *Coral Graphic Services, Inc.*

For permission to use copyrighted material, grateful acknowledgment is made to
the copyright holders on pp. C-1–C-2, which are hereby made part of this
copyright page.

Library of Congress Cataloging-in-Publication Data

Hult, Christine A.
    The brief new century handbook / Christine A. Hult, Thomas N. Huckin.—
    2nd ed.
        p.   cm.
    Includes index.
    ISBN 0–321–16421–0
        1. English language—Rhetoric—Handbooks, manuals, etc.   2. English
    language—Grammar—Handbooks, manuals, etc.   3. Report writing—
    Handbooks, manuals, etc.   I. Huckin, Thomas N. II. Title

    PE1408.H6877   2003
    808'.042—dc21

                                                            2003041027

Please visit our Website at http://www.ablongman.com/hult

ISBN 0-321-16421-0

12345678910—WCT—06050403

IT'S A NEW CENTURY!

Today we communicate with friends and colleagues more frequently and quickly than ever before; through email, Web sites, chat rooms, and instant messaging, the written word connects us all. *The Brief New Century Handbook*, Second Edition, will help you get your message across more effectively than ever before.

And in this edition of *The Brief New Century Handbook*, you get the power of technology FREE with your text.

- With this book, you'll receive the **Longman CompSolutions** plus **Interactive Ebook CD-ROM** that contains video clips that show ways to best use technology in writing; audio clips that deliver additional explanation from the authors aloud; exercises that help you develop and refine your skills in grammar, punctuation, and the mechanics of writing; and links directly to Web sites that provide supplementary information and explanations, as well as ways to practice what you learn in the text. Look for the icons in the margin of the text and the CD that indicate where to access this additional material.

- Also free with your text is an amazing **Companion Website**, at http://www.ablongman.com/hult that provides additional coverage of many of the book's important topics, writing assignments, and even more grammar exercises, links to related Web sites with guidance about where to find the best material for your needs in these Web sites, and much, much, much more! Look for the Web site icons in the margin of the text and the CD that indicate where to access this additional material.

How to Find It

There are a number of different ways to quickly locate the text sections you need:

- The **Quick Reference Guide**, on the book's inside front cover, provides a quick guide to the Handbook's entire contents.

- The colored **Tabs** that divide the sections provide a quick and easy way to turn to the section you need.
- The full **Table of Contents** on the book's inside back cover provides a listing of all of the sections of the book, with corresponding page numbers.
- **Chapter** and **section numbers, running heads,** and **page numbers** will all help direct you to your topic.
- The **Index** provides an alphabetical listing of every key term and topic in the Handbook, as well as the precise pages on which it is covered.

Colored tabs printed at the top of each page identify the chapter number and title (abbreviated) and the number of the section.

Running heads indicate the topic covered on a particular page.

Section numbers display the chapter number and letter corresponding to a particular topic and heading.

Margin icons identify an Audio, Video, or Web resource that can be accessed via the FREE companion CD-ROM.

Web links provide the exact addresses of important writing resources on the Internet.

Cross references direct you to related information elsewhere in the text.

Boldfaced terms are defined in the text and in the Glossary.

Subsection numbers identify topics within a section.

With all of these features, and more (CD-ROM, audio, video, and Web links, HELP boxes that provide detailed

---

Get to know the Internet and the Web   net **8b**   115

8a   Use Internet sources throughout the research process

AUDIO
The importance of Internet research.

Searching the Internet for information on a topic is similar in many respects to researching in the library. When beginning to research on the Internet, you should follow a search strategy, as outlined in 7a-5. Use the Internet for finding and exploring research topics, for background and focused searching, and even for collaboration with your peers and feedback from your instructor. Email and online discussion forums are ideal for trying out your topic ideas on your instructor and your peers. As you research and write your paper, take advantage of the forums the Internet provides for sharing information—trade ideas, drafts, research sources, and revision feedback. For more information on collaboration, see 2c, 3c, and 4e.

WEBLINK

http://www.lib.berkeley.edu/TeachingLib/Guides/index.html
Current information on Internet searching, from UC Berkeley librarians

WWW
8.1
Read this before starting an electronic search.

8b   Get to know the Internet and the Web

The **World Wide Web,** or the **Web** for short, is by far the easiest and most popular way of accessing information from the Internet. The Web provides a hypertext interface for "reading" Internet information. This means that information is presented in the form of a series of **links,** each leading to another document or another location on the Internet. Documents structured as text with a series of links to other texts are called **hypertexts.** One simply uses a mouse to click on the link (usually a graphic or a word or phrase in blue type with blue underlining) to connect with the hyperlinked document. Researchers navigate the Web through the use of an Internet browser. Two of the most popular browsers today are *Netscape Navigator* and *Internet Explorer*.

WWW
8.2
A tutorial and Internet research guide.

1 Surfing the World Wide Web: Browser tools and homepages

The World Wide Web, a huge spider web–like structure that encompasses computer networks throughout the world, seems to have been woven overnight. But no one spider wove this web; anyone and

---

instructions for computer functions, FAQs on each tabbed section page), you can see why *The Brief New Century Handbook*, Second Edition, is a resource that you'll want to consult time and again.

Preface

It is clear that computers have influenced our lives immensely—at home, at work, and at school. Most students these days do their writing on a computer in order to take advantage of the unique features afforded by word-processing software. They also make extensive use of the Internet—gathering information from the World Wide Web and communicating via email. It is logical that a handbook for writers should take such developments into account. Many college students have found that they need a handbook that provides guidance on using computers as an effective tool in the writing process. *The Brief New Century Handbook*, Second Edition meets this need.

WRITING

The first part of this handbook shows students how to apply critical reading and writing processes to their own work. In Chapter 1, student writers learn about critical thinking and the reading and writing processes. In Chapter 2, students explore means of finding topics through Internet searches; ways to brainstorm potential topics; and how to harness the power of computers to focus, develop, and organize ideas. In Chapter 3, students learn techniques for combining prewriting and outlining documents, for building a first draft from an electronic outline, and for composing with documents in two separate windows. In addition, the chapter encourages students to collaborate online with other student writers, using email and newsgroups. Chapter 4 guides students through the steps required to rewrite their work efficiently and effectively—from comparing and revising drafts to editing for effective wording and sentence structure. The next two chapters are devoted to two fundamental issues in writing academic papers: structuring paragraphs and formulating arguments. Chapter 5 explains how to construct paragraphs that guide readers through the text. Chapter 6 emphasizes the importance of audience analysis, sound reasoning, and considering alternative points of view; it explains how to devise an appropriate thesis and how to support that thesis with appropriate evidence.

RESEARCH

In addition to covering the research process, this handbook addresses how computers can facilitate researching and writing. Chapter 7 covers innovations such as computerized notebooks and note cards, document comments, footnote and bibliography software, Boolean searching, and online databases. Two chapters explain how to use sources on the World Wide Web. Chapter 8 shows students how to use the Internet to explore ideas, find topics, and conduct background and focused research. Chapter 9 helps students assess the credibility and reliability of sources they find in print and on the Internet. An entire chapter (Chapter 10) covers the use of appropriate and effective sources, offering guidance on avoiding plagiarism and on quoting, summarizing, and paraphrasing. In Chapter 11, students learn to plan, organize, draft, review, revise, and format research papers using their computers. Chapters 12 and 13 cover MLA, APA, CMS, and CBE documentation styles, and specific information on how to integrate sources and avoid plagiarism within these documentation formats. In addition to supplying explanations and illustrations of how to document conventional sources, this handbook provides extensive coverage of electronic sources.

DOCUMENT DESIGN

With the increased availability of computer graphics software, the "look" of documents has become more important than ever. Chapter 14 describes three basic design principles and explains how various formatting tools (such as itemized lists, frames, and columns) can be used to put these principles into practice. The chapter also discusses common types of graphical displays. Chapter 15 teaches students how to apply basic principles when designing Web pages. In this chapter, students learn the important ways in which Web texts differ from print texts and about the process of designing their own Web pages. In Chapter 16, students learn about writing for the Web. They are introduced to HyperText Markup Language (HTML) and receive step-by-step instruction on building a Web page.

SPECIAL PURPOSE WRITING

Part 6 of this handbook covers special types of writing students may encounter, from email to essay exams. Chapter 17 discusses the use of email and covers topics such as email addresses, email etiquette, instant messaging, and how to send file attachments. Chapter 18 gives students help in writing about literary topics. Chapter 19 provides basic instruction on writing letters, résumés, memos, and other forms of business correspondence. This chapter also devotes special attention to scannable résumés and homepage résumés. A new Chapter 20 teaches students how to prepare oral presentations. Chapter 21 covers essay exams.

GRAMMAR AND STYLE

Parts 7 through 11 of this handbook provide comprehensive coverage of grammar and style, including traditional topics such as sentence structure, pronoun case, subject-verb agreement, consistency, conciseness, parallelism, word choice, spelling, and punctuation. Because students are likely to use this material selectively, discussions and explanation are concise and various devices (such as consistent formatting, FAQs, and a comprehensive index) make it easy for students to look up a topic.

The handbook's unique emphasis on computers is continued throughout this section. Warnings about the shortcomings of style/grammar checkers are accompanied by suggestions about special ways to make good use of such checkers. Help boxes enumerate ways to search for particular style/grammar problems, use an electronic thesaurus, customize and streamline spell checking, and identify punctuation problems. In addition, the text includes many references to helpful Web sites.

ESL students will benefit as much as native-speaking students from the material presented in Part 12 of this handbook. Four chapters address specific ESL issues: the use of definite and indefinite articles (Chapter 50), verbs (Chapter 51), word order (Chapter 52), and vocabulary (Chapter 53).

NEW TO THIS EDITION

In writing the second edition, we listened to feedback from users of the first edition to make *The Brief New Century Handbook* even more useful. There are many revisions and substantive changes throughout the book to ensure that it remains the most current and up-to-date handbook on the market. Here are some major changes listed by chapter:

- Chapter 1, "Thinking and Reading Critically," features extensive new material on critical thinking and reading.
- Chapter 2, "Preparing," has expanded coverage of narrowing a topic, formulating a working thesis, and evaluating and revising a thesis, as well as new information on preparing a revision outline.

- Chapter 4, "Rewriting," features a new Help box that instructs students how to insert comments into a document for peer review.
- Chapter 6, "Constructing and Evaluating Arguments," has a new section on Visual Argument and an essay on Cyber-censorship. Also new to this edition is a section on Electronic Argument and a new section on Inductive vs. Deductive Reasoning.
- Chapter 7, "The Research Project," includes an expanded discussion of taking notes with photocopies and printouts and also features a new discussion of using library electronic full-text databases.
- Chapter 8, "Using the Internet for Research," contains the latest information on Internet browser tools, keeping track of your Internet search, understanding URLs, respecting copyright, and avoiding plagiarism. Coverage on using search tools effectively has also been considerably expanded and updated.
- Chapter 9, "Evaluating Electronic and Print Sources," includes updated coverage to help students discriminate among sources.
- Chapter 10, "Using Sources and Avoiding Plagiarism," has been totally revised to provide the guidance students need to avoid plagiarism, especially in the electronic age. Many new examples and illustrations are also included.
- Chapter 11, "Writing the Research Paper," outlines the process that a student followed when drafting her paper and refining her argument about cyber-shopping. The new model paper whose progress is followed in this chapter is located in Chapter 12 to illustrate MLA documentation.
- Chapters 12 and 13, "MLA Documentation" and "APA, CMS, and CBE Documentation," have been completely updated and expanded with many new models for electronic sources. Students will easily be able to find all the documentation styles for their bibliographies, particularly for citing Internet sources. The newest MLA (2003) and APA (2001) styles have been included. Each section also includes specific guidance on integrating sources and avoiding plagiarism.
- Chapters 14, 15, and 16 on Document Design have all been updated to include the latest information on design principles, graphics, designing and writing for the Web.
- Chapters 17 through 21, Special Purpose Writing, include a new section in Chapter 17 on Instant Messaging, and a new Chapter 20 on how to give an oral presentation, including the use of *PowerPoint* and other related tools.
- Chapter 50, "Tips on Nouns and Articles," has a new summary flow chart on ESL article usage.

COMPUTER FEATURES

Chief among this handbook's computer features are the Help boxes. Appearing throughout the handbook, these special boxes provide clear, succinct computer advice and explanations. On the backs of the tabbed pages are FAQs, or Frequently Asked Questions, many of which concern the use of computers in writing. The Weblinks are yet another unique feature of this handbook. Dozens of these links, scattered throughout the handbook, provide Internet addresses for valuable writer's resources. Additionally, within the text itself are several sample computer screens, which illustrate various points about computers or the Internet. At the end of the handbook, along with other useful glossaries, is a glossary of computer terms.

ACKNOWLEDGMENTS

We wish to acknowledge and thank the many people who helped to make *The Brief New Century Handbook*, Second Edition a reality. In addition to those specifically mentioned below, we owe a debt of gratitude to the researchers and writers in the fields of rhetoric, composition, and linguistics whose work informs our own.

We acknowledge and thank the entire team at Longman, who supported this handbook from the beginning. Specifically, we would like to thank Joseph Opiela, whose vision for this book both inspired its early beginnings and continued to shape it through development. To our developmental editors, Allen Workman, Ellen Darion and Judith Fifer, whose hands-on, in-the-trenches writing feedback made us write better and work harder, we owe our thanks as well. To the production editor, Bob Ginsberg, and his supporting staff, including many designers, copyeditors, and proofreaders, we are grateful for the careful attention to design and details that make this handbook inviting and accessible. Finally, we wish to thank our capable research assistants, Jana Kay Lunstad and Michelle van Tassel.

Throughout the handbook, we stress the principle that writing is not a solitary act, but rather is collaborative in the best sense of the term. Writers need feedback from readers in order to communicate better. We benefited tremendously from the timely feedback of the many reviewers who read our manuscript. In particular, we would like to thank those reviewers who helped us with the text revision: John Clark, Bowling Green State University; Ray Dumont, University of Massachusetts, Dartmouth; Lynne R. Graft, Saginaw Valley State University; Susanmarie Harrington, Indiana University-Purdue University, Indianapolis; Susan Lang, Texas Tech University; Todd Lundberg, Cleveland State University; Richard Marback, Wayne State

University; Bill Newmiller, United States Air Force Academy; Matthew Parfitt, Boston University; Kathryn Raign, University of North Texas; Scott R. Stankey, Anoka Ramsey Community College; Patty Strong, Virginia Commonwealth University; Scott A. Topping, Southwestern Michigan College; Mary Trachsel, University of Iowa; Katherine Wright, Northern Illinois University; and Jane Zunkel, Portland Community College. We are grateful to Kathy Fitzgerald, Utah State University, for help with a computer cross-platform review; Eric Hoffman, Northern Illinois University, for help with the Web links; and Joe Law, Wright State University, for help with the documentation chapters.

In addition, we would like to thank: H. Eric Branscomb, Salem State College; Susan Brant, Humboldt State University; Deborah Burns, Merrimack College; Joseph Colavito, Northwestern State University; Linda Daigle, Houston Community College; Carol David, Iowa State University; Kitty Chen Dean, Nassau Community College; Keith Dorwick, University of Illinois at Chicago; Scott Douglass, Chattanooga State College; John W. Ferstel, University of Southwestern Louisiana; Robert W. Funk, Eastern Illinois University; Casey Gilson, Broward Community College; Gordon Grant, Baylor University; Joseph Janangelo, Loyola University of Chicago; Michael Keller, South Dakota State University; Thomas P. Klammer, California State University at Fullerton; Richard Louth, Southeastern Louisiana University; Richard Marback, Wayne State University; Lawrence Millbourn, El Paso Community College; Kevin Parker, Orange Coast College; Donna Reiss, Tidewater Community College; Susan Romano, University of Texas at San Antonio; Jack Scanlon, Triton Community College; Allison Smith, Louisiana Technical University; Nancy Stegall, Devry Institute of Technology; Nancy Traschsel, University of Iowa; Audrey Wick, University of Texas at Arlington; and Donnie Yielding, Central Texas College.

We were fortunate to have in our classes student writers who were willing to share their fine work with us—and with the larger readership of this handbook. Student writers whose work appears in these pages include Brandy Blank, Wensdae Miller, Angela Napper, Wyoma Proffit, Heather Radford, Kirsten Reynolds, Sarah Smith, and Kaycee Sorensen.

Lastly, we say thanks to our friends and families who supported us in our personal lives so that we could free up the time and the energy to work on this challenging project. Specifically, we wish to thank our respective spouses, Nathan Hult and Christiane Huckin, and our children, Jen and Justin Hult and Jed and Neil Huckin.

CHRISTINE A. HULT
THOMAS N. HUCKIN

Writing

FAQs

▶ **Chapter 1**

What is critical thinking? (1a)
How do I read critically? (1b)

▶ **Chapter 2**

How do I decide what to write about? (2a)
How can brainstorming help? (2b-1)
What is a thesis, and why do I need one? (2d)
Can my computer help me outline? (2d-5)

▶ **Chapter 3**

Why should I review my prewriting? (3a)
How do I get over writer's block? (3b)
Can a computer help me collaborate? (3c)

▶ **Chapter 4**

Can I be an objective reader of my own writing? (4a)
How can the computer help me revise and edit my
    writing? (4b, 4c)
How do I proofread on screen? (4d)
How do I give effective feedback to my peers? (4e)

▶ **Chapter 5**

What is a topic sentence, and why is it important in my
    writing? (5a)
How long should my paragraphs be? (5f)
How should I link my paragraphs together? (5g)

▶ **Chapter 6**

What's the difference between a convincing argument and a
    personal opinion? (6a-1)
What makes a good, arguable thesis? (6a)
What's a *non sequitur?* (6g-3)
How can I make a good argument online? (6h)

CHAPTER 1

Thinking and Reading Critically

Throughout your life, you have been reading and writing—formally at school and work, informally with family and friends. The processes of reading and writing are closely interrelated. We read and write to understand our world, to communicate with others, and to share our thoughts and ideas. Everyone can improve both reading and writing abilities through practice.

As a college student, you have a unique opportunity to practice your reading and writing skills. Much college work revolves around the processes of reading and writing. Academic knowledge is both created and shared through these processes. Whether your course of study is mathematics or sociology or engineering, reading and writing are intimately involved in learning. You read to understand what others think and say about a topic; you write to share what you have learned or understand about a topic. This is how knowledge progresses.

AUDIO
Reading, writing, and thinking overlap.

1a Think critically

A term often used to describe the way in which educated people approach knowledge building is *critical thinking*. To think critically is to make a conscious effort to delve beneath the surface of things. Much of the process of obtaining a college education is designed to help you become a more critical thinker. The term *critical* in this case does not mean the same as *criticize*. Critical thinking does not imply a negative attitude; rather, critical thinking involves the ability to contemplate, question, and explore ideas in depth without accepting easy answers. When you identify the political propaganda as you listen to a political speech on your campus, you exhibit critical thinking. When you recognize the overblown claims for a product in an advertisement in the local newspaper, you also exhibit critical thinking. The processes involved in thinking critically are the same for all aspects of communication—speaking and writing as well as listening and reading.

1 Establishing your purpose and raising questions

The key first step in critical thinking is to have a clear sense of purpose. *Why* are you interested in this topic? Why do you want to learn about it in depth? What specific aspects of the topic most concern you? What is your goal? Having a clear sense of purpose is crucial, because it will guide you through the entire process of critical thinking. Among other things, knowing your purpose will allow you to formulate more specific questions about the topic. And these questions will help focus your exploration.

For example, let's say you're in the market for a used (or "pre-owned," as they say in the trade) car. If you're a careful buyer, you won't just head for the nearest used car lot and let yourself be talked into the first car that catches your eye. It's more likely that you'll do some research—by reading *Consumer Reports,* talking to your parents or knowledgeable friends, showing the car to a trusted mechanic, and so on. And if you know what kind of car you're looking for and why, you'll probably ask the right kinds of questions to elicit the kind of information you need to make a wise decision.

2 Analyzing the topic

Analyzing something means mentally dividing it into its parts. Sometimes, when the subject being analyzed has obvious component parts, this dividing into parts is straightforward. For example, a music reviewer will conventionally analyze a symphonic performance according to its different movements, and a drama critic will conventionally analyze a play according to its acts and scenes.

But critical analysis usually goes beyond such obvious procedures. Guided by particular purposes and questions (see 1a-1 above), a critical analyst will often see *other* ways to dissect a subject. For example, the music reviewer may choose to analyze the symphony according to the different instruments, and the drama critic may decide to focus on the acting, the costumes, or the sets. The mode of analysis, in short, is not necessarily predetermined by the object of analysis; more often it is governed by the purposes and interests of the analyst.

The purposes and interests of your sources of information should also be taken into account. Analysis often depends to some degree on information provided by other people, who have their own interests, biases, beliefs, and assumptions. As a critical thinker, you should always be aware of other people's orientations and try to keep them in mind as you absorb their information. Information from any source can be lacking in objectivity, so it's a good idea to routinely gather your information from multiple, independent sources and compare them. This is especially true when gathering information from the Web.

3 Synthesizing

Synthesizing is the opposite of analyzing. Instead of taking something apart, synthesis puts things together. But this does not mean that synthesizing merely restores something to the way it was before analysis. Rather, synthesis seeks to find *new* ways of assembling things, *new* relationships among the parts, *new* combinations. Like analysis, this process is governed by the critical thinker's purposes.

For example, let's say you live in the north country and you're looking for a car that will get you back and forth to school through the winter. You have looked at various cars and analyzed them in various ways, but you're uncertain which one is best for you. As you sit back and ponder the situation, you realize that what matters most to you is not the purchase price, the fuel efficiency, or the looks of a car, but rather how suitable it is for winter driving. You want a reliable car that has a good heating/defrosting system, a good ignition system, solid traction (either four-wheel or front-wheel drive) and all-weather tires in decent shape. Also, it should be dark-colored (for better visibility in snow). A combination snowboard/ski rack would be a plus.

This set of features is not one that would emerge from any standard analysis. Rather, it is the result of synthesizing, guided by your own purposes and needs.

4 Making inferences

Another important critical thinking skill is the ability to make inferences or "read between the lines." People often do not say exactly what's on their mind. Sometimes their lack of candor is just an effort to be tactful, sometimes it's due to uncertainty about what to say, sometimes it's more deceptive than that. When you interpret what people don't say, or don't say fully, you are making inferences. For example, if a used-car salesman evades your question about a car's heating system, and you thereby infer that there's something wrong with the heating system, you are exhibiting an important kind of critical thinking. (Note how *purpose* once again plays a key role—in this case, the purpose or intent of the message producer.)

Many of the logical fallacies discussed in 6g—such as the *non sequitur,* either/or reasoning, and begging the question—invite the listener or reader to make *faulty* inferences. The ability to detect such inferences is also a type of critical thinking.

5 Evaluating

1.1
An accessible
introduction to
critical thinking.

Once you've determined your purpose, analyzed your topic, synthesized new ideas, and made appropriate inferences, you are ready to "put it all together," that is, **evaluate** the results. Evaluation involves examining everything you have done up to this point and determining what it all adds up to. In the case of buying a used car, you would want to review what you have learned from going through the first four steps; in particular, you would check to see if the information you have gathered consistently points to the same conclusion. If not, you would want to identify the contradictions and try to resolve them. Perhaps your sources of information are not as knowledgeable as you had thought; perhaps you haven't asked them the right questions. In any case, this activity itself is a form of critical thinking—the willingness to confront and resolve inconsistencies in your reasoning and information gathering.

If at this point there are still troubling inconsistencies in your thinking about the topic, you may want to "change the playing field"—that is, broaden your inquiry. This can be done in either of two ways. First, you can use additional sources of information: talk to more people, consult other publications, gain some more firsthand experience. Alternatively, you can reexamine the initial premises of your investigation. It could be that these have changed in the course of your inquiry—or were never quite accurate in the first place. For example, in your search for reliable transportation that would beat the winter weather, perhaps you went too quickly for a used car when public transit might be just as good or even better. Sometimes it is only at this evaluation stage that nagging discrepancies and uncertainties are resolved and critical thinking fully rewarded.

1b Engage actively and critically in the reading process

VIDEO
Analyzing the
writing
situation.

A good reader reads actively. As you read, your mind must be actively engaged with what your eyes see on the page or on the computer screen. You need to see the text on multiple levels—the words, the sentences, the paragraphs, the text as a whole—and you need to think about how it relates to things *outside* the text, such as where it was published, what you know about the author, who its target audience might be, other readings, and your own life experience. In short, you need to situate the text, and make sense of it, in a context larger than itself.

A good reader also reads critically; that is, he or she reads with an open mind and a questioning attitude. To be a critical reader, you need to go beyond understanding what the author is saying; you need to challenge or question the author. You may question the validity of the author's main point or ask whether the text agrees or disagrees with other writings on the same topic and with your own experience.

1 Reading on three different levels

To fully understand a text, you should read it on three different levels: literal meaning, interpretation, and criticism. As you move from one level to the next, you increase your "resistance" to the text and thereby construct, in your mind, an alternative text.

Reading for Literal Meaning   The literal meaning of a text is its explicit meaning as determined by the words on the page and their conventional meanings. Put another way, it is the "surface" meaning of a text. It comprises all those aspects of a text that are available to anyone who reads that text. Literal meaning does not include insinuations, satire, irony, subjective impressions, tone, or other implicit meanings that must be inferred by the reader. (This type of meaning is discussed below.)

When readers start reading a novel, magazine article, textbook, or other published text, they expect to move from sentence to sentence in a smooth flow of literal meaning. (Certain kinds of poems might be an exception to this.) Authors, of course, are aware of this and work hard to provide "readable" texts. Indeed, there seems to be an implicit understanding among readers and authors that the linguistic surface of a text should be coherent, meaningful, and accessible to all. Since the deeper meanings of a text (see below) are derivative of this literal meaning, before you can engage in interpretive or critical reading you must fully understand the literal meaning of a text. (Use a good dictionary to help you with any words you don't know; see 38b.) At this stage, you should be a *compliant* reader trying to understand the text on its most basic terms. It is no different from a moviegoer enjoying a sci-fi film as sheer entertainment, rather than analyzing it as a movie critic would.

Reading for Interpretation   Once you have grasped the literal meaning of a text, you should go beyond it to the realm of interpretation. At this level, you are seeking a deeper understanding of the author's ideas, point of view, and attitude. You become more conscious of the author's role in constructing the text, giving it a certain "spin," and manipulating the reader. In short, you become a more detached, "resistant," and analytical reader. You look for clues as to what the author has implied rather than overtly stated, what assumptions the author is making, what audience the author seems to be addressing, and what the author's attitude seems to be as revealed by the tone of his or her writing.

This interpretive work should start with certain words, expressions, and statements found in the text, but instead of taking these textual details at face value, you contrast them with alternative words, expressions, and statements that the author opted *not* to use. For example, if an author consistently used the term *fetus* where he or she could have used the alternative term *unborn child,* you might infer that he or she supports reproductive freedom. These two terms have the same denotation but differ in connotation (see 36b); in choosing one term over the other, the author would probably be revealing something about his or her stance on abortion. In reading for interpretation, you should always ask yourself questions such as, "In what other way(s) could the author have said this?" or "What *didn't* the author say here, that he could have?" Usually the easiest way to get started in such analysis is with those words and phrases that draw attention to themselves, for example because they are loaded terms (as in *fetus* vs. *unborn child*), are deliberately "off-register" (see 36c) or figurative (36f), or are punctuated with scare quotes (44b,c).

AUDIO
Finding alternative views.

1.2
Apply your critical reading skills.

Reading Critically Finally, you want to read beyond the literal and interpreted meanings to evaluate the worth of the writing and the validity of the author's ideas or argument. In this mode, you should be even more detached, resistant, and analytical than you were in the interpretive mode. Critical evaluation should be done on two levels, internal and external. With **internal evaluation,** you restrict your attention, as before, to the text itself. This time, though, you focus on the overall logic of the text. Does it hang together? Does it make sense? If the author is making an argument, does it have enough supporting evidence (see 6b)? Does it consider alternative views (6c)? Is it appealing mainly to logic, to authority, or to emotion (6e)? Does it have any fallacies (6g)? With **external evaluation,** you go a step further. Here you evaluate the text against other texts and against your own experience. These other texts could include other writings by the same author—to get a sense of his or her general views or interests—or other writings on the same topic by other authors. Engaging in this kind of comparative analysis allows you to see the text in a larger perspective. This in turn enables you to make

Checklist for Critical Reading

Internal Evaluation

1. Is the text coherent? Does its logic "hang together" and make sense?
2. If it constitutes an argument, is it appealing mainly to logic, to authority, or to emotion (6e)?
3. Does it have enough supporting evidence (see 6b)?
4. Are there any fallacies in the author's reasoning (6g)?
5. Does the author consider alternative views (6c)?

External Evaluation

6. Where was this particular piece of writing published? Does this suggest an ideological slant of any kind?
7. Judging from the author's other writings, what are his or her general views or interests?
8. What purpose or "agenda" might the author have had in writing about this topic?
9. What do other writers have to say about this topic?
10. What might the author have *left out* of the text? Why?
11. How well does the author's representation of the world fit with your own experience?

an informed guess as to any "agenda" the author might have, and should give you insight into the author's purpose in writing the text. It also will make it easier for you to guess what's been *left out* of the text. Most writers who are trying to persuade readers to a particular point of view will tend to avoid mentioning things that might damage their cause. As a critical reader, it is important that you not allow yourself to be manipulated in this way. By looking at other texts and by interrogating your own life experience, you can often make an educated guess as to what's been left unsaid in a particular text.

2 Structuring your reading process

Reading thoroughly on all three levels is crucial to understanding a text well enough to discuss it intelligently and write about it knowledgeably. If you structure your reading process according to the three steps of previewing, reading, and reviewing, you will understand what you read more completely.

Previewing   Begin any reading session by previewing the material as a whole. By looking ahead, you will gain a general sense of what is to come. This sense will help you predict what to expect from the text as you read and will help you better understand what you are reading. Jot down in a journal or notebook any questions that occur to you during previewing.

WWW

1.3

Tips and strategies for academic success.

WEBLINK

http://www.dartmouth .edu/admin/acskills

Help with reading and other academic skills, from Dartmouth College

As you approach a textbook for the first time, look closely at the table of contents to preview the book's main topics. You can also learn the relative importance of topics by scanning the table of contents. Next, preview one chapter. Page through the chapter, reading all chapter headings and subheadings in order to gain a sense of the chapter's organizational structure. Look also at words in boldface or italic print. These words are highlighted because the author considered them especially important. Finally, preview any graphs, charts, or illustrations. These visuals are included to reinforce or illustrate key ideas or concepts in the chapter. You will want to remember these key ideas.

You should also preview shorter works, such as magazine or journal articles, prior to reading them. An article may include subheadings, which provide an idea of the article's structure. Again, look for highlighted words or graphics in the article, since these can provide clues about key ideas. You should read any biographical information about the author, both to note his or her credentials and to determine whether he or she has a particular bias on the subject. As the final step in previewing an article, read the opening and closing paragraphs to get an idea of the author's thesis and conclusion.

Reading   After you preview the text, read it carefully and closely. Pace your reading according to the difficulty of the material—the more difficult the material, the more slowly you should read it. You may find that you need to take frequent breaks if the text is especially dense or contains a lot of new information. You also may find that you need to reread some passages several times in order to understand their meaning. Material assigned for college classes often is packed with information and therefore requires not only slow reading but also rereading. As you read, pay attention to the three levels of meaning (see 1b-1). Do not be surprised if you find yourself having to go back over the text several times—that, too, is an essential part of the reading process.

Reviewing Once you have completed a thorough reading, go back to the text and review it. Pay particular attention to those areas of the text that you previewed. Have the questions you had when previewing been answered? If not, reread the relevant passages. It may help to review the text with a classmate or a study group; discuss the text with your peers to be sure that your understanding conforms with theirs. Talking about the text with others also will help you communicate your understanding in a meaningful way. If your class has a computer bulletin board or online discussion group, post any questions that you still have about the reading. Like discussing the text in groups, writing about the text in such forums will help you articulate your ideas, which will serve you well when you are asked to write about the material more formally, in an essay or exam. To gain a thorough understanding from your reading, plan to review the material several times.

3 Annotating the text while reading

One way to ensure that you are reading critically and actively is to annotate the text as you read. When **annotating** a text, you make summary notes in the margins, and underline or highlight important words and passages. Typically, it is best to preview material before annotating it. Annotating is important during the reading process. Your annotations should summarize the key ideas in the text. Take care, however, not to over-annotate. You need to be selective so that you do not highlight everything in the text.

WEBLINK

http://karn.ohiolink.edu/ ~sg-ysu/process.html
A Web page that breaks the writing process down into a series of steps, one leading to the next

AUDIO
Annotating texts.

CHAPTER **2**

Preparing

Novice and experienced writers tend to devote different amounts of time and attention to preparing. Novice writers often dive right into drafting a final version of their paper. Rather than experimenting, inventing, and planning, they spend most of their time struggling with the writing itself. Many experienced writers, however, spend a great deal of time thinking about what they want to say before they actually begin to write. Learn from these experienced writers—take time to prepare prior to drafting.

Taking sufficient time to prepare will:

- Save you time in the long run
- Make your drafting process much easier
- Help you to develop your ideas more fully

Your computer can help as you prepare for writing. You can designate folders on your computer's hard drive or on a floppy disk to

HELP

2.1
Step-by-step
instructions for
using folders.

How do I organize my files?

1. Using a file management program (such as *Windows Explorer*), create a directory or folder for each course in which you have written assignments (for example, English and History). To create the folders in *Windows Explorer,* click FILE>NEW>FOLDER; or in the FILE MENU of your word-processing program, click "OPEN" and then click on the "CREATE NEW FOLDER" icon.

2. Within each directory or folder, create subdirectories in which to store the work for each assignment.

3. Each time you begin a new writing assignment, save all the work in the appropriate assignment directory or folder.

organize your work. Many operating systems permit you to create a tree-like hierarchy of directories, folders, and document files. Using this capability, you can group related documents in the same location on the hard drive or disk, much as you might store related papers within a folder in a file cabinet. Using the power of computers, you can store the following kinds of information, each in its own folder: the experimental ideas you generate, the prewriting you do, and the preliminary information you gather.

2a Experiment and explore

AUDIO
The importance of experimentation.

During the first phase of the first stage of the writing process, you experiment and explore in preparation for writing. Writers have many ways of experimenting with language and exploring ideas.

1 Deciding what to write about

It is important that you write about something you are interested in, can develop an interest in, are somewhat familiar with, or have questions about. You will write much better if your interest level is high. If you attempt to write about something that you have

HELP

How do I use the Internet to find writing ideas?

1. Use your Internet browser to access a search directory, such as *Yahoo!* that has hierarchical subject categories.

2. On the subject tree, look for categories that interest you or that are related to the assignment you are working on (for example, "entertainment" or "politics").

3. Within each category, search for possible writing ideas. (For example, under "society," you might find the topic "environment" interesting.)

4. Each time you go one level deeper in the subject tree, jot down other categories that might provide possible ideas for you to write about.

WWW
2.2
Details for finding a topic with search engines.

NOTE: Not all search tools use subject trees. Some use only keyword searching. (See Search Tools in Chapter 8.)

www

2.3

A detailed resource for developing a topic

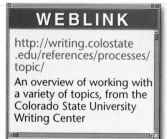

WEBLINK

http://writing.colostate
.edu/references/processes/
topic/

An overview of working with a variety of topics, from the Colorado State University Writing Center

absolutely no interest in, you may find yourself bored before you even begin. However, do not close your mind to topics that are not immediately appealing to you. It is possible to develop interest in something once you know a bit more about it. Use the following suggestions to help you explore some potential ideas to write about.

- Watch educational programs on television (PBS or Discovery).
- Converse with friends, family members, or teachers.
- Think about your own hobbies and interests.
- Think about your employment experiences.
- Think about your college major or other courses you have taken.
- Surf the Net.
- Browse through current periodicals in the library.

2   Considering your rhetorical stance

Once you have selected an area of interest to write about, you can begin to consider the approach that you will take, called your **rhetorical stance.** The term *rhetoric* refers to written or spoken communication that seeks to inform or convince someone of something. The rhetorical stance you adopt for a particular writing assignment reflects the way you define the components of the rhetorical situation: your purpose for writing the piece, your persona (how you wish to come across as a writer), and your readers (audience). You can visualize the rhetorical stance in terms of a triangle, as shown in Figure 2.1.

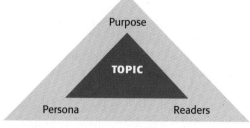

FIGURE 2.1 Rhetorical Triangle

Purpose At the top of the rhetorical triangle is your paper's *purpose*. You need to decide on some general goals for the piece of writing and some strategies for accomplishing these goals. For example, for a newspaper reporter covering an automobile accident, the goal might be to describe the scene clearly for the newspaper's readers. For each writing task, you should determine your purpose. Is it to inform your readers of the current state of knowledge on a subject, to persuade them to accept a particular point of view, to illustrate or describe a scene?

Persona Next you need to consider your **persona**—how you will present yourself to those who will read your work. Do you want to sound objective and fair, heated and passionate, sincere and persuasive, informative and impartial? The term *persona* is used to describe the identity that a speaker or writer adopts and the credibility that the speaker or writer establishes. Just as you play many roles in life, depending on the situation in which you find yourself, you can be flexible about how you portray yourself in your writing, changing your persona with your purpose and readership. For example, a scholarly audience demands a rather formal persona, whereas an audience of your peers probably does not. The language you choose goes a long way toward establishing your persona.

Readers or Audience Finally, try to identify as best you can your *readers or audience*. A piece of writing is often judged by how effectively it reaches its intended audience. Defining your potential audience will help you to make appropriate decisions about what to include in and exclude from your writing. Although your instructors are ultimately the audience for most writing you do in college, you may find yourself writing to others as well. Here are some questions about audience that you need to think through:

VIDEO
Considering the audience.

- Who are your readers likely to be? (Age, sex, income, belief systems, potential biases)
- Are they likely to agree with you, or will you need to persuade them of your point of view?
- What are your readers likely to know? (Educational level, prior knowledge, level of expertise)

2b Invent and prewrite

Writing begins with thinking. The words that appear on your computer screen are the result of the thinking you do prior to and during the writing process. In the prewriting stage, you invent or discover what you want to say about your subject. As the words *invent* and *discover* imply, during this period you delve into your subject, come up with new ideas, connect these new ideas with prior experiences and knowledge, read about and research your subject, and generally allow your thoughts to take shape. All of these activities will help you to decide what you will write.

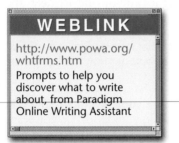

WEBLINK

http://www.powa.org/whtfrms.htm

Prompts to help you discover what to write about, from Paradigm Online Writing Assistant

2.4
The process of topic discovery.

As you prewrite, you can use several techniques to tap your own inner resources and knowledge. Many of these techniques also work well when you begin writing with a partner or in a small group. As we look at each technique, we will suggest ways to use it both on your own and with others.

1 Brainstorming

Brainstorming refers to generating random ideas or fragments of thought about a topic. You are probably familiar with brainstorming from writing classes you have taken in the past. It is possible to brainstorm as a group, calling out ideas to the instructor, who writes them on the blackboard; at a computer, either individually or with another classmate; or in your writing journal, as you jot down your ideas. Here is an example from Kirsten Parsons, a student whose progress we will follow in the next several chapters.

BRAINSTORMING EXAMPLE

Taking information from the Net. Is it legal? Can we swipe graphics? People copying CDs from each other. What is Net theft like? Maybe shoplifting? Copyright laws. Hackers and other Net criminals. What is a criminal? If I copied a graphic, was that a crime? Who are hackers? Do I know any? Are they always criminals? Maybe they're just having fun.

2 Freewriting

Freewriting is related to brainstorming in that it involves writing down thoughts as they come to mind. However, unlike brainstorming, freewriting is typically formulated in connected sentences rather than lists. The idea is to write rapidly in an informal style without conscious regard to details of usage, spelling, and punctuation. It is possible to freewrite with pen and paper or at the computer. Using either your word-processing program or a writing journal, you can freewrite on a topic to generate ideas and to discover information stored in your mind. After freewriting on a particular topic for five or ten minutes without stopping, read over your freewriting. As you read it, you may see relationships between ideas that you had not seen before. If you were freewriting at the keyboard, you can CUT and PASTE in order to group related ideas. If you were freewriting with pen and paper, circle important ideas and use arrows to show relationships.

3 Invisible writing

Invisible writing is a computer freewriting technique designed to release you from the inhibitions created by seeing your own words on the computer screen (see the Help box on writing invisibly). Compulsive revisers find it difficult to ignore the errors they see on the screen and so are unable to write freely at the computer. When you write invisibly, your words do not appear on the screen, so you are free to generate ideas without interruption. You can concentrate on the emerging thoughts rather than on the form those thoughts are taking.

HELP

How do I write invisibly?

You can reduce your anxiety about writing by turning off the computer's monitor.

1. On your computer, open a document in which to store your invisible freewriting.

2. Close down any other open windows or applications on your computer. (You do not want to lose valuable data if you should accidentally hit the wrong key.)

3. Turn down the contrast or turn your monitor off altogether, thus making your writing invisible.

4. When you have finished freewriting, turn the monitor back on and read what you have written.

2.5
Step-by-step instructions for writing invisibly.

4 Clustering

Clustering is a prewriting technique that can help you to see relationships among the ideas you have generated in brainstorming or freewriting exercises. You begin a clustering session by putting your topic, in the form of a word or a phrase, in the middle of a sheet of paper. Then, attach to your topic other words or phrases that come to mind, linking and connecting related ideas or subtopics. When you cluster, you free associate from one word or phrase to another, allowing your mind to trigger related ideas that may not have occurred to you before. When you have finished your clustering activity, look at the results closely for any new insights you might have uncovered. The results of Kirsten's clustering session on the topic of Net theft are shown in Figure 2.2.

5 Debating

Debating is a prewriting technique that can help you to explore a controversial issue from all sides. You might begin by writing down all the generalizations you can think of about the topic—either handwriting them in your journal or typing them into a computer file. For example, if you were writing about Net theft, you could list both pro and con arguments, writing contrasting general statements that could then be supported through examples and evidence:

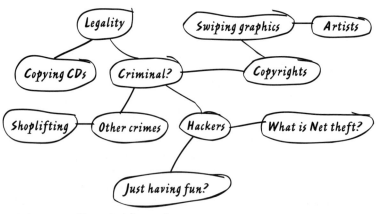

FIGURE 2.2 Clustering Example

PRO

1. Using other people's work from the Net is just another form of sharing.

2. The Internet should be "free." To regulate it goes against its very nature.

3. When people put their ideas out on the Internet, they should just assume they're public.

CON

1. Authors and artists who publish on the Internet should not have their work "stolen."

2. "Borrowing" creative ideas, texts, and graphics from the Net is a form of stealing.

3. Net theft is the same thing as shoplifting.

Under each general heading or statement, you then can insert examples or evidence to support the generalization. In this way, you build your arguments and counterarguments. If you generate your lists using a word-processing program, you can add to, delete, replace, and rearrange the information. The general statements and evidence you accumulate while debating the topic can be used to start an outline or an exploratory draft of your paper.

2c Gather information

Particularly if your assignment is to write a research paper, you will need to supplement whatever prewriting techniques you use by gathering information from external sources. The ideas you read about and formulate will lead you into a more systematic and extensive search that is focused on a specific topic. If your writing task involves a significant research component, refer to Chapters 8–10 for guidance.

AUDIO
Gathering preliminary sources.

There are several informal ways you can begin to gather information for your paper. You can discuss your ideas with classmates, friends, family members, and professors, who may be able to provide you with information. Browsing through periodicals in the current periodicals section of your library will tell you whether your topic is currently under discussion in the media. Or, you can use a search engine to browse the Internet, trying out a variety of keywords and subjects. As you begin your informal, preliminary research on a topic, you will also want to begin taking notes.

2d Plan and organize

Once you have explored your topic, done some prewriting, and consulted a few sources, you are ready to begin thinking about a logical order in which to present the ideas you have developed. The structure of your paper will be influenced by all of the items shown in the rhetorical triangle in Figure 2.1 (purpose, persona, readers). No matter how good your information, if your paper is not organized, your readers will not be able to understand what you are trying to say.

1 Narrowing your focus

Through prewriting, you develop an awareness of what you do and do not know about a topic. As you look back at your prewriting, think about ways in which you could narrow your topic to a manageable size. Think of any subdivisions there might be within the topic. Try to write down in one sentence what you take to be your specific, narrow topic.

For example, through brainstorming and clustering, Kirsten discovered that her broad topic of Net theft could be subdivided into legal issues, ethical issues, crimes on the Net, computer hackers, and so on. Out of all the possible subtopics, Kirsten decided to narrow the focus of her topic to the practice of "borrowing" information from the Internet.

2 Formulating a working thesis statement

AUDIO
Develop a
working thesis
statement.

Once you have written down your narrow topic, try to state in one or two sentences the main point you want to make about that topic. This will be your working **thesis statement.** A thesis statement concisely identifies the topic and main point of a piece of writing. Many writers like to formulate a working thesis statement early in the writing process (see 6a). Your working thesis should ideally have two parts: the first part defines the specific topic to be covered in the essay and the second part makes a strong point about the topic.

For her working thesis, Kirsten wrote a two-part sentence that defined the specific topic and articulated her main point.

KIRSTEN'S WORKING THESIS

When it comes to "borrowing" information from the Internet, we are gradually becoming a people that can accept lawbreaking as long as we can participate, too.

An effective thesis statement defines the specific topic and makes a strong point about it. It also provides the reader with a blueprint for the direction the paper will take. In other words, the thesis not only states the writer's opinion on the topic but also indicates how the writer intends to support that opinion. Kirsten's thesis implies that her essay will explain how borrowing information from the Internet is a kind of lawbreaking that society has begun to accept.

3 Evaluating and revising your working thesis

To evaluate your working thesis, ask yourself the three questions outlined in Evaluating a Working Thesis. Your answer to each of these three questions should be "yes." If it is not, you will need to revise your thesis accordingly. You may need to revise your working thesis several times as you draft your paper. This is why it is called a "working thesis": it can be clarified, modified, or even completely rewritten during the course of your writing process. Allow your thesis to evolve with your understanding of the topic.

WEBLINK

http://writing.colostate.edu/references/processes/topic/pop2j.cfm
Information about moving from a topic to a thesis, from the Colorado State University Writing Center

2.6

A guide to developing your thesis.

4 Organizing your information

In addition to constructing an effective thesis, another step in coming up with a blueprint for your paper's structure is to revisit your rhetorical stance, since your persona, purpose, and readers will also influence how you arrange information in your text. There is no one right way to organize material. However, since human beings habitually organize experience on the basis of time, space, and logic, these three factors often influence the organization of written work.

Organizing by *time* usually implies imposing a chronological order on information, whereas organizing by *space* implies a visual

Evaluating a Working Thesis

Below are three important questions to ask regarding your working thesis:

1. Does the thesis define a specific topic?
2. Does the thesis make a strong point about the topic?
3. Does the thesis provide a blueprint for the paper's development?

Sample Working Thesis 1: When it comes to "borrowing" information from the Internet, we are gradually becoming a people that can accept lawbreaking as long as we can participate, too.

Q1. The specific topic is borrowing information from the Internet.

Q2. The main point is that people accept lawbreaking if they can participate, too.

Q3. This thesis implies that the paper will explain how we have accepted lawbreaking in the Internet arena. We expect it to explain how easy it is for everyone to "participate" in this kind of lawbreaking.

Sample Working Thesis 2: Logging forests is a waste of resources.

Q1. This thesis is too broad and does not specify which forests are being discussed or in what ways they are being wasted. A broad thesis can be focused by using the journalists' questions: who, what, when, where, why, and how.

Q2. The main point of the thesis is not clear. The writer's opinion that logging is "a waste of resources" needs to be supported in the thesis; for example, "Logging is a waste of resources because . . . ."

Q3. It is not clear how the writer intends to develop this thesis.

orientation. Logical organization, the most frequently used pattern, is discussed in Chapter 5. With any logical organizational pattern, you are providing your reader with a familiar way of ordering experience.

HELP

How do I use a word processor's outline feature?

2.7

Step-by-step instructions for outline formatting.

1. With your word processor in OUTLINE mode, begin the outline (VIEW>OUTLINE).

2. Be sure to set the levels within your outline, as well as the outline style (FORMAT>BULLETS AND NUMBERING>OUTLINE NUMBERED).

3. Use the outliner's PROMOTE and DEMOTE features to move headings to different levels. Use the STYLE box to select the outline levels.

4. Rearrange major sections as needed by using CUT and PASTE.

5. When you have finished, end the OUTLINE feature (VIEW>NORMAL) and save your work.

NOTE: Programs differ in the ways they change levels and add text. Check your online HELP for details.

5 Writing an outline

Once you have decided which organizational pattern best suits your working thesis, you may find it useful to construct an outline for your paper. You need not be overly concerned with formal outline structure at this point, unless your teacher stipulates a particular outline format. An outline should serve as a guide as you write—not a constraint that confines and limits your thinking.

AUDIO

Outlines are flexible writing tools.

Formal Outlines A formal outline is typically structured in a conventional hierarchy, with numbered and lettered headings and subheadings. A formal outline can be either a topic outline, in which words or phrases are used, or a sentence outline, in which complete sentences are used.

VIDEO

Outlining with a word processor.

Formal Outline Pattern

Thesis Statement:

I. First main idea

   A. First subordinate idea

      1. First example or illustration

       2. Second example or illustration
         a. First supporting detail
         b. Second supporting detail
    B. Second subordinate idea
  II. Second main idea

Informal Outlines Informal outlines are not structured as rigidly as formal outlines. For example, in a formal outline, you are not allowed to have a number one subheading unless there is also a number two subheading. Informal outlines allow you to create any hierarchies you like, without paying close attention to issues of format.

Informal Outline Pattern

Thesis Statement:

First main idea
    Subordinate idea
        Example or illustration 1
        Example or illustration 2
Second main idea
    Subordinate idea

6 | Preparing a revision outline

One technique that may help you evaluate a piece of writing is preparing a revision outline. When you have a first draft and perhaps some peer or instructor comments on it, you can create a revision outline by updating the original outline for the piece to reflect the weaknesses of the draft. To begin to plan for revising, add comments in brackets to the revision outline concerning items you need to change in your draft. Kirsten used this revision outline to plan changes to her first draft on Net theft:

KIRSTEN'S REVISION OUTLINE

Net Theft

Thesis: When it comes to "borrowing" information from the Internet, we are gradually becoming a people who can accept lawbreaking as long as we can participate, too.

    I. Introduction

       A. Scenario

B. Definition of Net theft [I need to focus this better to correspond with my thesis.]

C. Thesis

II. Different medium, same crime

A. Compare to shoplifting

B. Compare difficulty of each crime

III. Standards of honor

A. Describe what is legal [I really don't do this very well. Need to expand this section to show where the law stands now.]

B. Ten commandments for computers [This section doesn't really fit the focus of the paper. Maybe just mention it.]

IV. Redefining a criminal

A. Why Net theft is accepted [I need to eliminate examples that don't fit the focus. Concentrate on why it's so widely accepted.]

B. What should we do about it? [I need a strong conclusion that restates the problem with Net theft and what--if anything--should be done about it.]

CHAPTER **3**

Composing

After paying conscious attention to prewriting and planning, you are ready to begin composing—that is, writing a first draft of your text. Of course, you already have done considerable writing—

through your brainstorming and freewriting, for example, and through your planning and outlining. But when we talk about composing a draft, we are speaking more specifically about the stage in the writing process when you put your ideas down in the form of connected sentences and paragraphs. To write your first draft, you may use pen and paper, a typewriter, a word processor, or some combination of these tools. Your first draft will be necessarily tentative and exploratory. It is important to understand that an effective piece of writing proceeds through a number of drafts, each of which is improved through revision. We discuss the revision process at length in Chapter 4.

3.1

Thorough introduction to the writing process.

WEBLINK

http://web.uvic.ca/wguide/Pages/StartHere.html

An introduction to various elements of the writing process

3a Review

When composing your first draft, you use the information and ideas you generated in your prewriting, as well as your working thesis and outline. In the composing stage of the writing process, your concern shifts from experimenting with ideas and gathering information to expanding on your ideas and structuring them into effective, coherent prose. Review that crucial prewriting information before you begin composing your first draft.

1 Reviewing your prewriting

You can use your prewriting as the raw material for your first draft. If you recorded your prewriting in an electronic journal, begin by printing it out. Reading your prewriting in a printed format may spark fresh thoughts about the ideas you have generated. If your prewriting is in a handwritten journal or notebook, reread the journal entries. As you read, jot down notes in the notebook margin or enter notes at the bottom of the page in your computer journal. If one idea stands out, highlight it using a marker or the highlighting function on your computer.

3.2
Step-by-step instructions for managing files.

HELP

How do I work with word-processing files and documents?

The FILE menu of many word-processing programs is used to work with documents (sometimes called "files"). Listed below are some of the options provided with the FILE menu. Many of these options are also included as icons on the standard toolbar.

NEW—begin a blank document or document template.

OPEN—open an existing document.

CLOSE—close an open document.

SAVE—save a new document with an appropriate name.

SAVE AS—save an existing document with a new name.

SAVE AS A WEB PAGE—save a word-processing document as a Web page.

PAGE SETUP—format a document's margins, paper size, page orientation, and so on.

PRINT PREVIEW—view the page as it will look when printed.

PRINT—send the document to a printer.

SEND TO—email or fax the document.

PROPERTIES—identify the document's writer, track its length, and so on.

LIST OF FILES—the most recent documents worked on will be listed here following the other menu items.

NOTE: The above listing is from Microsoft Word 2000. Your FILE options may differ from these, depending on which word-processing software you are using.

2 Reviewing your thesis and outline

Next, review your working thesis and outline. Add any new ideas you discovered while reading through your prewriting. If you think the main idea has shifted since you wrote your working thesis, rewrite it and adjust your outline. Finally, revisit your rhetorical stance—your purpose, persona, and readers—and make any needed adjustments to your plans.

It is a good idea to copy your prewriting and outline documents before you begin composing. Or, you can create a new document that contains both earlier documents (see the Help box). You can use this new document to manipulate the text and rewrite it into a finished product. If you change your mind about where your writing is headed, you will still have your original prewriting and outline documents to go back to.

HELP

How do I combine my prewriting and outline documents?

Word-processing programs provide multiple ways to accomplish the same task. Here are two ways to combine documents:

1. Inserting the two documents into a blank document using the INSERT command from the menu bar.
   a. Create a blank document.
   b. INSERT the contents of your prewriting document. (INSERT>FILE)
   c. INSERT the contents of your outline document. (INSERT>FILE)
   d. Move appropriate information from the prewriting document to the outline document (using CUT and PASTE).
   e. Save the combined document as a first draft with an appropriate new name.

2. Combining the two documents using multiple windows:
   a. Open (FILE>OPEN) your prewriting document and your outline document, each in its own window. Resize the windows to view them both at the same time. (WINDOW>ARRANGE ALL)
   b. Moving the cursor between the windows, COPY and PASTE appropriate information from the prewriting document to the outline document.
   c. Save the combined text to a new document with an appropriate name.

See Figure 3.1 for an illustration of multiple windows.

WWW

3.3
Instructions for adding notes to an outline.

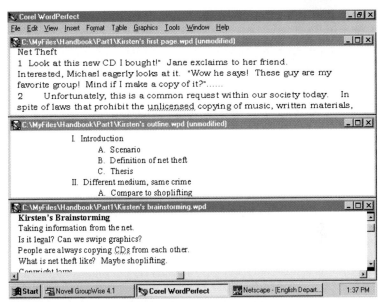

FIGURE 3.1 Three Windows Open at the Same Time

3 Using multiple windows

If you prefer, you can use your prewriting and outline documents for reference and begin composing from scratch in a new document. The WINDOW feature of many word-processing programs allows you to work on two or more documents simultaneously. Multiple windows are useful for keeping track of your ideas as you work—you can keep your prewriting, your outline, and your draft in separate windows. It is also possible to use separate windows to display different parts of your document at the same time. For example, you could insert your thesis into one window and your draft into another. Figure 3.1 shows three windows open simultaneously. (See the Help box for instructions on working with windows.)

3b Draft

When you are ready to begin composing, you can choose from a number of different approaches. Two possible approaches are the building-block technique and the top-down method.

1   Using the building-block technique

One approach to composing is to create a group of building blocks that you can use to construct your text a piece at a time. Many writers first compose a skeleton of the finished text and then expand it by adding new arguments, supporting examples and evidence, or illustrative details, the "building blocks" of a text. Word processing is particularly effective for this approach. Some writers like to write their central paragraphs—the middle blocks of a text—first and add the introductory blocks and concluding paragraphs later. You can decide which blocks will be easiest and write those blocks first, saving the more difficult parts for last. Once you have a preliminary draft, you can return to your text to amplify sections, one block at a time. To create blocks, you can use the new document you made from copies of your prewriting and outline documents. Use the headings in your outline to expand and build your text. CUT and PASTE text from your prewriting to place under the headings; then rewrite and amplify the text to create blocks. You can also COPY information from your prewriting window and PASTE it into your document in the other window. In this way, you avoid having to retype information from your prewriting document as you compose.

2   Using the top-down method

As an alternative to composing from building blocks, you may prefer to work from the beginning of your paper straight through to the end, thus moving from the top down. You can use your working thesis statement and the corresponding organizational plan to compose in this way. Type or COPY and PASTE your working thesis statement into a new document. As we discuss in Chapter 2, your thesis statement can provide you with a blueprint for composing. With the thesis statement at the top of your screen, begin writing your draft, following the blueprint suggested by your thesis. Save your draft into the appropriate folder on your hard drive so that you can return to it for more work at a later time. Remember, your working thesis is just that—working. You can revise it at any time (see 2d). Be flexible as you write and open to new directions that may occur to you while you are writing.

3   Avoiding writer's block

Each writer develops his or her own writing rhythms. It is a good idea to get into the habit of stopping a writing session when you know what comes next—making it easier the next time to pick up where you left off. However, if you find yourself "blocked" as a writer, set your work aside for a few hours or even a few days. Get up and stretch, grab a cup of coffee or a soft drink before returning to your draft. Do not expect perfection from a first draft. Remember that writing is essentially rewriting; everything you write should undergo extensive revision in a continuous cycle of writing, revising, editing, and writing again (see Suggestions for Overcoming Writer's Block).

3c Collaborate

As you compose, you might find it helpful to collaborate with others, either face to face or via a computer network. In college classes, as in the work force, writers often work on projects in writing

AUDIO
Keep an open
mind about
group projects.

Suggestions for Overcoming Writer's Block

- *Gain some distance.* Set your writing aside for a few days or hours. Take a coffee or snack break before coming back to your writing task.
- *Keep at it.* When your writing is flowing well, try to avoid interruptions so that you can keep the momentum going.
- *Stop when you know what's next.* This will make it easier to pick up where you left off.
- *Try freewriting.* Often, the act of writing itself will stimulate those creative juices.
- *Use visualization.* Picture yourself writing or picture some aspect of the topic you are writing about. Then describe what you see.
- *Change your point of view.* Try writing from another person's point of view. Or try writing in a different genre, such as a letter or a memo.
- *Write what you know first.* Rather than beginning with an introductory paragraph, start by writing the portion of your paper that you know the most about.
- *Change your mode of writing.* If you normally type at a computer, try using pencil and paper, or vice versa.

WWW

3.4
How famous
writers over-
come writer's
block.

groups or writing teams. Your teammates can serve as a sounding board for your ideas and arguments.

1 Working with a group

WWW

3.5
The benefits of collaborative learning.

Working with a group may be something you enjoy or something you dread, depending on whether your prior experience with group projects was positive or negative. In some group projects, one or two students may end up feeling that they are doing all the work. In other group projects, a few students may be bossy or controlling rather than cooperative. But if you pay attention to group dynamics and role assignments from the start of your collaborative project, you should do just fine.

2 Writing collaboratively

Once you have come up with an overall plan of action for your writing project, you can assign specific tasks or roles to group members. In one writing class, each group was assigned the task of developing a Web site on a topic related to cyberspace. The students in each group brainstormed together possibilities for their site, first deciding on the nature of the content their Web site would present and the audience it would address. They agreed to each write independently a two- to three-page piece that would be incorporated as a page at the site. Then, they assigned each person in the group a specific role, from site Webmaster to site publisher. Because each student knew exactly what his or her contribution would be, group members were able to work together cooperatively.

3 Collaborating via network

AUDIO
Using email for collaboration.

If you are involved in a joint writing project, forming an email discussion group can facilitate collaboration with others in the group. Students collaborating to write material for a Web site they were creating, for example, used a study group address so that they could email the first draft of each Web page to the entire writing group for review. Most email software offers the option INCLUDE EMAIL MESSAGE IN REPLY. That option places the entire message—in this case, the draft of a Web page—into the reply window. Members of the writing group could add their comments and suggestions in capital letters or italics to make them stand out from the draft itself. Then, by selecting the REPLY TO ALL option, they could send the reply

How do I collaborate on a computer?

If your instructor or lab supervisor has designated a common location (drive) on a local area network for your class, you can use it to share work with your classmates (step 1). Other ways to collaborate include using Web pages and email.

1. Post your work to the common drive by using the SAVE AS function in your word-processing program.
   a. Read and comment on the work that has been posted by your classmates (use italics, boldface type, or your word-processing program's INSERT>COMMENT feature).
   b. On a PC, use SAVE AS to save your classmates' work plus your comments in a new document under a new title.
2. If possible, post your work to a class Web site for others to read and review.
3. Use email to send your work to a peer.

3.6

Three ways to collaborate using computers.

message to everyone in the group, or, by selecting the REPLY TO SENDER option, they could send their reply to only the writer.

You can also use the email software's ATTACHMENT capability to facilitate collaboration with a writing group. This feature allows you to include a document (file) with the email message. In this way, you can send your actual word-processing document to the others in the group for their review. Group members can use the word-processing program's COMMENT feature (found in the INSERT menu) to insert their comments and suggestions for revisions. The paper and the comments can then be sent back to the writer, again as an email attachment.

3d Be flexible about your writing process

Although some students who do not have computers readily available may still be writing out rough drafts by hand, most students now compose their papers directly at a computer keyboard. You may need to become more flexible about your writing process if you are changing to a new writing tool or environment. Plan ahead and leave time to compensate for problems that may crop up—either

3.7

Using the writing process to your advantage.

AUDIO
Adapting your
writing habits.

with your own computer or in computer labs. For example, you may experience a computer virus on your home computer, or you may find that a computer network is down or a computer lab is overly busy. Work on developing a writing system that uses available computers—and your time—to best advantage.

CHAPTER **4**

Rewriting

AUDIO
The three
phases of
rewriting.

This chapter discusses three levels of rewriting—revising, editing, and proofreading. As you think about rewriting, imagine that you are viewing your writing through the lens of a camera. The first view is panoramic (revising): you look globally at the entire piece of writing with the goal of revising its focus, coherence, organization, development, tone, and format. The second view is at normal range (editing): you look locally at specific sentence-level features with the goal of eliminating wordiness, repetition, and ineffective or awkward language. Finally, you zoom in for a close-up (proofreading): you look for any distracting errors that might interfere with a reader's understanding, including errors in punctuation and mechanics.

4a   Shift from writer to reader

To be skillful revisers, writers must put themselves in the place of their readers. When writers read their own work, however, they may have trouble seeing what they have actually written. Instead, they often see what they *intended* to write.

If possible, allow at least a day between the time you finish a draft and the time you read it over to revise, edit, and proofread. You will be astonished at how much more clearly you can view your writing if you take a break from working on it. If you are facing a tight deadline, even several hours are helpful. Also, try to schedule more than one session for revising. When your writing is stored electroni-

HELP

How do I manipulate my text to make revising easier?

1. Change the way your text looks in any of these ways:
   a. Change the spacing of your text lines from double to triple.
   b. Change the font size from 12 point to 15 point.
   c. Insert a page break after each paragraph.
   d. Change the margin width from 1 inch to 2 inches.
2. Save the reformatted text under a different name.
3. Print out the reformatted text.
4. Read each paragraph of the printed text carefully, using the Critical Reading Questions for Revision.
5. Write suggestions for revision in the margins.

4.1
Formatting tips to make revising easier.

cally, it is much easier to revise because you do not need to retype or recopy the entire text after each change.

As you read your work critically, it will help if you pay attention to different major elements during each subsequent reading. These elements are focus, coherence, organization, development, tone, and format. (See Critical Reading Questions for Revision.)

Critical Reading Questions for Revision

Focus

- Do I have a clearly stated thesis that controls the content?
- Do all the major points refer back to and support my thesis?
- Are all of the examples and illustrations relevant to my point?

Coherence

- Are individual sentences and paragraphs held together by transitions?
- Are the transitions I have used the best available?
- Have I avoided overusing any transitions?

(continued)

Organization

- Are the major points arranged in the most effective order?
- Are my strongest arguments placed near the end?
- Are the supporting points arranged to best advantage?
- Have I followed through with the organizational pattern I selected?

Development

- Is my thesis adequately supported?
- Are my major points backed up by specific details and examples?
- Is there at least one paragraph for each major point?
- Are my paragraphs developed proportionately?

Tone

- Is my tone appropriate to my rhetorical stance and consistent throughout?
- Do my language choices reflect my intended tone?
- Have I eliminated contractions or first-person pronouns from a formal piece?

Format

- Does the "look" of my text help convey its meaning?
- Is the font I have used readable and appropriate to the topic?
- Are the headings descriptive and helpful in orienting the reader?
- Have I used graphics and illustrations appropriately?

4b Revise

AUDIO
One student's
revision process.

Critical reading can highlight problems of focus, coherence, organization, development, tone, and formatting in your paper. Revising involves the tasks of adding to the text, deleting from the text, and rearranging information within the text to fix those problems. Using a word-processing program makes these tasks easy. Knowing what to add, delete, and rearrange is the tricky part. In the next several sections, we will follow Kirsten's progress as she rewrites her paper on Net theft (see 4f).

1 Revising for focus

Revisit your working thesis, and revise it to more accurately reflect the overall point of your text. Then revise each paragraph, one by one, to ensure that it is focused on only one idea, which supports the thesis. Delete any paragraphs that are not related to the thesis.

Kirsten revised her second paragraph to focus more clearly on the idea of "borrowing" from the Internet. Notice how she eliminated references to phone cards and other products and included music, software, written texts, and graphics instead.

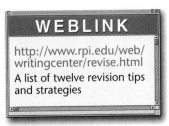

WEBLINK

http://www.rpi.edu/web/
writingcenter/revise.html
A list of twelve revision tips
and strategies

WWW

4.2

Some useful
suggestions for
revising.

Unfortunately, this is a common request ~~within our society~~

today. In spite of laws that prohibit ~~the~~ unlicensed copying of

~~music, written materials and movies,~~ *in some circles* it has become an accepted

practice to reproduce another's work without paying for it.

Similarly, this ∧*practice* has spread to the Internet where access to ∧software, *music,*

~~phone cards, and other products~~ ∧*written texts, and graphics* is convenient and fast. ~~Graphics,~~

~~quotes, articles and many other various things~~ ∧*These items* can be copied for

personal use with ease, but often no credit is given to the original

author.

2 Revising for coherence

Wherever you notice that sentences do not flow smoothly in your draft, add appropriate transitional words and phrases. Look particularly at the links between paragraphs. Insert transitions to help the reader follow the flow of the text. Such words or phrases as *however, on the one hand/on the other hand, but,* and *in addition* can help the reader see the relationships between ideas.

WWW

4.3

An example of
revising for
coherence.

HELP

How do I compare drafts of my text to track my changes?

Here are three ways you can use your word processor to track changes you have made to a draft:

1. When you begin to revise a document, turn on TRACK CHANGES (REVISION MARKING) from the TOOLS menu. This feature will mark any changes you make in the document. (Note: Not all word processors offer this feature.)

2. If you forgot to turn on TRACK CHANGES, you may still be able to compare two versions of a document by selecting the DOCUMENT COMPARE or COMPARE VERSIONS feature of the word-processing program.
   a. Select the files that you want compared (for example, draft1 and draft2).
   b. Look closely at the changes you have made between the two documents. (Revisions will be indicated with markings in the text.)
   c. Check to see that your revisions were substantive; that is, you did not merely tinker with the text but actually added, deleted, and rearranged.

3. If your word processor does not have DOCUMENT COMPARE, open both files concurrently in two windows and scan for differences.

WWW

4.4
Step-by-step
instructions
for tracking
changes.

3 Revising for organization

VIDEO
Revising with a
word processor.

Once you have decided how to improve the organization of your text, use the CUT, COPY, and PASTE commands to move parts of your text. Rearrange the words, sentences, and paragraphs that comprise your text into the most effective order. Be certain that you check for coherence after rearranging.

4 Revising for development

Your argument is stronger if you include many concrete examples or details. If you are writing an informal piece, do not hesitate to add anecdotes or narratives of personal experiences to give life and personality to your writing. If you are writing a formal paper, you can add information from sources that support your arguments. Place the cursor where additional explanatory details, evidence, examples, or illustrations need to be added to your text.

While working on her revision outline, Kirsten discovered that she needed to focus and develop her discussion of the legalities of the Internet (an item in her outline). Notice how Kirsten has rewritten this paragraph and developed it in an entirely new direction.

ORIGINAL PARAGRAPH

Information about copyright laws, what is legal and what isn't, is available on the Net as well. Web Issues at the Copyright Website (www.benedict.com) provides information about what can be copied from the Net and how to do it properly. ~~Another page specifically discusses using graphics (PageWorks available at http://www .snowcrest.net/kitty/hpages). Those who decide to break these "laws," run the risk of being ostracized by a group such as Netbusters! This vigilante group seeks to prevent what they call "bandwidth robbery" by informing Netusers about its devastating results. The Netbusters homepage has a place to report clandestine computer activities if you know of any perpetrators.~~

REWRITTEN PARAGRAPH

Organizations and individuals have tried to establish standards of conduct for Internet use. For example, the Computer Ethics Institute wrote its Ten Commandments for Computer Ethics, which includes such obvious "rules" as "Thou shalt not use the computer to steal" (Roach). But what is stealing when it comes to materials found on the Internet? The Copyright Website asserts that any texts or graphics that you find on the Internet are by their very nature published and thus are "copyrighted" (O'Mahoney). This means that in order to use anything from someone else's Web site, you need their permission. If you put a comic strip such as Calvin and Hobbes onto your home page, you run the risk of being sued for violation of copyright.

4.5
Advice on
revising style
and tone.

5   Revising for tone

In rereading, you may decide that your tone is either too formal or too informal. To revise your tone to be more formal, expand contractions into their full forms, combine some short sentences to make longer sentences, and change informal diction or slang into more formal wording.

6   Revising for format

WEBLINK

http://leo.stcloudstate.edu/acadwrite/intro.html
Information about writing effective introductions
http://leo.stcloudstate.edu/acadwrite/conclude.html
Ideas for writing an effective conclusion

To convey your information in a more visual way, you may want to add formatting more commonly found in a brochure or a newsletter. You can import and insert graphics to illustrate your text at appropriate points. Try using different fonts by selecting them from the FORMAT menu. Remember, though, that readability of your text is the most important goal; choose fonts accordingly. (See Chapter 14 for more information on fonts.)

7   Writing effective openings, closings, and titles

VIDEO
Composing
introductions.

Openings   Writers have very little time in which to grab the reader's attention—usually only a few seconds. That is why a piece's opening, or lead, is so important. But do not let concern over how you will begin become a stumbling block. Many writers find that leaving the opening for the last stages of revision works best. For further ideas on writing introductory paragraphs, see 5h-1.

4.6
The power
of effective
openings.

Closings or Conclusions   A conclusion usually takes the form of a summary, which points the reader back to the text itself, or speculation, which points the reader outside of the text. For additional suggestions on writing concluding paragraphs, see 5h-2.

A SUMMARY CONCLUSION

Few Interneters would disagree that stealing and reselling software or credit cards is wrong. But fewer still would feel guilty about copying the latest game version of *Doom*, or some such, rather than forking out $39.95. Unfortunately, that often admirable ethos makes it easier for genuine crooks to perpetrate—and justify—their crimes.

—Michael Meyer and Anne Underwood, "Crimes of the 'Net'"

A SPECULATIVE CONCLUSION

Nevertheless, in the litigations and political debates which are certain to follow, we will endeavor to assure that their electronic speech is protected as certainly as any opinions which are printed or, for that matter, screamed. We will make an effort to clarify issues surrounding the distribution of intellectual property. And we will help to create for America a future which is as blessed by the Bill of Rights as its past has been.

—John Perry Barlow, "Crime and Puzzlement"

Do not feel obligated to limit yourself to a summary conclusion. Sometimes a speculative conclusion will work better. This type of conclusion is most appropriate for papers that point the reader in a new direction, that reflect on the implications of some topic, or that suggest the need for further research.

Titles Because the title is the first thing a reader sees, it must make a good impression. The title also must help the reader anticipate the topic and perhaps the writer's particular point of view. Kirsten's title, "Net Theft," is descriptive and intriguing, if not particularly clever. It is more important that the title be related to the content than that it be cute or funny.

4c Edit

When editing a text, the writer's goal is to make it easier to read. During revision, the writer concentrates on making the piece focused, organized, and well developed. During editing, the writer concentrates on refining words and sentences. Like a car buff putting the final finish on a classic automobile, an editor "finishes" a piece of writing—in general, refining what has been done and making it aesthetically pleasing as well as functional. (See the Editing Checklist on page 40.)

Editing Checklist

Your response to each of the following questions should be "yes."

Sentence Structure

- Are all of my sentences complete (see Chapter 26)?
- Have I avoided comma splices and run-on sentences (see Chapter 27)?
- Do paired elements have parallel structures (see Chapter 33)?

Wordiness

- Have I avoided using unnecessary words, such as *in order to* (Chapter 31)?
- Have I replaced two-word phrases, such as *new innovation* and *repeating recurrence* (see Chapter 34)?

Repetition

- Have I avoided excessive use of a single word (see Chapter 36)?
- Have I avoided repetition of a single idea that is not the thesis (see Chapter 34)?

Verb Usage

- Have I used primarily active rather than passive voice (see 24g)?
- Have I replaced overused verbs with more vivid verbs (see 36a)?

Other Errors

- Is my end punctuation correct (see Chapter 39)?
- Is my internal punctuation correct—commas (see Chapter 40), semicolons (see Chapter 41), and colons (see Chapter 42)?
- Have I used quotation marks appropriately (see Chapter 44)?
- Have I used other punctuation marks appropriately (see Chapter 45)?

(continued)

Editing Checklist *(continued)*

- Is my spelling correct (see Chapter 49)?
- Are my mechanics correct—capitals and italics (see Chapter 46), abbreviations and numbers (see Chapter 47), and hyphens (see Chapter 48)?

4d Proofread

Proofreading is the final phase in rewriting. In this stage of the process, writers look closely for distracting punctuation and mechanical errors that will interfere with the reader's understanding. Proofreading prematurely, before there is a final, edited draft, may allow important revision and editing issues to be overlooked, in addition to wasting a lot of time. By proofreading after revising and editing, writers can concentrate on details related to manuscript preparation, such as typographical errors, missing words, and irregular spacing, as well as errors in punctuation that they may have missed in earlier stages.

AUDIO
Proofread for accuracy and correctness.

Some writers prefer to proofread on the computer screen. However, recent studies have shown that writers who read their texts on

Proofreading Strategies

1. Scroll rapidly through your text to check for spacing, margins, indents, widows and orphans (single lines and words left alone at the top or bottom of a page, respectively), page numbering, and so on.
2. Print the text; wait several hours before proofreading it.
3. Use a pointer or ruler to force yourself to read slowly.
4. Proofread the text several times; each time, you will pick up additional errors.
5. Change your reading technique to a proofreading one. Normal reading involves skimming; in contrast, proofreading requires looking at every word and punctuation mark.
6. Ask someone else—for example, a friend, a relative, or a classmate—to proofread the printed text as well.
7. Read your paper aloud—either to yourself or to a peer, friend, or writing center tutor.

screen may not see them as clearly or read them as carefully. Also, proofreading on a computer screen can be tiring to the eyes. Those who choose to proofread on screen should take frequent breaks. Experiment with your own proofreading technique, which may be a combination of on-screen proofreading and proofreading on paper.

4e   Give and receive feedback

VIDEO
Peer reviews.

In many writing classes, students work together in peer review groups, in which they exchange drafts for review, either electronically via a networked computer system (a local area network, or LAN) or in hard copy form. The instructor also may comment on early drafts and make revision suggestions. Or students may be asked to take their papers to a writing center, where a tutor will read them and offer suggestions. As a writer, you will find it helpful to receive feedback on your work from a variety of sources. Such feedback allows you to become increasingly sensitive to the needs of your readers. (See Giving and Receiving Peer Feedback.)

Giving and Receiving Peer Feedback

Giving Feedback

1. Read the piece through carefully, noting strengths and weaknesses.
2. Phrase your comments as suggestions and questions, not as criticisms.
3. Give positive feedback and praise where appropriate.
4. Respond generally first and then specifically.
5. Respond completely to any prompts provided by the teacher.

Receiving Feedback

1. Read peer comments with an open mind.
2. Consider all comments seriously.
3. Accept those comments that help you improve your piece.
4. Reject those comments that seem to be leading you in another direction.
5. Ask for clarification of a confusing peer comment or suggestion.

rew

HELP

How do I insert comments into a word-processing document?

Most word-processing programs will allow you to insert comments into a document that you are reading.

1. Commenting in *Microsoft Word:*

    To establish your identity, choose OPTIONS from the TOOLS menu. Under the USER INFORMATION tab, fill in your name and your initials. These will show up with your comments. Make sure that "Show Highlight" and "Screen Tips" are both checked on the VIEW tab on the OPTIONS screen.

    To insert a comment, choose COMMENT from the INSERT menu. A comment box will appear at the bottom of your screen. Type in your comment and close the box when finished. Your comment will not interfere with the text itself; rather, the presence of a comment will be indicated by highlighted words in your text. The comment inside a box will open when the mouse is held over the highlighted words. You can EDIT or DELETE your comments by using a mouse click (right mouse for PCs). You can also view all comments by selecting VIEW>COMMENTS from the VIEW menu or print the comments by selecting COMMENT from the "Print What" line on the print dialog box.

VIDEO

Inserting comments in documents.

2. Commenting in *WordPerfect:*

    To establish your identity, choose TOOLS>SETTING> ENVIRONMENT. Type your name and initials in the dialog box; choose a user color in which your comments will appear in the documents. Choose CREATE COMMENT from the INSERT menu and type your comment into the commenting window. When you close the window, your comments appear as marginal icons that will open when you click on them. As with *Word*, comments can also be edited, viewed, and printed.

WWW

4.7

How to insert comments into a document.

NOTE: Your commenting options may differ slightly from these depending on the word-processing software you are using.

4f Review a model student paper

4.8

View two
model student
essays.

Let us consider Kirsten Parsons's essay on Net theft. It is a truism in the writing field that there are no finished pieces of writing, only deadlines. Any piece can be revised and improved. In what ways do you think this draft can be improved? Are there elements Kirsten could still work on to make them more effective?

Parsons 1

Student and
course
identification

Kirsten Parsons

English 101-35

Professor Hines

April 15, 2003

Net Theft

Opening
scenario

"Look at this new CD I bought!" Jane exclaims
to her friend. Interested, Michael eagerly looks at
it. "Wow," he says. "These guys are my favorite
group! Mind if I make a copy of it?". . .

Introduction

Unfortunately, this is a common request today.
In spite of laws that prohibit unlicensed copying,
in some circles it has become an accepted practice
to reproduce another's work without paying for it.
Similarly, this practice has spread to the
Internet, where access to music, software, written
texts, and graphics is convenient and fast. These
items can be copied for personal use with ease, but
often no credit is given to the original author.
Not only is this wrong from a moral standpoint, but

Parsons 2

legally, it is forbidden as well. It has become a
situation where "legality collides with
practicality" (Meyer and Underwood 113). In other
words, breaking the law is more convenient than
obeying it, and since we know we can get away with
doing it, our conscience gives in. When it comes to
"borrowing" information from the Internet, we are
gradually becoming a people that accept lawbreaking
as long as we can participate, too.

Walking into a store and taking something
without paying for it is obviously not legal;
ironically, this principle seems to break down
where the Net is concerned. With available
technology, Net theft is commonplace. Written
texts, software, graphics, and music all are
vulnerable to cyber-shoplifting. Though it is not
encouraged per se, it is not really discouraged
either. Isn't this just stealing masked by softer
terms such as "sharing" or "borrowing"? Granted it
is less noticeable, but that doesn't change the
fact that you didn't pay for it.

Part of the problem is that the physical
element involved in actually traveling to a store
and taking something is not necessary for these Net
crimes. Imagine walking down the aisle of the local

Print source
authors and
page number

Thesis

Definition of
Net theft

Compare
difficulty of
each crime

Parsons 3

Wal-Mart with the intention of stealing a Hobbes
doll, your favorite cartoon character. Blood rushes
to your ears and your heart begins to pound, as
your body reacts to the rush of adrenalin. Casting
a nervous glance around the nearby aisles, you
decide that the coast is clear. You extend your
arm, grab the orange tiger, place it in your
backpack, and then walk nonchalantly towards the
exit. Then the alarm goes off and you are caught
holding the goods!

This scenario is only possible in a physical
world. Because the Net is so unphysical, the risk
of being caught, which may serve to deter many
thieves in a store, is minimal. Net theft is
committed within the reach of the refrigerator!
Imagine that while Net-surfing you find a cartoon
of Calvin and Hobbes on a commercial Web site. You
think it would look great on your home page. With a
click of the mouse, you grab the graphic and paste
it onto your own page. Who has ever heard of
someone being arrested for copying a graphic?
Because Net crimes often go ignored, and "everyone"
is guilty, more and more people engage in them. The
consequences seem to be less punitive, and thus we
give in to the influence of the Wild Net.

Parsons 4

Organizations and individuals have tried to
establish standards of conduct for Internet use.
For example, the Computer Ethics Institute wrote
its Ten Commandments for Computer Ethics, which
includes such obvious "rules" as "Thou shalt not
use the computer to steal" (Roach). But what is
stealing when it comes to materials found on the
Internet? The Copyright Website asserts that any
texts or graphics that you find on the Internet are
by their very nature published and thus are
"copyrighted" (O'Mahoney). This means that in order
to use anything from someone else's Web site, you
need their permission. If you put a comic strip
such as Calvin and Hobbes onto your home page, you
run the risk of being sued for violation of
copyright.

The problem, as Meyer and Underwood also point
out, is that the "wild West culture of the Internet
promotes an anything goes attitude in Net surfers"
(113). Most Internet users would agree that
stealing credit card numbers and selling them is
wrong. However, many would not agree that sharing a
pirated copy of a game was illegal or even wrong.
Similarly, many would not find that using a cool
graphic from someone else's page was unethical or

Standards of
conduct

Online
source
without page
number

Summary of
the conflict

Parsons 5

illegal. The free-wheeling world of the Internet considers capitalist rules like "copyright" to be offensive.

Conclusion   In the tangled world of the Internet, not all of the new dilemmas that have surfaced will be solved immediately. However, if the definition of a criminal is one who has committed a crime, then in the world of the Net, perhaps we all need to serve some time.

Parsons 6

Works Cited

Print source   Meyer, Michael, and Anne Underwood. "Crimes of the 'Net.'" CyberReader. Ed. Victor Vitanza. 2nd ed. Boston: Allyn & Bacon, 1999. 111-13.

Online Web site   O'Mahoney, Benedict. The Copyright Website. 2002. 1 Sept. 2002 <http://www.benedict.com>.

Online Web site   Roach, Kitty. PageWorks. 2 Jan. 2001. 1 Sept. 2002 <http://www.snowcrest.net/kitty/hpages>.

¶

CHAPTER **5**

Structuring Paragraphs

A **paragraph** is a sentence or group of sentences that develops a main idea. Paragraphs serve as the primary building blocks of essays, reports, memos, and other forms of written composition.

Well-written paragraphs facilitate quick skimming and help readers stay focused on the main ideas so that they can understand and evaluate the text. To promote this kind of readability, paragraphs should be unified, coherent, and adequately developed, while flowing from one to the next as smoothly as possible.

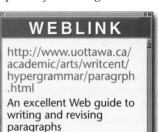

WEBLINK

http://www.uottawa.ca/ academic/arts/writcent/ hypergrammar/paragrph .html

An excellent Web guide to writing and revising paragraphs

AUDIO
Chapter overview.

WWW

5.1

Writing paragraphs from start to finish.

5a Write unified paragraphs

A **unified paragraph** focuses on and develops a single main idea. This idea is typically captured in a single sentence, called a *topic sentence*. The other sentences in the paragraph, the *supporting sentences*, should elaborate on the topic sentence in a logical fashion.

VIDEO
Achieving paragraph unity.

1 Using a topic sentence

A **topic sentence** serves the important purpose of giving readers a quick idea of what the paragraph as a whole is about. It is a good idea to place the topic sentence at the beginning of a paragraph, where it provides a preview of the rest of the paragraph. A topic sentence should, if possible, do four things: (1) provide a transition from the preceding paragraph, (2) introduce the topic of the paragraph, (3) make a main point about this topic, and (4) suggest how the rest of the paragraph will develop this point. The topic sentence in the following paragraph is underlined.

<u>During the past decade or two, children have slipped into poverty faster than any other age group.</u> One of six white U.S. children, two of every five Latino children, and almost one of every two African-American children are poor. These figures translate into incredible numbers—approximately *18 million* children live in poverty: 9 million white children, 4 million Latino children, and 5 million African-American children. [Underscores added.]

—James M. Henslin, *Sociology*

In a series of paragraphs, the first sentence of each paragraph should serve as a transition from the preceding paragraph. Often, you can make the first sentence both a topic sentence and a linking sentence.

2   Placing the topic sentence

Although topic sentences usually are best placed at the beginning of a paragraph, sometimes writers use the first sentence of a paragraph to provide a transition, making the second sentence the topic sentence, as in the following example.

Regardless of causes—and there are many—to say that millions of children live in poverty can be as cold and meaningless as saying that their shoes are brown. <u>Easy to overlook is the significance of childhood poverty.</u> Poor children are more likely to die in infancy, to go hungry and to be malnourished, to develop more slowly, and to have more health problems. They are more likely to drop out of school, to become involved in criminal activities, and to have children while still in their teens—thus perpetuating the cycle of poverty. [Underscores added.]

—James M. Henslin, *Sociology*

Occasionally a topic sentence falls at the end of a paragraph, either as a summary or as a restatement of a topic sentence appearing earlier in the paragraph. Sometimes no topic sentence is needed at all. If a paragraph continues the topic covered in the preceding paragraph or simply narrates a series of events or a set of details whose common theme is obvious, you may decide that an explicit topic statement is unnecessary.

5b   Use clear organizational patterns

All paragraphs should be *coherent:* each sentence should connect logically with those preceding and following it. Coherent paragraphs

HELP

How do I connect my ideas in a coherent way?

If you have problems connecting ideas and making paragraphs, try outlining the topics and subtopics within a section of your first draft.

1. From within the first-draft document, open the function that provides numbered or lettered lists (usually called OUTLINE).

2. Find your first topic idea, and list it as main heading 1. If you have a second and third main idea following the first, list them as main headings 2 and 3.

3. Under each main heading, find ideas that support or expand on it. List these as subheads a, b, and so on. Ideas subordinate to these subtopics can be listed as (1), (2), and so on.

4. Survey the outline for connections between the main items. How can you use the subheads to build a phrase or sentence that will connect to the next main heading?

5. Finally, write full paragraphs based on your outline, constructing or combining sentences so that they flow in the order of the outline.

allow readers to move smoothly from one idea to the next. One way writers create coherent paragraphs is through the use of organizational patterns.

Among the many possible ways to organize paragraphs, certain patterns are especially common: general to specific, cause and effect, comparison or contrast, definition, classification, problem and solution, narrative or process description, exemplification, and physical description. These organizational patterns mirror typical ways people categorize experience. Readers look for familiar patterns, so the more explicitly you signal those patterns, the easier it will be for readers to see the logic connecting your ideas.

1 Organizing by general to specific

The sample paragraphs in 5a-1 and 5a-2 both illustrate general-to-specific organization, in which a general statement is followed by specific supporting details. This is one of the most common of all paragraph patterns, and the general statement serves effectively as a topic sentence. Here is another example of general-to-specific ordering:

> Every society creates an idealized image of the future—a vision that serves as a beacon to direct the imagination and energy of its people. The ancient Jewish nation prayed for deliverance to a promised land of milk and honey. Later, Christian clerics held out the promise of eternal salvation in the heavenly kingdom. In the modern age, the idea of a future technological utopia has served as the guiding vision of industrial society. For more than a century utopian dreamers and men and women of science and letters have looked to a future world where machines would replace human labor, creating a near-workerless society of abundance and leisure.
>
> —Jeremy Rifkin, *The End of Work*

This paragraph leads off a chapter in Rifkin's book called "Visions of Techno-Paradise." Rifkin uses the general-to-specific pattern to first situate his discussion in universal terms ("every society") and then narrow his focus to the "near-workerless society" that will be the subject of the chapter.

It is possible to organize a paragraph in the reverse order—that is, from specific to general. Such a pattern is seldom used, however, even by professionals.

2   Organizing by cause and effect

Many pieces of writing link phenomena through cause-and-effect relationships. The cause-and-effect organizational pattern is especially appropriate for explaining why something happened the way it did or predicting some future sequence of events. Paragraphs organized with a cause-and-effect pattern usually include transitional words and phrases such as *therefore, thus, as a result, since, because, consequently, for this reason,* and *thereby*.

> Fetal alcohol syndrome (FAS) occurs when alcohol ingested by the mother passes through the placenta into the infant's bloodstream. *Because* the fetus is so small, its blood alcohol concentration will be much higher than that of its mother. *Thus,* consumption of alcohol during pregnancy can affect the infant far more seriously than it does the mother. Among the symptoms of FAS are mental retardation, small head, tremors, and abnormalities of the face, limbs, heart, and brain. [Italics added.]
>
> —Rebecca J. Donatelle and Lorraine G. Davis, *Access to Health*

3 Organizing by comparison or contrast

Many writing situations call for comparing or contrasting two or more ideas, issues, items, or events. Comparison focuses on similarities; contrast focuses on differences. In either case, the writer evaluates two or more subjects on the basis of one or more criteria. Transitional words and phrases commonly found in comparison or contrast paragraphs include *however, on the one hand/on the other hand, similarly, in contrast, just as, while, but,* and *like.*

A paragraph based on the comparison or contrast pattern should be structured either (1) by evaluating one subject completely and then turning to the other or (2) by focusing on each criterion, one at a time.

The following paragraph is organized according to subject. The liberal view of affirmative action is contrasted to the conservative view, and the criteria used (such as group fairness and individual fairness) are secondary.

> The role of affirmative action in our multicultural society lies at the center of a national debate about how to steer a course in race and ethnic relations. In this policy, quotas based on race (and gender) are used in hiring and college admissions. Most liberals, both white and minority, defend affirmative action, saying that it is the most direct way to level the playing field of economic opportunity. If white males are passed over, this is an unfortunate cost we must pay if we are to make up for past and present discrimination. Most conservatives, *in contrast,* both white and minority, agree that opportunity should be open to all, but say that putting race (or sex) ahead of people's ability to perform a job is reverse discrimination. They add that affirmative action stigmatizes the people who benefit from it because it suggests that they hold their jobs because of race (or sex), rather than merit. [Italics added.]
>
> —Adapted from James M. Henslin, *Sociology*

AUDIO
Multiple paragraph patterns working together.

4 Organizing by definition

In academic writing, important new terms sometimes require a complete paragraph for their definition. The term is usually introduced in a topic sentence at the beginning of the paragraph and elaborated on in the sentences that follow. Here is a typical example of a paragraph organized by definition, from an educational psychology textbook:

> Another tool for building a better understanding of the teaching and learning processes is *theory.* The common sense notion of theory

(as in "Oh well, it was only a theory") is "a guess or hunch." But the scientific meaning of theory is quite different. "A theory in science is an interrelated set of concepts that is used to explain a body of data and to make predictions about the results of future experiments" (Stanovich, 1992). Given a number of established principles, educational psychologists have developed explanations for the relationships among many variables and even whole systems of relationships. There are theories to explain how language develops, how differences in intelligence occur, and, as noted earlier, how people learn. [Italics added.]

—Anita E. Woolfolk, *Educational Psychology*

A paragraph organized by definition should include a formal definition—that is, a statement "X is a Y that _____," where X is the *term* being defined, Y is the *class* it belongs to, and _____ is a set of *distinguishing features.* In the above example, such a definition is found in the third sentence: "A theory in science is an interrelated set of concepts that is used to explain a body of data and to make predictions about the results of future experiments."

5 Organizing by classification

To make sense of the world, people routinely classify things according to their characteristic parts. In academic writing, an entire paragraph is often devoted to classifying some concept. Paragraphs organized by classification normally introduce the topic in the first sentence and the various subtopics in the following sentences. Using these subtopics as the grammatical subjects of their respective sentences, as in this example, creates grammatical parallelism (see 5e), which makes it easy for readers to see the structure of the paragraph:

Human development can be divided into a number of different aspects. *Physical development,* as you might guess, deals with changes in the body. *Personal development* is the term generally used for changes in an individual's personality. *Social development* refers to changes in the way an individual relates to others. And *cognitive development* refers to changes in thinking. [Italics added.]

—Anita E. Woolfolk, *Educational Psychology*

6 Organizing by problem and solution

In the problem and solution organizational pattern, a particular problem is identified and one or more solutions are proposed. Usually the writer states the problem explicitly, although sometimes it is only implied. Posing the problem in the form of a question is especially attention-getting.

> What can be done about drug abuse among students? First, we should distinguish between experimentation and abuse. Many students try something at a party but do not become regular users. The best way to help students who have trouble saying no appears to be through peer programs that teach how to say no assertively. The successful programs also teach general social skills and build self-esteem (Newcomb & Bentler, 1989). Also, the older students are when they experiment with drugs, the more likely they are to make responsible choices, so helping younger students say no is a clear benefit.
>
> —Anita E. Woolfolk, *Educational Psychology*

7 Organizing by narrative or process description

Narratives and process descriptions present events in a time-ordered sequence. A **narrative** tells a story; a **process description** depicts a step-by-step procedure. In either case, the writer recounts events in chronological order, using verb tenses consistently and not jumping from one time frame to another.

In narrating the plot of a literary work, you normally use the present tense, as in this brief description of Ibsen's *An Enemy of the People:*

> The play is set in a little town which makes its living from the tourists who come to take its famous baths. Dr. Stockmann discovers that the waters have been contaminated by the local sewage system. He insists that the facts must be revealed, and expects that the city authorities will be grateful for his discovery. To his astonishment he finds that he has become an enemy of the people because he insists that the truth be known and the evil corrected. Doggedly he decides to fight on for truth even though the whole community is against him.
>
> —Vincent F. Hopper and Bernard D. N. Grebanier,
> *Essentials of European Literature*

When writing a process description, keep the verb tenses consistent (see 24e), and use an occasional transitional word such as *first, second, finally, after, then,* or *while.* Notice the transitional words in this process description paragraph:

> Land reclamation is the careful burying and grading of refuse that is dumped into prepared sites, such as deep trenches, swamps, ponds, or abandoned quarries. *After* the refuse has been dumped, it

is sprayed with chemicals to kill larvae and insects. *Then* it is compacted by heavy equipment, covered with a thick layer of clean earth, and graded so that it blends with surrounding land. [Italics added.]

—*The New Book of Knowledge*

8 Organizing by exemplification

Examples are a powerful way to make difficult concepts understandable. A paragraph organized by **exemplification** usually follows a general-to-specific pattern. The concept to be explained is introduced in general terms at the beginning, and then one or more specific examples are offered to make it meaningful, as in this paragraph:

A general principle of human behavior is that we try to minimize our costs and maximize our rewards. Sociologist Richard Berk calls this a *minimax strategy.* The fewer costs and the more rewards we anticipate from something, the more likely we are to do it. For example, if we believe that others will approve an act, the likelihood that we will do it increases. Whether in yelling for the referee's blood at a bad call in football, or shouting for real blood as a member of a lynch mob, this principle applies. In short, whether people are playing cards with a few friends, or are part of a mob, the principles of human behavior remain the same.

—James M. Henslin, *Sociology*

9 Organizing by physical description

A descriptive paragraph paints a picture of a person, place, or object by appealing to the reader's senses (sight, sound, touch, taste, or smell). It emphasizes details, which should be carefully selected so as to give the reader a vivid sense of what is being described. The following example brings to life something that most people can only imagine—the microscopic structure of ordinary soil.

The spaces between the soil grains offer a variety of habitats. The smaller pores and channels are filled with water, the larger ones mostly with air. Clay soils have narrow, threadlike channels that twist and taper downward; in sand, as might be imagined from seeing it on the beach, there are air pockets in the tiny spaces between the grains. Draped upon the skeleton of the soil are the sinews and flesh of a teeming life: each particle, even the finest, has a tight-fitting film of oxides, water, bits of organic matter. This skin is what gives life to the soil underfoot.

—Peter Farb, *Living Earth*

10 Organizing by mixing patterns

Although many paragraphs can be structured using one of the organizational patterns just described, you may sometimes want to express ideas in a way that does not conform to any one pattern. In such cases, do not be afraid to mix two or more organizational patterns. Just make it clear what pattern you are following at any one time. Here is an example of a paragraph that mixes patterns:

> Popular music has never been a stranger to controversy or opposition. Herman Gray has noted three periods of particularly strong opposition: the response to jazz in the early part of the century, the reaction against rock 'n' roll in the 1950s and 1960s, and the most recent wave of controversy associated with heavy metal and rap. No matter what the genre, certain themes such as a fear of the connection between music and sexuality tend to run through all three periods. Such concerns may be expressed either as the fear that sensual rhythms can overcome rationality or that lyrics that push the boundaries of decorum can undermine moral values. Because of these fears, each genre has been linked at various times to drug abuse, lawless behavior, and general moral decline. In turn, all of these problems have been projected to some degree onto race.
>
> —Reebee Garofalo, *Rockin' Out*

This paragraph basically follows the exemplification pattern, with sentences 2–6 exemplifying the generalization stated in the first sentence. But sentence 2, describing "three periods," is a classification statement. And sentences 5–6, marked by "Because . . . ," follow the cause-and-effect pattern. As long as pattern shifts are clearly marked, mixed paragraphs can be comprehensible and coherent.

5c Use sentence-linking techniques

In addition to conforming to organizational patterns, writers increase the coherence of their paragraphs by developing connections between sentences through use of transitional expressions, repetition of words or phrases, or references to earlier information.

5.2
Details on developing an argumentative essay.

1 Using transitional words and phrases

Transitional words and phrases are useful for linking sentences. The various expressions listed under Common Transitional Words and Phrases (page 59) differ somewhat in degree of formality. For example, *furthermore* and *consequently* are more formal than *besides* and *so*. Being aware of these differences will help you strike a consistent tone in your writing (see 30c).

Notice how effective the transitional expressions are in making this paragraph more readable:

> Many of us live in awe of statistics. Perhaps nowhere is our respect for statistics so evident—and so exploited—as in advertising. If three out of four doctors surveyed recommend Pain Away aspirin, it must be the best. If Sudsy Soap is 99.9 percent pure (whatever that means), surely it will help our complexions. *And* if nine out of ten people like Sloppy Catsup in the taste test, we will certainly buy some for this weekend's barbecue. How can the statistics be wrong? *On the other hand,* some people are suspicious of all statistics. They have witnessed too many erroneous weather forecasts and election predictions. *In reality,* the truth about statistics lies somewhere between unconditional faith in numbers and Mark Twain's wry observation that "there are three kinds of lies: lies, damned lies, and statistics." [Italics added.]
>
> —Adapted from Steven A. Beebe and Susan J. Beebe,
> *Public Speaking*

2 Repeating key words

A paragraph almost always has key words. Repetition of these words helps the reader focus on the topic at hand. Exact repetition can become tiresome, however, so good writers use synonyms or paraphrases. (The THESAURUS feature of your word processor can help you choose synonyms.)

Notice how the writer of this paragraph about a teaching technique artfully uses repetition to maintain focus and coherence:

AUDIO

Keeping sentence subjects short.

> *Modeling* has long been used to teach dance, sports, and crafts, as well as skills in subjects such as home economics, chemistry, and shop. *Modeling* can also be applied deliberately in the classroom to teach mental skills and to broaden horizons—to teach new ways of thinking. Teachers serve as *models* for a vast range of behaviors, from pronouncing vocabulary words, to reacting to the seizure of an epileptic student, to being enthusiastic about learning. For example,

Common Transitional Words and Phrases

To show cause and effect	*therefore, thus, consequently, as a result, for this reason, so, so that*
To compare	*similarly, likewise, in like manner, also*
To contrast	*however, on the one hand/on the other hand, in contrast, conversely, but, yet, nevertheless, nonetheless, on the contrary, still*
To show addition	*and, in addition, also, furthermore, moreover, besides*
To indicate time	*before, now, after, afterwards, subsequently, later, earlier, meanwhile, in the meantime, while, as long as, so far*
To give examples	*for example, for instance, specifically, namely, to illustrate, that is*
To conclude or summarize	*in conclusion, to conclude, in summary, to summarize, in short, in other words, therefore, thus, in reality*
To generalize	*in general, for the most part, as a general rule, on the whole, usually, typically*
To emphasize a point	*indeed, in fact, as a matter of fact, even*
To signal concession	*of course, naturally, although it is true that, granted that*

a teacher might *model* sound critical thinking skills by thinking "out loud" about a student's question. Or a high school teacher concerned about girls who seem to have stereotyped ideas about careers might invite women with nontraditional jobs to speak to the class. [Italics added.]

—Anita E. Woolfolk, *Educational Psychology*

3   Referring to old information

Another way to link sentences is to refer to "old information," something readers are already familiar with, at the beginning of the new sentence. These references to old information usually consist of repeated words, pronouns, or words marked by *the* or *this,* inserted into the subject position (see 22b-1). Here is an example from a textbook on public speaking:

> In a classic study, Ralph Nichols asked both good and poor listeners what their listening strategies were. *The poor listeners* indicated that they listened for facts such as names and dates. *The good listeners* reported that they listened for major ideas and principles. *Facts* are useful only when you can connect them to a principle or concept. In speeches, *facts* as well as examples are used primarily to support major ideas. *You* should try to summarize mentally the major idea that the specific *facts* support. [Italics added.]
>
> —Steven A. Beebe and Susan J. Beebe, *Public Speaking*

5d   Be consistent with verb tense, person, and number

Verb tenses help create a time frame for readers (see 24e). When writers jump from one verb tense to another within a paragraph, they disrupt the paragraph's coherence and risk confusing the reader. Conversely, maintaining a consistent point of view in the use of pronouns helps readers. After using the first-person plural (*we, us, our*), do not switch to the singular (*I, me, my*) or to second or third person (*you, they, . . .*) unless there is a good reason to do so (see Chapter 30). The following paragraph illustrates how problems with verb tense and person might be solved.

Watching Monday Night Football on ABC has become a ritualistic practice for countless American sports lovers. Every Monday night during the NFL season, we would ~~gather~~ *millions of fans* gather to watch the "old pigskin" being thrown around. This activity can be experienced in the comfort of ~~your~~ *one's* own home, at parties, or in popular sports bars. ~~A typical viewer will~~ *Viewers* especially enjoy the opening segment of the program, with all its pyrotechnics and special effects. ~~They~~ *The producers* really know how to put on a show at ABC! ~~If you~~ *For those who* like football, MNF is not to be missed.

5e Use parallelism to make paragraphs coherent

Many paragraphs contain embedded "lists"—that is, sets of sentences that have equivalent values and roles. In such cases, it is important to establish **parallelism** between the sentences by giving them the same grammatical structure. Such parallelism helps the reader easily see the relationship between sentences. (Chapter 33 discusses parallelism *within* sentences.) Notice how the two parallel sentences in this paragraph set off the contrast between poor and middle-class African Americans:

> Sociologist William Julius Wilson argues that there are two worlds of African-American experience. *Those who are stuck in the inner city live in poverty, confront violent crime daily, attend underfunded schools, face dead-end jobs or welfare, and are filled with hopelessness and despair, combined with apathy or hostility.* In contrast, *those who have moved up the social class ladder live in good housing in relatively crime-free neighborhoods, work at well-paid jobs that offer advancement, and send their children to good schools.* Their middle-class experiences and lifestyle have changed their views on life. Their aspirations and values have so altered that they no longer have much in common with African Americans who remain poor. According to Wilson, then, social class—not race—has become the most significant factor in the lives of African Americans today. [Italics added.]
>
> —Adapted from James M. Henslin, *Sociology*

To make it easy for the reader to spot the "two worlds" that Wilson is talking about, the writer describes them in separate, grammatically parallel sentences (*Those who . . . , those who . . .*).

5f Decide on appropriate paragraph length

Each paragraph should be long enough to adequately develop its main point. Thus, paragraph length depends mainly on how complicated the topic is. The important thing is to make paragraphs complete and unified. A writer who does so is not likely to make them excessively long or excessively short.

Also, bear in mind that desirable paragraph length can vary from one type of writing to another. In college essays, most paragraphs are likely to be three to five sentences long. In contrast, paragraphs in the *Encyclopaedia Britannica* may contain twelve or more sentences.

5g   Link paragraphs with key words

In any series of paragraphs, a reader should be able to move easily from one paragraph to the next. If a paragraph picks up where the preceding one left off, provide at least one link in the first sentence of the new paragraph. Such links can be transitional words and phrases or expressions referring to old information and preceded by terms such as *this, these,* or *such.* Notice that the first sentence of the second paragraph below contains a phrase that continues a theme from the first paragraph:

> One of the major forms of social stratification is caste. In a caste system, status is determined by birth and is lifelong. In sociological terms the basis of a caste system is ascribed status. Achieved status cannot change an individual's place in this system. People born into a low-status group will always have low status, no matter how much they personally may accomplish in life.
>
> Societies with *this form of stratification* try to make certain that the boundaries between castes remain firm. They practice endogamy, marriage within their own group, and prohibit intermarriage. To prevent contact between castes, they even develop elaborate rules about ritual pollution, teaching that contact with inferior castes contaminates the superior caste. [Italics added.]
>
> —Adapted from James M. Henslin, *Sociology*

5h   Construct effective introductory and concluding paragraphs

The beginning and the end of a document are the two places where readers are most likely to give full attention to what they are reading. Thus, it is particularly important that you write effective opening and closing paragraphs (see 4b-7).

1   Writing an introductory paragraph that will draw the reader's attention

When readers start to read a piece of writing, they want to know what it will be about and whether it will be interesting—and they want to know these things quickly. Therefore, you should write an opening paragraph that is informative and interesting. The opening paragraph should always be appropriate to the genre: an academic essay requires a different sort of opening than does, say, a letter of

Some Effective Devices for Introductory Paragraphs

- *A personal anecdote.* Personal stories give readers a vivid sense of what a topic means.
- *A detailed description.* Another way of setting the scene is to describe the environment in detail.
- *A quotation.* If the relevance of the quotation to the rest of the writing is not entirely clear, add an accompanying explanation or comment.
- *A problem.* For most readers, stating the problem will pique interest in possible solutions.
- *An analogy.* If your topic is difficult to grasp, an analogy may clarify it. Note, however, that analogies are risky. For an analogy to work, there must be sufficient correspondence between the two things being compared (see 6g-7).
- *A provocative statement.* A statement that seems contradictory or nonsensical will certainly draw attention. Of course, for this strategy to be effective, you must be able to show that the statement is not contradictory or nonsensical at all.

complaint. In all genres, however, an introductory paragraph should accomplish four things:

1. Identify the topic of the piece
2. Stimulate reader interest
3. Establish a tone or style
4. Enable readers to anticipate what comes next

Here is an example of an effective introductory paragraph from an essay on gender differences in the electronic age:

As a longtime *Star Trek* devotee, Janis Cortese was eager to be part of the Trekkie discussion group on the Internet. But when she first logged on, Cortese noticed that these fans of the final frontier devoted megabytes to such profound topics as whether Troi or Crusher had bigger breasts. In other words, the purveyors of this *Trek* dreck were all *guys*. Undeterred, Cortese, a physicist at California's Loma Linda University, figured she'd add perspective to the electronic gathering place with her own momentous questions. Why was the male cast racially diverse while almost all the females were young, white, and skinny? Then, she tossed in a few lustful thoughts about the male crew members.

—Barbara Kantrowitz, "Men, Women, Computers"

Because it relates a personal anecdote about a popular TV program, this paragraph is likely to interest many readers. The topic ("the purveyors . . . were all *guys*") is identified by the end of sentence 3. A jocular tone is established with words like *dreck, skinny,* and *lustful thoughts.* And the final sentence enables readers to guess what comes next (male Trekkies responded by flooding her email box with nasty flames).

While some types of writing, such as business letters and memos (see Chapter 19), have fairly conventional openings, other types of writing give you more latitude in ways to draw reader interest. For example, if you are writing an exploratory essay, such as the one by Kantrowitz, you have some freedom in how you construct your opening paragraph. You can adopt a relaxed style, and you can hint at your thesis instead of stating it explicitly. On the other hand, if you are writing an argumentative essay, your readers will expect you to use a more formal style and tighter structure, and they will look for an explicit thesis in the first paragraph.

5.3

Seven examples of effective opening paragraphs.

2 Writing a concluding paragraph that creates a sense of completeness

The concluding paragraph of an extended piece of writing should not leave the reader hanging but, rather, should neatly tie things up. Except in a very short essay, the concluding paragraph should reiterate your main point, preferably not by simply restating it but by adding something to it. Ideally, it should also stimulate the reader to think beyond what you have already said. See Some Effective Devices for Concluding Paragraphs; sometimes two or more of these techniques work well together.

The following paragraph is the concluding paragraph of the Kantrowitz essay introduced in 5h-1. It includes a quotation, a story, and speculation about what the future may hold.

Ironically, gender differences could help women. "We're at a cultural turning point," says MIT's Turkle. "There's an opportunity to remake the culture around the machine." Practicality is now as valued as invention. If the computer industry wants to put machines in the hands of the masses, that means women—along with the great many men who have no interest in hot-rod computing. An ad cam-

Some Effective Devices for Concluding Paragraphs

- Present an apt quotation.
- Tell a story that illustrates your main point.
- Pose a thought-provoking question.
- Pick up on a theme or idea that was mentioned at the beginning of the essay.
- Speculate about the future.

paign for Compaq's popular Presario line emphasizes the machine's utility. After kissing her child goodnight, the mother in the ad sits down at her Presario to work. As people start to view their machines as creative tools, someday women may be just as comfortable with computers as men are.

—Barbara Kantrowitz, "Men, Women, Computers"

CHAPTER **6**

Constructing and Evaluating Arguments

A natural outcome of the critical thinking you are expected to do in college (see 1a–b) is speaking or writing in which you formulate and defend your own point of view. This is called *argument*. Argument in this sense does not mean quarreling; rather, it means taking a position on an issue and supporting it with evidence and good reasoning.

AUDIO
Chapter
overview.

WEBLINK

http://eslplanet.com/
teachertools/argueweb/
frntpage.htm

From Australia, an authoritative guide to writing
argumentative essays

Critical thinking for purposes
of developing an argument is more
creative than critical thinking in
reading. To prepare the ground for
an argument, you need to think
about an issue in a way that will
engage an audience's (and your
own) interest and lead to some res-
olution. It should be an issue that is
worth arguing about, one for
which you can assemble sufficient evidence and refute any counterevidence.

6a   Formulate an arguable thesis

VIDEO

Finding
arguable
topics.

WEBLINK

http://powa.org/argument
.htm

Thorough treatment of how
to formulate and develop an
arguable thesis

The first step in developing an
argument is to formulate a good
thesis, or claim (see 2d-2-3). In argument, as in exposition, a thesis is
a statement in which the writer or
speaker takes a supportable position on an issue—for example,
"Voting rights can be extended
safely to most of the mentally ill."

1   What constitutes an appropriate thesis?

To have an influence on others, a thesis should be *open to debate.*
That is, it should not make a claim that everyone would already agree
with. "Smoking is harmful to your health" is not an effective argumentative thesis because almost no educated person would disagree
with it. A more interesting, more arguable thesis would be "Smoking
should be prohibited in all public places, including restaurants." It
makes a better thesis because it would not meet with universal agreement or disagreement and thus would require argumentation.

Second, an appropriate thesis is *open to evidence and counterevidence*—you can gather and present evidence for and against this
claim. If a thesis merely expresses your own opinion about something ("I think smoking is cool"), without citing evidence beyond
your own feelings, it offers no claim that can be objectively assessed
by others.

An Arguable Thesis or Claim

- Is debatable. Not everyone will automatically agree with it.
- Can be supported with evidence available to everyone.
- Can be countered with arguments against it.
- Is a clearly stated claim of fact, value, or policy, with terms defined.
- Is not based just on personal opinion or subjective feelings inaccessible to others.

Third, a thesis should be *clearly stated*. It should leave no confusion in the mind of the reader as to what you are claiming. Provide definitions or paraphrases of any terms that may be unclear.

A thesis can be either a claim of fact, a claim of value, or a claim of policy. A claim of fact asserts that something is true ("Smoking is harmful to your health"). A claim of value asserts that something is or is not worthwhile ("People should protect their health by not smoking"). A claim of policy argues for a course of action ("Smoking should be banned in all public places"). Your thesis should make clear to the audience which type of claim you are making (see 2d-2–3).

2 Using inductive and deductive reasoning

If you have to develop your own thesis, there are two kinds of reasoning that can help you get there. **Inductive reasoning** begins with particular evidence and arrives at some general conclusion. For example, if your mail has been delivered three hours late for the past four days (particular evidence), you might conclude that a substitute carrier is now working your route (generalization). Or let's say the front tire on your bike needs frequent pumping but your rear tire doesn't; you might reasonably infer that your front tire has a small leak. As you can see from these examples, inductive reasoning is something we use routinely, every day. We use inductive reasoning to try to make sense of things and to come up with new ideas. Inductive reasoning relies on experience; it is sometimes referred to as "educated guesswork." Inductive reasoning deals with probability, not absolute truth or validity. Thus, the conclusions it arrives at are not necessarily "true"; rather, they are only probable or plausible.

Deductive reasoning goes in the opposite direction, from general to particular. You start with some generalization—a general claim, principle, or belief—and then you apply it to some specific fact and arrive at some specific conclusion or prediction. Deductive reasoning relies on a strict form of logic, conventionally expressed in a **syllogism.** A syllogism contains a major premise (the generalization), one or more minor premises (the facts), and a conclusion.

MAJOR PREMISE   People who work hard are usually successful.

MINOR PREMISE   Kevin works hard.

CONCLUSION   Kevin will probably be successful.

In deductive reasoning there is a difference between *validity* and *truth.* When a deductive argument conforms to the rules of logic, it is said to be a *valid argument.* In the above case, the minor premise fits logically the condition set up in the major premise ("People who work hard"), and so the conclusion logically follows. A deductive argument can be *true,* however, only if its premises are true, so if any premise is false, the argument itself is false. For example, if it turns out that Kevin does *not* work hard, the above argument, although valid, would be false.

In everyday use, deductive reasoning often leaves its major premise unstated. This is because major premises are often widely accepted assumptions in the particular culture. Thus, the syllogism given above might be expressed in everyday language as, "Kevin works hard—I think he'll be successful some day." Such abbreviated syllogisms (or **enthymemes**) are commonplace in daily life because they convey logical reasoning in shortcut fashion. Unfortunately, the very convenience of enthymemes makes them attractive to those who misuse them for deception. Here is an example from a political campaign: "The Congressman clearly supports family values. He has five children."

MAJOR PREMISE,   Anyone who has five children supports family
UNSTATED   values.

MINOR PREMISE   The Congressman has five children.

CONCLUSION   The Congressman supports family values.

By leaving the major premise an unstated assumption, the speaker avoided subjecting it to public scrutiny. If he had stated it explicitly, people in the audience might have raised questions about its truth, about the vagueness of the term *family values,* and so on. (This example illustrates the fallacy of begging the question; see 6g-2.)

Of course, there is no guarantee that simple uses of induction and deduction by themselves will lead to good, arguable theses. The claim that "Kevin will probably be successful" would not make a good thesis, as it is not open to evidence and counterevidence and is not a claim of fact, value, or policy. The claim that "The Congressman supports family values" holds better promise as a thesis, especially if it is a public issue in the Congressman's district. But it would first need to have the term *family values* defined in a way that allowed for evidence to be marshaled for and against it.

Inductive and deductive reasoning often work together, and this combination has a better chance of producing a good, arguable thesis. For instance, you might use inductive reasoning to formulate a generalization from particulars, and then use that same generalization as your major premise in deductive reasoning. Here is an example:

INDUCTIVE REASONING

PARTICULARS	You keep reading or hearing news reports about mass shootings in Southern and Western states.
PARTICULARS	You have read in several places that there are more guns per capita in Southern and Western states than in other states.
GENERALIZATION	More gun ownership leads to more gun-related violence.

DEDUCTIVE REASONING

MAJOR PREMISE	More gun ownership leads to more gun-related violence.
MINOR PREMISE	The new concealed weapon ordinance in our city is causing more people to buy guns.
CONCLUSION	The new concealed weapon ordinance will cause the rate of gun-related violence in our city to increase.

This conclusion would serve as a good thesis for an argument because it is an important public issue, is debatable, can be supported or refuted with evidence, is a clearly stated claim of fact (which, in this case, can be converted to a claim of policy), and is not just based on personal opinion. Note also how the underlying premises themselves satisfy these requirements.

3 Working through a thesis

Not every claim, or thesis, ends up the way it began; most writers develop a thesis somewhat by trial and error, refining their ideas as they gather more information. For an essay in her composition class, Angela Napper decided to write about cybercensorship. She had heard that administrators at her college were considering new rules that would prohibit students from accessing certain Web sites in the school's computer labs. She felt this would be an infringement on academic freedom, and so she decided that her thesis would be something like "Censoring Internet usage is inappropriate in a college environment." But this was only her *working thesis*. As she explored the subject and worked through her ideas, she realized that the issue of cybercensorship was far broader than just its effect on college students. She also decided that she should make her thesis more specific, more open to evidence—that is, more arguable. After further research and brainstorming, Angela decided to focus not on the inappropriateness of cybercensorship in college but on the constitutionality of such censorship in the broader public sphere. This resulted in a *revised thesis*: "Citizens need to take a stand to protect their rights to privacy and freedom of information on public computers as these rights are guaranteed to them in the Constitution under the Bill of Rights."

Angela's thesis is a good one. First of all, it is not a statement that everyone would automatically agree with. In fact, after the terrorist attacks of September 11, many people would argue that citizens must sacrifice some of these rights for the sake of greater national security. Second, the thesis can be debated with evidence and counterevidence. Angela could cite the relevant parts of the Constitution and court decisions that either support or undermine her thesis. Third, the thesis is a clearly stated claim of policy, alluding to several of the key subissues (right of privacy, freedom of information, the use of public computers, constitutional rights).

6b Generate good supporting evidence

VIDEO
Investigating
assumptions.

Central to the strength of an argument is the evidence cited to support it. There are five main types of evidence: factual data, expert opinion, personal experience, examples, and statistics.

Factual data include any information presented as representing objective reality. Factual data most often consist of measurable, or quantitative, evidence such as distances, amounts, and ratios. But factual data can include historical events, longstanding assessments, and other widely attested observations about the world. Objectivity makes factual data difficult to refute. Therefore, in most academic disciplines, factual data are considered to be the most powerful form of evidence you can present.

Expert opinion also can be persuasive, because it represents the studied judgment of someone who knows a great deal about the subject at hand. If a famous literary critic said that *Twelfth Night* was one of Shakespeare's finest plays, quoting this expert's statement would strengthen any argument you made along those lines. But expert opinion has its limitations. First, a quotation taken out of context may not convey what the expert really meant. Second, experts sometimes fall prey to the influence of some special interest. Not long ago, experts employed by the tobacco industry testified that tobacco was not addictive. Finally, experts can simply be wrong in their judgments and predictions.

Personal experience is less objective than either factual data or expert opinion, but it can be highly compelling. Personal experience is especially effective when presented in the form of a narrative. The story you tell may represent only your own experience— and thus lack generalizability—but since it is coming directly from you it has a certain vividness that is missing from more detached accounts. Personal experience is not the same as personal opinion: the former is an account of an experience—something you have personally tested against reality—whereas the latter may be nothing more than a snap judgment. Arguments do not go far on opinion alone.

Examples are effective because, like personal experience, they are concrete, vivid, and therefore easy for readers to relate to. (Just think of how much you appreciate good examples in the textbooks and other instructional materials you read!) Unlike personal experience, examples are supposed to be generalizations about a larger category. That is, they are good only to the extent that they are typical of an entire class of phenomena. If you present an odd case as a "typical example," you may justifiably be criticized for giving a misleading example.

A collection of numerical data, *statistics* usually are compressed in a way that points to a certain interpretation. Because statistics typically represent a large body of data, they can be compelling as evidence. But they can also be manipulated in deceptive ways. If you gather your own statistics, be sure you know how to analyze them correctly. If you take statistics from other sources, try to use only sources that are considered reliable (for example, the US government or prestigious academic journals).

Angela's essay on cybercensorship is printed on page 72. Note what kinds of evidence she used to support her thesis.

Angela Napper

Writing 2010-08

April 3, 2003

Cybercensorship

With more and more regulations being formed
about what citizens are allowed to view on the
Internet, concerns as to the constitutional rights
of these citizens are being raised. At public

Introduces the issue in attention-getting terms: "the debate rages"

libraries, at colleges and universities, and at
businesses the debate rages as to how much privacy
users should have, and whether censorship of
certain materials is needed to protect the public
welfare. More and more it is becoming clear that
citizens need to take a stand to protect their

Presents her thesis

right to privacy and freedom of speech on public
computers as these rights are guaranteed to them in
the US Constitution, specifically the First, Fifth,
and Fourteenth Amendments.

Libraries. Recently, the Chesterfield County
Board of Supervisors in Virginia passed a law

Gives an example as background information

making it illegal for any computer user in a public
library to access any material deemed by the
community as pornographic or obscene. This includes
any information on sex education and any Web sites
containing prohibited words. Consequently,

Napper 2

a site containing a recipe for chicken breasts
would be banned. The local chapter of the American
Civil Liberties Union (ACLU) is expected to
challenge the legislation. However, the new policy
seems to be popular with some of the locals. They
have even started a Liberty Watch group where
citizens make a point of monitoring what those
around them are accessing on the Web. Anything they
deem illegal by the new standards is reported to
the local authorities (Oder and Rogers).

With this type of a system in place, citizens'
right to access information--as guaranteed in the
freedom of speech and freedom of press clauses of
the First Amendment and the equal protection clause
of the Fourteenth Amendment--is greatly infringed
upon. The morals and beliefs of those in power have
been forced upon everyone. It is exactly this type
of regulation that the Founding Fathers were trying
to escape when they created the United States, a
country where everyone would be free to live their
lives as they chose, assuming they were not hurting
others. I fail to see how attempting to access a
recipe for chicken is hurting anyone. For that
matter, gaining information on sex education is not
infringing on the well-being of the community.

Presents
main
supporting
evidence for
her thesis

Napper 3

Rather, it is likely helping the overall well-being by preventing unwanted pregnancies and diseases. As educator David Thornburg states, "Libraries in schools and communities should be the last places to use censorship of any kind. Once the door to censorship is opened, how do we ever get it closed again?" (Thornburg).

Uses quotation from authority to reinforce her point

Colleges and universities. The debate between freedom of speech and censorship is also raging at a number of universities. At Snow College in Southern Utah, administrators added software that blocked student access to all information deemed nonacademic. They say the motivation behind their actions had nothing to do with moral censorship. Rather, they claim that students playing games and looking up pornography were using up too much computing time and power. Students who needed the computers for homework had to wait through long lines and deal with slower computers. With the new policy in effect, the rate of hits on blocked sites has gone from 35 percent to fewer than five per day. This speeds up the computers for those who need them for academic purposes. Students complained that they were never asked about their opinion beforehand and were not told about the

Introduces another site; should resonate with students

Napper 4

decision after it had gone into effect. When asked
what they would do if the student body voted
against the new policy, school officials say the
policy would be removed (Madsen).

Similarly, Indiana University recently banned
the downloading of MP3's on school computers
because it was using up too much of the school's
bandwidth. Opposition came from a group called
Students Against University Censorship who began
circulating a petition around the nation with the
goal of gaining popular support as well as legal
representation in their fight against these
censorship policies. Their aim was to gain public
support so as to have more power in a court of law
or in negotiations with officials who could strike
down censorship at universities nationwide
(Ferguson).

However, some universities are in favor of
giving students free reign. The University of
Nevada, Las Vegas, refuses to put limits on what
their students can access on school computers or in
the dorms. Officials state that they respect the
students' rights and they want to make them feel at
home when they are living in the dorms, which means
allowing them access to all sites. If anyone on

Another
example of
students
being
victimized

Napper 5

campus is offended by what another student is

viewing, that student is simply asked to relocate

to a more private computer. This type of policy

respect~~s the rights of all involved. It does not~~

infringe upon the freedom of speech rights of the

students, while at the same time anyone who feels

uncomfortable by material around them is

accommodated appropriately (Ferguson).

This more reasonable approach provides ~~support for~~ her argument

Businesses. More and more the battleground is

moving into the professional workplace. Employers

are looking to monitor what their employees access

during work hours, so as to prevent them from

wasting company time on personal entertainment.

Currently, over 2000 companies have begun using

Cyber-Patrol, software that filters out any Web

sites the company does not want its employees to

access. Microsystems Software Inc., the company

that designs this software for corporations, claims

it is not censoring anything, but only filtering.

It allows managers to personally inspect Web sites

that have been accessed by company employees. Since

every Web site Cyber-Patrol blocks has been viewed

by a person, there is not blanket censorship based

on what words a site may contain. All sites are

placed into one of three categories: CyberYes,

This counter-example serves nicely to restrict her thesis; gives her more credibility

Napper 6

CyberNo, and Sports/Entertainment. With this system, any company can choose whether it wants its employees to be able to access sports and entertainment sites during work hours. It can also restrict any sites that have been deemed pornographic or violent (Markels).

This type of restriction seems less in violation of citizens' rights because it is designed to be used only in the workplace where most would agree employers have the right to monitor what their employees are doing during office hours as they own the machines and are paying the employees for their time. Similarly, it might be argued that public libraries and universities also own their computers and consequently should have the right to censor them. It must be kept in mind, however, that those computers were purchased using taxpayers' money, so in reality they belong to the public. Cyber-Patrol is also improved in its format in that each Web site is individually viewed. Web sites with recipes for chicken breasts would consequently not be banned.

Highlights the public vs. private dimension of this issue, setting up the next section

Government surveillance. These same issues of the public's right to privacy have become a point

Napper 7

of controversy in recent government hearings. There is a push by the Bush administration led by Attorney General John Ashcroft to allow government officials access to private citizens' Web use and emails. New technology called Carnivore would allow officials access to the records of any Internet provider. "In order to find specific emails, Carnivore must sort through all the email of an Internet service provider. That opens up all the people using that provider to government surveillance without judicial review" (Puzzanghera). This same system has the ability to record all people who have hit on any given site, or all of the sites accessed by any given computer (Puzzanghera).

Ashcroft is pushing to have the legislation passed quickly. He claims that such laws are necessary to gain ground against further terrorist attacks in the US. Opposition to new proposed laws such as this is led by Jerry Bermann, the executive director for the Center for Democracy and Technology in Washington. He and his supporters claim that the government is moving too fast, not stopping to consider the long-term effects that this legislation would have. The Attorney General's

This example adds complexity to the issue, making it even more interesting

Napper 8

response to this claim is that Americans do not have time on their side if further attacks are to be prevented (Puzzanghera). This seems to be a scare tactic on the part of the government to pass legislation quickly before it can be debated and, if necessary, modified. While we may need new laws to stop future attacks by terrorists on the US, it is also vital to ensure that citizens' rights are not crushed in the process. As one human rights researcher has said, "If allowed to be controlled by a government, instead of a tool for democracy, the Internet may be employed as a tool by which more modern dictatorships can monitor and control its citizens" (Hansen).

Refutes the counter-example, making her argument stronger

Conclusion. With the debate raging as to how much privacy Americans are entitled to when it comes to the Internet and what information they should be able to access, it is the citizens' job to take a stand and fight for their rights. It is only by doing so that the ideals of freedom of speech and right to privacy that the founding fathers so highly valued will be preserved.

Concludes with a concise summary of the main points

Napper 9

Works Cited

Ferguson, Kevin. "Net Censorship Spreading on
    University Campuses." Las Vegas Business Press
    28 Feb. 2000: P20.

Hansen, Stephen A. "The Unhindered Use of the
    Internet in Human Rights Work." 22 Jan. 1999.
    Speech to the American Academy for the
    Advancement of Science. 15 Mar. 2003 <http://
    shr.aaas.org/Cybercensorship/Hansen.htm>.

Madsen, Grant. "Snow College Officials Defend Net
    Censorship; Blocking Pornography Was Not for
    Moral Reasons." Salt Lake Tribune 16 Jan.
    1999: D3.

Markels, Alex. "Screening the Net." Salt Lake
    Tribune 5 May 1997: B1.

Oder, Norman, and Michael Rogers. "VA County Public
    Library to Filter All Access." Library Journal
    126 (2001): 15.

Puzzanghera, Jim. "Privacy Advocates Argue Anti-
    Terrorism Plans Harm Free Society." San Jose
    Mercury News 27 Sept. 2001:1A.

Thornburg, David. "Children and Cybercensorship." 22
    Aug. 2002. PBS Teacher Source. 15 Mar. 2003
    <http://www.pbs.org/teachersource/thornburg/
    thornburg1098.shtm>.

What kinds of evidence does Angela use to support her argument? Mainly, she relies on a number of extended examples of situations where citizens' rights to privacy and freedom of speech are being eroded through the use of cybercensorship. By using a broad selection of settings (libraries, colleges, businesses, government surveillance), she conveys a sense of how widespread the danger is. She also cites the opinions of experts ranging from US Attorney General Ashcroft to Jerry Bermann, the executive director for the Center for Democracy and Technology. In addition, she gives source information for many of the statements in her paper. Angela uses factual data as well, in the form of objective accounts of the different cases and of the applicability of the US Constitution to them.

6c Take note of evidence for alternative views

VIDEO
Accommodating opposition.

In gathering evidence, do not go looking just for evidence that supports your case; take note of evidence supporting other positions as well, including evidence that argues directly against your case. On issues that are of any interest or value, the evidence will not be entirely one-sided; there will be evidence supporting alternative views. When you acknowledge the counterevidence, you gain credibility as a careful, conscientious thinker, thereby strengthening your argument rather than weakening it.

Angela's essay includes two different kinds of counterevidence to her thesis. First, she notes that some college administrators have been restricting students' Internet access not to censor their access to inappropriate material but to save on computing resources, thus ultimately giving students more access to appropriate uses of the schools' computer systems. Second, she says that private companies do have a legitimate right to restrict employees' use of company computers, since these computers are owned by the company and the employees are paid to do the company's work, not to entertain themselves. She also acknowledges the government's desire to promote greater security against terrorism as a reason for its increased cyber-surveillance of American citizens.

6d Develop and test the main points

Once you have formulated an appropriate thesis and compiled enough information to make a case for it, you need to develop and test the main points you want to make. This is the heart of an argument, where you lay out your reasoning in step-by-step fashion.

1 Deciding what your strongest points are

In any argument, some points are stronger than others: they are more central to the issue at hand, they make more sense in terms of logical reasoning, they have more evidence supporting them, and they have less counterevidence opposing them. In constructing your argument, you need to try to identify those points that seem to be strongest.

What do you do if your strongest points do not coincide with the main concerns of your audience? One strategy is to *redefine* their concerns and your points so that there is a closer fit. Another strategy is to accept the differences between yourself and your audience and prepare to make your argument anyway. Even a losing argument can have value, so long as it is a strong argument.

2 Developing and checking your points using Toulmin logic

Starting with your strongest point, use careful step-by-step reasoning to develop each point. Your main goal is to make sure that your points are logically sound, by analyzing their structure according to a method devised by the philosopher Stephen Toulmin. This structure consists of six parts: Claim (or point), Data (supporting reasons), Warrant (general principle connecting Data to Claim), Backing (for the Warrant), Qualifier (of the Claim), and possible Rebuttal (or counterargument, with a response). Here is an illustration of how Toulmin logic can be used to check one of Angela Napper's claims, namely that the Constitution guarantees citizens the right to access information:

POINT OR CLAIM	American citizens have the right to freely access information.
DATA	The Constitution guarantees freedom of speech and freedom of the press.
WARRANT [IMPLIED]	Freedom of speech and freedom of the press imply a freedom to *listen* to speech and *read* the press, that is, to access information.
BACKING	The Founding Fathers felt people should be free to live their lives as they choose, provided they do not hurt others.
QUALIFIER	The right to access information does not include making others uncomfortable or wasting company or university computing resources.

Checking Your Argument for Sound Reasoning

1. Have I arrived at a clearly stated, arguable thesis (6a)? What is it?
2. What is the evidence for my thesis, and how does it function as support for the thesis (6b)?
3. What are the main underlying assumptions—or *warrants*—that logically connect my claims to my evidence (6d-2)?
4. If these warrants are unstated, will they be obvious to everybody in my audience?

REBUTTAL   People should not be allowed to use public computers to view immoral material. (Response: People have a constitutional right to access whatever information they please, and no one else has the right to impose their own standards of morality on them.)

Notice that the validity of Angela's argument depends on an implied *warrant*—an underlying assumption that logically connects her claim to her evidence. Is this warrant valid? Many people in our culture might think so.

When careful readers judge your arguments, they will be scrutinizing your chain of reasoning. Thus, be aware of the warrant you use for each point you make. Often, the warrant is implicit rather than actually stated. But if critical readers do not share your assumptions, they will say that your claims are *unwarranted*. Any assumptions that might not be shared by your readers should be stated explicitly.

6e   Build a compelling case

The primary goal of any argument is to make the best case you can. The three basic ways to make a case are by using logical reasoning, by asserting your and others' authority, and by appealing to the readers' emotions.

1 Appealing to logic

In college, certainly the most important type of support you can give to an argument is logical reasoning (or *logos*). Indeed, one of the main purposes of education is to promote the ability to communicate effectively with a broad, skeptical audience (in both professional and public life), and logical reasoning is the primary tool for doing so. In particular, you should avoid logical fallacies (see 6g). In whatever field of study you undertake—sociology, history, mathematics, or biology—your instructors will always be paying close attention to the logical reasoning you use. They will want to know that you can develop an argument step by step, laying out a chain of reasoning that compels skeptical readers to respect your thinking.

6.1

Some terms used in formal logical reasoning.

WEBLINK

http://owl.english.purdue.edu/handouts/general/gl_argpers.html

A guide to logic in argumentative writing

There are many effective patterns for developing an argument. They include linking cause and effect, making comparisons and contrasts, defining and classifying, narrating a series of events, generalizing from particulars (or *induction*), drawing particular inferences from general rules (or *deduction*), and providing relevant examples and analogies. (Some of these approaches underlie the paragraph patterns discussed in Chapter 5.)

2 Appealing to authority

People usually are greatly influenced by the credibility or reputation of the person trying to persuade them. That is why advertisers like to use highly esteemed celebrities such as Tiger Woods and Jennifer Lopez to push their products, even when such celebrities know little about the product they are endorsing.

More discerning readers are not so likely to be influenced by celebrity endorsements, but they often are influenced by expert judgments. Thus, you can support an argument by invoking the authority of true experts. In doing so, it is important to (1) find experts who are addressing an issue within their field of expertise, (2) use actual quotes rather than paraphrasing, (3) include enough context to make the quote an accurate reflection of the expert's statement, and (4) provide a reference so that skeptical readers can look up the quote for themselves.

An even more important type of authority is your own. Since you are the person who has gathered the information and assembled the argument, your own credibility (or *ethos*) will be under scrutiny. If readers have any reason to doubt your honesty, fairness, or scholarly integrity, they will treat what you say with a good deal of skepticism. Here are some things you can do to safeguard and enhance your credibility:

1. Avoid making any exaggerated or distorted assertions.
2. Acknowledge opposing points of view and counterevidence.
3. If you use other people's ideas or words, give them explicit credit.
4. If appropriate, mention your credentials (without bragging).
5. Use good reasoning throughout.
6. Maintain a respectful, civil tone.
7. Pay attention to details of writing such as grammar, style, spelling, and punctuation.

3 Appealing to emotion

A third powerful way of supporting an argument is by enlisting the readers' emotions (or *pathos*). Although this type of persuasion is generally discouraged in academic and technical writing, it can occasionally be used in conjunction with a more logical appeal. In many other kinds of writing (such as political discourse, journalism, and advertising), emotional appeals are used frequently.

Here are some things you can do to add emotional power to an argument:

1. Describe the issue in a way that relates it to the readers' values or needs.
2. Include examples that readers can identify with, such as stories featuring sympathetic protagonists.
3. Occasionally use language that has emotive connotations (see Chapter 36).

6.2
Details on five major case-building strategies.

6f Structure the argument

There are a number of ways to structure an argument. Here are some of the most common ones.

1 Using the classic five-part method

The classic method, which dates back to antiquity, has five parts:

1. Introduce the topic, explain why it is important, and state or imply your thesis.

2. Provide enough background information so that readers will be able to follow your argument.

WEBLINK

http://www.winthrop.edu/
wcenter/wcenter/classica
.htm
Detailed description of the
classic method of argument

3. Develop your argument. If you did not state your thesis in step 1, state it here. Support it with appropriate evidence, compelling appeals, and sound reasoning.

4. Acknowledge and refute possible objections and counterarguments, using good evidence and reasoning. Various objections can be dealt with in different parts of the paper. For example, you may want to cite one or more counterarguments early in the paper in order to introduce some of your main points as refutations.

5. Conclude by re-emphasizing the importance of the issue and the main points of your argument.

2 Using the problem and solution method

The problem and solution method involves describing a problem and then proposing one or more solutions to it. This pattern is common in reports, memos, and other forms of business and technical writing. The key to this method is to clearly identify the problem before stating the solution. The problem and solution method is a good choice when (a) the audience agrees on the nature of the problem and (b) the possible solutions are few in number.

3 Using the Rogerian method

The aim of the Rogerian method is to defuse a hostile audience. The arguer begins by characterizing the opponent's position in terms the opponent can accept and then presents his or her own position in a form that respects both the opponent's and the arguer's views. Once a dialogue has been established, the differences between the two sides can be explored. For example, in her essay on Net theft

(4f), Kirsten Parsons begins by noting that unlicensed copying off the Internet has become "an accepted practice," one that "we know we can get away with." By framing the issue in this way (in particular, by using the collective pronoun "we"), she establishes common ground with her readers before going on to argue against Net theft.

> **WEBLINK**
>
> http://www.winthrop.edu/ wcenter/wcenter/rogerian .htm
>
> Good advice on Rogerian argument from Winthrop University

4 Using the narrative method

Storytelling is a powerful and persuasive form of presentation, especially if the narrator has a lot of credibility with his or her audience. But because a skeptical reader may not be willing to generalize from the experience of the narrator, the personal narrative is not effective in college writing unless it is backed up by other kinds of support.

HELP

How do I keep track of my argument?

1. Analyze your audience and topic, and then select an appropriate argument structure.

2. Open the outlining feature of your word-processing program.

3. List your main points from most important to least important, and plug them into the outline according to the argument structure you have selected.

4. Under each point, indicate your supporting evidence and basic line of reasoning.

5. Check the hierarchical structure of your outline. Make sure each point is distinct and independent. If two points say similar things, select one as a main point and make the other a supporting point under it.

6. Draft your paper as you normally would, but refer to your outline occasionally to make sure you are staying on track.

6g Avoid logical and emotional fallacies

VIDEO

Recognizing fa-
miliar fallacies.

As you work out your lines of reasoning, be sure to avoid any logical or emotional fallacies. Some of the most common ones are described in the following sections.

1 Overgeneralizing/oversimplifying

Overgeneralizing involves making a broad statement on the basis of too little evidence; oversimplifying is overlooking important differences. Usually the tipoff to the overgeneralization/oversimplification fallacy is the use of absolute qualifiers like *all, every, none, never,* and *completely,* as in "All Democrats are liberals" or "Corporations never look beyond quarterly profits." Examples are vulnerable to this fallacy because an example, by definition, makes a claim for generality.

2 Begging the question

Making an argument at a superficial level and leaving the underlying issue or issues unaddressed is known as begging the question, assuming what needs to be proved, or engaging in *circular reasoning.* Consider this statement: "Sex education should be eliminated from the public schools. We should not be encouraging our young people to engage in sex." It implies that sex education encourages students to engage in sex, which is unproven. Often, as in this case, begging the question involves leaving controversial warrants unstated (see 6d-2).

3 Using a *non sequitur*

In Latin, *non sequitur* means literally "It does not follow." A *non sequitur* is a statement that does not logically follow from—or is irrelevant to—previous statements. Consider the statement "Senator Jones voted for the Flag Burning Amendment—she's a true patriot." In a country that advertises freedom of speech as one of its basic values, prohibiting the burning of a political symbol does not necessarily count as true patriotism; indeed, some would say it is just the opposite!

4 Attacking the person instead of the evidence

Also called the *ad hominem* fallacy, the tactic of attacking the person instead of the evidence is common practice in public discourse. The speaker or writer, by discrediting his or her opponent, tries to divert attention from the real issue. An interesting variant of this fallacy is seen in much modern advertising (especially on TV), where the viewer's attention is directed to such diversions as a beautiful landscape, beautiful people, or funny dogs instead of to the merits of the product.

5 Using either/or reasoning

Assuming that there are only two possible solutions to a given problem leads to the fallacy of either/or (or "false dilemma") reasoning. This assumption is promoted heavily in the media, with its predilection for getting "both sides of the story"; in our adversarial system of justice; and in our two-party political system. But reality teaches us that there are typically *many* sides to a story. To be a good thinker, avoid falling into the either/or trap.

6 Using faulty cause-effect reasoning

The fact that two events occur closely spaced in time does not necessarily mean that one caused the other. As statisticians are careful to point out, correlation does not always imply causation. Here is an example of faulty cause-effect reasoning from an Internet posting: "Tax cuts can lead to higher economic growth. From 1990 to 1995, the ten states that raised taxes the most created zero net new jobs, while the ten states that cut taxes the most gained 1.84 million jobs, an in-

WEBLINK

http://www
.intrepidsoftware.com/
fallacy/welcome.htm
A guide to logical fallacies

crease of 10.8 percent." It could be that it was the lack of new jobs that caused the first group of states to raise taxes (to pay unemployment compensation, for example), not the other way around.

7 Making false analogies

False analogies arise when speakers and writers extend true analogies beyond reason, claiming similarities that do not exist. Here is an example of a false analogy: "Our Founding Fathers said that a well-regulated militia was necessary to the security of a free state. Similarly, modern-day militias like the Montana Freemen are the best guardians of our freedom."

8 Engaging in the bandwagon appeal

A common emotional ploy, the bandwagon appeal tries to pressure readers or listeners into going along with the crowd. Statements such as "Everyone agrees that a free-market economy is best" or "The general consensus is that Pearl Buck was not as great a writer as Toni Morrison" suggest that, since "everyone agrees," there must be something wrong with you if you do not agree.

9 Using a red herring

Anything that draws attention away from the main issue under discussion is a "red herring." Politicians often use this ploy when confronted with difficult questions from journalists. For example, when asked about the increasing shortage of affordable housing, the city mayor who responded by talking only about a new city park would be guilty of using a red herring.

10 Assuming that two wrongs make a right

Another way to deflect attention away from an issue is by using the two-wrongs-make-a-right fallacy. In this ploy, the arguer defends an accusation of wrongdoing on his or her part by claiming that the other side is guilty of similar or worse wrongdoing. For example, if a local politician defends the city's high crime rate by saying that crime is even worse in other cities, she would be diverting attention away from the real issue, her own city's crime rate.

11 Appealing to bias

Using words with strong positive or negative connotations can exploit the biases of an audience. As with other emotional fallacies, the appeal to bias disregards rational thought but can still be effective in influencing readers or listeners. A bumper sticker saying, "Your kids and my taxes go to St. Pedophiles," might be effective with readers with an anti-Catholic bias. More fair-minded readers, however, would notice its loaded language ("St. Pedophiles") and gross overstatement and quickly dismiss it.

6h Use special techniques for electronic argument

Traditional forms of argument, as described above, depend on a model of communication in which a writer (or speaker) produces a complete argument, which is then read and evaluated by a passive, "captive" reader. With the advent of new, Internet-based forms of communication, however, argument itself has taken on new forms. Email, newsgroups, listservs, and Internet relay chats (IRCs) all use an interactive, dialogic form of communication that promotes an equally interactive form of argument. In this conversation-like environment, there is great pressure on participants to take turns, with no one dominating the floor. This provides little opportunity for any one person to lay out an extended argument in its entirety; rather, one must be content to offer a quick, abbreviated argument or even, in some cases, just make a single point.

The give-and-take nature of these electronic forms of argument calls for some special adaptations:

1. If you want to contribute an argument to an ongoing discussion (for example, in a newsgroup or IRC), make sure you are up to date on how the topic has been discussed up to that point. By reading previous posts, you can avoid simply repeating what has already been said (which may only irritate other participants).

2. Do provide enough context, however, so that the reader knows what you are referring to. One or two sentences should suffice.

3. Limit your response to whatever you can say on a single screen. In most cases, this means making only one or two well-supported points. Most people do not want to scroll through page after page of print.

4. Consider adding links (see 16b-3) to Web sites containing relevant supporting information.

5. Make your point concisely and precisely. Take time to edit and proofread.

6. Before hitting SEND, read your message over and make sure you're comfortable with its content and tone. Remember that

electronic postings are often read by a larger and more diverse audience than the writer anticipates.

6.3

Three examples of effective electronic arguments.

Another, albeit less interactive, form of electronic argument can be found on Web sites. Unlike either traditional arguments (laid out in one piece from start to finish) or the interactive types of arguments just described, Web site arguments are dispersed over hypertextual links (see 15a-2). For example, the main claims may be on a single page, but the supporting evidence may be found on other pages or even at other linked sites. Visitors to a Web site can navigate the site in any number of ways, and so a Web site creator who wishes to present an argument has to somehow induce visitors to navigate the site in a way that brings out the full force of that argument. Following the general principles of good Web site design (see Chapter 15) should help, as should the more specific guidelines shown in the Help box.

6i   Enhance your argument with visual support

Although argument is normally conveyed through language, it can also occur through pictures, graphs, or other forms of visual representation. As mentioned at the beginning of this chapter, argument

HELP

How should I design a Web site argument?

1. Make the opening screen both visually and textually appealing, so as to capture the interest of your readers. Establish the issue that your argument addresses.

2. Decide on your main pieces of supporting evidence and put clearly labeled links to these items on the opening screen (see 16b-3).

3. Cluster your claims and your supporting evidence so that each page of your Web site has unified content.

4. Use graphics only as needed to support your argument, not for decoration.

5. Include a "For Further Reading" link to other Web sites dealing with the same topic, including some that present alternative views. This could enrich the reader's experience and, if nothing else, will enhance your credibility.

means taking and defending some point of view. Thus, if an advertisement from a tobacco company shows a beautiful model smoking a cigarette, that advertisement is taking the point of view that cigarette smoking is cool. In this way, even a simple photograph can be seen as making an "argument." In most cases, though, visual arguments do not stand alone; rather, they serve to provide supplementary support for more conventional verbal arguments.

Consider, for example, the following table about the worldwide HIV/AIDS epidemic:

TABLE 6.1
Global Summary of the HIV/AIDS Epidemic, 2000

	ADULTS	CHILDREN	TOTAL
Newly infected in 2000	4,700,000	600,000	5,300,000
Living with HIV/AIDS	34,700,000	1,400,000	36,100,000
Died from AIDS in 2000	2,500,000	500,000	3,000,000
Died from AIDS since 1981	17,500,000	4,300,000	21,800,000

(*Source:* Joint UN Program on HIV/AIDS. 2001 <http://www.unaids.org>)

Like most tables, this one presents words and numbers in a visual layout that suggests certain themes. If you were writing an argumentative essay about the global HIV/AIDS epidemic, for example, you could use Table 6.1 to support a claim that adults have suffered far more from HIV/AIDS than children have. Or you could use it to claim that children are especially vulnerable to the disease once they've contracted it: almost three-fourths of all children who contracted AIDS in the past twenty years have died from it.

Tables can provide an effective form of visual argument, but they are not as rhetorically powerful as more visual types of graphic, such as line graphs, bar charts, pie charts, maps, diagrams, and photographs. For example, the bar chart in Figure 6.1 shows more dramatically than a table the contrast between adults and children with regard to AIDS mortality. Through the stark visual differences of the two columns, one can immediately grasp the enormous difference in degree of victimization suffered by children. A chart such as this would add tremendous power to an essay about the effects of HIV/AIDS on children.

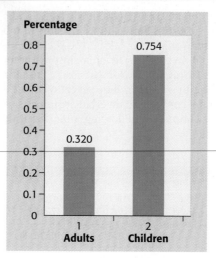

FIGURE 6.1 Worldwide AIDS
                Mortality, 1981–2000

Whenever you are constructing an argumentative paper or oral presentation (Chapter 20), look for ways to enhance your argument with visual support. (For further discussion of the use of graphics, see 14c.)

PART 2

Research

FAQs

CHAPTER 7

The Research Project

The process of writing a research paper does not differ markedly from the process of writing an essay. The difference is one of scope. A research paper is longer than most essays and contains more information from external sources, found by doing research. It would be a good idea to review the stages of the writing process briefly before you begin a research project. (See Chapters 2 through 4.)

WEBLINK

http://www.researchpaper.com

A site devoted to helping writers of research papers

VIDEO
Drafting a research paper.

7.1
Ideas and assistance for writing research papers.

7a Become a researcher

Why research? Work in many academic and professional disciplines, including law, medicine, engineering, and psychology, depends heavily on research. In all fields, researchers conduct studies to answer important questions, to solve problems, to prove cases, and to argue positions. In college, there are many purposes for research. Your professor may want you to join in an ongoing academic conversation that is published in journals; you may research to answer specific questions that you have about a subject, to make informal decisions about something, or to form reasoned opinions with support from other researchers. You also will need to read the research of others to help inform your own arguments.

AUDIO
Breaking research tasks into manageable parts.

The ability to research—that is, to explore a problem systematically—is a crucial skill for an educated person. A researcher is a careful, critical, systematic thinker who goes beyond memorizing facts on a subject to examine the bases on which claims and arguments rest.

Although you may not realize it, you probably have already researched many subjects. Have you ever purchased a DVD player or an automobile? How did you decide which one to choose? If you read about DVD players in *Consumer Reports* or other magazines, talked to friends about them and compared several models, or shopped around, you researched your purchase. The thinking processes you used are similar to those used to research a subject in a college course.

1   Understanding the research project

When you begin a research project, first think through what you will need to do. Ask yourself questions such as

- What will my purpose be?
- How should I sound as a writer?
- Who will my readers be?
- Where will I get my authority?

Deciding on a rhetorical stance (see 2a-2) will help you to determine a general approach to the assignment.

The two main types of research are primary research and secondary research. **Primary research** entails generating information or data through processes such as interviewing, administering questionnaires, or observation (see 7f-6). **Secondary research** involves finding information in secondary, or published, sources (see 7f1–5). You need to decide which type or types of research your project demands. Discuss with your instructor the kinds of sources that you should be locating and reading for your research project.

Does your assignment provide clues as to what your instructor expects from you? Look for keywords, such as *analyze, discuss, explain, define, evaluate, compare,* and *persuade,* in the assignment. These words can help you decide how to approach your research project.

2   Discovering what to research

Research typically begins with good questions. Experienced researchers do a great deal more than just find information in library books, encyclopedias, or the Internet and then report that information back in the form of a research paper. You need to think about how you can use the information you find in your research to answer a question that a particular subject has inspired in you. A good place to begin looking for a research question is in the textbooks you are currently using. Is there a debate that is discussed in the textbook that has not yet been resolved or that is arguable? For example, perhaps in your history textbook you read that there is a difference of opinion among historians concerning the nature of the interactions between the Native Americans and the Pilgrims. Out of this debate might come a question for you to research: "What was the relationship between the local indigenous population and the Pilgrims in the early colony of Plymouth Plantation?" Or, you might begin by browsing through a specialized encyclopedia, such as the *Encyclopedia of Psychology* or the *Encyclopedia of Educational Research,* for some ideas. Another place to begin looking for potential research questions is on the Internet (see the Help box in Chapter 2, p. 11). For additional information on Internet searching, see Chapter 8.

3 Selecting a specific topic and starting question

Kaycee Sorensen, the student whose research paper is included as a model in Chapter 12, was given the assignment of writing a research paper on a technological subject. She was not sure what technological issue she wanted to write about or what questions she should ask about it, so she decided to surf the Net as a way of generating some ideas (see 8c-1). After browsing around for a while in the *Yahoo!* search directory, Kaycee noticed the topic of "shopping and services" listed under the category "Business and Economy." She had been wondering about the prevalence of online shopping in our culture. Was the number of cybershoppers increasing? Was shopping via the Net a viable alternative for consumers? Was it safe to use a credit card for online shopping? And so on. These questions served as a starting place for Kaycee's research. Posing these questions allowed Kaycee to begin her background reading in search of answers, rather than reading aimlessly in an unfocused way.

4 Developing a hypothesis

As you work through the research process, attempting to answer your starting questions, you should come up with a hypothesis—a tentative statement of what you anticipate the research will reveal. A working hypothesis specifically describes a proposition that research evidence will either prove or disprove. As you begin to gather background information on your topic, you should develop a hypothesis that will help you to focus your research. Kaycee moved from her starting questions to a working hypothesis as follows:

TOPIC

    Cybershopping

RESEARCH QUESTIONS

    Is the number of online shoppers increasing? Is shopping via

the Internet a viable alternative for consumers? Is it safe to use a

credit card for online shopping?

The number of online shoppers is increasing, which means that cybershopping is becoming a convenient, affordable, safe option for consumers.

A working hypothesis should be stated in such a way that it can be either supported or challenged by the research. Kaycee's research will either support or challenge her working hypothesis that the number of online shoppers is increasing, which means that cyber-shopping is becoming a convenient, affordable, safe option for consumers. The hypothesis is called "working" because you may find that you need to change or revise it during the course of the research.

5 Developing a search strategy

7.2

Mastering Internet search techniques.

A search strategy is a plan for proceeding systematically with re-search. Once you have decided on your starting questions and working hypothesis, you are ready to outline your search strategy. Your first decision will be about the nature of your research. Will you be relying mostly on secondary (library and Internet) research or on pri-mary (field) research? Secondary research is discussed in 7f-1 through 7f-5. Primary research is discussed in 7f-6.

The goal of a search is to build a working bibliography—a list of possible sources that may or may not eventually be used in the final paper. A working bibliography is typically about twice as long as the final bibliography for a research paper (see 7d for more about work-ing bibliographies), because many of the sources you identify will turn out not to be applicable to your paper or not to be available in time for you to use in your research. By searching for sources in a sys-tematic way, you avoid aimlessly wandering around the library or surfing on the Internet.

7b Schedule a time frame

If you have never done a research project before, you may be overwhelmed at the thought of such a large and complex task. If you break the job down into smaller parts, however, it will seem much more manageable. It will help to formulate a time frame in which to complete your research project. If your instructor has not given you deadlines, set your own dates for accomplishing specific tasks. Give yourself enough time to plan, organize, and write a first draft and then several revisions.

Sample Schedule for Writing a Research Paper

(Allow approximately one week for each step.)

Step 1: Select a preliminary research area; articulate starting questions and hypothesis; begin background research; schedule a time frame; begin to answer your questions (see 7a).

Step 2: Build a working bibliography by using indexes, online catalogs, databases, and the Internet (see Chapter 9); begin to locate sources in the library and on the Net (see 7f).

Step 3: Read and evaluate sources; take notes on relevant sources; in a research notebook, comment on the importance of sources to the research questions and their relationship to other sources (see 9a); print out information from the Internet; write down complete bibliographical information for each source; write down Web site **addresses,** or URLs (see 7d), and note date of access.

Step 4: Arrange and conduct any primary research; complete the reading and evaluation of sources; identify gaps in the research and find more sources if necessary (see 7f). Confirm or refute your working hypothesis.

Step 5: Begin preliminary writing in a research notebook—summarize key information; begin brainstorming; write a few possible thesis statements designed to answer the starting questions (see 11a).

Step 6: Write a thesis statement that will guide the direction of the piece; sketch a tentative outline or plan of the research paper (see 11a-2, 11b).

Step 7: Write a rough draft of the research paper; keep careful track of sources through accurate citations; take care to distinguish quotations and paraphrases and to document all source information appropriately (see Chapter 10); write a Bibliography, Works Cited, or References list (see Chapters 12 and 13).

Step 8: Revise and edit the rough draft; spell-check; check sentence structure and usage; check documentation of sources; solicit peer responses to the draft (see 4b, 4c, 4e).

Step 9: Print and proofread the final copy; have a friend or classmate proofread it as well (see 4d, 4e).

7c Create a research notebook

It is important to create a notebook in which to record all the information relating to your research project. If you are using a word processor, you can take advantage of its storage capabilities to develop an electronic research notebook. Create a folder, and label it your research notebook (see Help box on p. 10). In this folder, you can create files or documents to record your topic and your starting questions, notes from your background research and focused research, and your working bibliography (if you do not have bibliography software). In your electronic research notebook, you can also begin to articulate answers to your starting questions as your understanding evolves through research. As you investigate your topic, record not only what others have said on the subject, but also your own impressions and comments. You also can use research notebook documents to develop your thesis statement and an informal outline or organizational plan for your paper, and to write all preliminary drafts of your paper. For suggestions on how to take usable, accurate notes, see 10a-2.

If you do not have a computer, you might set up a ring binder with dividers for all of the documents just described:

- Topic and starting questions
- Thesis statement and outline
- Photocopies and printouts of articles
- Research notes and comments
- Working bibliography
- Drafts 1, 2, 3, as needed

Many students like to record notes in their research notebooks, while others like to take notes on note cards.

1 Recording notes in a notebook

AUDIO
Insert your
comments into
research notes.

Whether the notebook in which you record your notes is handwritten or computer generated, be sure to keep your recorded notes separate from your comments. If your notebook is handwritten, you might use two columns when recording information: one for notes taken from the source and the other for comments, analyses, and queries. If your notebook is electronic, you can use your word-processing program's DOCUMENT COMMENTS feature to INSERT your comments and analyses into the notes taken from sources (see Help box on p. 43).

2 Taking notes on note cards

Like notebooks, note cards can be either handwritten or computer generated.

Handwritten Note Cards   If you choose to handwrite notes on index cards, give each note card a descriptive title and take notes on only one side of each card to allow for easy sorting and scanning of information later on. Provide a page reference on your note card for all notes, both quoted and paraphrased (see Chapter 10). In the upper right-hand corner of the note card, include a control number that identifies the source. Then consecutively number your notes for each source.

Computer-Generated Note Cards   Some computer operating systems and Internet browsers offer computerized note card systems. Such a system can be particularly useful if you own a laptop computer that you can use in the library. You can use the computer note cards just as you would use index cards: title each card by topic, and then type your notes onto the card provided by the computer. The computer note card system will sort the cards automatically by topic. The screen in Figure 7.1 contains four computerized note cards.

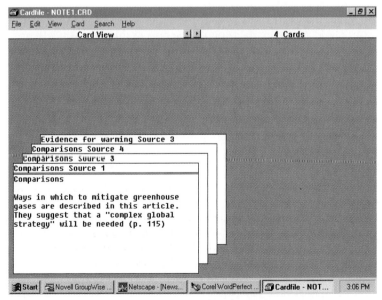

FIGURE 7.1 Example of Computerized Note Cards

3 | Taking notes with photocopies and printouts

Photocopies and Database Printouts With photocopy machines and computer printers readily available in libraries and computer labs, more researchers are making use of these tools to record source information. Making your own photocopies and printouts of sources has many advantages: first, you will have the actual wording of the authors at your fingertips, so you will not have to rely on your notes for accuracy when quoting (thereby reducing the chances for inadvertent plagiarism); second, you can highlight passages that are important to your own research for future reference; third, you can actually take notes on the photocopies or printouts (see Figure 7.2). Make certain that you record complete bibliographic information on all photocopies and printouts from books, newspapers, journal articles, or full-text library databases. You will make your life much more difficult if you have to retrace your steps because you neglected to write down the publication date from an article you photocopied. Refer to Chapters 12 and 13 for the complete bibliographic information that should be listed for each type of source you use in your research.

Printing Internet Sources When you are researching on the Internet, it will most likely be easiest for you to print out copies of relevant Web pages rather than taking notes by hand. If there is a specific section of a Web page that you wish to use as a source, you can highlight that section using your computer's mouse and then choose PRINT/SELECTION from the PRINT dialog box. In this way, you will print only the parts you need, and not the entire Web site. As with photocopies, printouts of sources from the Internet should also have complete bibliographic information. In addition to the usual information for all sources (the author, title, and publication data), for Internet sources you will need to note the complete URL of the page(s) you are referring to, the date you accessed the page, and the date the site was posted or last updated.

Downloading Internet Sources Another method of obtaining information from the Internet is to download or save Internet pages directly into your own computer files (using FILE>SAVE AS). When downloading or copying and pasting files from the Internet, you must be especially careful not to import source information directly into your own work without citing the source appropriately. To keep from inadvertently plagiarizing from the Internet, take special care to type into your computer notebook the complete bibliographic information from each source and to put quotation marks around any text that is copied and pasted from the Internet. Also, note for yourself the author of the quotation so that you can use that information in a

Need to learn more about this organization and its political motives

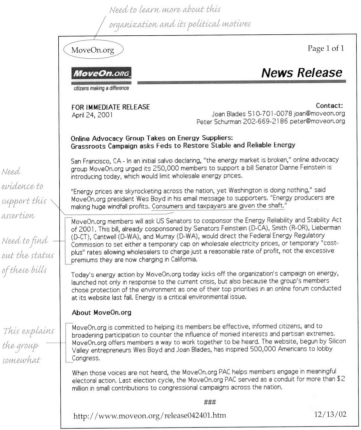

Need evidence to support this assertion

Need to find out the status of these bills

This explains the group somewhat

MoveOn.org Page 1 of 1

MoveOn.ORG *citizens making a difference* **News Release**

FOR IMMEDIATE RELEASE
April 24, 2001

Contact:
Joan Blades 510-701-0078 joan@moveon.org
Peter Schurman 202-669-2186 peter@moveon.org

Online Advocacy Group Takes on Energy Suppliers:
Grassroots Campaign asks Feds to Restore Stable and Reliable Energy

San Francisco, CA - In an initial salvo declaring, "the energy market is broken," online advocacy group MoveOn.org urged its 250,000 members to support a bill Senator Dianne Feinstein is introducing today, which would limit wholesale energy prices.

"Energy prices are skyrocketing across the nation, yet Washington is doing nothing," said MoveOn.org president Wes Boyd in his email message to supporters. "Energy producers are making huge windfall profits. Consumers and taxpayers are given the shaft."

MoveOn.org members will ask US Senators to cosponsor the Energy Reliability and Stability Act of 2001. This bill, already cosponsored by Senators Feinstein (D-CA), Smith (R-OR), Lieberman (D-CT), Cantwell (D-WA), and Murray (D-WA), would direct the Federal Energy Regulatory Commission to set either a temporary cap on wholesale electricity prices, or temporary "cost-plus" rates allowing wholesalers to charge just a reasonable rate of profit, not the excessive premiums they are now charging in California.

Today's energy action by MoveOn.org today kicks off the organization's campaign on energy, launched not only in response to the current crisis, but also because the group's members chose protection of the environment as one of their top priorities in an online forum conducted at its website last fall. Energy is a critical environmental issue.

About MoveOn.org

MoveOn.org is committed to helping its members be effective, informed citizens, and to broadening participation to counter the influence of monied interests and partisan extremes. MoveOn.org offers members a way to work together to be heard. The website, begun by Silicon Valley entrepreneurs Wes Boyd and Joan Blades, has inspired 500,000 Americans to lobby Congress.

When those voices are not heard, the MoveOn.org PAC helps members engage in meaningful electoral action. Last election cycle, the MoveOn.org PAC served as a conduit for more than $2 million in small contributions to congressional campaigns across the nation.

http://www.moveon.org/release042401.htm 12/13/02

FIGURE 7.2 Example of Annotated Internet Printout

signal phrase that introduces the quotation. For more information about citing electronic sources, see Chapters 12 and 13. For more information about avoiding plagiarism, see Chapter 10.

7d Create a working bibliography

A bibliography is a listing of books and articles on a particular subject. When you submit a research paper, you include a bibliography to show readers what sources you consulted to find your

AUDIO
Keeping accurate records of sources.

information. As you begin your research, start a working bibliography, which will grow as your research progresses. This working bibliography likely will contain some sources that you ultimately will not use in your research paper, so entries need not be in final bibliographic form. However, it is important to record accurately all the information you will need to compose your final bibliography so that you do not have to track down sources twice. Include the author's full name, a complete title including subtitle and edition, the city and state where the work was published, the name of the publisher, and the date of publication.

As discussed in 7c-3, if you are using sources from online databases or the Internet, you may want to print out copies for later review or download them onto your own computer (use FILE>SAVE AS). In either case, be sure that complete bibliographic information appears on the pages or files. If it does not, make a bibliography entry in your research notebook for the source, in addition to the printout. Include the following information: (1) author's name, if available; (2) publication information for print and online versions; (3) the URL; (4) the date of posting or updating; and (5) the date you accessed the site.

HELP

How do I use a computer bibliography program?

1. Open the bibliography software, such as *TakeNote!* from Pearson Education.

2. Follow the directions for entering data; usually you will be asked to enter information by category (author, title, publication data).

7.3

Instructions for using *TakeNote!* software.

3. Wait for the bibliography program to generate your bibliography, based on the information you provide. It will format the information appropriately for a particular documentation style and place it in alphabetical order. Some bibliography programs will convert from one documentation style to another—for example, MLA (see Chapter 12) to APA (see Chapter 13) style.

4. Name and save your bibliography, as well as any works cited lists you may have generated from it.

NOTE: You still need to check your bibliography carefully to be certain the program has generated it in the correct format.

You can prepare a working bibliography manually on index cards or electronically on a computer file. If you use index cards, record bibliographical information (author, title, and publication data) on one set of cards and content notes on a separate set.

7e Gather background information

Now is the time to gather background information, using your starting questions and working hypothesis as a guide. This information will help you conduct more focused research later on.

1 Starting with yourself

At the start of a research project, write down everything you already know about your topic. The list may be quite extensive or rather short. The important thing is to inventory your own knowledge first so that you can systematically build on that knowledge base. The more you know about your topic, the better you will be at judging the value of sources you read. Also, check your biases and assumptions about the topic, asking yourself the following questions:

1. Do I already have a strong opinion about this topic?
2. Have I "rushed to judgment" about it without looking at all the facts?
3. Am I emotionally involved with the topic in some way that might bias my judgment?

If your answer to any of the above questions is "yes," think seriously about whether you will be able to keep an open mind as you read about the topic. If you will not, you might want to choose another topic.

2 Compiling a list of subject headings and keywords

The cataloging system developed by the Library of Congress is the one most widely used for organizing library materials. In order to put information into related categories, the Library of Congress has developed a listing of subject headings. This listing is compiled in a multivolume set, called the *Library of Congress Subject Headings* (or *LCSH*), available in both printed and computerized form. The *LCSH* is a listing of all of the subject headings used by libraries to classify source materials (Figure 7.3).

This is the subject heading to use for online shopping

Used for

Broader term
Related term

> Online shopping Subject
> USE Teleshopping heading
> **Online stockbrokers** *(May Subd Geog)*
> UF Electronic stockbrokers
> Internet stockbrokers
> Web Stockbrokers
> BT Stockbrokers
> RT Electronic trading of securities
> Online trading of securities
> USE Electronic trading of securities

Subject heading

A subtopic

> **Teleshopping** *(May Subd Geog)* — Indicates the
> UF Home shopping presence of geographical
> Online shopping subdivisions to follow
> BT Shopping the heading
> Telecommunication systems
> **—Law and legislation** *(May Subd Geog)*
> **Teleshopping equipment industry**
> *(May Subd Geog)*
> HD9696.T45-HD9696.T454
> BT Telecommunication equipment
> industry

FIGURE 7.3 Library of Congress Subject Headings

Researchers use the subject headings in the *LCSH* to find both books and periodicals (magazines and journals) related to their topics. Whether you are using a regular library card catalog or a computerized catalog, the subject headings are the key to locating information on your topic. Searching a library's catalog is discussed in 7f.

Related to subject headings are **keywords** (sometimes called descriptors or identifiers), which are used to identify the subjects found in electronic databases, including the Internet. The keywords used to search for electronic sources may not be exactly the same terms that are used by the *LCSH* to categorize the subjects of books and periodicals. So, it is important at the outset of your research that you compile a comprehensive listing of both possible subject headings and possible keywords for your topic. In an electronic database search, keywords can be combined using what are known as **Boolean operators.** These operators are linking words, most commonly AND, OR, and NOT, that tell the computer to combine keywords in ways that it recognizes. (See Tips on Using Boolean Operators for Internet Searching, on page 125.)

3 Doing preliminary background reading in general reference books

We recommend that you begin your library search in the general reference section. Here you will find reference books that have condensed huge amounts of information into an accessible form. These sources can help you to define your subject area more clearly, to identify keywords and important authors, and to gain a general understanding of your topic. Most reference works are available both in book versions and in computerized versions (either on CDs or on the Internet). Many libraries provide access to computer-based dictionaries, encyclopedias, thesauruses, and bibliographies. Such computerized reference sources often are more up-to-date and can be searched faster than the printed forms.

Keyword Searching

1. *What is a keyword search for?* A keyword search allows you to search an electronic database for the term or terms that you have identified as being most important for your project.

VIDEO
Narrowing a subject online.

2. *Where does the computer search for the keywords?* The computer will locate all items in the database that include the particular keywords or terms anywhere in the work's record, from the title to the body to the bibliography.

3. *Can the computer supply other related words?* Typically the computer will not be able to supply synonyms for the keywords you have identified. You need to think of as many keywords as possible.

4. *What terms should I use as keywords?* You will have to use your knowledge of the topic, gained through background reading, to come up with keywords. For example, if you are searching the subject of UFOs, you might use *UFO* as a keyword. But you also might want to try *flying saucers* or *paranormal events*.

AUDIO
Tips for keyword searching.

5. *Can I do a keyword search on the Internet?* The same kind of keyword searching discussed here can be done on the Internet. (See Chapter 8 on Using the Internet for Research.)

Other Sources   The general reference section of a library contains many other sources that may be helpful in your research. Check with the reference librarian for the following types of sources, if they are relevant to your research: almanacs, which briefly present a year's events in government, sports, politics, and economics; yearbooks, which contain worldwide data; and handbooks, or fact books, which provide statistical data.

Even if your assignment does not specifically require primary research, it is a good idea to talk to experts in the field, if possible. By reading and talking about your topic, you can ascertain what is considered to be "common knowledge." Common knowledge is information that is generally known and, therefore, need not be cited as the idea of one particular author. If you read the same information in three or more general sources, you can assume it is common knowledge. However, any facts or data found in general sources still need to be cited in your paper, and the reference source listed in your bibliography. (For information on citing sources, see Chapters 12 and 13; see also Chapter 10 on using sources.)

7.4

Three resources
for Internet
research.

7f   Conduct focused research

Once background reading has helped you to understand your subject, narrow it to a manageable size, and formulate a hypothesis, you are ready to read in a more focused way on your topic. Conducting focused secondary research involves locating, through magazines, newspapers, journals, books, government documents, and the Internet, the specific information you need to write your paper.

AUDIO

Searching print
and online
sources.

1   Using library catalogs

Libraries have catalogs that list all the books and documents they have available. Although some libraries still use card files (which include cards for authors' names, subjects, and book titles), either by themselves or in combination with computerized catalogs, most libraries today house their catalogs on computers (see Figure 7.4). The computerized catalog is one of the most visible computer tools in libraries today. Computerized systems, which are replacing the traditional card catalog, are designed to handle various library functions, such as circulation, cataloging, and location of materials within the library collection. Like card catalogs, most computerized catalogs are searchable by author, title, and subject; in addition, computerized catalogs are searchable by keyword or by a combination of subject and keyword. (See Keyword Searching on page 107

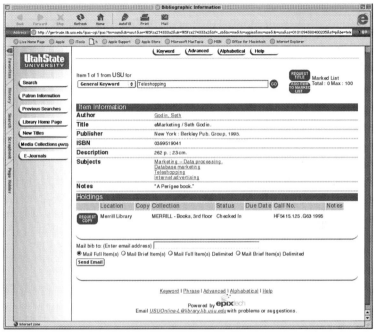

FIGURE 7.4 Library Catalog Entry

and Tips on Using Boolean Operators for Internet Searching on page 125.)

Typically, libraries divide their computerized catalogs into a general database, which indexes books, government documents, and audiovisual materials, and specialized databases, often organized by discipline. The articles that you find in a computerized catalog search may or may not be available in your own library, as most libraries can afford to subscribe to only a limited number of magazines, newspapers, and journals. If your library does not own a particular magazine, newspaper, or journal, do not despair. Through interlibrary loan or the Internet, often you can locate an article and obtain it for your own use. Check with the librarian to find out about such reciprocal services.

2   Using indexes to magazines and newspapers

In your library's general catalog, you'll find a listing of magazine and journal names, but you will not find a listing of specific articles within those publications. Private indexing services, such as ERIC (Educational Research Information Clearinghouse), have taken on the

7.5

Sites devoted to finding news.

job of listing (indexing) all of the individual articles found in specific journals on particular topics; in the case of ERIC, the articles indexed are related to the field of education. To locate articles in education journals on a particular topic, you would use the ERIC descriptors, which are keywords that ERIC uses to index the articles. As with the *LCSH* system discussed in 7e-2, to make the best use of such indexes, you need to first discover the keywords by which the subject has been indexed. These "controlled vocabularies" will vary by indexing service. Specialized subject indexes are often available both by computer searching and in print form.

Magazines Magazines and other publications that come out at regular intervals (usually longer than one day) are called *periodicals.* Articles in periodicals often can provide specific and up-to-date information on a topic. It is possible to locate magazine and newspaper articles both through computer searching and through print indexes. The most commonly used indexes to magazine articles are the *Readers' Guide to Periodical Literature* and the *Magazine Index.* In both sources, entries are arranged by subject and author.

Newspapers Libraries generally store back issues of newspapers on microfilm. You will need to use a newspaper index to locate relevant articles in newspapers. To gain access to articles in the *New York Times,* use the *New York Times Index,* which lists all major articles in the *Times* from 1913 to the present. The *Newspaper Index* lists articles from the *Chicago Tribune, Los Angeles Times, New Orleans Times–Picayune,* and *Washington Post.* Both indexes are arranged by subject. For business news, use the *Wall Street Journal Index.* Newspaper indexes are available in both print and computerized formats. Many search engines now offer a feature to help patrons keep track of the news headlines. Such "news tracker" services can also be customized to search for news stories related to particular subjects or topics. One of the best news tracker services is available from the *Google* search engine (see Weblink box).

WEBLINK

http://news.google.com/
Search and browse the latest headlines in the categories of World, US, Business, Technology, Entertainment, and Sports

3 Using indexes to professional journals

If you are researching a technical or academic subject, you will want to refer to articles written by professionals in the field. Professional journal articles are indexed by indexing services in much the same way as magazine and newspaper articles. However, you will need to find a specialized index or database for professional articles in the particular discipline or subject area you are working in. For example, the *Social Sciences Index* lists the titles of articles from journals in the social sciences, and the *General Science Index* lists articles from science journals. Discipline-specific indexes are available in most libraries, both in print and on computer. *Note:* these indexes are to article titles and do not provide the full text of the articles themselves.

4 Using CD-ROMs and other electronic databases

Locating specific information on a topic may require use of a variety of computerized search tools.

CD-ROM Databases In addition to your library's computerized catalog and computerized indexes to magazines, newspapers, and journals, investigate any CD-ROM databases available to you. As with any computerized searching, it is important when using CD-ROMs to know your keywords. Many CD-ROM databases use their own "controlled vocabulary," which may vary slightly from the subject headings used in other computerized catalogs. Check with the librarian to discern whether there is a thesaurus or listing of subject headings for the particular database you are using.

Figure 7.5 shows an example of an article listing from the *Environmental Periodicals Bibliography* CD-ROM. Notice the information that is listed for this article, including the keywords under which it has been indexed. You would need to use the information provided about the journal source—*Climate Change;* 1996 Vol. 33. No. 2 (June), page 145—to find the specific journal in which this article can be found. First, find out if your library carries the journal by looking up its title in the library's computerized catalog; then, if the library subscribes to this journal, you can locate it either in the serials collection in your library stacks or in the current periodicals section (for a very recent journal issue). If your library does not subscribe to the journal, do not despair. You may be able to locate the journal in a full-text database or through interlibrary loan.

Electronic Full-Text Databases Since it is clearly impossible for libraries to own all magazines and journals in a world of rapidly exploding information, many libraries instead choose to subscribe to full-text database services that provide library patrons with Internet access to copies of the actual articles from magazines, newspapers, and professional journals. Your library has to pay for such services

```
****************************************************************
                        NISC DISC REPORT
     ENVIRONMENTAL PERIODICALS BIBLIOGRAPHY JUNE 1997
****************************************************************
```

TITLE:	Uncertainties in global climate change estimates. An editorial essay.
AUTHOR:	Pate-Cornell, Elisabeth
SOURCE:	Climate Change; 1996 VOL. 33, NO. 2 (June), page 145
KEY TERMS:	Climate change; Uncertainty analysis; Policymaking; Science role; Risk assessment; Probability model
MAJOR TOPIC:	AIR
NOTES:	Assessing Uncertainty in Climate Change and Impacts
RECORD ID:	1997-018516
TITLE:	Evaluating the implementation of state-level global climate change programs.
AUTHOR:	Feldman, David L.; Wilt, Catherine A.
SOURCE:	Journal of Environment and Development; 1996 VOL. 5, NO. 1 (March), page 46
KEY TERMS:	Climate change, global; Environmental policy, national and international; Government compliance, state: policy implementation evaluation; Non-governmental organization role; Evaluation criterion
MAJOR TOPIC:	SOCIAL, POLITICAL AND PHILOSOPHICAL ISSUES
RECORD ID:	1997-015217

FIGURE 7.5 Listing from the *Environmental Periodicals Bibliography* CD-ROM

and they may be expensive to subscribe to—but not as expensive as trying to purchase every publication that's produced! Check with your librarian to find out if your library subscribes to an online database service such as *Lexis-Nexis* or *EBSCOHost*. If it does, you may be able to search the database via computer by subject or keyword to find not just a listing of the article's title and source, but an actual reproduction of the full text of the article itself.

5   Using Internet resources

The Internet is becoming an increasingly important research tool in all fields of study. A biologist observed that he can locate information crucial to his research in minutes via the Internet, when it used to take days or even weeks of searching through print sources. Since the Internet has become such an integral part of research, we devote an entire chapter in this handbook to the topic. You can find out more about how to use the Internet to enhance your research project by reading Chapter 8.

6   Doing primary, or field, research

In all disciplines, researchers use primary research methods to gather information and search for solutions to problems. (The researchers who read the printed reports generated from the primary research are using secondary research methods.) Of course, there is a great deal to learn about the primary, or field, research methods commonly used in various disciplines; we will consider just a few field research techniques that can be adapted for use in a research project—observation, surveys, and interviews.

Observation   The general goal of observation is to describe and perhaps evaluate customary behaviors. Observation is best suited to the collection of nonverbal data. The observer watches people behave in customary ways in a particular environment or setting and takes notes. You might observe where people stand in an elevator, for example, or how they cross a street at an unmarked crosswalk. Through observation, you accumulate "field notes," which are used to analyze trends and discern customary behaviors. The disadvantages of observation include lack of control over the environment, lack of quantifiable data, and small sample size. As you think about your research project, consider whether observational data would enhance your report.

Surveys   Ideally, an entire population would be studied to gain insights into its society. However, polling an entire population is seldom feasible, so surveys are used to sample small segments of the population selected at random. One common kind of survey is the questionnaire, a form that asks for responses to a set of questions. Designing questions is a science that has been developed over the years. Although the details are beyond the scope of this book, the basic principles are to be sure that the questions you write are clear and understandable and written in such a way that the responses will be easy to tabulate. Researchers generally agree that closed questions, which require checking a box or answering yes or no, yield more usable data, but open-ended questions, which require a short written response, can provide valuable insights (although they are harder to interpret). Think through your research topic to see if a questionnaire might yield useful data.

Interviews   Interviews are one particular type of survey. The advantages of the interview include flexibility (the questioner can interact with the respondent), speed of response (the questioner immediately knows the responses), and nonverbal behavior (the questioner can gather nonverbal as well as verbal clues). Here are some considerations in designing an interview:

1. Be certain that the questions are written down in advance and asked exactly as worded.
2. Be certain that you probe any unclear or incomplete answers.
3. Be certain that inadequate or brief answers are not probed in a biasing (directive) way.

After the interview, take time to review your notes and to clarify or supplement them as needed while the information is still fresh in your mind.

CHAPTER **8**

Using the Internet for Research

AUDIO

The importance of Internet research.

Much information published by educational institutions, libraries and service organizations, commercial and corporate providers, the public press, and the government can be located through an Internet search. This chapter introduces the ways in which the Internet can help with a research project.

8a Use Internet sources throughout the research process

Searching the Internet for information on a topic is similar in many respects to researching in the library. When beginning to research on the Internet, you should follow a search strategy, as outlined in 7a-5. Use the Internet for finding and exploring research topics, for background and focused searching, and even for collaboration with your peers and feedback from your instructor. Email and online discussion forums are ideal for trying out your topic ideas on your instructor and your peers. As you research

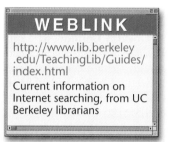

WEBLINK

http://www.lib.berkeley.edu/TeachingLib/Guides/index.html

Current information on Internet searching, from UC Berkeley librarians

8.1
Read this before starting an electronic search.

and write your paper, take advantage of the forums the Internet provides for sharing information—trade ideas, drafts, research sources, and revision feedback. For more information on collaboration, see 2c, 3c, and 4e.

8b Get to know the Internet and the Web

The **World Wide Web,** or the **Web** for short, is by far the easiest and most popular way of accessing information from the Internet. The Web provides a hypertext interface for "reading" Internet information. This means that information is presented in the form of a series of **links,** each leading to another document or another location on the Internet. Documents structured as text with a series of links to other texts are called **hypertexts.** One simply uses a mouse to click on the link (usually a graphic or a word or phrase in blue type with blue underlining) to connect with the hyperlinked document. Researchers navigate the Web through the use of an Internet browser. Two of the most popular browsers today are *Netscape Navigator* and *Internet Explorer.*

8.2
A tutorial and Internet research guide.

1 Surfing the World Wide Web: Browser tools and homepages

The World Wide Web, a huge spider web–like structure that encompasses computer networks throughout the world, seems to have been woven overnight. But no one spider wove this web; anyone and everyone can contribute (see Chapters 15 and 16 for information on designing and writing for the Web). This is probably the Web's greatest strength as well as its greatest weakness. It is a strength because no single organization could have compiled the varied and vast amounts of information placed on the Web for anyone to access. It is a weakness because the lack of control creates an information hodge-podge, with the trivial alongside the profound.

Getting Connected   You will probably be accessing the Internet either through a direct connection in a campus computer lab or through a dial-up modem, cable, or DSL service from home. Direct connections (cable and DSL) are much faster than dial-up modems. If you intend to use your home computer to access the Internet, it is a good idea to check with your campus computing center to find out what they recommend as the best way to connect to the campus computer network. Many campuses offer students a dial-up modem connection—an option that can be considerably cheaper than an Internet Service Provider (ISP) such as Prodigy or AOL. You will also need to be sure that your home computer has an up-to-date network card or modem.

AUDIO

Take advantage of Internet browser tools.

Internet Browser Tools   Once you have an Internet connection, you need an Internet **browser** in order for your computer to display Web pages. If you are using a computer in a campus lab, there will probably be icons on the opening screen for the two most popular browsers, *Netscape Communicator* or *Internet Explorer*. They contain comparable features and are free. If you are using a recent version of *Windows* or the Macintosh operating system, you will find that *Internet Explorer* has already been installed on your computer. Upgrades for both of these browsers can be found at their respective Web sites and downloaded to your own computer. Be aware, however, that **downloading** software from the Internet via a dial-up modem can be extremely slow.

> ## WEBLINK
>
> To find out if upgrades are available for your browser, go to the following Web sites
>
> *Internet Explorer*
> <http://www.microsoft.com/ie>
>
> *Netscape Navigator*
> <http://www.netscape.com>
>
> or
> <http://www.mozilla.org>

Both *Explorer* and *Netscape* include many useful tools that will help you as you conduct your research on the Internet. The most frequently used features that you will want to become acquainted

Internet Browser Tools

Selected *Netscape Communicator* **Menu Bar Tools**

File

NEW: Adds a new window

OPEN: Opens a page

SAVE AS: Saves Web page

SEND PAGE: Emails a Web page

OFFLINE: Views pages from cache

PRINT: Prints a Web page

Edit

CUT, COPY, PASTE: Allows copying text to another file

SELECT ALL: Selects all the text in a file

PREFERENCES: Allows you to customize the appearance of your pages, set a homepage that will open first, and generally customize your browser

View

SHOW: Allows you to display certain toolbars

RELOAD: Reloads the Web pages to show any updates or revisions

PAGE SOURCE: Reveals the HTML code behind the page

Selected *Internet Explorer* **Menu Bar Tools**

File

NEW WINDOW: Adds a new window

OPEN FILE: Opens a file

SAVE AS: Saves a Web page

SEND: Emails a page

WORK OFFLINE: Allows work while not connected to the Internet

PRINT: Prints a Web page

Edit

CUT, COPY, PASTE: Allows copying text to another file

SELECT ALL: Selects all the text in a file

FIND (ON THIS PAGE): Searches for information on the page

View

TOOLBARS: Display toolbars

GO TO: The GO menu

REFRESH: Reloads the Web pages to show any updates or revisions

TEXT SIZE: Allows you to choose how large the font is on your screen

ENCODING: Allows you to choose character sets and languages

(continued)

Internet Browser Tools *(continued)*

Selected *Netscape Communicator* Menu Bar Tools	Selected *Internet Explorer* Menu Bar Tools
PAGE INFO: Provides information about the page and its files	SOURCE: Reveals the HTML code behind the page
	Favorites
Go Shows the Web pages you have visited in a given session	Keeps track of your favorite sites (called "bookmarks" on *Netscape* toolbar)
Communicator Netscape's mail and messaging system	**Tools** Allows you to customize mail, news, and Internet options (similar to EDIT>PREFERENCES in *Netscape*)
Bookmarks Keeps track of your frequently visited sites (called "favorites" on *Internet Explorer*)	
	Help Explorer's help files
Help Netscape's help files	

with are described in the box on pp. 117–118. (Please note: depending on the version of the browser you are currently using, some of these tools may vary.)

Keeping Track of Your Search   Both *Netscape* and *Explorer* help you to keep track of important Web sites and to retrace the steps of your Internet search. The GO feature keeps a running list of the Web sites you have visited during your current Internet session. It will disappear when you close down your browser. The GO command is found on the menu bar in *Netscape* and within the VIEW menu in *Explorer*. You can also find the same listing by clicking the arrow to the right of the location box.

If you have found a page that you want to visit frequently, you can add this site's address to your list of bookmarks (*Netscape*) or favorites (*Explorer*). You can add a page to your bookmarks/favorites by visiting that page and then choosing ADD BOOKMARK or ADD TO FAVORITES from the bookmark menu or button. You can also arrange your bookmark/favorite sites into folders (see the HELP box on p. 129). Note: if you are working in a computer lab, you will not be able to individualize your bookmarks or favorites since they would become available to anyone using a particular lab computer.

To retrace your steps after an Internet search, you can use the HISTORY feature of your browser (found as a button on the toolbar in *Explorer* and within the COMMUNICATOR>TOOLS command on the menu bar in *Netscape*). You can customize your HISTORY to keep track of Web pages visited within a certain length of time. This is a very useful tool if you visited a site recently but you can no longer recall its address or how you found it (see the HELP box on p. 129)

Designating a Homepage on Your Browser When you are working at your home computer, you will want to identify which page your browser will display when you first open it (your "homepage"). Both *Explorer* and *Netscape* allow you to determine that **homepage.** To do so in *Explorer*, you first open the page you want designated and then click on TOOLS>INTERNET OPTIONS. You should see the site's address displayed and click on CURRENT to select that homepage. In *Netscape* you select your homepage via the EDIT>PREFERENCES menu. You can click USE CURRENT PAGE if the correct page address is displayed, or you can browse until you find the page you wish to use as your homepage. You might want to designate your campus's Web page as your homepage or some other page that you use frequently. You can get to your designated homepage quickly in either browser by clicking on the HOME icon.

2   Understanding URLs

In order to facilitate finding information on the Internet, a system of unique names was devised so that each resource on the Internet has a different name from any other resource. As long as you have the correct name of the resource, you should be able to locate it on the Internet. Names on the Internet are called **URLs** (Uniform Resource Locators). You can ask your browser to locate the resource by typing its URL into the browser's location bar. Or, you can go directly to the resource by clicking on a link found on another Web page. The link itself contains the URL as embedded code. A link on a Web page can be indicated by highlighted or colored text or by a graphical icon. Even without such signals, you can tell when your mouse is pointing to a link because, when it's over a link, the arrow will turn into a hand.

AUDIO
Tips for working with URLs.

Each URL is divided into several parts that provide you with important information about the resource itself. The major parts are separated by periods (called "dot" in Internet shorthand). The parts of a URL are illustrated below:

8.3
More on the
anatomy of
URLs.

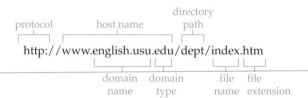

protocol   host name   directory
path

http://www.english.usu.edu/dept/index.htm

domain   domain   file   file
name   type   name   extension

The first part, the **protocol,** indicates the type of link itself (ftp, http, gopher, etc). The Hyper-Text Transfer Protocol (http) is the protocol used by resources found on the World Wide Web. This abbreviation is followed by a colon and two slashes. Next comes the **host name** (which typically begins with *www* to indicate a World Wide Web site); the **domain name** is the part of the host name which is registered by the organization that "owns" the Web site, in this case the English Department at Utah State University. Part of the domain name is the **domain type,** in this case *edu*, which indicates the type of organization sponsoring the Web site. The domain type can give you important information about a site's purpose: whether it is commercial (*com*), educational (*edu*), or a nonprofit organization (*org*), and so on. After the domain type comes the **directory path,** in this case a directory named *dept* for department. There may be several directories or subdirectories within a directory path. Finally you will find a **file name** that the site author(s) have used to identify a particular document located at the site. The **file extension** for a Web page will usually be *.htm* (hypertext markup) or *.html* (hypertext markup language). Your browser may allow for shortcuts on the address bar—that is, it is usually not necessary to type the *http://* at the beginning of a Web address. The browser will fill it in for you. *Explorer* and *Netscape* also have an AUTO COMPLETE feature that recalls previous addresses and types them in for you to select from. If the address is a **root URL,** that is, a URL without a specific file name, it is the address used by an organization or company for their **index page** or "homepage." For example, the root URL for Amazon books is simply *<amazon.com>*.

3   Respecting copyright and avoiding plagiarism

VIDEO
Understanding
online citation.

As a student, you need to be careful to behave ethically and responsibly when using Web materials and when publishing your own work on the Web. In any piece of writing, including Web pages, be certain that you cite all sources, including Internet sources, in a way that readers can find the sources themselves (see Chapters 12 and 13 for guidelines to citing Internet sources). Because it is so easy now to simply copy and paste information from the Internet into your own document files, you need to be especially vigilant. See Chapter 10 for more information about using sources responsibly and avoiding plagiarism.

When writing your own Web pages, also be sure to only download images or texts that are considered "shareware," offered by the site to users free of charge. If you are not certain, you should email the author or site sponsor for permission to either download the material or link to it from your own page. If you wish to use a portion of another's work on your Web page, the rule of thumb commonly used is that duplicating ten percent or less of the work constitutes fair use. Note: You still need to cite the source of the information. Using more than this amount from a source requires you to also secure permission. Be sure to include "reprinted by permission" after you have obtained permission. Of course, you should also include appropriate citation information for the original source regardless of whether you secured permission. If you are unsure about the use of Internet material, it is best to ask the author or site sponsor via an email message for permission to reproduce the work.

8.4

Learn more about Web ethics.

8c   Search the Internet and the Web

Many corporations, nonprofit organizations, and special interest groups maintain information-rich Web sites. The purposes of these sites vary from disseminating information to peddling propaganda to luring customers into spending money. When you use information from an Internet source, remember that unless it is part of a well-known professional organization's site, it probably has not been reviewed by anyone other than members of the organization that maintains the site.

AUDIO

Practice Internet searching.

1   Using search tools to locate information

How do you go about finding specific information on a particular topic? The most reliable way is to use one of the Internet **search tools.** Search tools use different methods of sorting Web pages. Some search tools, often called **search engines,** use an automated system to sort pages based primarily on the use and placement of keywords. *Altavista* and *Excite* are examples of search engines. Search engines automatically find and catalog new sites as they are added to the

8.5

Getting the most from search engines and news pages.

Web, indexing information by title and keywords. Other search tools, such as *Yahoo!*, are actually search directories with a system of categories in a hierarchy. *Yahoo!* uses real people to screen sites and sort them into categories. There are also meta search tools available, which search multiple databases at the same time. *Ixquick, Zworks*, and *ProFusion* are all examples of meta search tools. You might wish to begin with a meta search tool first and then choose one or two search engines or web directories as you fine tune your search. *Excite, Google, HotBot, Yahoo!, AltaVista,* and *Lycos* are some of the biggest Internet databases that index a large number of Web pages (see the list of search tools on p. 123).

Searching via Subject Directories   A subject directory is basically an organized index of topics and subtopics. The *Infoseek* guide to information on the World Wide Web, for example, starts with the following subject areas on the opening screen: Arts & Entertainment, Business & Finance, Computers & Internet, Education, Government & Politics, Health & Medicine, Living, News, and Reference. Using this subject directory, you can narrow the scope of your search. For example, if you were interested in finding out about Brazil's form of government, you could select the "Government & Politics" subject list. Then, once you were in that subtopic, you could type in the keyword *Brazil. Yahoo!* is a popular subject directory because it is both fast and comprehensive. Other subject directories include *Lycos* and *HotBot* (see Figure 8.1).

VIDEO
Conducting
online keyword
searches.

Searching with Keywords   Once you have selected a search tool and narrowed your way down a subject directory, you need to determine what search terms to try. If you searched your library's collection (see 7e-2), you may already have identified subject headings and keywords that you can use. Enter a keyword that identifies your topic and search for **hits** of that keyword—Web pages on which the word appears. Many search tools also permit more sophisticated, customized searches, but the options differ from one to another. Check the search tool's HELP screen to discover ways in which you can customize your search, particularly if you are getting hundreds or even thousands of hits for your search term.

Using Boolean Operators   One of the ways in which search tools allow you to focus is by means of Boolean operators—for example, AND and NOT (see Tips on Using Boolean Operators for Internet Searching on p. 125). The same principles used to search by keyword in a library database also apply to searching on the Internet. For example, if you type *childcare in Utah,* you may get all of the hits for *childcare* in addition to all of the hits for *Utah,* yielding thousands

Search Tools

AltaVista *http://www.altavista.com*	Large, comprehensive database. Keyword searching only. Supports Boolean searching.
Excite *http://www.excite.com*	Subject directory and keyword searching available. Supports Boolean searching.
Google *http://google.com*	Subject directory and keyword searching available.
HotBot *http://hotbot.com*	Subject directory and keyword searching available. Includes newsgroups and email. Supports Boolean searching.
Infoseek *http://infoseek.go.com*	Subject directory and keyword searching available. Does not support Boolean searching.
Ixquick *http://ixquick.com*	One of the world's largest meta search engines. Searches in many languages.
Lycos *http://lycos.com*	Subject directory and keyword searching available. Supports Boolean searching.
ProFusion *http://www.profusion.com*	Searches multiple search tools simultaneously, using keywords. Supports Boolean searching.
Yahoo! *http://yahoo.com*	Subject directory and keyword searching available. Includes news, chat, and email. Does not support Boolean searching.
Zworks *http://www.zworks.com*	Searches multiple search tools simultaneously. Includes the Web, Usenet, ftp, and newswires.

8.6

Access to on-line search tools.

of sources. But if you combine the terms using the Boolean operator AND, you ask the search engine to find only those sources that include both *childcare AND Utah* in the same source (the AND limits the search). To limit the search even more, you could add the Boolean operator NOT: *childcare AND Utah NOT preschool*. Then, any sources mentioning preschool would be eliminated from the list.

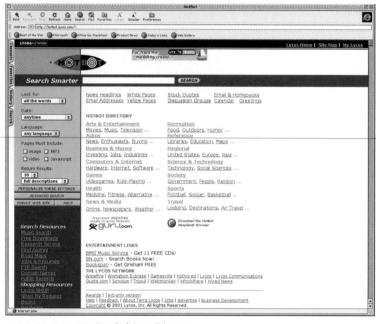

FIGURE 8.1 *HotBot* Subject Directory

Using Quotation Marks Another way to focus the search is by using quotation marks, which indicate that the words must appear in a particular order in the text. For example, *"global warming"* would tell the search tool that you are not interested in either *global* or *warming* by themselves; you want only the two terms in combination, exactly as written inside the quotation marks. In her search on cyber-shopping (see 8d), Kaycee found that *Yahoo!* yielded 17,000 hits for *online shopping* without quotation marks and 1,050 hits for *"online shopping."*

2 Using Internet library and periodical collections

Many libraries make some of the information from their collections available via the Internet; such a collection is known as a *virtual library*. If you are working in a particular academic subject area, it may be more efficient to use virtual library collections instead of (or in addition to) search tools. Virtual libraries are often organized in much the same way as traditional libraries—with separate listings for periodicals, dictionaries, government documents, and so on.

Tips on Using Boolean Operators for Internet Searching

Online databases use Boolean operators to combine two or more terms in ways that the computer recognizes. The Boolean operators most commonly used are AND, OR, and NOT.

1. Be sure to use the appropriate Boolean operator.

   a. AND (&) limits the search, because both keywords must be found in the search. For example, if you wanted to find information only on cats as pets, you could limit your search with the AND operator, typing in *pets AND felines*. The search would then be limited to those sources that included both words.

   b. OR (|) expands the search, because any text with either keyword will be included in the search results. For example, if you wanted to expand your search to include both dogs and cats, you would use the OR operator, typing in *dogs OR felines*. Both groups would then be included in your search.

   c. NOT (!) limits the search by excluding any text containing the keyword after the operator. For example, if you wanted to exclude dogs from your search of pets, you could do so with the NOT operator, typing in *pets NOT dogs*.

2. Enter Boolean operators in UPPERCASE letters (unless you use the symbols).

3. Leave a white space before and after each Boolean operator.

4. If your phrase is complex, involving several Boolean operators, use parentheses: *(pets AND felines) AND (NOT dogs)*. The same search can be indicated using symbols: *(pets & felines) & (! dogs)*.

They are generally more limited than regular libraries, so you should not rely on them exclusively. Rather, use a virtual library search as a supplement to a traditional library search.

Searching Government Documents   The federal government maintains numerous sites that you may want to use for research. The

Internet Libraries and Collections

Academic Info *http://academicinfo.net*	Gateway to quality educational resources categorized by discipline
AskERIC Virtual Library *http://ericir.syr.edu*	Includes the ERIC database and materials
CARL *http://www.carl.org*	Access to virtual libraries, tools, and databases
Internet Public Library *http://www.ipl.org*	Reference site built by the University of Michigan
LibCat *http://www.metronet.lib.mn.us/lc*	Links to hundreds of online libraries
Purdue's Virtual Library *http://thorplus.lib.purdue.edu/vlibrary*	Lists many online journals by academic subject
University of California—Berkeley, LibWeb *http://sunsite.berkeley.edu*	Links to online documents and image collections around the world
University of California—Riverside, Infomine *http://infomine.ucr.edu*	Lists many online sources by academic subject
Virtual Information Center *http://lib.berkeley.edu/Collections*	Links to many reference sites in many academic subjects

8.7
Access to on-
line libraries
and collections.

White House Web site offers an online photographic tour of the White House and provides links to important information about the federal government, including pending legislation, recently produced government documents, and Cabinet activities and reports. (See also the Thomas Web site for legislation.) At the site produced by NASA, you can find information on space flights, space research, and aeronautics. By using a search tool, you can locate specific information on hundreds of other government Web sites, including city and state sites.

Searching Online Periodicals   Journals and magazines that are published on the Web can be good sources for a research paper. Several publishers now offer online versions of their print publications.

Internet Sites for Government Documents

Bureau of the Census *http://www.census.gov*	Social, demographic, and economic information; index a–z; searchable by place, location, and word
Bureau of Justice Statistics *http://www.ojp.usdoj.gov/bjs*	Statistics on all criminal justice topics—law enforcement, drugs, crime, and so on
Bureau of Labor Statistics *http://stats.bls.gov*	Statistics by region, searchable by keyword; economy at a glance
Congressional Quarterly *http://www.cq.com*	*Congressional Quarterly* publishes world-class information and insight on government and politics
Department of Education *http://www.ed.gov*	Educational initiatives; news; publications; programs
Library of Congress *http://lcweb.loc.gov*	Centralized guide to information services provided by the Library of Congress
National Institutes of Health *http://www.nih.gov*	Health information, grants, health news; database searchable by keyword
Statistical Abstract of the U.S. *http://www.census.gov/statab/www*	Collection of statistics on social, economic, and international subjects
Thomas (congressional legislation) *http://thomas.loc.gov*	Full text of current bills under consideration by US House and Senate
White House *http://www.whitehouse.gov*	Information on federal government initiatives, tours, and the President, Vice President, and First Lady; includes a help desk

8.8

Access to online government documents.

Internet Sites for Online Periodicals

CNN Interactive *http://www.cnn.com*	CNN news from around the world; includes audio and video clips
Electronic Library *http://www.elibrary.com*	Keyword searching of online magazines and newspapers; subject tree
Excite NewsTracker *http://news.excite.com*	News headlines from *Excite* (includes Reuters and UPI)
Google NewsTracker *http://news.google.com*	News headlines by topic
Lycos News *http://news.lycos.com*	News headlines from *Lycos* news service (includes CNN, ABC, Reuters, and others)
New York Times *http://nytimes.com*	Daily contents of the *New York Times*
Yahoo! Today's News *http://dailynews.yahoo.com*	News headlines from *Yahoo!* news service (includes CNN, ABC, Reuters, and others)

WWW

8.9
Access to on-line periodicals.

Often you can access the full texts of articles that appear in the print version.

8d Follow a student Internet search

To show you how a search might work, in this section we follow the Internet search of Kaycee Sorensen, the student who was interested in online shopping. Her starting questions were

```
Is the number of online shoppers increasing?

Is shopping via the Internet a viable solution for consumers?

Is it safe to use a credit card for online shopping?
```

Her search strategy included looking for current sources on the Internet. She used the *Yahoo!* directory as a launching point for her Internet search.

HELP

How do I use the bookmark/favorites and history features?

Your Internet browser may have features that allow you to mark sites for future use and find out where you have been in a given search.

1. Marking Internet sites:
   a. When you locate a site that interests you, add this site to your list of bookmarks or favorites. The browser will link this site so that all you need to do to launch the site is select it from the bookmark/favorites list.
   b. Check the list of bookmarks/favorites: the site you just selected should now be listed. The next time you want to visit the site, use the bookmark/favorites feature to locate it quickly.
   c. As you collect more bookmarks/favorites, take advantage of your browser's organization feature. (Different browsers offer different ways to organize bookmarks/favorites.)

8.10

Instructions for using bookmarks and favorites.

2. Using the HISTORY feature to retrace your steps in an Internet search:
   a. Select the HISTORY icon from the menu bar to display the history of an Internet session. All of the sites you visited in the current session will be displayed.
   b. Use the history listing to recall sites that you visited but neglected to bookmark. You can customize your history using EDIT>PREFERENCES.

8.11

Instructions for using the history feature.

NOTE: If you are working in a computer lab, you may not be able to save your individual bookmarks/favorites except to your own disk.

When Kaycee opened the *Yahoo!* guide to information on the World Wide Web, she saw several potentially interesting subject categories listed. Kaycee noticed the topic of "Shopping and Services" listed under the category "Business and the Economy." Since she was interested in the online shopping topic, she decided to see if there were any relevant sources listed in that category. She typed the

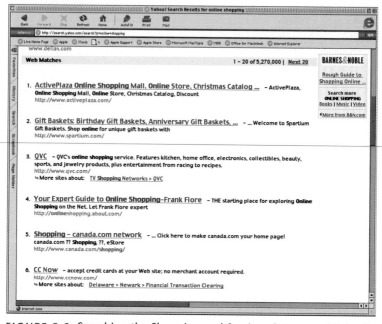

FIGURE 8.2 Searching the Shopping and Services Category of *Yahoo!*

words *online shopping* into the search screen and asked *Yahoo!* to search just the "Shopping and Services" category (see Figure 8.2).

That search yielded more than 15,000 hits for Web sources that contained either the word *online* or the word *shopping*. Kaycee also noticed that many of the sites were commercial businesses that offered consumers online shopping opportunities. Kaycee realized that she was using search terms that were much too broad and that she needed to narrow her search further, especially since many of the links appeared to be irrelevant to her research topic. She first decided to focus her search by putting the search terms in quotation marks so that *Yahoo!* would look for the keywords together in sequence rather than separately. When she typed *"online shopping"* in quotation marks and clicked SEARCH JUST THIS CATEGORY, *Yahoo!* informed her that there were now 744 hits, a more focused result, but still too broad. Kaycee then tried combining *ecommerce* and + *security* to further focus her search. She used the + sign to indicate that all results must have both the term *ecommerce* and the term *security* in them. The result of this search was closer to what she was after—51 hits with a range of articles and Web sites that were both commercial and non-commercial (see Figure 8.3).

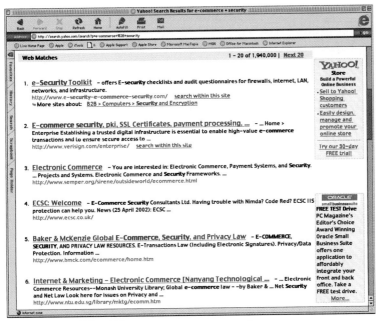

FIGURE 8.3 *Yahoo!* Hits on *ecommerce + security*

After browsing through the 51 sources, following the links and reading some of them to evaluate the sites for ther relevance to her research questions, Kaycee printed out a few for later use, including the "cyberatlas" and the shopping guide from Hypermart.net. Kaycee then went to her library's database for access to books, magazines, newspapers, and journal articles. By using her library's computer search capabilities, she was able to locate several more sources that were useful in her research, including *Money* magazine and *Capital Times*. Remember that you should be seeking a combination of different types of sources rather than relying exclusively on the Internet.

CHAPTER 9

Evaluating Electronic and Print Sources

AUDIO

The challenge of evaluating sources.

WWW

9.1

Guidelines for evaluating Web resources.

As a researcher in today's information environment, one of your most important tasks is to evaluate what you read. The tendency to believe everything one reads is dangerous, especially with respect to Internet sources. Some, but by no means all, print sources may undergo a process of peer review and evaluation before they are published. (Peer review refers to the practice of sending written material out to experts in the field for evaluation before it is actually published.) Peer-reviewed sources can generally be trusted to present information accurately. In contrast, the screening process for Internet materials is often determined by the author. Many people who create Web sites have a sense of personal integrity, but others are less than forthright in the ways they use the medium to promote themselves or their viewpoints. Reading with a critical eye is always important, but it is particularly crucial in dealing with Internet information.

> ## WEBLINK
>
> http://muse.widener.edu/
> Wolfgram-Memorial-
> Library/webevaluation/
> webeval.htm
>
> A fabulous collection of
> materials to help you
> evaluate all kinds of
> electronic and print texts

9a Choose legitimate sources

WWW

9.2

Detailed steps for critically analyzing sources.

Because you will be relying on your sources to provide the evidence and authority to support your hypothesis, it is crucial that you choose legitimate sources. Your reputation as a researcher may be at stake.

1 Deciding whether the source is worth reading

To save yourself a great deal of time, quickly assess a source by skimming for a few key elements.

HELP

How do I find a site's homepage?

To locate a site's homepage, you can travel up the URL's directory path.

1. Open your browser and locate the site that interests you.
2. Look at the URL, listed on the LOCATION line of your browser.
3. Back your way up the URL by deleting the last section of the address, following the last slash. Hit ENTER to retrieve the new page.
4. Look at the URL of the page you have now located.
5. Continue backing up in the URL until you reach the site's homepage.

NOTE: A well-designed Web site contains a link to the site's homepage.

9.3
Instructions for finding a site's homepage.

Relevance   Is the source relevant to your research? That is, does it address the topic you are researching? Sometimes a title will mislead you; a source will turn out to be on another topic entirely or on an aspect of the topic that does not interest you. If a source is not relevant, quickly move on.

Publisher or Sponsor   Who is the sponsoring organization or publisher? Is the article in a popular magazine, such as *Ladies' Home Journal*, or a professional journal, such as *Journal of Behavioral Sciences*? Depending on the nature of the research project, it may or may not be appropriate to use information from the popular press, which tends to be less scholarly than information found, for example, in a professional journal. For many college papers, however, the popular press—including major newspapers such as the *New York Times* and magazines such as *Time* and *Newsweek*—can certainly be useful.

Although determining the sponsoring organization or individual is no less important for an Internet site than for a print source, it may not be as easy to accomplish. One clue to the nature of the sponsoring organization is the URL itself. Internet conventions have been established to identify a standardized suffix for Web addresses, also called a **domain type** (see 8b-2). These domain types tell you something about the nature of the sponsoring organization. Looking at the

VIDEO
Comparing on-line sources.

domain type of a Web site's URL will help you to understand the purpose behind the page—whether educational or commercial, for example. Common domain types include

- Education (*.edu*)
- Government (*.gov*)
- Nonprofit organization (*.org*)
- Commercial (*.com*)
- Network (*.net*)
- Military (*.mil*)
- Other countries (*.ca* for Canada; *.uk* for United Kingdom)

9.4

A sample author search using *AltaVista*.

Author In addition to a sponsoring organization, is an individual author listed? Look carefully at both print and online sources to evaluate the author's credentials. Does he or she work for a government agency, a political group, a commercial industry, or an educational institution? Often the author's professional affiliation will be noted at the bottom of a journal or magazine article. A Web site may have an "About the author" page. If no author is listed, you should question the site's reliability.

Timeliness Be sure that you check the date of any piece you encounter. In many fields, the timeliness of the information is as important as the information itself. For example, if you are researching a medical topic, you want to be certain that your sources include the most up-to-date research. One of the many benefits of the Internet is that it allows information to be updated continually, but unfortunately not all Web sites list the dates on which they were first posted and last updated. With print sources, you need to be especially careful about when a piece was written. Months or even years may go by between when something is discovered and when it finally appears in print. Thus, research conducted many months or years ago may just now be appearing in print. In fields where information is changing rapidly, such as medicine, access to current information can be crucial.

Cross References Is the source cited in other works? You can sometimes make decisions about a work's credibility by considering how it is cited by other sources. When you are researching a topic, sometimes one author's name will come up repeatedly in references and in discussions. This author is probably an expert on the topic; it would be worth your while to check into sources written by that person.

2   Deciding whether the source is worth using

Once you have decided that a source is worth reading, read and evaluate the source to determine whether or not you want to use it in your paper. First look at the author's rhetorical stance (see 2a-2). Then evaluate the content of the piece itself.

Rhetorical Stance   Who is the intended audience for the piece? Does the title help you to understand which readers the piece is targeting? Is there evidence that the author has taken a particular stance in a controversy on his or her subject? Journals and magazines typically write for particular target audiences, whom they assume share certain biases and opinions. If you are aware of that bias before you read a piece, you will be able to keep the information in context. As well as considering the audience, think about the purposes for writing and publishing the piece. What are the author and sponsoring organization trying to accomplish? If the source is a magazine or newspaper, turn to the opening pages and read the editorial policy to get an idea of the publication's purpose. Regardless of the source, you need to exercise caution as an information "consumer." Check to see if the site includes an "About our site" page, which describes the site's purpose or agenda. Knowing this purpose will help you to evaluate the credibility of the information.

9.5

A sample site evaluation reveals a parody.

Elements to Examine to Assess a Potential Source's Appropriateness

Print Sources	Electronic Sources
Title and Subtitle: Check both the title and the subtitle for relevance to your topic. For example, you could not be sure that a book entitled *Wishes, Lies, and Dreams* was appropriate without reading the subtitle: *Teaching Children to Write Poetry.*	**Title and Subtitle:** Check the Web page title (found on the top line of your screen, above the browser window) and the title on the page itself for their relevance to your topic.

(continued)

Elements to Examine *(continued)*

Print Sources	Electronic Sources
Copyright Page: Check this page, just after the title page, to find out who published the book, where it was published, and when.	**Copyright Information and Sponsorship:** At the bottom of the home page, you should find information about who sponsors the site. Knowing the sponsor can give you clues to a site's reliability.
Table of Contents: Check the titles of parts, chapters, and sections. The outline of a book can show you the topics covered and the detail of that coverage.	**Major Links to Secondary Pages:** Check to see if the site includes links to secondary pages that elaborate on subtopics.
Abstract: Read the abstract, if included. It will provide you with a concise summary.	**Abstract:** Read the abstract, if included. It will provide you with a concise summary.
Preface: Read the preface. This is where the authors generally set out their purpose.	**Introduction:** Read any introductory material on the homepage. It should tell you about the site's purpose.
Chapter Headings and Subheadings: Check the headings and subheadings to find out what specific subtopics will be discussed.	**Headings and Subheadings:** Look closely at the major divisions on the homepage. They may tell you how detailed the site is.
Conclusion: Read any conclusion or afterword. It may give you another sense of the authors' stance.	**Conclusion:** Read any concluding material on the final page of the site. It may give you another sense of the authors' stance.
Author Note: To evaluate credibility, read anything provided about the author.	**Author Page:** To evaluate credibility, read any "About the author" or "About our site" pages or information. Conduct a search on the author's name, using a search tool.

(continued)

Elements to Examine *(continued)*

Print Sources	Electronic Sources
Index: If available, check the index for a listing of topics included in the book.	**Glossary:** If the Web site includes a glossary of terms, use it to help you understand the topics covered.
Bibliography: Look at the list of references at the end of the article or book. It can tell you how carefully an author researched and also lead you to other related information.	**Links to References or Related Sites:** Look at the links to related sites or to sources referenced. They can tell you about the site's research and also lead you to other related information.

Content   Pay close attention to the content itself. Does the language seem moderate and reasonable, or are there terms that might be considered inflammatory or prejudiced? Does the writer seem overly emotional? Is the tone strident or preachy? Other factors to consider as you read closely include how the piece uses source evidence, how logically the argument is developed, and how the content matches (or contradicts) what others have said on the subject.

9b   Follow a student's evaluation of Weblinks

To give you a sense of how you might go about evaluating information you find via an Internet search, we will follow a student's search for information related to smoking. Mark Robb had been reading about the debate on smoking and addiction. He wanted to find out about both sides of the debate, in an effort to answer the question "Is smoking addictive?" Mark knew that the tobacco industry had argued recently that smoking was not addictive, but rather habit-forming.

AUDIO
Conduct your own Internet search.

Mark began by turning to the Lycos search tool, located at <http://www.lycos.com>. Browsing through the subject directory, Mark noted a category "Health" (see Figure 9.1). He clicked on "Health" and found the subcategory "substance abuse" and under that "smoking and tobacco-related dependencies."

Checklist for Evaluating Information

The Sponsoring Organization

1. Where does the information appear—in the popular press, in a scholarly report, on a Web site?
2. Who is the sponsor of the source—an academic society, a publishing house, an organization?
3. For a Web site, what is the domain of the URL—educational, governmental, commercial?

The Author

1. Who is the author? Have you run across the name in other sources?
2. What are the author's credentials?
3. What kind of language does the author use?
4. What kind of tone has the author adopted?

The Audience

1. Who is the intended audience for the publication?
2. Does the publication target obvious biases in its audience?
3. What are the characteristics of the audience members?

The Purpose

1. What are the author and sponsoring organization trying to accomplish?
2. Is an idea or product being marketed?
3. Are you being urged to adopt a particular point of view?

The Timeliness

1. When was the piece published?
2. When was the Web site posted and/or updated?
3. How important is it that your information be current?

Mark found 49 hits for his search term. These were mainly sites to help smokers quit (see Figure 9.2 on p. 140). He wanted to find information on both sides of the question. One link caught his eye: Smoking from All Sides.

FIGURE 9.1 Homepage for *Lycos* Search Tool

Mark clicked on the link to find out what this site was all about. He found links to newsgroups, articles, and homepages that discussed smoking. The introductory material on the page stated

> I've tried to include links about all perspectives of smoking: health aspects, statistics, tobacco news, anti-smoking groups, smoking cessation, tobacco history, commentary, pro-smoking documents, and smoking glamour.

Mark wondered about the author of this page. He wanted to find out if the person who had collected the links at this site was reliable. He followed the link to the author's page and discovered that the author, Loring Holden, was a software engineer in the Brown University Computer Science Department. Although Mark was not sure that these credentials related in any way to expertise on the tobacco industry, he decided to give the author the benefit of the doubt and read the site.

Since Mark knew that he could find lots of anti-smoking information, he used Holden's page to locate pro-smoking sites. There

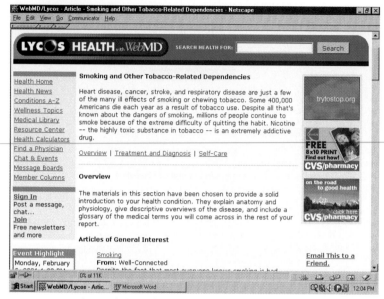

FIGURE 9.2 *Lycos* Listing of Sources Related to Tobacco

were about a half-dozen such sites, with names like "Smoke and Be Cool," and "Smoker's Home Page." Mark went to each of these links in turn. "Smoke and Be Cool" was a diatribe by an individual smoker against anti-smoking regulation. The language used by the author of the site was strident and even offensive. The author's tone clued Mark in to the author's agenda of irritating those in the anti-smoking campaign.

"Smoker's Home Page," updated recently, was a bit less harsh in tone but equally militant in its arguments against any regulation by the government of the tobacco industry. On "Smoker's Home Page" was a category called "Issues," which included articles with such titles as "Second Hand Smoke: The Big Lie" and "Addiction." These articles were authored by Joe Dawson. Mark could not find any information at the site about Joe Dawson, but it was obvious from his arguments that he was extremely suspicious of all government-sponsored studies having to do with smoking. The main thrust of his arguments was to keep the government out of the lives of individuals.

Mark read the addiction article with interest. The argument focused on making a distinction between a substance that was "habit-forming" and a substance that was "addictive." The article concluded that smoking was habit-forming rather than addictive and that the efforts to have nicotine classified as an addictive drug were part of the government's attempts to control smoking and infringe on smokers' rights. Mark printed out this article for later reference. It was the only article he found that explicitly argued that nicotine was not addictive.

Next Mark turned to the link for *Smoke* magazine, also on Holden's page. The magazine was touted as promoting the cigar-lover's lifestyle. Mark wondered just what type of journal this might be. He followed the link to the journal's Web page and glanced at the glitzy cover and the glossy photographs. He opened the site's page about the journal's sponsor and discovered that *Smoke* was a trade journal for the tobacco industry published by the Lockwood Publications Corporation, which Mark discovered, through further digging, had also published the weekly trade journal *Tobacco* since 1872. Mark knew that any information found in articles in this publication would have to be read with the magazine's obvious bias in favor of the tobacco industry in mind.

Mark's brief researching tour through the Internet illustrates the importance of evaluating everything you read. In thinking critically about the sites he encountered in his search, Mark posed all of the questions on the Checklist for Evaluating Information (page 138). By using these evaluative questions, Mark was able to get a sense of the reliability of the information he encountered.

CHAPTER **10**

Using Sources and Avoiding Plagiarism

Writers gain credibility through the use of information from experts. It is the responsibility of research authors to be certain that any information from another author, whether paraphrased, summarized, or quoted, is accurately relayed and clearly acknowledged. Integrating source information into one's own writing is a skill that takes practice.

AUDIO

Using sources accurately.

Being careless about your sources can lead to a serious academic offense called plagiarism—with serious consequences, such as a failing grade for the course or even expulsion from school. **Plagiarism** is defined as the unauthorized or misleading use of the language and text of another author. Whenever you use exact words from a source, this must be indicated clearly through the use of a signal phrase, quotation marks, and an in-text citation at the point in the text where the source information is quoted. When you paraphrase or summarize ideas from a source, in the same way you need to give proper attribution to the source from which you obtained the ideas (see Chapters 12 and 13 for information about in-text citations). It is not enough to list the authors in footnotes or bibliographies. Readers must be able to tell as they are reading your paper exactly what information came from which source and what information is your own contribution to the paper.

10a Use sources responsibly

WEBLINK

http://www.wisc.edu/writing/Handbook/QuoSuccessfulSummary.html

Detailed explanations and examples of using quotations, paraphrases, and summaries

www

10.1
Avoid plagiarism with these in-depth guidelines.

When writing a research paper, you must acknowledge any original information, ideas, and illustrations that you find in another author's work, whether it is in print or on the Internet. Acknowledging the work of other authors is called documenting sources. (The appropriate forms for documentation are discussed in Chapters 12 and 13.)

1 Reading critically

Your main task as a researcher is to make sense of the subject you have chosen to research. To understand the subject and come to some conclusions of your own about it, you need to read widely and critically. If you rely on only one source throughout your paper, you immediately lose credibility with your readers. Readers will question the depth of your research and the level of your knowledge; your competence as a researcher will be called into question. On the other hand, if you use a number of authors to provide supporting evidence, you gain credibility with your readers. So, it is important to read and evaluate several sources.

Previewing   Preview the source first. As you preview, pay attention to key words or phrases and try to get a general idea of the work's purpose and structure.

Reading   Read the work a first time at a relatively rapid pace, either a section or a chapter at a time. This first reading should be more than skimming, however, as the goal is to understand in general what you have read. Then read the work again, carefully and slowly. When you are reading your own books or photocopied articles, use a highlighter or a pencil to underline key ideas. Stop frequently to take notes (see 7c).

Reviewing   As part of your review, assess and evaluate each source, including those you find as you search the Internet. As discussed in Chapter 9, assessment is a two-step process of deciding whether or not the source is worth reading and whether or not the source is worth using in your paper. Evaluating involves thinking carefully about key elements in the work.

Synthesizing   As you read your sources, you should also seek to determine relationships among them. What kinds of "conversations" are happening between the authors that you are reading? Does one source contradict another, or does it serve to reinforce what you've read other places? Does a particular source serve as an example of something explained in a more general source? Or perhaps one source gives an excellent definition of the topic you are researching while another serves to describe something in more detail. In your research notebook, be sure that you not only summarize the individual sources, but also look for relationships among the ideas in these sources.

2   Taking accurate, usable notes

If you do not take good notes while you read, you may have to retrace your steps in an attempt to relocate a particular source. In the worst-case scenario, the source you need to reference will have been checked out by another library patron or the Internet site will be gone. So, it is important to take accurate, usable notes when you first encounter a source. For information concerning how to take notes, see 7c.

The most successful research papers incorporate information from several sources into the flow of the paper. The least successful papers tend to make one of the following major mistakes. Either they rely too heavily on just one source for support of the argument or they cobble together the opinions of three or four authors, one right after the other, without interpreting their meanings or relationships. To avoid these mistakes, make your notes both substantive and interpretive.

When you record content notes from a source, you typically either paraphrase or summarize what you have read. If the information seems especially significant to your research topic or if it provides new insights or ideas that you have not encountered before in your research, you will probably want to paraphrase it. Paraphrasing is an almost line-by-line rewording of the source information. (See 10b for examples of appropriate paraphrasing.) If the information seems less crucial to your topic or if you need little detail to make your point, you may wish to summarize instead. A summary, in contrast to a paraphrase, condenses information. Reserve direct quotations for those infrequent times when nothing but the author's own words can make the point as well.

3 Avoiding plagiarism

10.2

Recognizing and preventing plagiarism.

If you use source information carefully and accurately, you will avoid any charges of plagiarism. By following the guidelines in this chapter when you paraphrase, summarize, and quote, you will never plagiarize.

Acknowledgment Required   Any word, phrase, or sentence that you copied directly from a source must be placed in quotation marks, and complete bibliographic information must be given, including the page reference for the quotation. Similarly, you must acknowledge paraphrases and summary restatements of ideas taken from a source, even though you have cast them in your own words.

If you find information on a Web site, it is a relatively simple matter to download it onto a disk or into your computer's hard drive. However, you need to be careful to use the information fairly. When you summarize, paraphrase, or quote from a Web site, you must give proper acknowledgment to the source. It is not acceptable to CUT and PASTE text or graphics from the Internet without acknowledging the source or, for graphics, receiving permission. The same general principles about paraphrasing, summarizing, and quoting apply to other online sources found through the Internet.

No Acknowledgment Required   You need not document "common knowledge." This term refers to information that is generally known or accepted by educated people. Information that you can find readily in general reference works such as encyclopedias or in the popular media is probably common knowledge and need not be documented, although it must be stated in your own words. Common knowledge should be verified. Be certain that several sources provide the same information before assuming that it is common knowledge. Well-proven historical facts and dates need not be documented. As a general rule, it is better to over-document than to under-document and be accused of plagiarizing. When in doubt, document.

Unintentional Plagiarism Your notes should accurately record source information in your own words, when possible. You should be able to tell at a glance from your notes when information is from a source and when it is your own commentary or thoughts on a source. Students taking notes from a source sometimes commit *unintentional* plagiarism by carelessly copying words and phrases from a source into their notes and then using these words and phrases without acknowledgment in a paper. One way to avoid this problem is to read a piece carefully and then set it aside while you write your notes. If you follow the reading and notetaking procedures outlined above, paraphrasing and summarizing in your own words what you have read, you are unlikely to use the author's exact wording inappropriately in a research paper.

AUDIO
Take accurate notes to avoid plagiarism.

Intentional Plagiarism Sometimes plagiarism is *intentional;* that is, a writer knowingly copies the work of another without proper acknowledgment of the source. Whenever you use words from a source, this must be indicated clearly through the use of quotation marks and documentation at the point in the text where the source information is used. It is not enough to list the author in the footnotes or bibliography. Readers must be able to tell as they are reading your paper exactly what information came from which source and what information is your contribution to the paper. That way, they can follow your research trail and form their own judgments.

An Example of Plagiarism A *Newsweek** article reported on a Stanford University business school lecturer who used several pages from an article by Greg Easterbrook in his book, word for word, without acknowledging the original author. When the plagiarism came to light, the Stanford author apologized to Easterbrook, but insisted that he had not plagiarized because he had included Easterbrook's name in the book's footnotes. Easterbrook's response

WWW
10.3
Myths and excuses about plagiarism exposed.

* Easterbrook, Greg. "The Sincerest Flattery: Thanks, But I'd Rather You Not Plagiarize My Work." *Newsweek* 19 July 1999: 45–46.

explains an important distinction: "Footnotes my foot. Footnotes mean the place a fact can be found; they do not confer the right to present someone else's words as your own work" (Easterbrook 46). The distinction being made here is that whenever you use words or ideas from a source, this must be indicated clearly through the use of quotation marks and documentation at the point in the text where the source information is used. It is not enough to list the author in the footnotes or bibliography. Note how in this example we have used signal phrases that indicate that information in this paragraph comes from a *Newsweek* article by Easterbrook ("A *Newsweek* article reported . . ." and "Easterbrook's response explains . . ."), and how we have included specific documentation regarding the source itself along with quotation marks around the exact quotation from Easterbrook. This is an example of proper attribution of source information.

10b Paraphrase sources accurately

10.4

Examples of paraphrasing sources.

Instead of directly quoting from sources, writers have the option of paraphrasing source information. The objective of paraphrasing is to present an author's ideas clearly, using your own words and phrases instead of the author's. This important skill not only deepens your understanding of the author's ideas but also helps you to avoid plagiarism (see 10a-3). Here are some suggestions to help you paraphrase.

1. *Place the information in a new order.* When paraphrasing, you must rework a passage. One way to do this is to reorder the information. In the following example, the good paraphrase inverts the sentence structure of the original, whereas the poor paraphrase copies both words and sentence structure from the source.

ORIGINAL QUOTATION

"If you're coping with an illness or want to exchange views about a medical topic, you'll want to find your way to a newsgroup. Despite the name, these are not collections of news items. They are, in effect, virtual bulletin boards open to anyone who cares to participate. The messages generally consist of plain text" (Schwartz 28).

POOR PARAPHRASE [COPIES WORDS AND SENTENCE STRUCTURE DIRECTLY FROM SOURCE]

NO   If you're faced with an illness or want to exchange views about a medical topic, you'll want to find your way to a newsgroup.

Despite the name, these are not news items. They are virtual bulletin boards open to anyone. The messages generally consist of ordinary text (Schwartz 28).

GOOD PARAPHRASE [WITH INVERTED SENTENCE STRUCTURE AND DIFFERENT WORDS]

YES   In a recent *Consumer Reports* article, the author suggests finding a relevant newsgroup if you have a particular medical problem or if you want to talk with others about a medical subject. Newsgroups are online bulletin boards that are available to anyone; in spite of their name, they are not news reports. Anyone who wishes to may join in a newsgroup discussion (Schwartz 28).

2. *Break the complex ideas into small units.* If the author has expressed himself or herself in a rather complicated way, paraphrasing gives you the opportunity to state the complex ideas of the source more simply:

ORIGINAL QUOTATION

"The 'perfect' search engine would guide users to every relevant location, ranked in order of usefulness, without leaving anything out and without including anything irrelevant. That engine doesn't yet exist" (Schwartz 29).

PARAPHRASE [WITH SIMPLIFIED SENTENCE STRUCTURE]

Schwartz states that no Internet searching tool is yet able to be "perfect." If it were, it would lead you to all the appropriate locations on your topic. It would rank all the Web sites by how useful they were. It would never leave something out that was relevant. It would never include anything that was irrelevant (29).

3. *Use concrete, direct vocabulary in place of technical jargon.* If the author has used technical vocabulary, you can replace some of the technical jargon with more direct, familiar words as you paraphrase. Here are some examples of jargon from these examples that might be changed in a paraphrase:

newsgroup = online discussion group

search engine = Internet searching tool

users = those who are using the Internet

location = Web site found at a unique Internet address

4. *Use synonyms for words in the source.* Just as you can replace jargon with more familiar terms, you can use synonyms (words that

AUDIO
Three sets of
guidelines.

Guidelines for Effective Paraphrasing

1. Place the information in a new order.
2. Break the complex ideas into small units.
3. Use concrete, direct vocabulary in place of technical jargon.
4. Use synonyms for words in the source.
5. Accompany each important fact or idea in your notes with the source page number.
6. Incorporate the paraphrase smoothly into the grammar and style of your own writing.

mean roughly the same thing) in the place of words from the source. Here are some of the synonyms used in the paraphrases above:

illness = medical problem

exchange views = talk to others

medical topic = medical subject

available to = open to

despite = in spite of

news items = news reports

5. *Accompany each important fact or idea in your notes with the source page number.* With paraphrases, as with quotations, you must indicate exactly on what page in the source you found the information. Ideally, anyone else reading your work should be able to locate the exact wording from which your paraphrase was taken. If the source has no pages, as is true of many Internet documents, you might wish to use a screen number or a paragraph number instead. (See Chapters 12 and 13 for more information on documenting electronic sources.)

WWW
10.5
Examples of
summarizing
sources.

10c Summarize sources briefly

Summaries condense the information found in sources. Like paraphrasing, summarizing involves restating the author's ideas or information in your own words, but summaries are typically much briefer than the original information. To be sure that your summary accurately reflects the author's most important ideas, you first must read the source carefully in order to understand it thoroughly. Summaries typically leave out extended examples, illustrations, and long explanations. The goal of a summary is to record the gist of the piece—its primary line of argument—without tangential arguments, examples, and other departures from the main ideas. As with paraphrasing, you need to be sure that the summary is stated in your own words.

1 Recording summaries in notes

When you first preview a source to determine its relevance to your research, you can also decide how much of the source you are likely to use in your paper. You would not want to paraphrase an entire article, for example, if only the introduction related to your topic. Rather, you could simply summarize the relevant portion.

Here are some additional suggestions to help you summarize effectively:

1. *Identify key points.* A summary must reflect the main ideas of the source accurately, so you need to read carefully before you write a summary. As you read your own books or photocopied articles, underline or highlight key ideas, words, or phrases. Ask yourself, "What is the central idea of this passage?" Try to articulate that idea in your own words, using just a sentence or two.

2. *Record information.* As you record the key ideas, be certain that you separate your own interpretive comments from the source information itself. You can do this by using a two-column notebook or document comments (see 7c-1).

3. *Create lists and tables.* When you are condensing ideas, sometimes it helps to write them down in the form of a list or a table. In this way, you can capture the most important ideas in the simplest form possible and present them to readers as a listing of key ideas.

4. *Check for accuracy.* Just as you did when quoting or paraphrasing from a source, you need to check your summaries to ensure their accuracy. Check to make sure that the words and phrases are your own. Place any of the author's unique words or phrases in quotation marks and include a page reference. It is a good idea to reread the source after you have summarized it, just to be certain that you have not inadvertently altered the author's meaning.

2 Integrating summaries into a paper

Summaries are incorporated into a paper in much the same way as direct quotations and paraphrases. Introduce a summary with a signal phrase, place it in a context for the readers, or perhaps use the author's name or article title in the introduction. As with quoting and paraphrasing, you need to provide documentation indicating the source of the summarized information.

3 Avoiding plagiarism when summarizing

As mentioned above, using your own words and providing documentation for the source will produce a summary that avoids plagiarism. In the following examples, the unacceptable summary makes the mistake of using the same wording and sentence structure of the original source (the underlined words are plagiarized) as well as failing to provide documentation. The acceptable summary identifies and recasts the main idea into the student's own words and provides proper attribution to the source itself.

DIRECT QUOTATION FROM ORIGINAL SOURCE: "FREE MUSIC, FREE RIDE?"

"It should come as no surprise that Napster and other free Internet services that allow their users to share files containing such things as recorded music have got copyright holders reaching for their lawyers. Indeed, the Record Industry Association of America (RIAA) is now dragging Napster through the courts to try to shut it down (a final decision is expected in late September). But the users of such systems—at least those who make their files freely available—might soon get angry, too. For a study by Eytan Adar and Bernardo Huberman, who work at the Xerox Palo Alto Research Center in California, suggests that most of the inhabitants of this bit of cyberspace are not altruists concerned with the common good, but 'leeches' who suck up files without making their own available in exchange" ("Free Music" 68–69).

UNACCEPTABLE SUMMARY [COPIES WORDS AND SENTENCE STRUCTURE DIRECTLY FROM SOURCE AND LEAVES OFF ATTRIBUTION]

NO   We shouldn't be surprised that Napster and other free Internet services have copyright holders reaching for their lawyers. Often they are not altruists concerned with the common good but rather are leeches who suck up files of others.

GOOD SUMMARY [RECASTS THE MAIN IDEA INTO STUDENT'S OWN WORDS AND PROVIDES SOURCE ATTRIBUTION]

YES   According to an article in the *Economist*, we should not be surprised that the recording industry is suing free Internet music providers such as Napster. However, the article also points out that users of such file-sharing systems do not always exchange

Guidelines for Effective Summarizing

1. Identify the main points as you read the source.
2. Put those main points into your own words.
3. Condense the original, keeping the summary short.
4. Use a table or a list, when appropriate, to summarize the information.
5. Be objective rather than interpreting or judging source ideas.
6. Integrate the summarized ideas into the flow of your prose.
7. Provide proper documentation for the source.

files equitably. The article cites a study by Xerox researchers that implies many who use such systems do not also freely share their own files ("Free Music" 68).

10d Quote sources sparingly

Quotations are exact wordings taken from sources. Use direct quotations sparingly in a research paper. A string of quotations can be confusing for readers, especially if each presents information in a different writing style. By paraphrasing and summarizing instead of quoting, you can more smoothly incorporate the ideas from sources into your own writing. However, if an author uses unique language or an interesting image, a brief quotation may be an effective addition to a paper.

1 Using quoted material

When you quote from a source, it is important to be accurate. Unless you download text from the Internet, you are most likely copying from a source into your notes and then into your paper, so it is easy to make a transcription error. Making photocopies or printouts of a source can help you to quote exactly because you can recheck the wording from the original. Every time you copy information from a source, indicate through quotation marks on your note card or in your research notebook that you have taken the exact wording from the original so that you will not be confused later on. As mentioned before, take care to record the source and page number for the quotation.

2 Integrating quotations into a paper

10.6

Examples of integrating quotations into a paper.

When you use a direct quotation, you must integrate it smoothly into the flow of your ideas. Many teachers report that students have trouble with this skill. You need to use signal phrases to alert your reader that a quotation is coming (see Verbs to Use in Signal Phrases for Quotations below). You also need to attribute the source appropriately (see Chapters 12 and 13 on documentation formats) and punctuate it correctly (see Chapter 44 on Quotation Marks). The quotations that you use should be relatively short to minimize interruption. If you decide to use a long quotation in your paper, you are obliged to explain your choice to the readers. Otherwise, they are likely to just skim over the long quotation.

Verbs to Use in Signal Phrases for Quotations

acknowledges	confirms	observes
advises	contends	offers
advocates	criticizes	opposes
affirms	declares	recommends
agrees	denies	remarks
alleges	describes	replies
allows	disagrees	reports
answers	discusses	responds
asserts	disputes	reveals
avows	emphasizes	says
believes	explains	states
charges	expresses	suggests
claims	interprets	thinks
concludes	lists	writes
concurs	objects	

Techniques for Incorporating Quotations   Observing the four suggestions outlined below for incorporating quotations will help to improve the flow of your paper.

1. Integrate the quotation smoothly into the grammatical flow of your sentence.

NO   Carnegie Mellon researchers, "Scientists disagree about whether climate change will be a serious problem in the next 50 to 100 years" (U.S. Global Change 46). [Grammar problem—fused sentence]

YES   According to researchers at Carnegie Mellon University, "Scientists disagree about whether climate change will be a serious problem in the next 50 to 100 years" (U.S. Global Change 46).

2. Provide an explanation as to why you are using a particular quotation.

NO   "Everyone in the group contributes to the overall level of emotional intelligence, but the leader holds special sway in this regard. Emotions are contagious, and it's natural for people to pay extra attention to the leader's feelings and behavior" (Goleman, Boyatzis, and McKee 174) [No introductory explanation]

YES   Goleman et al. confirm that it is only when groups exhibit the qualities of emotional intelligence that they can be perceived as smarter than individuals. The authors assert "Everyone in the group contributes to the overall level of emotional intelligence, but the leader holds special sway in this regard. Emotions are contagious, and it's natural for people to pay extra attention to the leader's feelings and behavior" (174). [Includes introductory explanation with signal verbs *confirm* and *assert*]

3. Use a signal phrase to introduce the quotation. If you provide the author's name in the signal phrase, you need only put the page number in parentheses.

NO   "During the years with The Nature Conservancy and IUCN, I did some science, some conservation, and a little writing. What I always came back to was the writing—the more heart-filled, the better. In the end, I think I always knew the words would win out" (Pyle 59). [No signal phrase]

YES   As Robert Michael Pyle explains, "During the years with The Nature Conservancy and IUCN, I did some science, some conservation, and a little writing. What I always came back to

Guidelines for Effective Quoting

1. Use direct quotations sparingly as support for your own ideas.
2. Use primarily short quotations (one or two sentences).
3. Be extremely careful to be accurate when copying a quotation.
4. Attribute quotations to their sources and punctuate them correctly (see 44a).
5. Integrate quotations smoothly into the stylistic flow of the paper.
6. Incorporate quotations in a way that is grammatically correct (see 44e).
7. Provide an explanation to place the quotation in context.
8. Use the author's name or the work's title to introduce the quotation.
9. Use ellipses when words or phrases are omitted from the quotation (see 45k).

was the writing—the more heart-filled, the better. In the end, I think I always knew the words would win out" (59). [Signal phrase with the verb *explains*]

4. Use indentation to set apart a block quotation.

Quotations longer than four lines should be set off from the regular text by indenting every line of the quotation ten spaces from the left margin (MLA). Because the format sets apart the quotation, it is not necessary to use quotation marks. The line spacing and right margin remain the same as for the regular text. A long quotation should also be introduced by a signal phrase followed by a colon. Notice the punctuation at the end of the block quotation: the period comes before the page number in parentheses rather than at the end as it does for regular quotations that run into the text.

YES   Aronson describes the isolation that is commonly felt by those caring for patients suffering from Alzheimer's disease:

> As the chronic illness develops and the physical and behavior signs of the patient become more

> pronounced, the caregiver senses his or her isolation even more intensely. Friends and relatives may socialize less frequently. Telephone calls and visits may become few and far between, and the physical and emotional burdens of caring for the patient increase. (167)

The author goes on to describe the other experiences common to caregivers, including frustration, resentment, and trouble with letting go (167-168).

Deletions Using Ellipses and Brackets   Indicate with **ellipses,** or three spaced periods (see Chapter 45), when you delete any words or phrases within quoted information. If you use ellipses, you need to make certain that what remains is still readable and coherent. Put brackets around the ellipses and any words that you have changed from the original.

YES   According to researchers at Carnegie Mellon University, "Scientists disagree about whether climate change will be a serious problem . . . [since] nobody knows for sure whether climate changes caused by human actions will be large enough and fast enough to cause serious damage" (U.S. Global Change 46).

CHAPTER **11**

Writing the Research Paper

AUDIO
Organizing and presenting research data.

11.1

A complete guide to writing a research paper.

Now that you have gathered and evaluated your information, you need to step back and assess just where all this research has taken you. Although the writing process that you will follow in writing your research paper is not radically different from the writing process outlined earlier in this handbook, there are some important differences. The first difference is one of scope; a research paper is longer than most essays. Sometimes students find themselves overwhelmed by the sheer volume of information they have collected. It is indeed a huge challenge to organize and present research. Another major difference between a research paper and most essays is that you will be using information from sources, in addition to your own ideas, as support for your thesis. The suggestions in this chapter will help you to write a successful research paper. (For an example of a research paper, see 12d.)

11a Review the rhetorical stance and thesis

Chapter 2 suggests that you decide on a rhetorical stance, which will help you determine the direction of your research. It would be a good idea to review your rhetorical stance at this time, reassessing your topic, purpose, persona, audience, and hypothesis.

1 Reassessing purpose, persona, and audience

Remind yourself of your intended purpose for writing the research paper and of your persona (see 2a-2, 7a). Ask yourself, "Who is my audience?" You may not be able to determine for certain who your readers will be, but you can assume that they will be intelligent people who have an interest in the topic you are writing about. It is unlikely that they will be experts in the field you are discussing; therefore, you should define any terms carefully and avoid using jargon or technical vocabulary.

2 Refining your argument

Your starting questions and working hypothesis helped you to focus your research. Reassess your working hypothesis at this time. Does it still reflect the position you wish to take in your paper? If not, revise the hypothesis. Remember that a hypothesis usually takes a side on a debatable issue.

Testing Your Hypothesis   Kaycee Sorensen's starting questions about online shopping had to do with its growth, its convenience, and its safety (see 7a for a description of Kaycee's starting process). As she looked over the material gathered in her research, Kaycee was convinced that online shopping was an excellent option for consumers. In other words, she confirmed that her research had supported her working hypothesis:

```
The number of online shoppers is increasing, which means
cybershopping is becoming a convenient, affordable, safe alternative
for consumers. [Yes, Kaycee determined that this hypothesis was
supported by the research.]
```

Writing a Thesis Statement   A thesis statement for a research paper is similar to a thesis statement for an essay (see 2d-1–3). That is, it states for readers the central idea that the paper will argue. Many times, the working thesis statement is revised during the actual writing process. Kaycee decided to write a thesis that stated her conclusions about online shopping:

```
Working thesis: Cybershopping is a safe alternative for
consumers.
```

Revising the Thesis   Most research papers argue a position. However, some research papers are informational; that is, they report on information without taking a position. Your teacher may require that your thesis (and thus your research paper) have an argumentative edge. If so, make sure that you have taken a stand that can be supported through arguments in the paper (see Chapter 6). If your research paper is informational rather than argumentative, your thesis should reflect the fact that you are reporting information rather than taking a stand on an issue.

After Kaycee had written a first draft of her paper, she went back and revisited her working thesis statement. Although it stated in brief form her central idea for the paper, it was not really specific enough to provide an accurate blueprint of what she had argued in the paper itself. She revised her thesis to be more specific and to reflect her argumentative stance. The revised thesis now states both the central idea and her opinion about it.

```
Revised thesis: Consumers should shop online because, despite
fears of safety and identity theft, the simplicity, convenience of
comparison-shopping, and access to a variety of merchandise makes
online shopping the logical and best choice for consumers.
```

3   Deciding on a voice and tone

Academic papers should be informative and serious, but they need not be dull or dry. You can still put your own personality into a piece. Although it is generally not appropriate to adopt too informal a tone for an academic research paper, taking yourself out of the piece entirely may leave readers with the impression that the piece is lifeless and uninteresting. Try to strike a balance in your tone, making it pleasing to readers (see 2a-2).

11b Plan a structure

Some writers like to work from an organizational plan or outline, fleshing out the skeleton by incorporating additional information under each of the major points and subpoints. Others prefer to begin writing and have the structure evolve more organically. You need not be overly concerned about formal structure at this point, unless your teacher stipulates a particular outline format.

As you write your outline (see 2d-5), remember that you are trying to make the information or argument accessible to readers as well as clear and comprehensive. If you used note cards, sort them by heading and subheading into related ideas and information. If you used a computer research notebook, sort your materials by using the CUT, COPY, and PASTE features of your word-processing program.

In an argumentative research paper, it is crucial to present the counterarguments—that is, the arguments on the side opposite the position you are taking. In her paper, it was important for Kaycee to acknowledge that some consumers are reluctant to do their shopping online. In her revised thesis, she acknowledges those concerns ("despite fears of safety and identity theft"). Then, she refutes these concerns on pages 8 and 9 of the research paper by showing that security can be insured if consumers take reasonable precautions. As she wrote the paper, Kaycee was conscious throughout of possible opposing viewpoints and was careful to acknowledge their concerns and counter their views with her own arguments.

11c Write a draft

11.2
How to start
the first draft.

Now you should be ready to begin drafting your research paper. Remind yourself of your general understanding of the topic, of your starting questions and hypothesis, and of the answers to the questions as stated in your thesis. When writing your first draft, use concrete and simple language to explain in your own words your research conclusions. Ideally, you should type your draft on a computer to make revisions easier. Be certain to back up your computer documents and save to a disk frequently so as not to lose any of your hard work.

1 Choosing a drafting strategy

You will need to establish your own strategy for writing a first draft, one that fits your writing style. Here are a few different ways in which writers of research projects proceed:

- Write a draft systematically from a plan, using the building-block technique (see 3b).
- Write a draft from piles of notes arranged according to a blueprint suggested by the thesis (see 3b).
- Write a sketchy first draft without looking at the notes—just writing down everything remembered from the research; follow up by fleshing out the partial draft with a more complete version while referring to the notes.
- Write a rough first draft and then write a revision outline that suggests ways in which the draft needs to be changed.
- Write a draft by cutting and pasting information from an electronic research notebook (see 7c).
- Write a draft while viewing electronic note cards in a second window (see 7c-2).

2 Applying the drafting strategy to blend material

As you draft, you blend your own knowledge and material from sources. In writing a first draft, it is best to put down your own understanding of the topic first, rather than relying too heavily on your sources. After you have written your draft, you can go back and add specific sources to support your arguments. Readers want to know what *you* think about the subject. They do not want to read a string of quotations loosely joined by transitions.

3 Writing a working title

Writing effective titles is discussed in 4b-7; it would be helpful to review that section of the handbook at this time. Writing a title can help you to state succinctly the topic your research paper will cover. Try out a few titles before deciding on one. The title you choose should be brief yet descriptive.

4   Writing an introduction and conclusion

Composing introductions and conclusions is discussed in 4b-7 and 5h. Because a research paper typically covers more information than an essay, it may take a couple of paragraphs to introduce the topic effectively. Kaycee used two opening paragraphs for her research paper; the first paragraph provides an interesting opening anecdote that leads the reader into the topic of the paper. In the second paragraph, leading up to her thesis, she explains to readers how prevalent online shopping is becoming. In her conclusion, Kaycee sums up the major points to her argument and restates her stance on the subject. You should make certain that both your introduction and your conclusion help readers to understand your research paper's main point (see also 5h).

11d   Review and revise the draft

A great deal of important work remains to be done on your paper once you complete a rough draft. You must revise the paper to make the most effective possible presentation of the research. Readers expect you to be clear and correct; they should not be distracted by ambiguous source references, confusing language, or incorrect punctuation. It is a good idea to set your draft aside for a day or two, if time allows, so that you can look at it with a fresh eye. It is also a good idea to gather as much feedback as you can from peers. Plan to exchange drafts with a classmate or two for their suggestions (see 4e for more on giving and receiving feedback).

You need to reread your rough draft several times, both on the computer screen and in hard copy. Each time you read it, pay attention to a different aspect of the paper. The first time, think about the overall structure and style of the paper (see 4b). The second time through, check grammar and punctuation (see 4c, 4d). The third time, make sure source materials are incorporated smoothly and accurately into the text (see 10b, 10c, 10d).

11e   Follow formatting conventions

VIDEO
Understanding
footnote and
endnote
options.

Research paper formatting conventions are those customary ways of presenting information that have developed in various disciplines. Ask your instructor if there is a particular format you should use. If not, select the format from the discipline most closely related

Checklist for Revising a Research Paper

1. Does the paper fulfill the promise made by the thesis (see 2d-3, 11a)?
2. Do the arguments flow smoothly and logically (see 11b)?
3. Is sufficient attention paid to counterarguments (see 11b)?
4. Does the introduction lead effectively into the paper (see 4b-7, 5h)?
5. Does the conclusion either summarize or describe implications (see 4b-7, 5h)?
6. Is the paper focused, adequately developed, and coherent (see 4a)?
7. Are paraphrases, summaries, and quotations of sources integrated smoothly into the flow of the paper (see 10b, 10c, 10d)?
8. Is information in quotations, paraphrases, and summaries accurately related and clearly acknowledged (see Chapter 10)?
9. Are the parenthetical citations clear and accurately tied to the works cited (see Chapters 12 and 13)?
10. Are the works cited in the proper format (see Chapters 12 and 13)?
11. Is the format of the piece appropriate for a research paper (see 11e)?
12. Has the paper been edited and proofread to eliminate errors (see 4c, 4d)?

AUDIO
Revision checklist.

to your research topic. (Chapter 12 includes a model paper that uses MLA documentation style; Chapter 13 includes APA, CMS, and CBE documentation formats.)

MLA Documentation

FAQs

3 MLA Documentation

CHAPTER **12**

MLA Documentation

The Modern Language Association (MLA) system of documentation has been adopted by many scholarly writers in the fields of language and literature (Joseph Gibaldi, *MLA Handbook for Writers of Research Papers,* 6th ed., New York: MLA, 2003). The MLA system consists of in-text citations (found in parentheses) and an alphabetical listing of works cited (found at the end of the paper). For humanities researchers, specific sources and the pages on which information can be found are more important than the date on which the source was published. Thus, in-text citations in the MLA system include the author's last name and the page number of the source information.

A Directory to the MLA System

In-Text Citations

1. Author named in the narrative   168
2. Author not named in the narrative   169
3. Multiple sentences paraphrased   169
4. Work by two or three authors   169
5. Work by four or more authors   170
6. Work by a corporate author   170
7. Work in more than one volume   170
8. Different works by the same author   170
9. Two or more authors with the same last name   171
10. Work cited indirectly   171
11. Two or more sources within the same citation   171
12. Anonymous work   172
13. Work of literature   172
14. Work in an anthology   172
15. Bible   173
16. Entire work or one page article   173

(continued)

(continued)

12a Integrate sources and avoid plagiarism in the MLA system

In Chapter 10, "Using Sources and Avoiding Plagiarism," we talked in general about the importance of using sources accurately and responsibly in your research papers. To help you do so, the MLA citation format provides for a two-part system of source identification: (1) parenthetical references within the body of the paper (discussed in 12b below), and (2) a Works Cited list at the end of the paper (discussed in 12d below). By using the MLA system, you can integrate your source information appropriately and ethically without inadvertently committing plagiarism.

Plagiarism, a serious academic offense, is often committed by students inadvertently in the following two ways:

1. Failing to acknowledge a summary or paraphrase of a source in the body of the paper through a signal phrase and parenthetical citation.

2. Using the original authors' words without putting the borrowed words or phrases in quotation marks or including a parenthetical citation.

1 Acknowledge all sources

A successful research paper will be written as an argument in the writer's own words, expressing an understanding of the answers to

The MLA Citation System

1. Introduce your source using a *signal phrase* that names its author: According to Jones, . . . (see 10d-2; see box on p. 152 for suggested verbs to use in signal phrases).

2. Paraphrase or summarize the information from your source. It's best to use direct quotations sparingly. Rather, recast the source information into your own words. If you do use any words or phrases from the author, however, be sure to include them in quotation marks (see 10d).

3. At the conclusion of your paraphrase, summary, or quotation, insert in parentheses the page number on which the information was found, followed by a period: (332). (see 12b).

4. At the end of your paper, list the source in alphabetical order with complete bibliographic information on your Works Cited page (see 12d).

specific research questions. In such a paper, sources are used as evidence in support of the writer's argument. Source support is integrated into the flow of the research paper through the use of paraphrases and summaries in the writer's own words; each source is acknowledged by a parenthetical citation. Failing to acknowledge a source results in plagiarism. In addition to paraphrases and summaries, any other source material must also be acknowledged, such as specific facts, graphics or visuals, cartoons, diagrams, or charts, using the two-part MLA citation system (see 10a-3).

2 Indicate original source words and phrases with quotation marks

The best research papers use direct quotations sparingly as support for their own ideas and integrate those quotations smoothly into the flow of the paper. A signal phrase alerts the reader that a direct quotation follows; the quotation marks show exactly which words and phrases are being quoted. Long quotations are formatted using indentation rather than quotation marks (see 44a-2 or 10d-2). When students get into trouble by borrowing words and phrases without attribution to a source, it is very often the result of sloppy notetaking. Your notes should accurately record source information in your own words, and you should be able to tell at a glance when looking at your notes which information is from which source. Carelessness at the notetaking stage can result in unintentional plagiarism (see 10a-3).

12b Use the MLA system for in-text citations

In the MLA documentation system, citations within the body of the paper are linked to the Works Cited list at the end. The in-text citations are sometimes called *parenthetical references,* because the documentation is placed within parentheses. Both the author who is being cited and the page number of the source (when known) are included in the in-text citation in the MLA system. Following are some guidelines for incorporating parenthetical citations in the text of your research paper.

1. Author Named in the Narrative

If a paraphrase or direct quotation is introduced with the name of the author in a signal phrase, simply indicate the page number of the source in parentheses at the end of the cited material.

Attempting to define ethnic stereotyping, Gordon Allport states that "much prejudice is a matter of blind conformity with prevailing folkways" (12).

No page number is necessary when an entire work is cited. (Note that titles of independently published works are underlined.)

Conrad's book Lord Jim tells the story of an idealistic young Englishman.

2. Author Not Named in the Narrative

If the author's name is not used to introduce the paraphrased or quoted material, place the author's last name along with the specific page number in parentheses at the end of the cited material. Do not separate author and page number with a comma. Note that the parenthetical material precedes the sentence's end punctuation.

When Mitford and Peter Rodd were first engaged, "they even bought black shirts and went to some Fascist meetings" (Guinness 304).

3. Multiple Sentences Paraphrased

Indicate every instance of paraphrased or summarized material. If an entire paragraph is paraphrased from a single source, mention the author's name at the beginning of the paragraph and cite the page number where appropriate.

As Endelman shows, the turbulence of the interwar years--"political agitation, social discrimination, street hooliganism" (191)--culminated in the formation of the British Union of Fascists. He states that anti-Semitism "was common enough that few Jews could have avoided it altogether or been unaware of its existence" (194).

4. Work by Two or Three Authors

Include the last names of all the authors (the last two connected by *and*) either in the text or in the parenthetical reference. Because the following reference is to the entire work, no page number is necessary.

Goodsell, Maher, and Tinto write about how the theory of
collaborative learning may be applied to the administration of a
college or university.

5. *Work by Four or More Authors*

In citing a work by four or more authors, either provide the last
names of all the authors or provide the name of the first author followed by the abbreviation *et al.* ("and others").

In The Development of Writing Abilities, the authors present a
theory of writing based upon whether a writer assumes a participant
or a spectator role (Britton et al.).

6. *Work by a Corporate Author*

When the author is an organization or corporation, treat the
group's name the same way as the name of an individual author. If
the name is long, try to incorporate it into the text rather than including it in a parenthetical note.

The book The Downsizing of America, by the New York Times, quotes a
report as showing "that 131,209 workers had been cast out of their
jobs in just the first quarter of 1996" (220).

7. *Work in More than One Volume*

If the work consists of more than one volume, provide the volume number, followed by a colon, just before the page number.

In Ward's introduction to the collected works of Sir John Vanbrugh,
he states that "the Vanbrugh family seems to have been both ancient
and honorable" (1: x).

When referring to an entire volume of a multivolume work, add a
comma after the author's name, followed by *vol.* and the volume
number.

8. *Different Works by the Same Author*

When the Works Cited list refers to two works by the same author, include in the parenthetical reference the title (which may be ab-

breviated), as well as the author and the page number of the source. If the author's name is included in the text, cite only the title and page number in parentheses.

Her first volume of memoirs, published in 1975, tells the story of her brother's friend (Mitchison, All Change Here 85). In her pre-war novel, Mitchison, who was the housebound wife of an Oxford don, derives a strange solution to England's economic problems (We Have Been Warned 441).

9. *Two or More Authors with the Same Last Name*

Include both the authors' first and last names in the signal phrase or in parentheses to distinguish two authors who have the same last name.

Luci Shaw reveals deep spirituality in her poem entitled "Made Flesh" (31).

10. *Work Cited Indirectly*

If possible, take information directly from the original source. However, sometimes it is necessary to cite someone indirectly—particularly in the case of a published account of someone's spoken words. To indicate an indirect quotation, use the abbreviation *qtd. in* (for "quoted in") before listing the source.

High school teacher Ruth Gerrard finds that "certain Shakespearean characters have definite potential as student role models" (qtd. in Davis and Salomone 24).

11. *Two or More Sources within the Same Citation*

When referring to two or more sources within the same parenthetical reference, use semicolons to separate the citations. For the sake of readability, however, take care not to list too many sources in a single citation.

The works of several authors in the post-war years tend to focus on racial themes (Mitchison 440; Mosley 198).

12. Anonymous Work

Sources such as magazine articles, Web sites, and reports by commissions may not list an author. Such works are listed by their title on the Works Cited page. For the in-text citation of an anonymous work listed by title, use an abbreviated version of the title, in parentheses.

```
The article points out the miscommunications that can occur between

men and women because of differences in communication styles ("It

Started").
```

13. Work of Literature

Classic works of literature are often available in different editions. It is therefore helpful to include location information, such as chapter number, section number, or act and scene number, in the parenthetical reference so that the reader can locate the reference in any edition of the work. Include this location information after a page reference, where appropriate. When citing classic poetry or plays, use the line numbers instead of page numbers. Generally, use arabic numbers rather than roman numerals.

```
In the novel Lord Jim, Conrad describes the village of Patusan and

its inhabitants (242; ch. 24).
```

```
In Paradise Lost, Satan's descent to earth is described in graphic

detail (Milton 4.9-31).
```

```
As Laertes leaves for France, Polonius gives the young man trite and

unhelpful advice such as "Beware / Of entrance to a quarrel; but being

in, / Bear't that th' opposed may beware of thee" (Hamlet 1.3.65-67).
```

14. Work in an Anthology

If you are citing a work found in an anthology (collection), use the name of the author of the particular work you are citing, not the editor(s) of the anthology. List the page numbers as they are found in the anthology.

```
    The American Dream crosses many ethnic boundaries, as

illustrated by Papaleo (88).
```

15. Bible

When quoting from the Bible, give the title of the version (e.g., *The Revised Standard Version*), the book of the Bible, the chapter and verse (separated by a period). If using a signal phrase, spell out the book of the Bible being quoted. In parentheses, abbreviate the book of the Bible if its name is five or more letters (e.g., Phil. for Philippians).

In his letter to the Philippians, the apostle Paul says "There must be no room for rivalry and personal vanity among you, but you must humbly reckon others better than yourselves. Look to each other's interest and not merely to your own" (The New English Bible, Phil. 2.3-4).

16. Entire Work or One Page Article

When citing an entire work or a work that is only one page long, refer to the text in a signal phrase by the author and title without any page numbers.

In his book Losing My Mind: An Intimate Look at Life with Alzheimer's, Thomas DeBaggio chronicles his battle with Alzheimer's disease.

17. Work with No Page Numbers

If you are citing a work that does not have any page numbers listed, you may omit the page number from your citation. If a work uses paragraph numbers instead of page numbers, use the abbreviation *par(s)*.

The reporter from a recent Family Law Conference sponsored by the American Bar Association, Sarah H. Ramsey, stated that "High-conflict custody cases are marked by a lack of trust between the parents, a high level of anger and a willingness to engage in repetitive litigation" (par. 24).

18. Electronic Source or Web Site

When information is from an electronic medium, usually the entire work is referenced. In such cases, incorporate the reference to the work within the sentence by naming the author of the source (or the title, if no author is listed) just as it is listed on the Works Cited page.

One of the features of <u>The Encyclopedia Mythica</u> Web site is its

archive of cultural myths, such as those prevalent in Native-

American society.

When citing a Web site with secondary pages, list separately each secondary page used in the research paper. Be sure that the Works Cited list includes the correct URL for each secondary page and lists each page independently by its title.

According to <u>Britannica Online</u>, in Native-American mythology, a

feather often symbolizes a prayer ("Feather").

When quoting or paraphrasing directly from an electronic source, either give the section title in quotation marks (as in the example above) or cite the paragraph number (with the abbreviation *par.*), if provided, so that a reader will be able to find the section used in the paper. If no numbering is provided, list the source author or title only.

The writer discusses his reasons for calling Xerox's online site "a

great place to visit" (Gomes, par. 5).

The average global air temperature has risen between 0.3 and 0.6

degree Celsius (Hileman).

12c Format bibliographic footnotes according to the MLA system

Generally, footnotes and endnotes are not used in the MLA system of documentation. However, notes may be included to refer the reader to sources that contain information different from the content of the paper. In the text, indicate a note with a superscript number typed immediately after the source that is referred to. Number notes consecutively throughout the text.

Use a note to cite sources that have additional information on topics covered in the paper.

[1] For further information on this point, see Barbera 168, McBrien 56, and Kristeva 29.

Use a note to cite sources that contain information related to that included in the paper.

[2] Although outside the scope of this paper, major themes in the novel are discussed by Kristeva and Barbera.

Use a note to cite sources containing information that a reader might want to compare with that in the paper.

[3] On this point, see also Rosenblatt's Literature as Exploration, in which she discusses reader response theory.

For the endnote format, start a new page following the end of the text, before the Works Cited list. Type the title "Notes," centered horizontally one inch from the top of the page. Double-space to the first note. Indent the first line five spaces (or ½ inch) from the left margin, and type the note number slightly above the line (or use the superscript format on a word processor). Follow this number with one space, and then the text of the note. Double-space between and within all notes.

For the footnote format, position the text of the note at the bottom of the page on which the reference occurs. Begin the footnote four lines below the text. Single-space within a footnote, but double-space between footnotes if more than one note appears on a page. On the Works Cited page, include all the sources mentioned in the notes.

12d Format the Works Cited page according to the MLA system

The alphabetical listing of all the sources used in a paper, usually entitled Works Cited, comes at the end of the paper. Other names for this listing include Bibliography, Literature Cited, Works Consulted (which includes works not directly cited), and Annotated Bibliography (which includes brief summaries of sources). Check with your instructor to determine which format she or he prefers. The purpose of this listing is to help readers find the information used in the paper, so the entries must be complete and accurate.

List sources alphabetically by the last name of the author, using the letter-by-letter system of alphabetization. When no author is given, alphabetize by the first word of the title (excluding *A, An,* or *The*). Type the first word of each entry at the left margin. Indent subsequent lines of the same entry five spaces (or $\frac{1}{2}$ inch). Double-space the entire reference page, both between and within entries.

When you have more than one work by the same author, arrange the titles alphabetically. Give the author's name for the first entry only. For subsequent works by the same author, substitute three hyphens (followed by a period) for the author's name.

Books   A citation for a book has three basic parts:

Author's Name. <u>Book Title</u>. Publication Information.

For books, monographs, and other complete works, include the author's full name as given on the title page—start with the last name first, followed by a comma; then put the first name and middle name or initial, followed by a period. After the author's name, give the complete title of the work as it appears on the title page (underlined), followed by a period. Important words in the title should be capitalized. Include the subtitle, if there is one, separated from the title by a colon. Next, include (if appropriate) the name of the editor, compiler, or translator; the edition of the book; the number of volumes; and the name of the series. Finally, indicate the place of publication, followed by a colon (if several cities are listed, include only the first one); the publisher's name as it appears on the title page, followed by a comma; and the date of publication from the copyright page, followed by a period.

In MLA style, the publication information is abbreviated as much as is possible in the bibliographic entry. The city where the book was published is given without a state abbreviation, unless the city may be unfamiliar (*Redmond, WA*) or confused with another city (*Springfield, MA*). A country abbreviation may be needed for clarity for some foreign publications (for example, *Ulster, Ire.; Bergen, Norw.*). But if a foreign city is well known (such as *London* or *Paris*), a country abbreviation is unnecessary. Shorten the publisher's name to one word wherever possible (for example, McGraw-Hill, Inc. to *McGraw*; Houghton Mifflin Co. to *Houghton*). Similarly, abbreviate the names of university and government presses: *Columbia UP* stands for Columbia University Press; the letters *GPO* for Government Printing Office. (For guidelines on citing electronic books, see page 194.)

(Note)   Unless your instructor directs you differently, show the title of a complete work or a journal in underlined form, even though such titles appear in italics in most printed documents.

1. Book by One Author

Author's Name	Book Title	Publication Information

Allport, Gordon W. The Nature of Prejudice. Palo Alto: Addison, 1954.

Haire-Sargeant, Lin. H. New York: Pocket, 1992.

Manguel, Alberto. A History of Reading. New York: Viking, 1996.

2. Book by Two or Three Authors

Write multiple authors' names in the order in which they are given on the book's title page. Note that this order may not be alphabetical. Reverse the name of the first author only, putting the last name first; separate the authors' names with commas.

Goodsell, Anne S., Michelle R. Maher, and Vincent Tinto.

Collaborative Learning: A Sourcebook for Higher Education.

University Park: National Center on Postsecondary Teaching,

Learning, and Assessment, 1992.

3. Book by More than Three Authors

For a book with more than three authors, either write out the names of all the authors listed on the book's title page or write only the first author's name, followed by a comma and the Latin phrase *et al.* (for "and others").

Britton, James, Tony Burgess, Nancy Martin, Alex McLeod, and Harold

Rosen. The Development of Writing Abilities. London: Macmillan,

1975.

or

Britton, James, et al. The Development of Writing Abilities. London:

Macmillan, 1975.

4. Organization as Author

When an organization rather than an individual is the author, give the name of the organization as listed on the title page instead of the author, even if the same group also published the book.

Alzheimer's Disease and Related Disorders Association. Understanding

Alzheimer's Disease. New York: Scribner's, 1988.

5. Book by a Corporate Author

A book by a corporate author is any book whose title page lists as the author a group, rather than individuals. Start with the name of the corporate author, even if it is also the publisher.

Conference on College Composition and Communication. The National

Language Policy. Urbana: NCTE, 1992.

6. Unknown Author

If no author is listed, begin the entry with the title. List the work on your references listing alphabetically by the first major word in the title instead of by the author.

The American Heritage Dictionary of the English Language. 3rd ed.

Boston: Houghton, 1996.

7. Book with an Editor

For books with editors rather than authors, start with the editor or editors, followed by a comma and the abbreviation *ed.* (for "editor") or *eds.* (for "editors").

Barbera, Jack, and William McBrien, eds. Me Again: The Uncollected

Writings of Stevie Smith. New York: Farrar, 1982.

8. Chapter or Selection from an Edited Work

An entry for a particular selection needs to begin with the author's name and the title of the selection. The title is underlined if the work is a book or a play; it is enclosed in quotation marks if the work is a poem, short story, chapter, or essay. Note that the name of the editor or editors follows the book title and is preceded by the abbreviation *Ed.* (for "Edited by"). The inclusive page numbers of the work follow the publication information.

Bambara, Toni Cade. "Raymond's Run." The Norton Anthology of

African American Literature. Ed. Henry Louis Gates, Jr., and

Nellie Y. McKay. New York: Norton, 1997. 2307-13.

9. Book with Author and Editor

When citing the book itself, begin with the author's name, followed by the editor's name, introduced by *Ed.* after the title.

L'Engle, Madeleine. O Sapientia. Ed. Luci Shaw. Wheaton, IL:

    Harold Shaw, 1984.

When citing the editor's contribution to the work, begin with the editor's name followed by a comma and *ed*. Then list the author's name, introduced by *By*, following the title.

Shaw, Luci, ed. O Sapientia. By Madeleine L'Engle. Wheaton, IL:

    Harold Shaw, 1984.

10. *Two or More Items from an Anthology*

When citing more than one work from an anthology, list the anthology itself in your Works Cited.

Madison, Soyini D., ed. The Woman That I Am: The Literature and

    Culture of Contemporary Women of Color. New York: St. Martin's,

    1994.

11. *Two or More Books by the Same Author*

Alphabetize entries by the first word in the title. Include the author's name in the first entry only. In subsequent entries, type three hyphens in place of the author's name, followed by a period.

Rose, Mike. Lives on the Boundary: A Moving Account of the Struggles

    and Achievements of America's Educationally Underprepared. New

    York: Penguin, 1989.

---. Possible Lives: The Promise of Education in America. Boston:

    Houghton, 1995.

12. *Article in a Reference Book*

An entry for an article in a reference book follows the same pattern as an entry for a work in an anthology. Note, however, that the editor's name and full publication information need not be provided; it is sufficient to provide the edition (if known) and the year of publication. If the article is signed, provide the author's name. (Often the author's name is given in abbreviated form at the end of the article and included in full form elsewhere.)

Robins, Robert Henry. "Language." Encyclopaedia Britannica. 1980 ed.

If the article is unsigned, start with the title of the article:

"Lochinvar." Merriam-Webster's Encyclopedia of Literature. 1995 ed.

13. Introduction, Preface, Foreword, or Afterword

Start with the name of the author of the specific part being cited, followed by the name of the part, capitalized but not underlined or enclosed in quotation marks. If the writer of the specific part is the same as the author of the book, give the author's last name, preceded by the word *By*. If the writer of the specific part is different from the author of the book, give the book author's complete name after *By*. Provide complete publication information and inclusive page numbers (even if they are given as Roman numerals) of the part being cited.

```
Tompkins, Jane. Preface. A Life in School: What the Teacher Learned.

    By Tompkins. Reading: Addison, 1996. xi-xix.
```

14. Book in Translation

Begin the entry with the author's name and the title of the book. After the book's title, insert the abbreviation *Trans.* (for "Translated by") and give the translator's name. If the book also has an editor, give the names of the editor and the translator in the order in which they are listed on the title page.

```
Kristeva, Julia. Powers of Horror: An Essay on Abjection. Trans.

    Leon S. Roudiez. New York: Columbia UP, 1982.
```

15. Second or Subsequent Edition of a Book

If a book is not a first edition, identify the edition in the way that it is identified on the book's title page: by year (*1993 ed.*), by name (*Rev. ed.* for "Revised edition"), or by number (*2nd ed., 3rd ed.*).

```
White, Edward M. Teaching and Assessing Writing. 2nd ed. San

    Francisco: Jossey-Bass, 1994.
```

16. Work in More than One Volume

When citing more than one volume of a multivolume work, insert the total number of volumes in the work before the publication material.

```
Doyle, Arthur Conan. The Complete Sherlock Holmes. 2 vols. Garden

    City: Doubleday, 1930.
```

17. One Volume of a Multivolume Work

Provide the author and title followed by the volume number of the volume you are citing. At the end of the citation, following the date, MLA recommends providing the number of volumes in the complete work.

Poe, Edgar Allan. <u>The Complete Poems and Stories of Edgar Allan Poe</u>.

   Vol 1. New York: Knopf, 1982. 2 vols.

18. Book in a Series

If the title page indicates that the book is part of a series, insert the series name (do not underline it or enclose it in quotation marks) and the series number, if any, before the publication material.

Berlin, James A. <u>Rhetorics, Poetics, and Cultures</u>. Refiguring

   College English Studies. Urbana: NCTE, 1996.

19. Republished Book

Insert the original publication date, followed by a period, before the publication material of the work being cited.

Dewey, John. <u>Experience and Education</u>. 1938. New York: Collier, 1963.

20. Government Document

If the author of a government document is unknown, start with the name of the government, followed by the name of the agency that issued the document, abbreviated. The title of the publication, underlined, follows, and the usual publication material completes the entry.

United States. FBI. <u>Uniform Crime Reports for the United States:</u>

   <u>1995</u>. Washington: GPO, 1995.

(*GPO* stands for Government Printing Office.)

21. Published Proceedings of a Conference

Write an entry for proceedings in the same way as for a book. Provide information about the conference after the title of the proceedings.

Kelder, Richard, ed. <u>Interdisciplinary Curricula, General Education,</u>

   <u>and Liberal Learning</u>. Selected Papers from the Third Annual

   Conference of the Institute for the Study of Postsecondary

   Pedagogy, Oct. 1992. New Paltz: SUNY New Paltz, 1993.

22. Pamphlet or Newsletter

Cite a pamphlet the same way that you would cite a book.

Presbyterian Peacemaking Program. Peacemaking Pamphlets. Louisville:

Presbyterian Church USA, 1996.

23. Title within Another Title

If there is a title of another book within the title of the book you are citing, do not underline that title within another title.

Steinbeck, John. Journal of a Novel: The East of Eden Letters. New

York: Viking, 1969.

24. Sacred Book

When citing an individual published edition of a sacred book, begin the entry with the title, including the specific version.

The Torah: The Five Books of Moses. Philadelphia: The Jewish Society

of America, 1962.

Periodicals A citation for an article in a periodical follows a format similar to that for a book:

> Author's Name. "Title of the Article." Publication Information.

In the publication information, the title of the journal, as it appears on the journal's title page (without introductory articles such as *A* and *The*), is underlined. The volume and issue numbers, if provided, go after the journal title and are followed by the publication date, in parentheses. A colon follows the parentheses. Then, inclusive page numbers are provided for the entire article.

When citing magazines and newspapers, list the day and month (abbreviated except for May, June, and July) of publication, with the day before the month, followed by the year (*19 Dec. 1997*). Provide page numbers for the entire article. Note that if the article is not printed on consecutive pages, you need to provide only the first page number and a plus sign, with no space between them. (For guidelines on citing articles in online periodicals, see page 195.)

25. Article in a Journal Paginated by Volume

Many professional journals are numbered continuously, from the first page of the first issue to the final page of the last issue within a volume. Do not include an issue number when citing this kind of journal.

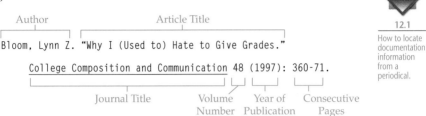

Author | Article Title

Bloom, Lynn Z. "Why I (Used to) Hate to Give Grades."

College Composition and Communication 48 (1997): 360-71.

Journal Title | Volume Number | Year of Publication | Consecutive Pages

12.1

How to locate documentation information from a periodical.

When there are two or more authors, write the authors' names in the order in which they are given on the first page of the article. Note that this order may not be alphabetical. Reverse the name of the first author only (putting the last name first).

Kidda, Michael, Joseph Turner, and Frank E. Parker. "There Is an

Alternative to Remedial Education." Metropolitan Universities 3

(1993): 16-25.

26. Article in a Journal Paginated by Issue

If each issue of the journal is numbered separately, starting with page 1, include both volume and issue numbers. Put a period after the volume number, and write the issue number after the period—for example, 12.1 signifies volume 12, issue 1.

Mohanty, S. P. "Us and Them: On the Philosophical Bases of Political

Criticism." Yale Journal of Criticism 2.2 (1989): 1-31.

27. Magazine Article

If the article is unsigned, begin with the title. For a weekly or bi-weekly magazine, provide the day, the month (abbreviated, except for May, June, and July), and the year; followed by a colon and the inclusive page numbers.

"It Started in a Garden." Time 22 Sept. 1952: 110-11.

For a monthly or quarterly magazine, give only the month or quarter and the year before the inclusive page numbers. (If the article is not printed on consecutive pages, give the first page number followed by a plus sign.)

MacDonald, Heather. "Downward Mobility: The Failure of Open

Admissions at City University." City Journal Summer 1994: 10-20.

28. *Newspaper Article*

Provide the name of the newspaper, but do not use the article (*The, An, A*) that precedes it (*Boston Globe*, not *The Boston Globe*). If it is not included in the newspaper's title, add the city of publication in brackets following the title. Nationally published newspapers, such as *USA Today*, do not need a city of publication in the reference. Next, provide the day, month (abbreviated, except for May, June, and July), and year. (Do not list volume or issue numbers; however, if the edition is given on the newspaper's masthead, do include it, followed by a colon.) Conclude the entry by providing the page numbers, preceded by the section number or letter if each section is separately paginated.

Doherty, William F. "Woodward Jury Seeks Definitions." Boston Globe

29 Oct. 1997: B1+.

"Twenty Percent Biased Against Jews." New York Times 22 Nov. 1992:

A1.

29. *Editorial*

Provide the name of the editorial writer (last name first), if known, and then the title of the editorial (in quotation marks). Next, write the word *Editorial*, but do not underline it or enclose it in quotation marks. End the entry with the name of the newspaper, magazine, or journal and the standard publication information.

Paglia, Camille. "More Mush from the NEA." Editorial. Wall Street

Journal 24 Oct. 1997: A22.

30. *Letter to the Editor*

Include the designation *Letter* after the name of the letter writer, but do not underline it or enclose it in quotation marks. End the entry with the name of the newspaper, magazine, or journal and the standard publication information.

Schack, Steven. Letter. New York Times 1 Dec. 1997, late ed.: A20.

31. *Review*

Start with the name of the reviewer and the title of the review. Then insert *Rev. of* (for "Review of"), but do not underline it or enclose it in quotation marks. Next, provide the title of the piece reviewed, followed by a comma, the word *by*, and the name of the author of the piece being reviewed. If the name of the reviewer is not given, start with the title of the review; if no title is given either, start with *Rev. of.* End the entry with the name of the newspaper, magazine, or journal and the standard publication information.

Ribadeneira, Diego. "The Secret Lives of Seminarians." Rev. of The

   New Men: Inside the Vatican's Elite School for American

   Priests, by Brian Murphy. Boston Globe 31 Oct. 1997: C6.

32. Abstract from an Abstracts Journal

Begin by providing publication information on the original work. Then provide material on the journal in which you found the abstract: the title (underlined), the volume number, and the year (in parentheses), followed by a colon and the page or item number.

Johnson, Nancy Kay. "Cultural and Psychosocial Determinants of

   Health and Illness." Diss. U of Washington, 1980. DAI 40

   (1980): 425B.

(*Diss.* means "Dissertation," and *DAI* is the abbreviation for *Dissertation Abstracts International.*)

Juliebo, Moira, et al. "Metacognition of Young Readers in an Early

   Intervention Reading Programme." Journal of Research in Reading

   21.1 (1998): 24-35. Psychological Abstracts 85.7 (1998): item

   22380.

33. Unsigned Article

If an article has no known author, begin with its title, alphabetizing the citation by the first major word of the title on your references list.

"What You Don't Know About Desktops Can Cost You." Consumer Reports

   Sept. 2002: 20-22.

Other Sources

34. Film or Video Recording

Begin with the film's title (underlined), followed by the director, distributor, and year of release; also provide other pertinent material, such as the names of the performers, writers, and producers, between the title and the name of the distributor.

Wayne's World. Dir. Penelope Spheeris. Prod. Lorne Michaels. Perf.

Mike Myers, Dana Carvey, and Rob Lowe. Paramount, 1992.

35. *Television or Radio Program*

Provide the title of the episode (enclosed in quotation marks), if known; the title of the program (underlined); the title of the series (not underlined or enclosed in quotation marks), if any; the network; the call numbers or letters and local city, if any; and the date of broadcast.

"Commercializing Christians." All Things Considered. Natl. Public

Radio. WBUR, Boston. 8 Dec. 1997.

"The Great Apes." National Geographic Special. PBS. WGBH, Boston.

12 July 1984.

36. *Sound Recording*

For a sound recording that is available commercially, provide the name of the artist, the title of the recording (underlined, unless the piece is identified only by form, number, and key), the manufacturer, and the year of issue. Indicate the medium, if other than a compact disc, before the manufacturer's name.

Ball, Marcia. Blue House. Rounder, 1994.

Ormandy, Eugene, cond. Symphony no. 3 in C minor, op. 78. By Camille

Saint-Saëns. Perf. E. Power Biggs, organ. Philadelphia Orch.

Sony, 1991.

Raitt, Bonnie. "Something to Talk About." Luck of the Draw.

Audiocassette. Capitol, 1991.

37. *Performance*

An entry for a play, concert, opera, or dance begins with the title (underlined), includes information similar to that given for a film, and ends with the performance site (for example, the theatre and city) and the date of the performance.

Blues for an Alabama Sky. By Pearl Cleage. Dir. Kenny Leon. Perf.

Phylicia Rashad, Tyrone Mitchell Henderson, Sean C. Squire,

Deidre N. Henry, and John Henry Redwood. Huntington Theatre,

Boston. 5 Feb. 1997.

38. Work of Art

Provide the name of the artist, the title of the work (underlined), the name of the site that houses the work, and the city. If it is available, include the date the work was created immediately after the title. If the work is part of a private collection, provide the collector's name.

Cassatt, Mary. Breakfast in Bed. 1886. Private collection of Dr. and

Mrs. John J. McDonough, Youngstown, OH.

---. Five O'Clock Tea. Museum of Fine Arts, Boston.

39. Published Interview

Provide the name of the person being interviewed; the title of the interview (enclosed in quotation marks), if any; the title of the source in which the interview is published; and any other pertinent bibliographic material.

Faulkner, William. "The Meaning of 'A Rose for Emily.' " Interview.

1959. The Story and Its Writer: An Introduction to Short

Fiction. Ed. Ann Charters. Compact 4th ed. Boston: Bedford-

St. Martin's, 1995. 772-73.

40. Unpublished Interview

Provide the name of the person being interviewed, the designation *Personal interview* (not underlined or in quotation marks), and the date of the interview.

Jensen, Steven. Personal interview. 12 Apr. 1997.

41. Personal Letter to the Author

Bush, George W. Letter to the author. 8 Sept. 2002.

42. Dissertation—Published

Cite a published dissertation as a book, but add dissertation information before the publication data. Underline the title of the dissertation, followed by the abbreviation *Diss.* (for "Dissertation"), the name of the degree-granting institution, date, and the publication information.

Deatherage, Cynthia. A Way of Seeing: The Anglo-Saxons and the

   Primal World View. Diss. Purdue U, 1997. Ann Arbor: UMI, 1997.

   9821728.

UMI stands for University Microfilms International. (For an example of a dissertation abstract, see page 185.)

43. Dissertation—Unpublished

Cite an unpublished dissertation as follows:

Balkema, Sandra. "The Composing Activities of Computer Literate

   Writers." Diss. U of Michigan, 1984.

44. Speech or Lecture

Provide the name of the speaker; the title of the presentation (in quotation marks), if known; the meeting and sponsoring organization, if applicable; the place where the speech or lecture was given; and the date.

Booth, Wayne. "Ethics and the Teaching of Literature." College

   Forum. NCTE Convention. Cobo Center, Detroit. 21 Nov. 1997.

45. Map or Chart

Cite a map or a chart the same way you would cite a book with an unknown author, but add the label *Map* or *Chart* to distinguish it.

Wyoming. Map. Chicago: Rand, 1990.

46. Cartoon or Comic Strip

Schultz, Charles. "Peanuts." Cartoon. Herald Journal 15 Aug. 2002:

   C6.

47. Advertisement

First name the item being advertised; then add the word *Advertisement* and supply the rest of the citation, indicating the source where the ad appeared.

Benadryl Severe Allergy & Sinus Headache. Advertisement. Prevention

   Sept. 2002: 55.

Electronic Media Because electronic sources tend to be less permanent and subject to fewer standards than printed works, their citations need more information than is required for print sources. Coverage of electronic references in MLA format is given in the *MLA Handbook for Writers of Research Papers, 6th ed.*, by Joseph Gibaldi (New York: MLA, 2003). The *MLA Handbook* points out that citations for electronic publications may need to include information in addition to the three divisions (author, title, publication data) typically used for print sources (see p. 176), in order to accurately describe the electronic publication itself and how to access it. Thus a citation for an electronic source may have the following five divisions: (1) author's or site creator's name, (2) title of the document, (3) information about a corresponding print publication, (4) information about electronic publication, (5) access information.

WEBLINK

http://www.mla.org
MLA's Web site includes information about citing electronic media.

AUDIO
Ways to document electronic media are evolving.

WWW
12.2
The MLA Web site provides the most recent updates on MLA citation style.

Division number five above is especially important in light of the fact that electronic information can be changed quickly, easily, and often. Therefore, the version available to your readers may be different from the one you accessed during your research. MLA recommends listing the last date of posting or updating the electronic source as well as the date of access (that is, the date you read the source). It would also be wise to print out or save to a disk the electronic source on the day you accessed it so that you have an accurate record. MLA also recommends including the electronic address (URL) within angle brackets to distinguish it from the surrounding punctuation of the citation itself.

Below are tips on citing some of the most commonly used electronic sources for the five divisions outlined. In its guidelines for electronic style, the MLA acknowledges that not all of the information recommended for a citation may be available. Cite whatever information is available. It might be wise to consult your instructor before finalizing your Works Cited list to ensure that you are conforming to his or her requirements for electronic sources.

Item 1: Author's or site creator's name

Begin your citation of electronic sources with the name of an author, listed in the same way as you would for a printed book (p. 177), that is, with the last name first, comma, first name, period.

Cohn, Dorritt.

Item 2: Title of the document

List next the full title of the document, enclosed in quotation marks. Exceptions include citations of entire Internet sites or online books (see #48 and #52 below). If no author's name is given, begin the entry with the document's title.

Cohn, Dorritt. "'First Shock of Complete Perception': The Opening

Episode of The Golden Bowl, Volume 2."

Item 3: Information about the print publication

If the document was simultaneously printed as well as posted to the Internet, list the print information next, following the guidelines for print publications.

Cohn, Dorritt. "'First Shock of Complete Perception': The Opening

Episode of The Golden Bowl, Volume 2." The Henry James Review

22.1 (2001): 1-9.

Item 4: Information about electronic publication

Next comes information about the electronic publication, including the title of the site (underlined), the date of electronic publication or the last date the site was updated, and the name of any sponsoring organization. If an editor's name or a version number is provided, include that information after the title. Since it is possible for print and electronic versions to vary, it is necessary to include both types of publication information in your citation. If there is no print version, provide the electronic publication information only.

Cohn, Dorritt. "'First Shock of Complete Perception': The Opening

Episode of The Golden Bowl, Volume 2." The Henry James Review

22.1 (2001): 1-9. Project Muse Journals. 2003. Johns Hopkins

University Press.

Item 5: Access information

Finally, you want to provide your readers with enough information to be able to locate the source for themselves. The date you

Print publication data   URL   Sponsoring organization

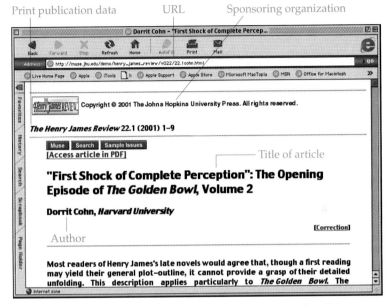

FIGURE 12.1 Online Journal Article with a Corresponding Print
Version

last accessed the source comes next in your citation. For works
such as the one cited here, you will find three dates (date of print
publication, date of electronic publication, date of access). After
the date of access comes the URL (uniform resource locator), that
is, the address by which the document may be found on the Internet. It is important to be very accurate in your listing of the URL.
Enclose the URL in angle brackets. If you need to divide a long
URL between two lines, make the break after a slash in the
address.

Cohn, Dorritt. "'First Shock of Complete Perception': The Opening

     Episode of The Golden Bowl, Volume 2." The Henry James Review

     22.1 (2001): 1-9. Project Muse Journals. 2003. Johns Hopkins

     University Press. 24 Apr. 2003 <http://muse.jhu.edu/demo/

     henry_james_review/v022/22.1cohn.html>.

You should provide the URL for the exact document you were using. However, in some cases the URL is so long that it is impractical to include the entire address. If that is the case, provide the address of the site's search page, if available. Sometimes, though, a reader proceeds to a certain page via a series of links. If so, you will need to provide your reader with the navigation path. After the URL of the site's homepage, type the word *Path* followed by a colon, and then indicate the links to be followed. Use semicolons as separators between the items in the path.

URL for Search Page:

"Anarchist Archive." <u>Voice of the Shuttle Web Site for Humanities</u>

> <u>Research</u>. Ed. Alan Liu. 2003. University of California,
>
> Santa Barbara, English Department. 1 May 2003
>
> <http://vos.ucsb.edu/search-results.asp>.

URL for Main Page plus Path:

"Anarchist Archive." <u>Voice of the Shuttle Web Site for Humanities</u>

> <u>Research</u>. Ed. Alan Liu. 2003. University of California,
>
> Santa Barbara, English Department. 1 May 2003
>
> <http://vos.ucsb.edu/index.asp>. Path: History;
>
> Anarchist Archive.

12.3
Citing an entire
Web site.

48. Entire Internet Site

Many times it is appropriate to reference an entire Internet Web site, such as a scholarly project or an information database. Include the information available at the site, in the following sequence:

1. The title of the site or project (underlined)

2. The creator or editor of the site (if given and relevant)

3. The electronic publication information: version number (if relevant), date of electronic publication or latest update, the name of the sponsoring organization or institution (if provided)

4. The date of access and the URL within angle brackets

URL   Navigation links   Search tool   Title of the Web project

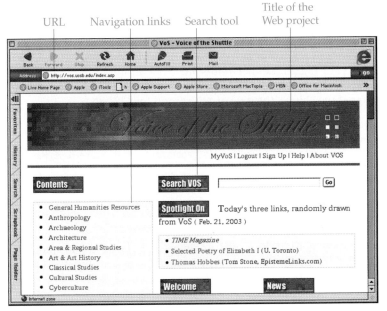

FIGURE 12.2 An Internet Site with Navigation Path or Search Option

The Encyclopedia Mythica. Ed. M. F. Lindemans. 1995-2003.

3 Mar. 2003 <http://www.pantheon.org/mythica>.

MSN.com. 2003. Microsoft Network. 28 Feb. 2003 <http://www.msn.com>.

The Pew Center on Global Climate Change: Advancing the Debate

Through Credible Analysis and Cooperative Approaches.

2003. Pew Center on Global Climate Change. 15 May 2003

<http://www.pewclimate.org>.

Victoriana Online. Ed. Sylvania Dye. 1996-2002. 12 Jan. 2002

<http://www.victorianaonline.com>.

12.4
Citing a course
home page.

49. Course Home Page

If you wish to cite a course home page, first list the name of the instructor (last name first), then the title of the course (neither underlined nor in quotation marks). Next comes a description, like *Course home page* (again, neither underlined nor in quotation marks), the dates of the course, the names of the department and institution that offered the course, the date of access, and the URL.

Edwards, Farrell. General Physics. Course home page.

Jan. 2003-May 2003. Physics Department, Utah State U. 6 May

2003 <http://www.physics.usu.edu/classes/2210spr03/index.htm>.

50. Academic Department's Home Page

Begin a citation for a department with its name, then a description, such as *Dept. home page* (neither underlined nor in quotation marks), the institution's name, the date it was last updated (if provided), the date of access, and the URL.

Department of English. Dept. home page. Utah State U. 16 June 2003

<http://websites.usu.edu/english>.

51. Personal Home Page

When citing someone's home page, begin with that person's name, followed by the title of the site or, if none is provided, with the description *Home page* (neither underlined nor in quotation marks). Next provide the date the site was last updated (if provided), the date of access, and the URL.

Avila, Alejandro Perez. Home page. 17 Feb. 2003. 1 May 2003

<http://www.u.arizona.edu/~aperezav>.

52. Online Book

The complete texts of many books are now available online as well as in print. Provide the following items when citing such works:

1. The name of the author (if only an editor, compiler, or translator is mentioned, give that person's name first, followed by *ed.*, *comp.*, or *trans.*)

2. The title of the work, underlined

3. The name of any editor, compiler, or translator (if not given earlier)

4. Publication information from the printed work, if the work has been printed

5. Electronic publication information, such as the title of the Internet site, editor of the site, version number, date of electronic publication, name of any sponsoring organization

6. The access date and URL in angle brackets

```
Woolf, Virginia. The Voyage Out. London: Faber, 1914. The EServer.

    Ed. Geoffrey Sauer. May 2003. U of Washington. 1 June 2003

    <http://eserver.org/fiction/voyage-out.txt>.
```

53. Part of an Online Book

Sometimes you will be referring to a part of an online book. In such a case, list the title of the part after the author's name. If the part is a work like a poem or an essay, use quotation marks. If the part is a customary section like an introduction or a preface, do not include quotation marks. Be sure to give the complete URL of the specific part of the book if it is different from the entire book's URL.

```
Pope, Alexander. "Epistle I." Essay on Man. The EServer.

    Ed. Geoffrey Sauer. 2003. U of Washington. 1 June 2003

    <http://eserver.org/poetry/essay-on-man/epistle-i.txt>.
```

54. Online Government Document

When citing government documents, start first with the information from the printed version and conclude with the electronic citation information.

```
United States. Dept. of Commerce. U.S. Census Bureau.

    How the Census Bureau Measures Poverty. 24 Sept. 2002. 5 May

    2003 <http://www.census.gov/hhes/poverty/povdef.html>.
```

55. Article in an Online Periodical

Many magazines, newspapers and scholarly publications are now available in online formats. Generally, citations for online

12.5
Citing an online periodical.

periodicals follow the same sequence as citations for print periodicals. They should include the following:

1. The author's name (if provided)
2. The title of the work, in quotation marks
3. The name of the journal, magazine, or newspaper, underlined
4. The volume and issue number (or other identifying number if provided)
5. The date of publication
6. The range or total number of pages, paragraphs, or sections, if they are numbered
7. The date of access and URL in angle brackets

All of this information may not be available, so cite what you are able.

Sheikh, Nabeela. "True Romance." Jouvert: A Journal of Postcolonial

    Studies 7.1 (2002). North Carolina State University,

    College of Humanities and Social Sciences. 23 Mar. 2003

    <http://social.chass.ncsu.edu/jouvert/v7is1/sheik.htm>.

NOTE: This journal is only published online and has no page or paragraph numbers. If page or paragraph numbers were provided, they would be listed after the publication date, for example, (2002): 21-25.

56. *Article in an Online Scholarly Journal via a Journal Database*

In addition to scholarly journals that are published online independently (see example above), others can be accessed via an online journal database. If the journal is included in a database, include the name of the database (underlined) following the print information for the article; end with the date of access and relevant URL within the database.

Reinhardt, Leslie Kaye. "British and Indian Identities in a

    Picture by Benjamin West." Eighteenth Century Studies

    31.3 (1998). Project Muse. 12 July 2000

    <http://muse.jhu.edu/journals/eighteenth-century_studies>.

57. *Article in an Online Newspaper or on a Newswire*

Dedman, Bill. "Racial Bias Seen in U.S. Housing Loan Program."

New York Times on the Web 13 May 1998. 14 May 1998

<http://www.nytimes.com/archives>.

58. *Article in an Online Magazine*

Ricks, Delthia. "Sickle Cell: New Hope." Newsday 12 May 1998.

12 May 1998 <http://www.newsday.com/homepage.htm>.

59. *Online Review*

Bast, Joseph L. Rev. of Our Stolen Future, by Theo Colborn et al.

Heartland Institute 18 Apr. 1996: 27 pars. 25 June 1997

<http://www.heartland.org/stolen1.htm>

60. *Online Abstract*

Reid, Joy. "Responding to ESL Students' Texts." TESOL Quarterly

28 (1994): 273-92. Abstract. 12 July 2000

<http://vweb.hwwilsonweb.com/cgi-bin/webspirs.cgi>.

61. *Anonymous Article*

"N. Korea May Build New Reactors." MSNBC News Service 16 Feb. 2003.

16 Feb. 2003 <http:www.msnbc.com/news/850567.asp?0sl=-31>.

62. *Online Editorial*

"A Nuclear Threat from India." Editorial. New York Times on the Web

13 May 1998. 14 May 1998 <http://www.nytimes.com/archives>.

63. *Online Letter to the Editor*

Lowry, Heath. Letter. Deseret News Online 23 Mar. 1998. 25 Mar. 1998

<http://www.desnews.com/archst.html>.

64. FTP Site

Deutsch, Pater. "archie-An Electronic Directory Service for the

    Internet." Mar. 1993. 15 Apr. 1995 <ftp://ftp.sura.net/

    pub/archie/docs/whatis.archie>.

65. TELNET Site

Gomes, Lee. "Xerox's On-Line Neighborhood: A Great Place

    to Visit." <u>Mercury News</u> 3 May 1992. 5 Dec. 1996

    <telnet://lambda.parc.xerox.com_8888>.

66. Information Database or Scholarly Project

<u>CNN Interactive</u>. 12 July 2000. Cable News Network. 12 July 2000

    <http://www.cnn.com>.

<u>The Electronic Text Center</u>. Ed. David Seaman. 2002. U of Virginia

    Library. 1 Jan. 2003 <http://etext.lib.virginia.edu>.

12.6
Citing a document from an information database or scholarly project.

67. Document from an Information Database or Scholarly Project

To cite a poem, short story, article, or other work within a scholarly project or database, begin with the author's name, if given, followed by the title of the work in quotation marks. If no author's name is given, begin with the title. Continue with relevant information on the project, including the access date and URL. Be sure to give the URL of the specific document rather than the URL of the database itself (if they are different). In the event the specific URL is too long and complicated to include, list the browser path instead. For example, the exact URL for Angelou's poem below is as follows:

<http://etext.lib.virginia.edu/etcbin/toccer-new2?id=AngPuls

    .sgm&images=images/modeng&data=/texts/english/modeng/parsed&tag=

    public&part=all>

Angelou, Maya. "On the Pulse of the Morning." <u>The Electronic Text</u>

    <u>Center</u>. Ed. David Seaman. 2002. U of Virginia Library. 1 Jan.

2003 <http://etext.lib.virginia.edu>. Path: Collections;

English; Online holdings; African American; Angelou, Maya.

68. Document or Full-Text Article Found Via a Personal Subscription Service

If you are using a personal subscription service, such as AOL, that allows you to locate documents by using keywords, provide the name of the online service (underlined) and the date of access, followed by the keyword.

"Dr. Phil's Relationship Rescue." Online With Oprah. 12 July 2000.

America Online. 15 Aug. 2000. Keyword: Oprah.

69. Document or Full-Text Article Found Via a Library Subscription Service

12.7
Citing a document from a full-text article found via a library subscription service.

To cite online documents or articles that you derive from a service that your library subscribes to (e.g., Lexis-Nexis, ProQuest, or EBSCO Host), follow the citation for the source itself with the name of the service (underlined), the library, and the date of access. If you know the URL of the database service's home page, provide it in angle brackets at the end of the citation. If the library service only provides a starting page for the article's original printed version rather than numbering the pages, provide the number followed by a hyphen, a space, and a period: "115- ."

King, Marsha. "Companies Here Ponder Scout Ruling." Seattle Times

6 July 2000: A1. Academic Universe. Lexis-Nexis. Utah State U

Lib., Logan, UT. 15 Aug. 2000 <http://web.lexis-

nexis.com/universe>.

Bozell III, Brent L. "Fox Hits Bottom Or Does It?" Human Events

57.4 (2001): 15- . Academic Search Elite. EBSCO. Utah State U

Lib., Logan, UT. 15 Oct. 2002 <http://www.epnet.com>.

70. Nonperiodical Publication on CD-ROM, Magnetic Tape, or Disc

Often, works on CDs, discs, or magnetic tape are published in a single edition, much as books are. To cite such publications, use a format similar to that used to cite print books, with the addition of the publication medium.

Corel WordPerfect Suite 8. CD-ROM. Ottawa, CA: Corel, 1998.

DeLorme Mapping. "Paris." Global Explorer. CD-ROM. Freeport, ME:

    DeLorme Mapping, 1993.

NOTE: DeLorme Mapping is the corporate author of this CD-ROM.

"Symbolism." The Oxford English Dictionary. 2nd ed. CD-ROM. Oxford:

    Oxford UP, 1992.

71. Database Periodically Published on CD-ROM

When citing periodically published reference works, include the information on the printed source, plus the publication medium, the name of the vendor (if relevant), and the electronic publication date.

Arms, Valerie M. "A Dyslexic Can Compose on a Computer." Educational

    Technology 24.1 (1984): 39-41. ERIC. CD-ROM. SilverPlatter.

    Sept. 1990.

72. Multidisc Publication

To cite a CD-ROM publication on multiple discs, list the number of discs or the specific number of the disc you used.

Great Literature Plus. CD-ROM. 4 discs. Parsippany, NJ: Bureau of

    Electronic Publishing, 1993.

73. Work in More Than One Medium

When a work is published in more than one medium (for example, both as a book and as a CD or both as a CD and as a disc), you may specify all the media or only the medium you used.

Hult, Christine A., and Thomas N. Huckin. The New Century Handbook.

    2nd ed. Book, CD-ROM. Boston: Longman, 2002.

74. Work in an Indeterminate Electronic Medium

If you cannot tell what medium the source is in (perhaps you accessed the work from a library's Web site and are unsure whether it is on CD-ROM or stored on the library's Internet server), use the designation *Electronic* for the medium.

Delk, Cheryl L. Discovering American Culture. Ann Arbor:

    U of Michigan P, 1997. Electronic. Berkeley Public Lib.

    20 June 1998.

75. *Electronic Television or Radio Program*

Lifson, Edward. "Clinton Meets Kohl." Morning Edition.

    13 May 1998. Natl. Public Radio. 20 June 1998 <http://www.npr

    .org/programs/morning/archives/1998>.

76. *Electronic Sound Recording or Sound Clip*

Beethoven, Ludwig van. "Symphony no. 5 in C, op. 67." June 1998.

    New City Media Audio Programs. 20 July 1998

    <http://newcitymedia.com/Radiostar/audio.htm>.

77. *Electronic Film or Film Clip*

Anderson, Paul Thomas, dir. Boogie Nights. 1997. Trailer.

    New Line Cinema. 13 May 1998 <http://hollywood.com>.

78. *Online Work of Art*

Van Gogh, Vincent. The Starry Night. 1889. Museum of Mod. Art, New

    York. 20 Mar. 1998 <http://www.moma.org/paintsculpt/index.html>.

79. *Online Interview*

Gregson-Wagner, Natasha. Interview. Hollywood Online. May 1998.

    15 May 1998 <http://hollywood.com/pressroom/interviews>.

80. *Online Map*

"Mellow Mountain: Park City, Utah." Map. MapQuest. 17 Feb. 2003

    <http://www.mapquest.com/maps/map.adp?historyid=0>.

81. Online Cartoon

Trudeau, Gary. "Doonesbury." Cartoon. <u>New York Times on the Web</u>

    13 May 1998. 13 May 1998 <http://www.nytimes.com/archives>.

82. Online Advertisement

3D RealAudio. <u>Advertisement. 20 Aug. 1998 <http://www.real.com>.</u>

83. Online Manuscript or Working Paper

Hendrickson, Heather. "Art: Impractical but Essential." Working

    paper, n.d. 28 Aug. 1998 <http://english.usu.edu/W98/204honors/

    index.htm>.

[NOTE: n.d. stands for "no date."]

84. Email Communication

For email messages that you wish to cite, provide the writer's name (or alias or screen name); the subject or title of the communication, if any (in quotation marks); the designation *Email to*; the name of the person to whom the email is addressed; and the date of the message.

Gillespie, Paula. "Members of the NWCA Board." Email to Michael

    Pemberton. 1 Aug. 1997.

Gardner, Susan. "Help with Citations." Email to the author.

    20 Mar. 2002.

85. Online Posting

For a message posted to an email discussion list, in addition to the information provided for an email citation, also include the description *Online posting* and the date of the posting. Provide the name of the discussion list, if known. Then give the date of access. Last, provide the URL, if known, or the email address of the list's moderator or supervisor in angle brackets.

Glennon, Sara. "Documenting Sessions." Online posting. 11 Dec. 1996.

NWCA Discussion List. 12 Dec. 1997 <wcenter@ttacs6.ttu.edu>.

When possible, cite an archival version of the posting so that readers can more easily find and read the source:

White, Edward. "Texts as Scholarship: Reply to Bob Schwegler."

Online posting. 11 Apr. 1997. WPA Discussion List. 12 Apr. 1997

<http://gcinfo.gc.maricopa.edu/~wpa>.

Citation of a posting to a World Wide Web discussion forum follows the style of an online posting.

Hochman, Will. "Attention Paid This Sunday Morning."

Online posting. 5 Apr. 1998. Response to Selfe. 7 May 1998

<http://www.ncte.org/forums/selfe/#forums>.

Citation of a posting to a Usenet newsgroup also follows the style for an online posting. Be sure to include the name of the newsgroup in angle brackets with the prefix *news:*

Shaumann, Thomas Michael. "Technical German." Online posting.

5 Aug. 1994. 7 Sept. 1994 <news:comp.edu.languages.natural>.

86. Online Synchronous Communication

To cite an online synchronous communication (e.g., an online chat or MOO), begin with the name (or alias or screen name) of the speaker, if available and if you are citing only one. Include a description of the event, the date of the event, the forum (for example, the name of the MOO), the access date, and the electronic address.

Pine_Guest. Personal interview. 12 Dec. 1994. MediaMOO. 12 Dec. 1994

<telnet://moo.mediaMOO.com_7777>.

87. Downloaded Computer Software

Fusion. Vers. 2.1. 30 June 2002 <http://www.allaire.com>.

12e Review a sample research paper in MLA format

The following research paper, written by Kaycee Sorensen, is formatted according to the MLA system of documentation. Annotations that explain various conventions are included in the margins.

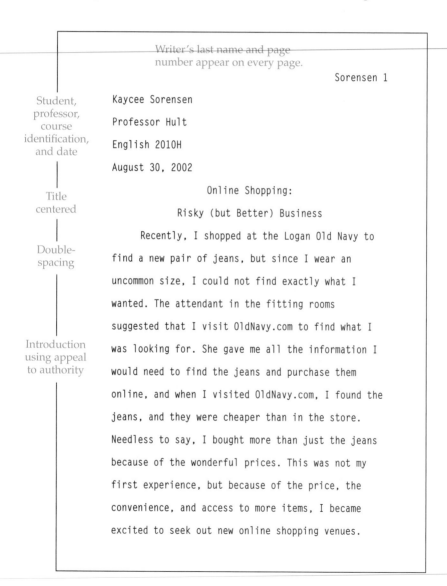

Writer's last name and page number appear on every page.

Sorensen 1

Student, professor, course identification, and date

Kaycee Sorensen

Professor Hult

English 2010H

August 30, 2002

Title centered

Online Shopping:

Risky (but Better) Business

Double-spacing

Recently, I shopped at the Logan Old Navy to find a new pair of jeans, but since I wear an uncommon size, I could not find exactly what I wanted. The attendant in the fitting rooms suggested that I visit OldNavy.com to find what I

Introduction using appeal to authority

was looking for. She gave me all the information I would need to find the jeans and purchase them online, and when I visited OldNavy.com, I found the jeans, and they were cheaper than in the store. Needless to say, I bought more than just the jeans because of the wonderful prices. This was not my first experience, but because of the price, the convenience, and access to more items, I became excited to seek out new online shopping venues.

Sorensen 2

I am not alone in my growing interest in online shopping. According to Nielsen-Netratings, 498 million people worldwide now have access to the Internet from home, and just as these people are using the Internet for quick access to information and electronic communication, millions of them are also turning to the Internet for shopping purposes (Hupprich and Bumatay). Consumers should shop online because, despite fears of safety and identity theft, the simplicity, convenience of comparison-shopping, and access to a variety of merchandise makes online shopping the logical and best choice for consumers.

The convenience of online shopping not only became clear to me as a consumer, but also as a retailer. During the holidays, I work for Sears in Frisco, TX. Our store is new and we still only serve the urban areas, so many people travel from rural areas to shop. While working over Christmas I helped one such woman who needed to shop for items for the baby she was expecting. She could not purchase everything she needed in this one trip and did not want to have to make the drive numerous times, so I suggested she go online to see what Sears.com had to offer. After visiting the site she

Internet source without a page number

Thesis: main point

Sorensen 3

decided to order all of her baby furniture from the
comfort of her own home. She informed me that
though she was able to buy most of the items she
needed online, she would come back to the store to
shop for baby clothes, which were not available
online.

Rural customers are not the only consumers who
benefit from online shopping. More and more
shoppers use the Internet to comparison-shop before
purchasing items online or in a store, so they save
money. There are price-comparison tools on the
Internet, and some, such as PriceGrabber.com, find
the best price for a particular item and then
calculate the tax and shipping costs. This site and
others can be used to get price quotes for items
varying from airline tickets to cashmere sweaters.

Many customers may want to try on a cashmere
sweater to see how it looks on them before buying
it, even if they have to pay more to do so. For
example, Ahmad Kushairi says, "For me, I would like
to browse the shelves and feel the products before
deciding if I even want to purchase" (2). Online
retailers are aware of this and try to target these
consumers by providing new technologies. For
example My Virtual Model Inc. has created a tool

No citation
needed for
common
knowledge

Transitional
sentence

Direct
quotation
from a print
source

Sorensen 4

that allows customers to "try clothes on" before
purchasing them. This technology has "increased
online sales" by leading to 26% more purchases than
average and increasing the average order size by
13%. Virtual models are being used by numerous
online retailers, such as Lands End, Limited Too,
Lane Bryant, and Nutri/System ("Virtual Model Tech"
6E).

Retailers also target consumers by offering
deals through special online promotions such as
credit card companies offering deals to their
cardholders. For example, American Express, Visa,
MasterCard, and Discover have promotions that
include free shipping and discounts ranging from 5%
to 25%. To receive these deals though, the customer
must first visit the credit card site, and will
usually have to use promotion codes or visit the
retailers' sites from a link on the credit card
company's site. The discounts change frequently and
vary among the various credit card companies.
Credit card companies can also offer promotions
for local businesses and attractions, so
consumers can register their email address to learn
of the offers before they are posted on the site
(Frey T8).

Summary of
a print
source

Sorensen 5

Development
of topic

In addition to good deals and access to new
technology, online shopping offers a place for
consumers to shop quickly and easily online, as
well as quickly and easily offline. One segment of
the population that has benefited the most is
teenagers. Jared Blank, an analyst for Juniper
Matrix, points out that teens today "use the
Internet as a shopping mall--a place to meet
friends, play games, and shop--even without the
intent to purchase. Teens spend almost as much time
on Amazon.com as adults, even though few of those
teens can make purchases on the site" (qtd. in
"Nearly One-Third of Teens").

Teens are not the only segment of the consumer
population who browse for goods online and then
choose to shop in brick-and-mortar stores.
According to The NPD Group, Inc., 92% of online
consumers use the Internet to shop and/or purchase
online (qtd. in Pastore). Cyber journalist, Michael
Pastore, points out that NPD's data show that even
those consumers not making purchases online are
still influenced by what they see on retailers' Web
sites. Eighty-four percent of occasional buyers,
who made only one or less online purchase in the
past six months, describe their usual use of the

Paraphrase
of an Internet
source

Sorensen 6

Internet for shopping online and then going offline
to purchase. Pamela Smith, Vice President of NPD
Online Research, explains:

> Measuring online sales alone cannot
> capture the full benefit of a retailer
> having an Internet presence. We know that
> even consumers who don't typically
> purchase online are using retailers'
> web sites to browse and decide what to
> buy. . . . Although it may not result
> in a purchase at that time, it could
> translate directly into an offline sale.
> (qtd. in Pastore)

The following chart, which outlines how online
shoppers describe how they typically use the
Internet for shopping, illustrates Smith's point:

All Shoppers	Percentage
Shop Online, Purchase Offline	51%
Shop Online, Purchase Online	40%
Shop Offline, Purchase Online	9%

(qtd. in Pastore).

Since the NPD study was completed, our nation
has experienced an economic downturn, but online
spending has increased. A recent study entitled
"The State of Retailing Online 5.0," reports that

Indented quotation

Ellipses to show part of quotation left out

Introducing a source within a source

Sorensen 7

"fully 56 percent of holiday retailers reported online profits in 2001, compared to only 43 percent in 2000" (Cox). Profits from online shopping ~~usually come from holiday shopping.~~ According to Nielsen/NetRatings, online shoppers were expected to spend 43% more than the $6.9 billion from the 2000 holiday season. One hundred six million users were estimated to shop online for the 2001 holidays, which would be a 27% rise over the 85 million shoppers in 2000. Categories normally reserved for traditional stores are climbing in online preference (Chan et al.).

Introducing a counter-argument to the thesis

Although online shopping trends and spending are growing, there are still consumers who resist purchasing products through the Internet. One reason why many people may choose to browse for goods online and then purchase them offline is their concern of identity theft. In fact, a report by Taylor Nelson Sofres points out "Almost one-third (30 percent) of Internet users who have not shopped online stated that they didn't want to give credit card details (up by 5 percent from 2001) and 28 percent cited general security concerns" (qtd. in Greenspan). In order to confidently shop online, consumers must be sure that the retail site is safe

and secure and that no one can steal personal
information from the site. According to the <u>Online
Shopping Guide</u>, which is an online shopping
directory sponsored by Microsoft Internet, consumers
can protect themselves by considering three things:
transaction security, privacy, and credit card fraud
("Online-Shopping Safety and Security").

    Transaction security is the first thing to be
aware of when shopping on the Internet, and data
encryption provides the most secure way to send
information from site to site, without having
anyone in between being able to read it. When an
Internet user sends information, the data is
encrypted, or put into code. If anyone tries to
read the information while en route to the site,
they would find it impossible to read. Secure
Sockets Layer (SSL), the standard for sending
secure data, protects against snooping and possible
tampering, and then verifies that the site to which
the data is sent is authentic. <u>Netscape Security
Center</u>, which is an informational site published on
the Internet browser's homepage, explains that
shoppers should make sure that their data is always
being checked by SSL when sending or receiving
confidential information. SSL works with certain

Refuting the counter-argument

Topic sentence

Sorensen 9

versions of browsers, such as Netscape, Internet

Explorer, and AOL, and can also be verified by

simply calling the vendor. Oftentimes, a padlock

will appear in the bottom left corner to tell you

if the site is secure ("How Encryption Works").

Transaction security can also be ensured by

checking the credibility of a source. One way to do

this is to look for the Better Business Bureau

Online Reliability Seal, which guarantees that a

retailer has been in business for at least one

year, has become a member of a local Better

Business Bureau (BBB), and has agreed to

arbitration in case of a dispute over sale. The

Better Business Bureau says that online

advertisements or emails with excessive capital

letters, dollar signs ($$$$$) and exclamation

points (!!!!) at every turn, misspellings, and

grammatical errors may indicate a sleazy operation

(Better Business Bureau Program).

Privacy is another important consideration for

online shopping and consumers may worry that once

their data gets to the receiver safely, a hacker

may come in and steal uncoded information. Most

retailers will move data off their Internet server

after receiving it, so it would be inaccessible to

In-text
citation
without an
author

Sorensen 10

hackers. Each company has a different policy, so it
is best to check with customer support or the help
section for specifics.

The Online Shopping Guide also advises that
shoppers need to check the policy on credit card fraud   Appeal to
                                                                           logic
and to be aware of any guarantees that online
retailers make about identity theft ("On-line
Shopping"). Ellen Stark reminds us that despite what
policies individual companies have, the Fair Credit   In-text
                                                                           citation of
Billing Act ensures that a bank cannot hold a customer   print source
                                                                           with a page
liable for more than $50 in fraudulent charges (41).   number
So, no matter what concerns consumers have about a
hacker stealing their identity and charging products
to stolen credit card numbers, the federal government
has provided consumers with protection.

Despite concerns about safety and identity   Summary
                                                                           conclusion
theft, more and more people are turning to the
Internet to meet their consumer needs. Retailers
are aware of this trend and are anxious to attract
new customers to their sites, and are therefore
willing to improve site-safety and user-friendly
technology to entice shoppers. While some people
choose to shop online because they find shopping in
brick-and-mortar stores annoying and time consuming,
others just enjoy the fact that they can not only

Sorensen 11

shop without leaving their homes, but also without
even getting dressed. Others would rather simply
click on a button to order goods than stand in
checkout lines or battle for parking spaces in a
crowded mall lot. Whatever the reason for initially
shopping online, many consumers, like myself, not
only enjoy the benefits of ease and convenience of
e-commerce, but also believe that it will only get
better.

Action to be
taken

Now that you know about online shopping, you
are probably wondering where to shop online. These
are just a few links to some of my favorite online
shopping sites. Just remember, just because you shop
online, does not mean you buy online. You can shop
around and then visit the store as you normally
would; this will just save you a few hours, or days!

amazon.com

bn.com

fossil.com

landsend.com

oldnavy.com

sears.com

shop.com

target.com

wal-mart.com

Alphabetical listing
of all sources used.

Works Cited

Better Business Bureau Program. 2002. 22 July 2002

    <www.bbbonline.org>.

Chan, Christine, et al. "Online Spending to Reach

    $10 Billion for Holiday Season 2001."

    Nielsen/NetRatings 20 Nov. 2001. 28 July 2002

    <http://www.nielsennetratings.com/pr/pr_011022

    .pdf>.

Cox, Beth. "E-commerce: Color it Green." Cyberatlas

    3 Aug. 2002. 12 Aug. 2002

    <http://cyberatlas.internet.com/markets/

    retailing/article/0,,6061_1364801,00.html>.

Frey, Christine. "Online Shopper: Advantages of

    Plastic." Los Angeles Times 18 Oct. 2001: T8.

Greenspan, Robyn. "E-shopping Around the World."

    Cyberatlas 5 Aug. 2002. 23 Aug. 2002

    <http://cyberatlas.internet.com/markets/

    retailing/article/0,,6061_1431461,00.html>.

"How Encryption Works." Netscape Security Center.

    5 Aug. 2002 <http://wp.netscape.com/security/

    basics/encryption.html>.

Hupprich, Laura, and Maria Bumatay.

    "Nielsen/Netratings Reports a Record Half

    Billion People Worldwide Now Have Home

    Internet Access." Nielsen/Netratings 3 June

*Online:
Professional
site*

*Title of
article*

*Name of
professional
site*

*Date of
publication*

*Date of
access*

*Print:
Newspaper*

*Internet:
Online
newsletter*

Initial
capitals are
used in
article titles,
which are
also put in
quotation
marks.

Library
Reference
databases
full-text
article

Print:
Magazine

2002. 3 Aug. 2002 <http://www.nielsen-

netratings.com/pr/pr_020306_eratings.pdf>.

Kushairi, Ahmad. "The Buying Experience Is Still

with Offline Shopping." New Strait Times Press

12 Aug. 2002: 2.

"Nearly One-Third of Teens Make Offline Purchases

after Window Shopping Online." PR Newswire

Association, Inc. 18 July 2001: Financial

News Section. Academic Search Elite. EBSCO.

Utah State U Lib., Logan, UT. 20 Aug. 2002

<http://www.epnet.com>.

"Online-Shopping Safety and Security." The Shopping

Guide 8 Aug. 2002. 12 Aug. 2002

<http://shoppingguide.hypermart.net/safety.html>.

Pastore, Michael. "Web Influences Offline

Purchases, Especially Among Teens." Cyberatlas

3 Aug. 2002. 18 Aug. 2002

<http://cyberatlas.internet.com/markets/

retailing/article/0,,6061_804141,00.html>.

Stark, Ellen. "There's Help on the Way If You Face

a Credit Card Dispute." Money May 1996: 41.

"Virtual Model Tech Hikes Lands' End Sales."

Capital Times 27 Sept. 2001: 6E.

APA, CMS, and CBE Documentation

FAQs

CHAPTER 13

APA, CMS, and CBE Documentation

This chapter provides an overview of three styles of documentation, codified by the American Psychological Association, the *Chicago Manual of Style,* and the Council of Science Editors.

AUDIO
Why are there so many documentation systems?

APA System

The documentation system commonly employed in the social sciences was developed by the American Psychological Association (APA). Detailed documentation guidelines for the APA system are included in the *Publication Manual of the American Psychological Association,* 5th ed. (Washington, DC: APA, 2001). The social sciences use an author/date method of documentation. In-text citations identify the source by the author's name and the date of publication so that the reader knows immediately whether the research cited is current. The date of publication is also emphasized in the References list at the end of the paper.

A Directory to the APA System

In-Text Citations

1. Author named in the narrative 222
2. Author not named in the narrative 222
3. Specific page or paragraph quoted 222
4. Work by two authors 223
5. Work by more than two authors 223
6. Anonymous work 223
7. Work by a corporate author 224

(continued)

(continued)

13a Integrate sources and avoid plagiarism in the APA system

In Chapter 10, "Using Sources and Avoiding Plagiarism," we talked in general about the importance of using sources accurately and responsibly in your research papers. To help you do so, the APA citation format provides for a two-part system of source identification: (1) parenthetical references within the body of the paper (discussed in 13b below), and (2) a References list at the end of the paper (discussed in 13d below). By using the APA system, you can integrate your source information appropriately and ethically without inadvertently committing plagiarism.

Plagiarism, a serious academic offense, is often committed by students inadvertently in the following two ways:

The APA Citation System

1. Introduce your source using a *signal phrase* that names its author, immediately followed by the date of publication in parentheses: Jones (1995) states that . . . (see 10d-2; see box on p. 152 for suggested verbs to use in signal phrases).

2. Paraphrase or summarize the information from your source. It's best to use direct quotations sparingly. Rather, recast the source information into your own words. If you do use any words or phrases from the author, however, be sure to include them in quotation marks and to provide a page number in parentheses (see 10d).

3. If you did not name the author in a signal phrase, at the conclusion of your summary insert in parentheses the author's last name, a comma, and the date of publication: (Jones, 1995). For a direct quotation or close paraphrase, also provide a page number: (Jones, 1995, p. 75) (see 13b).

4. At the end of your paper, list the source with complete bibliographic information on your References page (see 13d).

1. Failing to acknowledge a summary or paraphrase of a source in the body of the paper through a signal phrase and parenthetical citation.
2. Using the original authors' words without putting the borrowed words or phrases in quotation marks or including a parenthetical citation.

1 Acknowledge all sources

A successful research paper will be written as an argument in the writer's own words, expressing an understanding of the answers to specific research questions. In such a paper, sources are used as evidence in support of the writer's argument. Source support is integrated into the flow of the research paper through the use of paraphrases and summaries in the writer's own words; each source is acknowledged by a parenthetical citation. Failing to acknowledge a source results in plagiarism. In addition to paraphrases and summaries, any other source material must also be acknowledged, such as specific facts, graphics or visuals, cartoons, diagrams, or charts, using the two-part APA citation system. Note that the APA system stresses the publication date of a source by including that date in the parenthetical citation along with the name of the author. This custom has grown out of a desire of researchers in the social sciences to know immediately that the information found in a particular source is current and up to date (see 10a-3).

2 Indicate original source words and phrases with quotation marks

The best research papers use direct quotations sparingly as support for their own ideas and integrate those quotations smoothly into the flow of the paper. A signal phrase alerts the reader that a direct quotation follows; the quotation marks show exactly which words and phrases are being quoted. Long quotations are formatted using indentation rather than quotation marks (see 44a-2). When students get into trouble by borrowing words and phrases without attribution to a source, it is very often the result of sloppy notetaking. Your notes should accurately record source information in your own words, and you should be able to tell at a glance when looking at your notes which information is from which source and on what page that information is located. Carelessness at the notetaking stage can result in unintentional plagiarism (see 10a-3).

13b Use the APA system for in-text citations

In the APA documentation system, reference citations found in the body of the paper are linked to the References list at the end. Both the author's last name and the year of publication are included in the in-text citation.

1. Author Named in the Narrative

If the author is mentioned in the narrative, provide the year of publication in parentheses just after the name.

```
Hacking (1995) covers much that is on public record about
multiple personality disorder.
```

2. Author Not Named in the Narrative

If the author is not mentioned in the narrative, provide the author's last name and the year of publication in parentheses at an appropriate place. Include a comma between the author's name and the date of publication.

```
In antiquity and through the Middle Ages, memory was a valued
skill (Hacking, 1995).
```

3. Specific Page or Paragraph Quoted

When quoting or directly paraphrasing the author's words, provide a page number (or a paragraph number if the electronic source includes one). Precede the page reference with the abbreviation *p.* (to cite one page), *pp.* (to cite more than one page), or the word *paragraph.*

```
There may be a causal explanation for multiple personality
disorder, because "multiplicity is strongly associated with early
and repeated child abuse, especially sexual abuse" (Hacking, 1995,
p. 73).
```

If the quotation from an electronic source does not have pages or paragraph numbers, provide author and year only.

```
Vault Reports makes the following request on its Web site: "If
you work (or have worked) for a company we write about . . . please
fill out our Survey and tell us about your experience" (1998).
```

4. Work by Two Authors

In citing a work by two authors, provide the last names of both authors. Use the word *and* to separate their names in the narrative, but use an ampersand (&) to separate their names in an in-text parenthetical citation.

As Sullivan and Qualley (1994) point out, many recent

publications take the politics of writing instruction as their

central concern.

or

The explanation for recent turmoil in the academy may be found

in politics (Sullivan & Qualley, 1994).

5. Work by More than Two Authors

In the first reference to a work by three, four, or five authors, provide the last names for all authors. In subsequent citations, use the first author's last name and the Latin phrase *et al.* (for "and others"). When a work has six or more authors, include only the name of the first author, followed by *et al.*, in the first and in all following citations.

According to Britton et al. (1975), mature writers consider

their readers more than themselves.

6. Anonymous Work

If no author's name is provided, use either the title or an abbreviated form of the title (usually the first few words) for the in-text citation. Italicize the title of a book, periodical, brochure, or report; use quotation marks around the title of an article or chapter.

Public schools have become overly dependent on the IQ test as

an indication of academic potential (*Human Abilities in Cultural*

Contexts, 1988).

An individual's success in life depends in large measure on the

cultural context in which he or she was raised ("Beyond IQ," 1994).

7. Work by a Corporate Author

Generally, provide the full name of a corporate author in in-text parenthetical citations.

Recently published statistics show the gap between the rich and poor to be widening (New York Times, Inc., 1996).

If the name of the corporate author is long (such as United Cerebral Palsy Association) or if its abbreviation is easily recognized (such as APA), use the abbreviation after including both the complete name and the abbreviation in the first text reference.

FIRST TEXT REFERENCE

There is a Web site that explains citing information from the Internet (American Psychological Association [APA], 2001).

SECOND AND SUBSEQUENT TEXT REFERENCES

The documentation system commonly employed in the social sciences is presented in great detail (APA, 2001).

8. Works by Authors with the Same Last Name

When the reference list includes two or more primary authors with the same last name, provide those authors' initials in all citations, even if the publication dates are different.

G. A. Fraser (1990) writes about abuse as the cause of multiple personality disorder.

S. Fraser (1987) has written a memoir about incest and its effect on multiplicity.

9. Two or More Sources

To cite several different sources within the same parenthetical citation, list the sources in alphabetical order by the authors' names and use a semicolon to separate the entries.

Several studies (Prinsky & Rosenbaum, 1987; *Record Labeling*, 1985; Thigpen, 1993) show concern about songs with themes of drugs and violence.

10. *Personal Communication*

Personal correspondence, such as letters, telephone conversations, lecture notes, and email, should be cited only in the text itself. Do not list the communications on the References page because readers cannot access them. Provide the initials and the last name of the correspondent, the designation *personal communication*, and the date.

```
J. Tompkins suggests that fear of authority prevents true

learning in elementary, secondary, college, and university

classrooms (personal communication, August 7, 1997).
```

11. *Email Communication*

Email communication from individuals should be cited as personal communication within the text and is not included on the Works Cited list. The in-text citation is formatted as follows:

```
L.L. Meeks provided researchers with the pertinent

information regarding teacher training (personal communication,

May 2, 2000).
```

12. *Web Sites*

When referring to an entire Web site (as opposed to a specific document or page on the site) it is sufficient in APA style to give the address of the Web site within the text itself. Such a reference is not included on the Works Cited page.

```
Patricia Jarvis's homepage includes a great deal of information

about recent archaeological digs in the Great Basin (http://www.asu

.edu/~students).
```

13c Format any content notes according to the APA system

The APA discourages use of content notes. They should be included only if they enhance or strengthen the discussion. Number notes consecutively throughout the text, using a superscript number. List the notes on a separate Notes page at the end of the text.

13d Format the References page according to the APA system

The research paper's References page (the equivalent of the Works Cited listing in MLA style) contains an alphabetical listing of all the works used as sources. The purpose of the References list is to help readers find the materials used in writing the paper, so the entries must be complete and accurate. List sources alphabetically by the last name of the author. When no author is given, alphabetize by the first word of the title (excluding *A, An,* or *The*). Format the References list in a paper according to the APA style for a final text: type the first word of each entry at the left margin, and indent subsequent lines of the same entry five spaces (or one-half inch). Double-space the entire References page, both between and within entries.

Books   A citation for a book has four basic parts:

Author's Name. (Publication Date). *Title of work.* Publication Information.

Begin a book citation with the author's last name, followed by a comma and the first and middle initials. Next include the year of publication, enclosed in parentheses and followed by a period. Italicize the title and subtitle of the book. Capitalize the first word of the title and the first word of the subtitle. Follow the title with publication information: the city of publication and the publisher, separated from each other with a colon. If the city is not well known or could be confused with another city, include a state or country abbreviation. Omit the word *Publisher* and abbreviations such as *Inc.* and *Co.* from the publisher's name. Include the complete names of university presses and associations. (For guidelines on citing books in electronic format, see page 234.)

1. Book by One Author

Publication
Author   date   Title of work

Bolick, C. (1988). *Changing course: Civil rights at the crossroads.*

New Brunswick, NJ: Transaction Books.

Publication information

2. Book by Two or More Authors

When a book has two to six authors, provide all the authors' names (last name first, followed by initials) in the order in which they appear on the title page. Note that this order may not be alphabetical. Connect the final two names with an ampersand (&). Abbreviate the seventh and subsequent authors as *et al.*

Hindelang, M. J., Hirschi, T., & Weis, J. G. (1981). *Measuring*

delinquency. Beverly Hills, CA: Sage.

3. Book by a Corporate Author

Begin the entry with the full name of the group; alphabetize the entry by the first important word in the name. Should the same group be listed as author and publisher, include the word *Author* at the end of the entry in place of the publisher's name.

National Commission on Excellence in Education. (1984). *A nation at*

risk: The full account. Cambridge, MA: USA Research.

4. Book with an Editor

For an edited book, provide the editor's name in place of an author's name. Include the abbreviation *Ed.* (for "Editor") or *Eds.* (for "Editors") in parentheses immediately following the editor's name.

Dilts, S. W. (Ed.). (1991). *Peterson's guide to four-year colleges*

(21st ed.). Princeton, NJ: Peterson's Guides.

5. Chapter or Selection from an Edited Book

Start with the author's name, the year of publication, and the title of the selection. Do not underline the title or enclose it in quotation marks. Next, provide the names of the editors in normal order as they appear on the title page, preceded by the word *In* and followed by the abbreviation *Ed.* or *Eds.* (in parentheses). End the entry with the book's title (underlined), the inclusive page numbers for the selection (in parentheses), and the publication information.

Kadushin, A. (1988). Neglect in families. In E. W. Nunnally, C. S.

Chilman, & F. M. Cox (Eds.), *Mental illness, delinquency,*

addiction, and neglect (pp. 147-166). Newbury Park, CA: Sage.

6. Two or More Books by the Same Author

Arrange the entries by the date of publication, with the earliest first. If you have two or more works by the same author published in the same year, alphabetize by title and distinguish the entries by adding a lowercase letter immediately after the year: (1991a), (1991b).

Flynn, J. R. (1980). *Race, IQ, and Jensen*. London: Routledge.

Flynn, J. R. (1991). *Asian Americans: Achievement beyond IQ*.

  Hillsdale, NJ: Erlbaum.

7. Article in a Reference Book

If an encyclopedia entry is signed, start with the author's name; if it is unsigned, start with the title of the article. The publication date follows the author's name or, if no author's name is given, the title of the article. Provide the volume number and page numbers of the article (in parentheses) after the title of the reference book.

Davidoff, L. (1984). Childhood psychosis. In *The encyclopedia of*

  psychology (Vol. 10, pp. 156-157). New York: Wiley.

8. Book in Translation

Indicate the name of the translator in parentheses after the book's title, with the abbreviation *Trans.*

Freire, P. (1993). *Pedagogy of the oppressed* (New rev. 20th anniv.

  ed., M. B. Ramos, Trans.). New York: Continuum.

9. Subsequent Edition of a Book

If a book is not a first edition, indicate the relevant edition in parentheses immediately following the title of the book. Use abbreviations to specify the type of edition: for example, *2nd ed.* stands for "Second edition" and *Rev. ed.* stands for "Revised edition."

Lindeman, E. (1987). *A rhetoric for writing teachers* (2nd ed.). New

  York: Oxford University Press.

10. Republished Book

Provide the original date of publication in parentheses at the end of the entry, with the words *Original work published.*

Dewey, J. (1963). *Experience and education*. New York: Collier.

  (Original work published 1938)

11. *Government Document*

Unless an author's name is given, begin an entry for a government document with the name of the agency that issued the publication.

National Center for Educational Statistics. (1996). *The condition of education 1996*. Washington, DC: U.S. Department of Education, Office of Educational Research and Improvement.

12. *Published Proceedings from a Conference*

Van Belle, J. G. (2002). Online interaction: Learning communities in the virtual classroom. In J. Chambers (Ed.), *Selected Papers from the 13th International Conference on College Teaching and Learning* (pp. 187-200). Jacksonville, FL: Community College at Jacksonville Press.

13. *One Volume of a Multivolume Work*

Doyle, A. C. (1930). *The complete Sherlock Holmes* (Vol. 2). Garden City: Doubleday.

Periodicals   A citation of an article in a periodical or a journal follows a format similar to that for a book:

Author's name. (Publication date). Article title. Publication information.

When citing magazines and newpapers, include the month and date of publication. The article title and subtitle appear without quotation marks or italics. The publication information begins with the name of the publication as it appears on the publication's title page, with all major words capitalized. Italicize the journal name. Include the volume number (italicized and not preceded by the abbreviation *vol.*) and the issue number (in parentheses and not italicized) for journals that are not numbered consecutively throughout the volume. End with the inclusive page numbers for the article. (Use the abbreviation *p.* or *pp.* with articles in newspapers but not with articles in journals or magazines.) (For guidelines on citing articles in online periodicals, see pages 235–236.)

14. Article in a Journal Paginated by Volume

Popenoe, D. (1993). American family decline, 1960-1990: A review and

appraisal. *Journal of Marriage and Family, 55,* 527-555.

15. Article in a Journal Paginated by Issue

If each issue of a journal begins with page 1, provide the issue number (in parentheses) immediately following the volume number.

Alma, C. (1994). A strategy for the acquisition of problem-solving

expertise in humans: The category-as-analogy approach. *Inquiry,*

14(2), 17-28.

16. Article in a Monthly Magazine

Include the month, not abbreviated, following the year in the publication date.

Katz, L. G. (1994, November). Perspectives on the quality of early

childhood programs. *Phi Delta Kappan, 76,* 200-205.

17. Article in a Weekly Magazine

Provide the year, month, and day of publication.

Ives, D. (1994, August 14). Endpaper: The theory of anything. *The*

New York Times Magazine, 58.

If the article has no known author, start the entry with the title of the article, and alphabetize by the first important word in the title (usually the word that follows the introductory article).

The blood business. (1972, September 7). *Time,* 47-48.

(In the References list, this entry would appear in the B's.)

18. Newspaper Article

Provide the complete name of the newspaper (including any introductory articles) after the title of the article. List all discontinuous page numbers, preceded by *p.* or *pp.*

Fritz, M. (1992, November 7). Hard-liners to boycott German anti-

racism rally. *The Dallas Morning News*, pp. 1, 25.

19. Editorial

Add the word *Editorial*, in brackets, after the title of the editorial.

Paglia, C. (1997, October 24). More mush from the NEA [Editorial].

The Wall Street Journal, p. A22.

20. Letter to the Editor

Add the designation *Letter to the editor*, in brackets, after the title of the letter or after the date if there is no title.

Schack, S. (1997, December 1). [Letter to the editor]. *The New York*

Times, p. A20.

21. Review

Provide the name of the reviewer, the date of publication (in parentheses), and the title of the review, if given. Then, in brackets, write the designation *Review of* and the title of the piece that was reviewed.

Ribadeneira, D. (1997, October 31). The secret lives of seminarians

[Review of the book *The new men: Inside the Vatican's elite*

school for American priests]. *The Boston Globe*, p. C6.

22. Unsigned Article

Quacks in European solidarity (2002, August). *The Economist*, 50.

23. More than One Work by the Same Author in the Same Year

List the works alphabetically by title and use the lowercase letters *a, b, c,* etc. after the dates to distinguish the works.

Hayles, N. K. (1996a). Inside the teaching machine: Actual feminism

and (virtual) pedagogy. *The Electronic Journal for Computer*

Writing, Rhetoric and Literature, 2. Retrieved Nov. 15, 1996,

from http://www.cwrl.utexas.edu/cwrl

Hayles, N. K. (1996b). Self/Subject. In P. Vandenberg & P. Heilker

(Eds.), *Keywords in composition* (pp. 217-220). Portsmouth, NH:

Heinemann/Boynton-Cook.

Other Sources

24. *Film or Video Recording*

Begin with the names of those responsible for the film and, in parentheses, their titles, such as *Producer* and *Director*. Give the title (italicized), and then designate the medium in brackets. Provide the location and the name of the distributor.

Rosenthal, J., et al. (Producers), & Ramis, H. (Director). (2002).

Analyze That [Motion picture]. Hollywood: Warner Brothers.

25. *Television or Radio Program*

Identify those who created the program, and give their titles— for example, *Producer, Director,* and *Anchor.* Give the date the program was broadcast. Provide the program's title (italicized), as well as the city and the station where the program aired.

Miller, R. (Producer). (1982, May 21). *Problems of freedom.* New

York: NBC-TV.

26. *Technical Report*

Write an entry for a technical report in a format similar to that for a book. If an individual author is named, provide that information; place any other identifying information (such as a report number) after the title of the report.

Vaughn Hansen Associates, in association with CH2M Hill and Water

Research Laboratory, Utah State University. (1995).

Identification and assessment of certain water management

options for the Wasatch Front: Prepared for Utah State Division

of Water Resources. Salt Lake City, UT: Author.

27. *Published Interview*

For a published interview, start with the name of the interviewer and the date. In brackets, give the name (and title, if necessary) of the person interviewed. End with the publication information, including the page number(s), in parentheses, after the title of the work in which the interview is published.

Davidson, P. (1992). [Interview with Donald Hall]. In P. Davidson,

 The fading smile (p. 25). New York: Knopf.

28. Unpublished Interview

Follow the format for a published interview.

Hult, C. (1997, March). [Interview with Dr. Stanford Cazier, past

 President, Utah State University].

29. Unpublished Dissertation

Provide the author's name, the date, and then the title of the dissertation, italicized and followed by a period. Add the phrase *Unpublished doctoral dissertation,* a comma, and the name of the degree-granting institution.

Johnson, N. K. (1980). *Cultural and psychological determinants of*

 health and illness. Unpublished doctoral dissertation,

 University of Washington.

30. Speech or Lecture

For an oral presentation, provide the name of the presenter, the year and month of the presentation, and the title of the presentation (italicized). Then give any useful location information.

Meeks, L. (1997, March). *Feminism and the WPA.* Paper presented at

 the Conference on College Composition and Communication,

 Phoenix, AZ.

31. Paper Presented at a Conference

Provide information about the location of the meeting as well as the month in which the meeting was held.

Klaus, C. (1996, March). *Teachers and writers.* Paper presented at

 the meeting of the Conference on College Composition and

 Communication, Milwaukee.

Electronic Media The electronic documentation formats found in *Publication Manual of the American Psychological Association,* 5th ed., have been updated in the new edition. The formats discussed in this section are based on models found in the 5th edition of the manual.

13.1

An overview of APA documentation style.

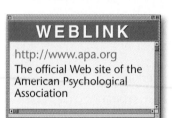

WEBLINK

http://www.apa.org
The official Web site of the American Psychological Association

When citing electronic media, use the standard APA format to identify authorship, date of origin (if known), and title, much as for print material; the Web information is placed in a retrieval statement at the end of the reference. If you are referencing an electronic version that duplicates exactly a print source, simply use the basic journal reference format for print sources. Indicate the electronic version by including the terms [Electronic Version] in brackets immediately following the article's title.

32. *Online Professional or Personal Site*

To comply with APA style, present information in the following general sequence when citing online sources:

1. The author's or editor's last name and initial(s)
2. The creation date of the work, in parentheses; use *n.d.* (no date) if the electronic publication date is not available
3. The title of the complete work, italicized
4. The relevant subpage (if the document is contained within a large, complex site)
5. The phrase "Retrieved (date) from" http:
6. The access protocol or path or URL. [Note: Only break URL lines after a slash or before a period; do not follow the URL with a period.]

Jarvis, P. (n.d.). *My Homepage.* Retrieved December 3, 1997, from

   http://www.mtu.edu/~students

McCarthy, B. (1997). *Reflections on the past--Antiques.* Retrieved

   January 20, 1998, from Resources for Victorian Living Web site:

   http://www.victoriana.com

33. *Online Book*

Provide any data on the print publication before giving details on where the electronic version may be located.

Aristotle. (1954). *Rhetoric* (W. R. Roberts, Trans.). Retrieved April

8, 1997, from *The English Server* at Carnegie Mellon University:

http://www.rpi.edu/~honeyl/Rhetoric/index.html

34. *Article in an Online Work*

Generally, citations for articles in online works follow the same sequence as citations for their print counterparts.

Women in American history. (1998). In *Encyclopaedia Britannica*.

Retrieved May 25, 1998, from http://www.women.eb.com

35. *Article in an Online Newspaper or on a Newswire*

Schmitt, E. (1998, February 4). Cohen promises "significant"

military campaign against Iraq if diplomacy fails. *The New York*

Times on the Web. Retrieved from http://www.nytimes.com/

archives

(Note) No need to repeat the date of retrieval if it is the same as the publication date.

36. *Article in an Online Magazine*

Thakker, S. (1998, May). Avoiding automobile theft. *Ontario Police*

Crime Prevention Magazine. Retrieved May 26, 1998, from

http://www.opcpm.com/inside/avoidingautomobile.html

37. *Online Review*

Spiers, S. (1998). [Review of the report "Blood poisoning" by

Prevention/NBCToday.] *OBGYN.net*. Retrieved August 3, 1998,

from http://www.obgyn.net/women/articles

38. *Online Abstract*

Reid, J. (1983). Computer-assisted text-analysis for ESL students.

Calico Journal, 1(3), 40-42. Abstract retrieved August 2, 1998,

from DIALOG database (ERIC Item: EJ29870).

39. *Online Editorial*

Spilner, M. (1998, May). Walking club welcome [Editorial].

    Prevention. Retrieved June 20, 1998, from

    http://www.prevention.com/walking/welcome.html

40. *Online Letter to the Editor*

Rivel, D. (1998, May 6). Art in the schools [Letter to editor]. *The*

    New York Times on the Web. Retrieved May 6, 1998, from

    http://www.nytimes.com/yr/mo/day/letters

41. *Article in an Online Scholarly Journal*

Britt, R. (1995). The heat is on: Scientists agree on human

    contribution to global warming. *Ion Science*. Retrieved November

    13, 1996, from http://www.injersey.com/Media/IonSci/features/gwarm

42. *Document or Full-Text Article Found Via a Reference Database*

To cite a full-text article you derive from a service that your library subscribes to (e.g., *Lexis-Nexis, EBSCOHost,* or *ProQuest*), follow the citation for the source itself (the same as for its print counterpart) with the name of the service (italicized) and the library. Provide the date of access and the URL of the service's home page in a retrieval statement.

King, M. (2000, July 6). Companies here ponder scout ruling. *Seattle*

    Times, A1. *Lexis-Nexis*. Utah State U. Library., Logan, UT.

    Retrieved August 15, 2000, from http://web.lexis-

    nexis.com/universe

43. *Nonperiodical Publication on CD-ROM, Magnetic Tape, or Disk*

ClearVue, Inc. (1995). *The history of European literature* [CD-ROM].

    Chicago: Author.

44. *Online Work of Art*

Seurat, G. (1884). *A Sunday afternoon on the island of la Grande Jatte*. Art Institute of Chicago. Retrieved August 3, 1998, from http://www.artic.edu/aic/collections

45. *Online Interview*

Jorgenson, L. (1998, May 26). For a change, Jazz feel bullish [Interview with Jeff Hornacek]. *Deseret News,* 15 paragraphs. Retrieved May 27, 1998, from http://www.desnews.com/playoffs

46. *Online Posting*

Although unretrievable communication such as email is not included in APA References, public or retrievable Internet postings from newsgroups or listservs may be included.

Shaumann, T. (1994, August 5). Technical German. *Technical German Discussion List*. Retrieved September 7, 1994, from USENET@comp.edu.languages.natural

47. *Online Synchronous Communication*

WorldMOO Computer Club. (1998, February 3). Monthly meeting. Retrieved February 3, 1998 from telnet:world.sensemedia.net1234

13e Review a sample research report in APA format

The following research paper, written by two students in a general education course, is formatted according to the APA system of documentation. Annotations that explain various conventions are included in the margins.

Title page
Shortened title appears with page number on every page
Introverts & Extroverts   1

Running Head: INTROVERTS AND EXTROVERTS

If the paper is being submitted for publication, include the shortened title to be used as a header on every page of the printed version

Title

A Study of the Study Habits of Introverts

and Extroverts

Student and course identification

Group: True Colors

Brandy Black

Sarah Summers

Liberal Arts & Sciences 124

Professor Long

October 30, 2002

An abstract, a brief summary of the paper, is often included as the second page in social science papers

Introverts & Extroverts   2

A Study of the Study Habits of Introverts

and Extroverts

Research about personality types and their

study habits has become increasingly important. In

particular, psychologists have studied how to

recognize personality types of students and how to

teach different kinds of students. Because of this

national interest, we decided to investigate the

study habits of two personality types, introverts

and extroverts. We began this study with two

general assumptions. First, we thought that

introverts would be less socially active in their

study habits, spend more time studying, and have a

higher degree of academic success. Second, we

thought that extroverts would study in groups,

study less, and have slightly lower grades. In

order to investigate our assumptions, we read

several articles in journals such as *Psychological

Reports*, *Personality and Individual Differences*,

and *The Journal of Research in Personality*.

We constructed a four-page survey about

academic success and study habits which we asked

fifteen students to answer. In addition, we also

created a six-day study log to chart the length of

study time, duration of breaks, and type of

Title

*Double-
spaced text*

Hypothesis

*Background
information*

Introverts & Extroverts   3

studying done by the students. The purpose of this
research report is to review the literature and to
present information from our own research. This

<u>report shows that our own research, for the most</u>
part, replicated the findings of many of the
national studies. Information in this paper will be
presented in two sections. First, findings from the
larger, national studies will be summarized. Then,
findings from our study will follow.

Literature Review

According to national studies, there are three
major trends used in tracing the academic life of
extroverts and introverts. The first trend is the
academic success of the student, classified into
self-rated academic success and actual degree of
success. The second trend is preferred study
locations and situations. The third trend is the
number of study breaks taken by extroverts and
introverts, measured by frequency and duration.

Academic Success

Several studies chart the success of
extroverted and introverted students. These have
divided academic success into two categories: self-
rated academic success (Irfani, 1978) and the
actual degree of success (Furnham & Medhurst, 1995;

Marginal notes:

Thesis

Others' research is reviewed and summarized in the literature review

In APA style, source citations include last name and date, with a comma

Introverts & Extroverts   4

Olympia et al., 1994). One study showed that more
extroverts rated themselves as academically
successful than introverts (Irfani, 1978). So,
according to this study, "the possibility [that] a
student will rate himself academically successful
is likely to be greater when the student is
extroverted rather than introverted" (Irfani, 1978,
p. 505).

 In contrast, another national study found that
"stable introverts [are] the highest academic
performers" (Furnham & Medhurst, 1995, p. 197).
Students went on to review the literature
related to the second and third trends.

Methods: The State University Study

 To determine how State University students
would compare to reports found in our literature
review, we administered a four-page questionnaire
to fifteen students. We also asked the students to
keep a six-day study log. The methodology used to
create this questionnaire follows.

Developing the Research Questions

 We designed a questionnaire to learn about the
academic life of introverts and extroverts. The main
areas we wanted this questionnaire to address were:

1. How do students view themselves? as introverts
  or extroverts? as successful academically?

Brackets show wording change

Direct quotations require a page number in the citation

First-level heading is centered

The primary research study is described and the results discussed

Second-level heading is set flush on left margin and underlined

Introverts & Extroverts   5

2. Do introverts or extroverts do better in
   school?

3. Do introverts and extroverts study differently?

By writing these research questions, we were then
able to design the actual questionnaire. We
randomly selected fifteen students in the library
who agreed to answer the questionnaire. The
students were given a brief personality survey to
determine if they were introverted or extroverted.
The subjects were divided into two groups: 8
introverts and 7 extroverts. Thirteen of the
students also agreed to keep a six-day study log.

Results and Discussion

In the Results section of the paper, students analyzed
demographics—age, years in school, gender, marital status,
number of roommates, and number of children. Then, they
analyzed the academic success, time management skills,
study habits, and preferred study situations and locations
of their subjects by using the questionnaire and study log
data.

Conclusions

Results of the
study are
compared to
the
hypothesis

In comparing the national studies with our
State University study, we made several
observations about the three major trends we had
intended to address. Our first trend dealt with
academic success. Both studies agreed that the GPA
is only slightly different between introverts and

Introverts & Extroverts   6

extroverts. In the national studies, more extroverts rated themselves as academically successful. In contrast, our study showed more introverts rated themselves as academically successful.

The second trend dealt with the preferred study locations and situations of introverts and extroverts. The national studies concluded that introverts liked quiet environments; however, our study showed that the majority of introverts preferred to listen to music while studying. Both the national studies and our study concluded that introverts like to be alone while studying and that extroverts prefer group study. Our final trend dealt with the frequency of study breaks. Our study showed that introverts took fewer study breaks than extroverts, which agreed with the national studies.

In one area, results run counter to hypothesis

APA citation style

Only first word and proper nouns are capitalized in article or book title

Introverts & Extroverts   7

References

Initials

Publication date

Campbell, J. B. (1983). Differential relationships

of extroversion, impassivity, and sociability

to study habits. *Journal of Research in*

Personality, 17, 308-313. ——— Page numbers

Campbell, J. B., & Hawley, C. W. (1982). Study

Journal name, in capital and lowercase letters, is italicized

habits and Eysenck's theory of extroversion-

introversion. *Journal of Research in* No quotation marks around title

Personality, 16, 139-146.

Furnham, A., & Medhurst, S. (1995). Personality

correlates of academic seminar behavior: A

study of four instruments. *Personality and*

Individual Differences, 19, 197-208.

Irfani, S. (1978). Extroversion-introversion and

self-rated academic success. *Psychological*

Volume number is italicized

Reports, 43, 505-510.

Internet journal

Olympia, D. E., Sheridan, S. M., Jenson, W. R., &

Andrews, D. (1994). Using student-managed

interventions to increase homework completion

and accuracy. *Journal of Applied Behavior*

Analysis, 27, 88-99. Retrieved September 25,

1998, from http://www.envmed.rochester.edu/

www.rap/behavior/jaba.htm

CMS System

The documentation system used most commonly in business, communications, economics, and the humanities and fine arts (other than languages and literature) is outlined in *The Chicago Manual of Style,* 14th ed. (Chicago: The University of Chicago Press, 1993). This two-part system uses footnotes or endnotes and a bibliography to provide publication information about sources quoted, paraphrased, summarized, or otherwise referred to in the text of a paper. Footnotes appear at the bottom of the page; endnotes appear on a separate page at the end of

WEBLINK

http://www.press.uchicago.edu/Misc/Chicago/cmosfaq.html

For answers to questions about CMS style

www

13.2

FAQs about CMS documentation.

paper. The Bibliography, like the Works Cited page in the MLA documentation style, is an alphabetical list of all works cited in the paper.

13f Integrate sources and avoid plagiarism in the CMS system

In Chapter 10, "Using Sources and Avoiding Plagiarism," we talked in general about the importance of using sources accurately and responsibly in your research papers. To help you do so, the CMS citation format provides for a two-part system of source identification: (1) footnote superscript numbers and footnotes within the body of the paper (discussed in 13g & h below), and (2) a Bibliography at the end of the paper (discussed in 13i below). By using the CMS system, you can integrate your source information appropriately and ethically without inadvertently committing plagiarism.

Plagiarism, a serious academic offense, is often committed by students inadvertently in the following two ways:

1. Failing to acknowledge a summary or paraphrase of a source in the body of the paper through a signal phrase and parenthetical citation.

2. Using the original authors' words without putting the borrowed words or phrases in quotation marks or including a parenthetical citation.

The CMS Citation System

1. Introduce your source using a *signal phrase* that names its author, with a superscript footnote number following the source information: Jones states that . . .[1] (see 10d-2; see box on p. 152 for suggested verbs to use in signal phrases).

2. Paraphrase or summarize the information from your source. It's best to use direct quotations sparingly. Rather, recast the source information into your own words. If you do use any words or phrases from the author, however, be sure to include them in quotation marks (see 10d).

3. Format your footnotes (which are listed on the page on which the source was cited) or endnotes (which are typed in one consecutive list at the end of the paper before the bibliography) according to the CMS style (see 13h).

4. At the end of your paper, list the source with complete bibliographic information on your Bibliography page (see 13i).

1 Acknowledge all sources

A successful research paper will be written as an argument in your own words, expressing an understanding of the answers to specific research questions. In such a paper, sources are used as evidence in support of the writer's own argument. Source support is integrated into the flow of the research paper through the use of paraphrases and summaries in the writer's own words; each source is acknowledged by a parenthetical citation. Failing to acknowledge a source results in plagiarism. In addition to paraphrases and summaries, any other source material must also be acknowledged, such as specific facts, graphics or visuals, cartoons, diagrams, or charts, using the CMS footnote citation system (see 10a-3).

2 Indicate original source words and phrases with quotation marks

The best research papers use direct quotations sparingly as support for their own ideas and integrate those quotations smoothly into the flow of the paper. A signal phrase alerts the reader that a direct quotation follows; the quotation marks show exactly which words and phrases are being quoted. Long quotations are formatted using indentation rather than quotation marks (see 44a-2). When students get into trouble by borrowing words and phrases without attribution to a source, it is very often the result of sloppy notetaking. Your notes should accurately record source information in your own words, and you should be able to tell at a glance when looking at your notes which information is from which source and on what page that information is located. Carelessness at the notetaking stage can result in unintentional plagiarism (see 10a-3).

13g Use the CMS system for in-text citations

In the text, indicate a note with a superscript number typed immediately after the information that is being referenced. Number notes consecutively throughout the text.

In A History of Reading, Alberto Manguel asserts that "we, today's readers, have yet to learn what reading is."[1] As a result, one of his conclusions is that while readers have incredible powers, not all of them are enlightening.[2]

13h Format notes according to the CMS system

For footnotes, position the text of the note at the bottom of the page on which the reference occurs. Separate the footnotes from the text by skipping four lines from the last line of text. Single-space within a note, but double-space between notes if more than one note appears on a page.

For endnotes, type all of the notes at the end of the paper, in a section entitled Notes. The title, centered but not in quotation marks, should appear at the top of the first page of the notes. List the notes in consecutive order, as they occur in the text. Double-space the entire endnote section—between and within entries.

The other details of formatting are the same for both footnotes and endnotes. Indent the first line of each note five spaces (or $\frac{1}{2}$ inch). Use a number that is the same size as and is aligned in the same way as the note text (do not use a superscript); follow the number with a period and a word space to the note itself. Begin with the author's name (first name first), followed by a comma. Then provide the title of the book (underlined or italicized) or article (enclosed in quotation marks). Finally, provide the publication information. For books, include (in parentheses) the place of publication, followed by a colon; the publisher, followed by a comma; and the date of publication. Conclude with the page number of the source, preceded by a comma. For articles, include the title of the periodical (underlined or italicized), followed by the volume or issue number. Then add the date of publication (in parentheses), followed by a colon and the page number.

BOOK

> 1. Alberto Manguel, A History of Reading (New York: Viking, 1996), 23.

ARTICLE

> 2. Steven Brachlow, "John Robinson and the Lure of Separatism in Pre-Revolutionary England," Church History 50 (1983): 288-301.

In subsequent references to the same source, it is acceptable to use only the author's last name and a page number:

> 3. Manguel, 289.

Where there are two or more works by the same author, include a shortened version of each work's title:

> 4. Merton, Mystics, 68.

Books

Book by One Author

> 5. Iris Murdoch, The Sovereignty of Good (New York: Schocken Books, 1971), 32-33.

Book by Two or Three Authors

List the authors' names in the same order as on the title page of the book.

> 6. Anne S. Goodsell, Michelle R. Maher, and Vincent Tinto, Collaborative Learning: A Sourcebook for Higher Education (University Park, Pa.: National Center on Postsecondary Teaching, Learning, and Assessment, 1992), 78.

Book by More than Three Authors

In the note itself, use the abbreviation *et al.* after the first author's name; list all authors in the accompanying bibliography entry.

7. James Britton et al., The Development of Writing Abilities (London: Macmillan, 1975), 43.

Book by a Corporate Author

8. American Association of Colleges and Universities, American Pluralism and the College Curriculum: Higher Education in a Diverse Democracy (Washington, D.C.: American Association of Higher Education, 1995), 27.

Book with an Editor

9. Jane Roberta Cooper, ed., Reading Adrienne Rich: Review and Re-Visions, 1951-1981 (Ann Arbor: University of Michigan Press, 1984), 51.

Book with an Editor and an Author

10. Albert Schweitzer, Albert Schweitzer: An Anthology, ed. Charles R. Joy (New York: Harper & Row, 1947), 107.

Chapter or Selection from an Edited Work

11. Gabriele Taylor, "Gossip as Moral Talk," in Good Gossip, ed. Robert F. Goodman and Aaron Ben-Ze'ev (Lawrence: Kansas University Press, 1994), 35-37.

Article in a Reference Book

The publication information (city of publication, publisher, publication year) is usually omitted from citations of well-known reference books. Include the abbreviation *s. v.* (*sub verbo,* or "under the word") before the article title, rather than page numbers.

12. Frank E. Reynolds, World Book Encyclopedia, 1983 ed., s. v. "Buddhism."

Introduction, Preface, Foreword, or Afterword

13. Jane Tompkins, preface to A Life in School: What the Teacher Learned (Reading, Mass.: Addison-Wesley, 1996), xix.

Work in More than One Volume

14. Arthur Conan Doyle, The Complete Sherlock Holmes, vol. 2 (Garden City, N.Y.: Doubleday, 1930), 728.

Government Document

15. United States Federal Bureau of Investigation, Uniform Crime Reports for the United States: 1995 (Washington, D.C.: GPO, 1995), 48.

Periodicals

Article in a Journal Paginated by Volume

16. Mike Rose, "The Language of Exclusion: Writing Instruction at the University," College English 47 (1985): 343.

Article in a Journal Paginated by Issue

17. Joy S. Ritchie, "Confronting the 'Essential' Problem: Reconnecting Feminist Theory and Pedagogy," Journal of Advanced Composition 10, no. 2 (1989): 160.

Article in a Monthly Magazine

18. Douglas H. Lamb and Glen D. Reeder, "Reliving Golden Days," Psychology Today, June 1986, 22.

Article in a Weekly Magazine

19. Steven Levy, "Blaming the Web," Newsweek, 7 April 1997, 46-47.

Newspaper Article

20. P. Ray Baker, "The Diagonal Walk," Ann Arbor News, 16 June 1928, sec. A, p. 2.

Abstract from an Abstracts Journal

21. Nancy K. Johnson, "Cultural and Psychological Determinants of Health and Illness" (Ph.D. diss., University of Washington, 1980), abstract in <u>Dissertation Abstracts International</u> 40 (1980): 425B.

Other Sources

Speech or Lecture

22. Wayne Booth, "Ethics and the Teaching of Literature" (paper presented to the College Forum at the 87th Annual Convention of the National Council of Teachers of English, Detroit, Mich., 21 November 1997).

Personal Letter to the Author

23. George Bush, letter to author, 8 September 1995.

Electronic Media Because *The Chicago Manual of Style,* 14th ed., primarily covers citation formats for electronic journals with a print equivalent, researchers continue to adapt to new electronic formats by modifying some of the basic CMS conventions. Melvin E. Page of East Tennessee State University has developed a CMS-based style sheet. This section reflects features of that style sheet, which has been recommended by H-Net, a consortium of email lists aimed at historians. One feature of Page's proposed style is the convention of enclosing URLs within angle brackets. Another is the provision of any publicly recorded email addresses (but not privately recorded ones) as part of the author's identification. The date of posting, if available, follows the Internet address without parentheses; a date of access is provided when no date of posting is available.

WEBLINK

http://h-net.msu.edu/
~africa/citation.html
A CMS-based style sheet for
citing Web sources and
other online material

13.3
How to document Internet sources using CMS.

Online Professional or Personal Site

24. Academic Info., "Humanities," <http://www.academicinfo.net/index.html>, 1998-2000.

25. Michelle Traylor, "Michelle Traylor Data Services," <http://www.mtdsnet.com>, 1989-2002.

26. John C. Herz, "Surfing on the Internet: A Nethead's Adventures Online," Urban Desires 1.3, ⟨http://www.desires.com⟩, March/April 1995.

13i Format bibliography entries according to the CMS system

The style for Bibliography entries is generally the same as that for Works Cited entries in MLA style. Follow the formatting conventions outlined in Chapter 12 when creating a Bibliography page.

CBE System

Although source citations in the sciences are generally similar to those recommended by the APA, there is no uniform system of citation in the sciences. Various disciplines follow either the style of a particular journal or the style outlined in a style guide, such as the guide produced by the Council of Biology Editors: *Scientific Style and Format: The CBE Manual for Authors, Editors, and Publishers,* 6th ed. (New York: Cambridge University Press, 1994).

The Council of Biology Editors (CBE) became the Council of Science Editors (CSE) on January 1, 2000. The new name, which was voted on by the membership during 1999, more accurately reflects its expanding membership. More information about the organization can be found at their Web site (listed in the box). The Council of Science Editors aims to improve communication in the sciences by educating authors, editors, and publishers; by providing means of cooperation among persons interested in publishing in the sciences; and by promoting effective communication practices in primary and secondary publishing in any form. Until it is revised and updated by the CSE, the CBE style will remain the preferred system for science citations.

13.4
An overview of CBE documentation style.

WEBLINK

http://councilscienceeditors.org

The official Web site of the Council of Science Editors.

13j Integrate sources and avoid plagiarism in the CBE system

In Chapter 10, "Using Sources and Avoiding Plagiarism," we talked in general about the importance of using sources accurately and responsibly in your research papers. To help you do so, the CBE citation format provides for a two-part system of source identification: (1) parenthetical references or reference numbers within the body of the paper (discussed in 13k below), and (2) a References list that is either alphabetical or numerical at the end of the paper (discussed in 13l below). By using the CBE system, you can integrate your source information appropriately and ethically without inadvertently committing plagiarism. Since the CBE citation system closely resembles the APA system, for more on integrating sources and avoiding plagiarism please see the information in 13a on p. 220.

13k Use the CBE system for in-text citations

The CBE system of documentation offers two alternative formats for in-text citations: the name-year (or author-year) system and the citation sequence (or number) system.

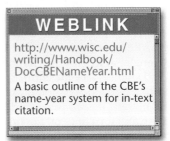

WEBLINK

http://www.wisc.edu/ writing/Handbook/ DocCBENameYear.html

A basic outline of the CBE's name-year system for in-text citation.

13.5
A guide to CBE in-text citation.

Name-Year System If the author's name is used to introduce the source material, include only the publication date in the citation.

> According to Allen (1997), frequency of interactions and context of occurrence were unknown.

or

> Frequency of interactions and context of occurrence were unknown (Allen 1997).

Note that there is no comma between author and year in CBE style.

Citation Sequence System In the citation sequence system, numbers are assigned to the various sources, according to the sequence in which the sources are initially cited in the text. Then the sources are listed by number on the References page. Set citation numbers within the text as superscripts.

> Temperature plays a major role in the rate of gastric juice secretion.[3]

Multiple sources are cited together:

```
Recent studies[3,5,8-10] show that antibodies may also bind to
microbes and prevent their attachment to epithelial surfaces.
```

131 Format the References page for the citation sequence system in CBE style

Like the MLA's Works Cited page, the CBE's listing of references contains all the sources cited in the paper. The title of this page may be References or Cited References. Since the purpose of this list is to help readers find the materials used in writing the paper, information must be complete and accurate.

The format of the References page will depend on whether the name-year system or the citation sequence system is used. Since the References page for the CBE name-year system basically resembles the APA References page discussed in 13d, we will consider here the References page for the citation sequence system.

Double-space the entire References list, both between and within entries. Type the citation number, followed by a period, flush left on the margin. Leave two word spaces to the first letter of the entry. Align any turn lines on the first letter of the entry. List the citations in order of appearance in the text.

List authors with last names first, followed by initials. Capitalize only the first word of a title and any proper nouns. Do not enclose titles of articles in quotation marks, and do not underline titles of books or journals. Abbreviate names of journals, where possible. Include the year of publication. Cite volume and page numbers when appropriate.

(Note that initial numerals accompany citations in the list *only* when the citation sequence system is used. The citations appear in alphabetical order when the name-year system is used.)

Books

Book by One Author

```
1. Kruuk H. The spotted hyena: a study of predation and social
   behavior. Chicago: University of Chicago Pr; 1972.

2. Abercrombie MLJ. The anatomy of judgment. Harmondsworth (Eng.):
   Penguin; 1969.
```

Book by Two or More Authors

3. Hersch RH, Paolitto DP, Reimer J. Promoting moral growth. New York: Longman; 1979.

Book by a Corporate Author

4. Carnegie Council on Policy Studies in Higher Education. Fair practices in higher education: rights and responsibilities of students and their colleges in a period of intensified competition for enrollment. San Francisco: Jossey-Bass; 1979.

Book with Two or More Editors

5. Buchanan RE, Gibbons NE, editors. Bergey's manual of determinative bacteriology. 8th ed. Baltimore: Williams & Wilkins; 1974.

Chapter or Selection from an Edited Work

6. Kleiman DG, Brady CA. Coyote behavior in the context of recent canid research: problems and perspectives. In: Bekoff M, editor. Coyotes: biology, behavior, and management. New York: Academic Pr; 1978. p. 163-88.

Government Document

7. Mech D. The wolves of Isle Royal. National Parks fauna series. Available from: United States GPO, Washington; 1966.

Periodicals

Journal Article by One Author

8. Schenkel R. Expression studies of wolves. Behavior 1947; 1:81-129.

Journal Article by Two or More Authors

9. Sargeant AB, Allen SH. Observed interactions between coyotes and red foxes. J Mamm 1989; 70:631-3.

Article with No Identified Author

10. Anonymous. Frustrated hamsters run on their wheels. Nat Sci 1981; 91:407.

Newspaper Article

11. Rensberger B, Specter B. CFCs may be destroyed by natural process. Washington Post 1989 Aug 7; Sect 1A: 2 (col 5).

Magazine Article

12. Aveni AF. Emissaries to the stars: the astronomers of ancient Maya. Mercury 1995 May: 15-8.

Electronic Media Internet formats are covered briefly in *Scientific Style and Format: The CBE Manual for Authors, Editors, and Publishers,* 6th ed. The CSE Web site refers users to the following publication "National Library of Medicine Recommended Formats for Bibliographic Citation," which expands basic CBE citation conventions to encompass electronic journals and print-based Internet sources.

WEBLINK

http://www.nlm.nih.gov/pubs/formats/internet.pdf
A Web document summarizing this style

Online Professional Site or Homepage

13. Gelt J. Home use of greywater: rainwater conserves water--and money [Internet]. 1993 [cited 1996 Nov 8]. Available from: http://www.ag.arizona.edu/AZWATER/arroyo/071 .rain.html

Online Book or Monograph

14. Merck. The Merck index on-line [monograph on the Internet]. 10th
    ed. Rahway (NJ): Merck; 1972 [cited 1990 Dec 7]. Available from:
    http://www.merck.com/pubs

Article in an Online Periodical

15. Lechner DE, Bradbury SF, Bradley LA. Phys Ther J [serial on the
    Internet]. 1998 Aug [cited 1998 Sept 15]. Available from:
    http://www.apta.org/pt_journal/Aug98/Toc.htm

13.6
Practice
documenting
sources.

PART 5

Document Design

FAQs

▶ **Chapter 14**

Are there special ways to design a page? (14a)
What is the best typeface to use? (14b-7)
When is one type of graphic better than another? (14c)

▶ **Chapter 15**

What does it mean to design a Web site? (15a, 15b-4)
What is hypertext? (15a-2)
How can I transfer my Web files to the Internet? (15b-1)
How can I help readers navigate my Web site? (15b-3)

▶ **Chapter 16**

How do I save a word-processing document into HTML? (16a)
How do I add a link to another site? (16b-3)
Where can I find images to use in my Web site? (16b-4)
How should I refine my Web site? (16c)

CHAPTER 14

Design Principles and Graphics

In today's consumer-oriented, message-dense society, people are inundated with advertisements, solicitations, entertainment, news reports, and all other manner of electronic and print documents. In this environment, people tend to read selectively, focusing only on documents that are interesting, inviting, and clear.

This is where *document design* comes in. By using headings, itemized lists, graphics, white space, effective layouts, and special typefaces, you can increase the chances that people will read your writing. These design elements also can help you emphasize the most important parts of your writing.

WEBLINK

http://www.impressive printers.com/EightRules .html

Eight rules of document design

AUDIO
Chapter overview.

14a Follow the three basic design principles

Adhering to the three basic principles of graphic design will make your documents more meaningful and more readable. These principles, which we will refer to as "the three C's," are clustering, contrasting, and connecting.

1 Clustering: grouping closely related items

Ideas or concepts that are closely related in nicative value should be clustered together w page from a student paper shown at the ⊦ is neat and centered, but there appe mation, none of them having any Logically, the title and subtit course and the name of the instru the revised version at the bottom ri cause the reader can now see at a g pieces of information instead of five. (Devon Johnson) stands out more.

Nature and the Poetic Imagination

Death and Rebirth in
"Ode to the West Wind"

Devon Johnson

English 202

Professor Baker

Nature and the Poetic Imagination
Death and Rebirth in
"Ode to the West Wind"

Devon Johnson

English 202
Professor Baker

2 Contrasting: highlighting differences

A second way of using design to make documents more meaningful and readable is to create visual contrasts that mirror important differences in content. Contrast can be seen in Devon Johnson's title page, where the main title is set larger and in bolder type than the subtitle. This formal difference makes it immediately clear to the reader that, although these four have something in common (and thus should be clustered together), they differ in content and purpose.

3 Connecting: relating every part to some other part

The third way of employing design to make text more coherent is to repeat important graphical or typographical elements—that is, visually connect different parts of a document so that no single element is left stranded. These connections should not be made haphazardly but, rather, in a way that underscores connections in meaning, value, or purpose. In this handbook, for example, the headings and subheadings are set off in different colors, to make it easier for readers to skim through the chapters and see how sections are related.

WWW

14.1
A business card illustrating the three C's.

14b Use formatting tools

Formatting is another powerful way of using visual representation to make a document easier to read and more emphatic in its message. Formatting can be done for decorative reasons only, but it is more effective if it also helps readers understand the text. Today's word-processing programs provide all the formatting tools you are likely to need, from boldface type to hanging indents.

AUDIO
Avoiding the overuse of formatting tools.

1 Headings

Headings (and subheadings and titles) draw attention, mark off parts of a text, and give the reader a quick sense of what those parts are about. Headings are especially beneficial for readers who only skim a text instead of reading it closely. Headings should give the reader an idea of what the paper, section, or illustration is about. They should be no longer than four or five words.

Headings also are useful during the writing process, to help you keep track of your overall writing plan. If you write an outline before composing, you can often convert the main points of the outline into headings and subheadings for your paper.

VIDEO
Designing academic papers.

2 Itemized lists

Itemized lists are a powerful form of visual clustering, as they show how several things form a closely related set. There are two main types of list formats. A *numbered list* or *lettered list* has ordered numbers or letters, suggesting either a ranking of the items or a step-wise procedure, as in the Help box. A *bulleted list,* which uses bullets (•), diamonds (♦), dashes (—), or some other symbol, is useful for an unordered set of items.

Since itemized lists attract a lot of attention, be careful not to overuse them. If you have too many lists too close together, their effectiveness will be lost. Try to have no more than one itemized list per manuscript page or computer screen.

3 Indentation and spacing

In academic papers, the first line of each paragraph is customarily indented five spaces or $\frac{1}{2}$ inch. With a word processor, you can set this indentation automatically, using either the ruler or the PARAGRAPH feature on the FORMAT menu. Quotations longer than four lines of prose or three lines of poetry are set off as a block, with each line indented ten spaces (see Chapter 44). In bibliographies, résumés, bulleted lists, and certain other types of writing, you may want to use *hanging indents,* where the first line begins at the left margin and fol-

HELP

How do I create an itemized list?

1. Introduce the list with a title or brief sentence describing the topic covered.

2. Set off each item with a number, letter, bullet, dash, asterisk, or other marker, and align the markers. Most word-processing programs will automatically do this formatting for you—check the user's manual or online HELP to make sure you are taking full advantage of the LIST feature.

3. Put all of the items in the same grammatical form (see Chapter 33). You will have to do this yourself, as no computer can do it for you.

lowing lines are indented. Hanging indents can usually be set on the PARAGRAPH menu.

Normally, your instructor will want you to use double-spacing throughout your paper (except perhaps in footnotes). You should leave a space after all end punctuation, such as periods, question marks, and exclamation points, and after commas, semicolons, colons, and each dot in ellipses.

4 Margins

For academic papers, the standard margin is 1 inch all around, to give the instructor space in which to write comments. These are also the default margins used by most word-processing programs. Word processors are normally set to *left-justify* your text—that is, start lines at the left margin and leave the right margin ragged, thus avoiding the need to hyphenate at the end of a line (see Chapter 48). Academic papers are usually written with left justification.

If you prefer the formal look of a commercial publication, you can *block-justify* your text, starting lines at the left and ending them evenly at the right; just click the appropriate icon in the toolbar. Block justification sometimes looks more elegant (especially in documents with columns, such as newspapers or brochures), but it can leave unsightly gaps in lines unless you use appropriate hyphenation.

5 Frames and boxes

An effective way to highlight a paragraph, graphic, or other part of a document is by putting a rectangular frame or box around it. Frames and boxes are especially useful for summarizing main points or procedural steps, because they simultaneously cluster these points or steps and set them off, through contrast, from the rest of the text. Frames and boxes are commonly found in textbooks, handbooks, user manuals, and other instructional documents (including this one). They are rarely found in academic writing and can be tricky to position, so you should use them only with caution. (You may want to check with your instructor to see whether he or she finds them acceptable.)

14.2

More on frames and boxes.

6 Columns

Putting text into columns is a useful way of clustering information in documents such as brochures, newsletters, résumés, and Web pages. There are basically two kinds of columns: newspaper and tabular. In *newspaper columns,* the text starts on the left, flows down the first column, and then continues at the top of the next column to the right. Newspaper columns are created with the COLUMNS feature on the FORMAT menu.

Tabular columns consist of independent texts side by side. They are useful if you want to have text in one column and numerical data in another, as in a table, or different kinds of corresponding entries, as in a résumé. Tabular columns are created by using the TABLE feature on a word processor.

7 Typography

Typography refers to all the features associated with individual letters, numbers, and other symbols: font type, font style, font size, color, and case.

Font type refers to the distinctive design of the typeface; some of the most common font types are Courier, Times New Roman, Garamond, and Arial. Font types that have little extra lines (*serifs*) at the ends of the letter strokes are called *serif fonts. Sans serif* (literally, "without serif") *fonts* lack such extra lines.

This sentence is written in a serif font.

This sentence is written in a sans serif font.

Because the extra lines help the eye move from letter to letter, serif fonts are often considered better for extended prose; the extra lines create a visual connectedness between the letters. Sans serif fonts have a more contemporary look and are often preferred for short texts such as advertisements, signs, and instructions. More unusual fonts such as *Mistral*, **Impact**, and *Brush Script* should be avoided in academic writing.

Font style (or *font weight*) refers to the particular variant of a single typeface: regular, *italic,* **bold,** or ***bold italic.*** Italic, bold, and bold italic typefaces can all be used for emphasis, but they have other uses as well. Italic typeface, for example, is commonly used for book titles (see 46e) and for words that are set off as vocabulary items (see examples in Chapter 36). Bold typeface is often used for introducing new terms, as in this handbook, and for headings.

The standard *font size* range for academic papers is 10 to 12 points, with section headings often set in 14-point type and the title of the paper in 20- or even 24-point type. More specialized bulletins or reports may use a wider range of heading sizes and styles.

Color is another option that has become available with the widespread use of computers. Like bold and italic type, however, color should be used sparingly—and systematically.

One other typographical variable is *case*. Academic writers normally use the standard combination of lowercase (small) and uppercase (capital) letters, except for acronyms and other abbreviations (see Chapter 46).

WWW

14.3
Use color effectively.

8 Page numbering

In a multipage document, it is a good idea to number the pages. Consult your word processor's documentation on how to operate the PAGE NUMBERING feature, as well as how to adjust numbering if you create section breaks in your document. Headers and footers can be used to put other interesting types of information—such as your name, a file name, the date and time, or even a company logo—at the top or bottom of the page along with the page number.

14c Use graphics

Graphics include tables, line graphs, bar graphs, pie charts, clip art, photographs, cartoons, drawings, maps, and other forms of visual art.

AUDIO
Choosing the most appropriate graphic.

1 Tables

Tables are the best type of graphic for presenting a lot of data in compressed form. Table 14.1 illustrates how information-rich a table can be.

Guidelines for Using Graphics

1. Place the graphic near the text to which it relates.
2. Introduce each graphic with a text reference. For example, precede the graphic with a sentence ending in a colon or a brief parenthetical comment such as "(see Figure 2)."
3. Use a caption that makes the graphic self-explanatory.
4. Keep the graphic as simple and uncluttered as possible.

TABLE 14.1
Annual World Carbon Dioxide Emissions
(million metric tons carbon equivalent)

	1990	1999	2010	2020
Industrialized Countries	2,849	3,129	3,692	4,169
E. Europe/FSU	1,337	810	978	1,139
Developing Countries	1,641	2,158	3,241	4,542
Asia	1,053	1,361	2,139	3,017
Middle East	231	330	439	566
Africa	179	218	287	365
Central & S. America	178	249	377	595
Total World	5,827	6,097	7,910	9,850

Sources: **1990 and 1999:** Energy Information Administration (EIA), *International Energy Annual 1999*, DOE/EIA-0219(99) (Washington, DC: February 2001). **Projections:** EIA, World Energy Projection System (2002).

Current word-processing programs offer a variety of table formats to choose from. Just click on TABLE and explore the options your program gives you.

Once you have the data laid out in a table, you can convert to other formats (such as line graphs and bar graphs) by selecting certain cells and importing them into whatever graphics program you have on your computer.

2 Line graphs

Line graphs generally do not contain as much data as tables do. But they can make data more understandable and are especially effective for showing changes over time. Figure 14.1 is a line graph representing the data in Table 14.1.

If a graph has more than one line, be sure to distinguish the various lines clearly (for example, by having one solid, another dotted, and a third dashed). Do not use more than three lines in a graph, as too many lines will produce a cluttered effect.

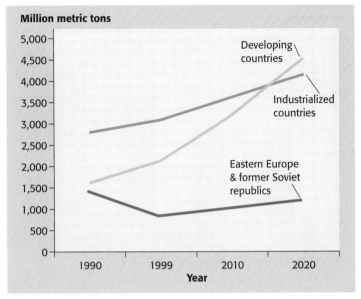

FIGURE 14.1 World CO_2 Emissions by Region, 1990–2020

3 Bar graphs

Bar graphs emphasize discrete points rather than continuity, but they can also show changes over time, sometimes more dramatically than line graphs. For example, the sheer weight of the bars in the bar graph in Figure 14.2 emphasizes the increase in global carbon dioxide emissions that we will likely experience in the next two decades.

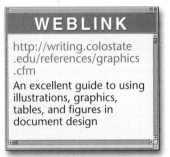

WEBLINK

http://writing.colostate.edu/references/graphics.cfm

An excellent guide to using illustrations, graphics, tables, and figures in document design

4 Pie charts

Pie charts are effective in showing how a fixed quantity of something is divided into fractions. Generally, the entire "pie" should represent 100 percent. Figure 14.3 shows the projected CO_2 emissions for all developing countries in 2020.

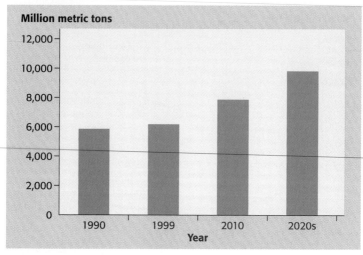

FIGURE 14.2 Global CO_2 Emissions, 1990–2020

5 | Clip art

Clip art, or ready-made images, can add a decorative touch to a document. Do not get carried away, though; too much of a good thing may only distract or annoy readers. Be especially cautious about using clip art in academic papers.

WEBLINK

http://www.clip-art.com

A great list of links to free graphics, icons, and other stuff on the Web

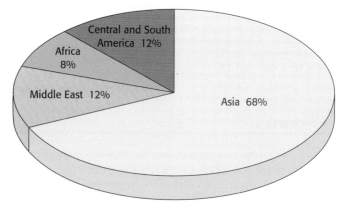

FIGURE 14.3 CO_2 Emissions in Developing Countries, 2020

6 Photographs, cartoons, drawings, and maps

The advent of graphical scanners and Internet downloading has made it easy to incorporate photographs and other images (such as cartoons, drawings, and maps) into documents. But remember that you cannot use copyrighted materials, such as cartoons or photographs created by someone else, without that person's permission.

14d Review your document

Before you print out a document, review it to be sure that the page numbers and headers or footers are set up as you want them to be. Reviewing the document is particularly important if you change from one printer to another, as you may need to adjust the formatting of the document to accommodate the fonts, spacing, and different graphics of the new printer.

The best way to review a document on a computer is by selecting either PAGE LAYOUT (VIEW menu) or PRINT PREVIEW (FILE menu) and then scrolling through to simulate a reader leafing through the document. A two-page view is especially useful with newsletters and brochures.

In reviewing a document, check for the following features:

- *Widowed or orphaned lines.* Single lines left stranded at the top and bottom of a page are known as widowed and orphaned lines, respectively. Particularly irritating to readers are orphaned headings.

- *Interrupted lists.* Like widowed or orphaned lines, short lists that start on one page and end on another have an adverse effect on readability.

- *Misplaced graphics or boxes.* Graphics and boxes should appear on the same page as their text reference. Your word-processing program will prevent such elements from being placed on a different page from their reference, provided you anchor the graphic or box properly to the reference. Otherwise, you will have to make manual adjustments.

- *Errors in page or section numbering.* You can usually avoid page numbering errors by having the word-processing program do the page numbering automatically.

- *White space.* Unused space is important because it makes different elements of a text (such as graphics, lists, and titles) stand out. By surveying your document in the PAGE LAYOUT or PRINT PREVIEW mode, you can decide whether specific elements are getting proper emphasis. White space also is important simply for aesthetic reasons. As readers leaf through your document, they should find its look appealing—neither too crowded nor too empty.

CHAPTER **15**

Designing for the Web

As you begin to think about designing Web documents, it is important to remember that writing for the Web is not all that different from writing for other purposes. The basic rhetorical principles outlined in Part 1 of this handbook still apply. Web authors need to consider carefully their rhetorical stance (purpose, persona, and audience) and let it dictate the content and structure of their Web sites. However, Web documents differ from print documents in two important ways: they tend to include more graphics than print documents, and they are hypertextual and Web-like (that is, they have electronic links). This chapter discusses these differences and what they mean to writers.

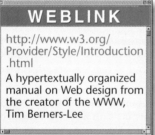

WEBLINK

http://www.w3.org/ Provider/Style/Introduction .html

A hypertextually organized manual on Web design from the creator of the WWW, Tim Berners-Lee

15.1
A hypertextual manual on Web design from the W3C.

15a Generate a basic design for the Web

AUDIO
Web design begins with preplanning.

A third grader in Huntsville, Alabama, and a research scientist in Osaka, Japan, have equal access to a worldwide audience on the Web. And, like anyone else who authors a Web site, both proceed through a design planning process in which they generate ideas and then plan, draft, revise, and publish the Web site. When a Web page is well designed, the author's message is successfully conveyed to readers, and the look and content of the page match the purposes of the author. Thus, effectively designed Web sites make good use of both graphics and hypertext.

1 Using graphics effectively

In print media, the printed words convey most of the text's meaning. But even printed texts contain other meaningful visual cues in addition to the words themselves—for example, by indenting five spaces at the beginning of a paragraph, using italics for titles of books, and using boldface for chapter titles, we also convey meaning. When Web authors consider document design, formatting, and graphics, they make decisions similar to those made by writers of print documents. However, the role of visual features in conveying meaning is greater in Web documents than in print documents. Web authors typically use images instead of words to show readers how to find information and to help them understand concepts. They employ such visual tools as color, background images, typographical distinctions, spacing, graphics and icons, lists, and tables and frames (see Figure 15.1). Increasingly, Web sites are becoming multimedia; they use sound and even movement to convey their message to readers. However, Web designers still need to pay close attention to the size of multimedia files (see the Help box on p. 299).

2 Using hypertext effectively

Effective writers accommodate the busy, selective reader through the use of headings, itemized lists, and graphics (see Chapter 14). Hypertext goes a logical step beyond print by allowing busy readers to choose among short chunks of text on specific topics, deciding what to read and what to ignore. **Hypertext** is text that is broken down into discrete pieces, which are then connected through electronic links. The first page of a Web site appears to be a flat, one-dimensional document, but it is not. It is hypertext, linked to other pages that will appear on-screen at the click of the mouse. These links are embedded in "hot" words, phrases, and graphics, which lead the reader to related texts within the same Web site (relative links), graphics and other media (hypermedia), and other Web sites (remote links). One of the greatest challenges in writing hypertext is to make it easy for readers to navigate through the links. Careful design is the key to constructing a successful Web site.

Site table of elements
with links to secondary
pages on the Web site

Colorful
image

Table used to position
elements on the page

Black graphic
on light background

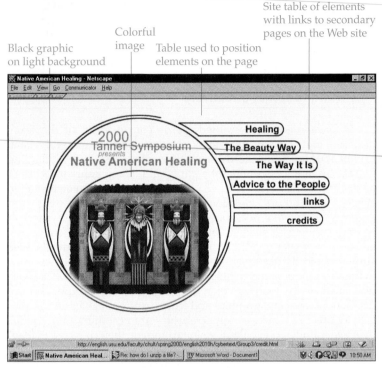

FIGURE 15.1 Web Page Illustrating Several Design Features

15b Plan your Web document

As you think about how you want your Web site to look, you should keep in mind the basic strengths and limitations of this medium. Although the Web allows you to be extremely creative in using graphics, photos, colors, and even video and sound, the Web authoring language HTML (HyperText Markup Language) is not as versatile as many desktop publishing programs. For example, constructing columns for a Web page is more difficult than producing a newsletter in columns using a word-processing program. In addition, the number of fonts available may be limited.

1 Learning about design technology

You do not compose a Web site directly on the World Wide Web. Instead, you create the text and graphics as files on your computer's hard drive or on disk. When the files are complete and stored in appropriate folders and directories, you transfer them from your computer or the lab's server to your college's Internet server or to an Internet service provider (ISP).

Naming and Storing Your Web Files

Naming Conventions.   When you begin any Web project, it is important to get organized from the start. Since servers may be picky about what file names they will accept, you need to decide on a simple yet understandable system of naming the files that will make up your Web project. For example, you should use only lowercase letters in Web file names and you should not use any spaces or characters such as periods since those can also cause problems for servers. Web file names should be kept short and must end in either *.htm* or *.html*. These extensions at one time distinguished Mac from PC Web files, but they have since become interchangeable. Graphics files will end in either *.gif* or *.jpg* since these are the image formats recognized by Web browsers.

15.2
Organizing
your Web files.

Creating a Directory for Your Project.   It is a good idea to create a project directory or folder on your computer's hard drive or disk in which to store all documents and graphics related to a particular Web project. As you construct your Web site, you will probably create a number of separate documents and graphics files that will later be connected to each other with hypertext links. If you keep them all in the same location on your disk or hard drive, you will find it easier to organize your Web site. Furthermore, if they all reside in the same folder, you will be able to transfer all of the related files at once to your Internet server. Be certain to make backup copies of everything you are using for your Web site, and remember to save frequently as you work on the project.

Understanding How Web Files Are Stored.   Before you begin your Web project, it is also important to understand how Web files are stored on your college's or service provider's computer system. If your college provides Internet access for students and faculty, it will have dedicated storage space on a large computer that is used as the campus Internet server. To use your college server, you will need to secure an account, which will include a user name and password unique to you.

Publishing Your Web Pages with a Browser.   The major Internet browsers, *Netscape* and *Explorer*, both provide you with a method to publish your Web pages, once you have set up an account on a server. For example, on *Netscape Composer*, click the PUBLISH icon to send your Web page to the campus server. It will ask you for information such as the server address, as well as your user name and password. *Composer* will send all the files associated with your Web page, including image files, if you so desire. If you decide to make a change to a file, simply send it again and it will replace the old file on the server (see Figure 15.2).

Publishing Your Web Pages with FTP. Another way to publish your Web pages is by using **FTP** or File Transfer Protocol. You can use ftp with *Internet Explorer* by typing ftp:// followed by the URL of the server (instead of http://URL) in the location box. Once *Explorer* has located the destination server, use COPY and PASTE to transfer files from your home computer to the destination server. Alternatively, you can use ftp software to transfer your files. There are several versions of ftp software, but the most commonly used is *Windows FTP* (WS_FTP). When you open the ftp software, it asks you to supply the information about the destination server and the location on that server for your files. You will need to find out from your lab supervisor or instructor the correct information to provide so that your files will be transferred to the proper location on the destination

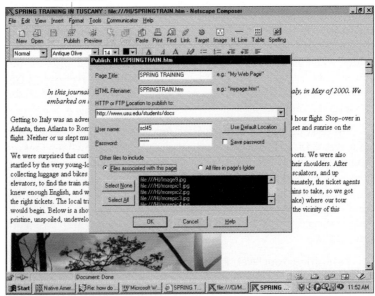

FIGURE 15.2 Publishing a Web Page with *Netscape Composer*

server (see Figure 15.3). In Figure 15.3, notice that there are basically two windows; the one on the left shows the drives, directories, and files on your local computer system (that is, the computer and network you are currently using); the one on the right shows those on the destination computer system (that is, the host server, called here the "remote system"). The arrows in between the two windows are used to transfer the files back and forth between the two computer systems.

Publishing Your Web Pages with an ISP. Finally, in addition to publishing your Web pages on your campus server, it is also possible to publish them on other Internet Service Providers (ISPs), such as AOL or Microsoft Network or on "free" sites offered by such companies on the Web as GeoCities (http://geocities.com) or Angel Fire (http://angelfire.com). The downside of these free sites is that advertising banners will automatically be included along with your Web pages.

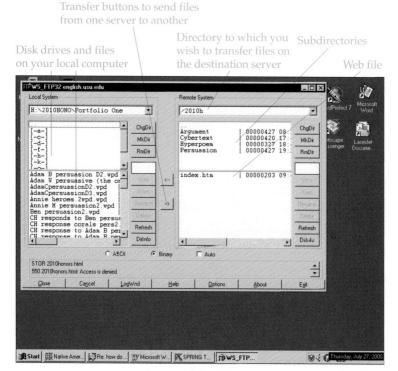

FIGURE 15.3 Publishing a Web Page with *Windows FTP*

AUDIO

Organize content with basic design elements.

Basic Design Elements. As you think about your Web site, you will need to consider whether to use some basic design elements to structure the Web pages, such as tables, frames, style sheets, and java script. Depending on your site's purpose and the needs of your audience, you can select among these design options. We will provide a brief explanation below, but you will need to research them further if you wish to try them yourself (see also 16b-8).

WWW

15.3

Using tables and frames to design Web pages.

Using Tables. Tables are used by Web page authors to control page layout so that text and graphics appear on the page where they'd like them to appear. When using tables, you can decide on the number of columns and rows that will be used on each page and what data will "fill" cells formed by the intersection of those columns and rows. If you select a zero width as the table border, the table itself will not appear on the page. Instead, the table will provide you with "cells" in which you can insert appropriate data (see Figure 15.4).

Using Frames. Frames are used like tables to organize the text and graphics on a Web site. They differ from tables, though, in their ability to show in the browser window multiple files displayed in different portions of the frame. The frame itself consistently appears on

Column 1 of table   Column 2 of table

FIGURE 15.4 Using Tables to Organize Content on the Page

the page, but different Web pages may be displayed within the frame windows (see Figure 15.5).

Using Style Sheets. Style sheets provide another sophisticated way to format your Web pages. Style sheets for the Web work in much the same way as style sheets for word-processing programs. They allow you to set default elements such as fonts and colors that will then be applied uniformly to your document. For example, if you wanted all of your first-level headings to be black on a red background, you could define the header 1 style to associate the colors, fonts, and type style that you'd like them to appear in throughout your Web document.

Using Java. Java is a programming language that allows for miniature programs to be embedded into Web pages as **applets.** These

WEBLINK

http://java.sun.com
To learn more about using Java in your Web pages, go to the Sun Microsystems Web site

Table of contents with relative links to secondary pages

Scroll bar

Linked secondary pages will appear in this window

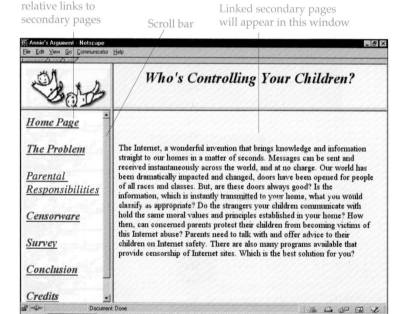

FIGURE 15.5 Using Frames to Organize Content on the Page

applets can perform functions within a larger Web page, generating information that would otherwise have been sent over the Internet. Java is a complicated language to learn and beyond the scope of this book (see Figure 15.6).

2 Deciding on a rhetorical stance

The kinds of writing decisions you must make in determining a rhetorical stance for your Web site are similar to those you confront in writing any paper (see 2a-2). Think about what knowledge and information you will need in order to write a successful Web site. You should have a clear *purpose* in mind before you start. What specific goals do you want to accomplish with your Web site? Do you intend to share your creative work? Educate your audience? Provide links as a service to readers? You should think about the *persona* that will be conveyed by your site. Do you want to seem whimsical and humorous? Professional and serious? Finally, consider your *audience*.

JavaScript Applet: Spotlight ball roves across the title.

JavaScript Applet: Scrolling text that prints the first line of the poem, "I wandered lonely as a cloud."

FIGURE 15.6 JavaScript Applets

Readers appreciate a balance between graphics and text. They like a hypertext structure that allows them to choose their own paths through the site. Finally, they appreciate helpful elements such as navigational buttons.

3 Planning navigation

Web sites begin with a homepage (the first page), which also serves as an introduction to the site. It often includes several secondary pages (relative links), which are accessed from the homepage. Each page (designated by a different filename) should be no more than two or three screens long. For high-impact pages, try limiting the length to what will fit on one screen so that readers can see the entire page at a glance without scrolling. **Links** are highlighted words and phrases within a document that allow readers to get from one page to another. **Navigational buttons** are graphical icons, such as arrows, symbols, buttons, or pictures, that will take readers in a particular direction or to a particular location. Navigational buttons may be included at the top, bottom, or one side of each page within a multipage Web site.

AUDIO
Navigational links connect content on the Web.

4 Applying the basic design principles to a Web site

Given the vast quantity of information on the World Wide Web, accommodating the busy, selective reader is imperative. The homepage is the first page readers will see when they access your site, so it should introduce your site concisely, providing an overview of the content and the organization of the site. Do not waste readers' time with decorative design elements; rather, include elements that will enhance readers' understanding of your message. Observing the basic design principles (see Chapter 14) exemplified by the three C's—clustering, contrasting, and connecting—may be even more critical to Web design than to print design. Note that some Web sites offer the reader a choice between two versions: one that is intensively graphical and one that is text-based. This option allows viewers to read the page even if they do not have a graphics-capable browser.

WWW
15.4
Examples of effective Web design.

WEBLINK

http://webdesign.about.com

Yet another fantastic Web design resource

AUDIO
Apply design principles for print to the Web.

Clustering When designing Web pages, position chunks of information that are related in meaning close to one another. Emphasize clusters of information by placing white space around them. Group important elements at the top left and lower right of the screen, as readers of the English language are trained to move their eyes from left to right. Use numbered and bulleted lists to show relationships among items in a group.

Contrasting Use contrasting fonts or font sizes to highlight basic elements. For example, you might use the largest HTML headings (H1) for titles and smaller HTML headings (H3) for any subtitles (see 16b-2). Use colors or patterns to contrast other elements on the page.

Connecting Adhering to the principle of connectedness is especially important for Web authors. Since readers can access the pages within a site in any sequence, use a design template and a consistent graphic, title, or logo to foster visual connectedness. Furthermore, because readers can easily become lost when reading hypertext, it is important to include navigational aids to connect all pieces of the Web site. One way to do so is to provide a "home" link on every secondary page that takes readers back to the homepage. You might also supply a site map on the homepage, showing how all of the pieces are connected (see Figure 15.7). It is a good idea to provide readers with alternative routes through the site's pages so that they are not forced along a single path. Busy, selective readers will appreciate the optional routes.

Some Dos and Don'ts of Web Design

Do organize your information before designing your site.

Do aim for pages that are no more than two or three screens long.

Do accommodate text-only browsers.

Do use a template and repeat visual elements.

Do study other Web pages as a way to learn new code (see 16b).

Don't include unnecessary design elements.

Don't use graphics files of over 30 K (kilobytes).

Don't use copyrighted text or graphics without permission and acknowledgment.

FIGURE 15.7 A Site Map

CHAPTER **16**

Writing for the Web

This chapter addresses some of the basics of writing for the Web—how to use HyperText Markup Language (HTML) and an HTML editor to construct basic Web pages and how to add links that attach graphical images and other documents to pages in a hypertextual "web." Even though there are Internet composers available to help you write your Web pages, it is still important to know the basics of HTML coding in order to understand how browsers are reading the code and in order to read the code of others' Web pages yourself.

VIDEO

Understanding Web compositions.

The homepage of your Web site is the first page that readers will come to when they locate your Web site by using its URL (uniform resource locator). From the homepage, you can provide **relative links** to secondary pages that you have written. You also can include on your pages **remote links** to other Web sites located elsewhere on the Internet. Although one chapter cannot possibly discuss everything there is to know about writing for the Web, you will be off to a good start if you work your way through the information provided here.

16a Construct good Web pages

AUDIO
Composing
content for
your Web
pages.

Once you have an overall plan for your Web site (see Chapter 15), you can begin to compose your Web pages. The text of a Web site—what it "says" to the reader—is as important as how it looks; Web pages communicate through both text and graphics. Thus, it is important to begin any Web project with a carefully thought-out design.

There are several methods by which to compose your Web pages—or you may use a combination of these methods:

AUDIO
Formatting
content for
your Web
pages.

1. *Use an HTML editor or composer, software that is designed to help with writing Web pages.* Some commonly used commercial HTML editors include *Macromedia Dreamweaver, Adobe PageMill, Microsoft Front Page,* or *Claris Home Page.* There are also HTML editors available in free shareware versions that can be downloaded from the Internet (e.g., *HomeSite*). To find these HTML editors, consult the Shareware Directory, which is located at <http://www.sharewaredirectory .com>. Or, you can type "HTML Editor" as a search term in a search engine (see 8c-1). The most popular Internet browsers, *Netscape* and *Explorer,* also include their own HTML editor/composer, along with useful advice and tutorials on writing Web pages. *Netscape,* for example, provides software called *Composer* that allows you to construct Web pages. Newer versions of *Explorer* allow you to move from writing Web pages in *Microsoft Word* to viewing those pages via *Explorer.* We will discuss this process in more detail in 16b-1.

2. *Use a translator program that changes a word-processing or database file into a Web file.* Newer versions of *Microsoft Word, WordPerfect, Excel,* and *PowerPoint,* for example, all include a SAVE AS HTML command, typically found in the FILE>SAVE AS menu. You may wish to elect this option when you have already written an extensive text in a word-processing program that you wish to convert into a Web file. Another plus of the translation method is that you can take full advantage of all the features found in a word-processing program (such

as spell checker, grammar checker, or thesaurus) which may not be available to you in an HTML editor or composer. (See also the HELP box on p. 284.)

3. *Use a text editing or word-processing program (e.g., Windows NotePad or Microsoft Word) and enter the HTML code by hand.* When authors first began writing in HTML for the Web, this is the method they used—that is, they typed in all of the HTML codes that the browser would need to interpret and display the Web pages. This is the most difficult and time-consuming method for composing Web pages. However, despite the help of the sophisticated editors and composers available today, sometimes it is still necessary to insert HTML codes by hand in order to achieve exactly the result you desire. It is important to understand enough HTML coding to be able to revise and rewrite the code that underlies any of your Web pages.

16b Use HTML editors and HTML codes

HyperText Markup Language (HTML) is not really a language but rather a system for embedding codes into text. These codes tell a Web browser how to display the text in the browser window. To introduce yourself to HTML, surf the Web until you find a site that you think is lively and well designed. Then view the source code by following the instructions in the Help box on page 285. In writing the code for your own pages, you can analyze the code from other Web sites

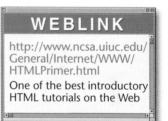

WEBLINK

http://www.ncsa.uiuc.edu/General/Internet/WWW/HTMLPrimer.html

One of the best introductory HTML tutorials on the Web

16.1

Using the NCSA's *Beginner's Guide to HTML.*

and use it as a model, as long as your pages are for educational and not commercial purposes. However, if you rely heavily on another Web page's design, be sure to credit the original site.

1 Using *Microsoft Word* or *Netscape Composer* to compose a Web page

As we mentioned in 16a, there are three methods currently used to generate HTML files: (1) using an HTML editor or composer, (2) using a translator program to save a word-processed document as an HTML file, or (3) embedding the HTML code by hand. Most Web authors begin with either method 1 or 2 but also find that they need to embed some codes by hand. So, even if you are

AUDIO

Use *Netscape Composer* and *Microsoft Word* to write Web pages.

16.2

Steps for converting a document into HTML.

HELP

How do I save a word-processing document in HTML format?

1. If your word processor allows you to save a document as HTML, just use its SAVE AS feature and specify HTML.

2. If your word processor will not save a file as HTML, then you must follow these steps:
   a. Highlight the text you want to convert to HTML, and copy it.
   b. Open your HTML editor, and paste the copied text into it.
   c. Use the HTML editor's features to format the text for the Web.

using an HTML editor that is WYSIWYG ("What You See Is What You Get"), you will still, in all probability, need to know enough HTML coding to be able to make adjustments and refinements to your HTML files. We discuss the most commonly used HTML codes in 16b-2 below. In this section of the chapter, we will spend most of our time discussing the first method—using an HTML editor or composer. As examples, we will use two common HTML editors: *Microsoft Word/Explorer* and *Netscape Composer*. For method 2, see the HELP box on this page.

16.3

Building Web pages with *Word* and *Explorer*.

Using *Microsoft Word* and *Internet Explorer* to Create Web Pages   The newest Microsoft products have been attempting to integrate Web authoring and word processing. Not only can you use the SAVE AS command in *Word* to save your document as an HTML file, but you can also construct the Web files directly in *Word* and then preview them on *Internet Explorer*. To do so, you need to be sure that the *Word* Web templates have been loaded onto your computer. These templates provide you with the HTML editor necessary to begin writing Web pages. To find the Web templates, go to the FILE menu and click on NEW. One of the tabs of templates available to you should be WEB PAGES. You will see several options (depending on your version of *Word*), including a BLANK WEB PAGE, MORE COOL STUFF, and WEB PAGE WIZARD. If you click on BLANK WEB PAGE, *Word* will construct a Web page for you that includes the basic underlying codes necessary to begin any Web document (see Figure 16.4). *Word* uses a WYSIWYG editor, so you will not see the underlying HTML codes unless you go to the VIEW menu and view the HTML source. If you

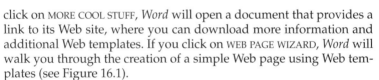

HELP

How do I view the source code of a Web page?

1. On many browsers, you can view the HTML source code of a document by selecting the appropriate menu item. Often, the command VIEW HTML SOURCE or VIEW PAGE SOURCE will bring the source code onto the screen.

2. If you cannot find a VIEW command, you can save the document to a file and then view the source code in a text editor (such as *Windows Notepad*) or word-processing program:

   a. On the FILE menu of your browser, select the SAVE or SAVE AS command to save the document to a file. (Remembering where you saved the file will be helpful when you want to view it.)

   b. Start your text editor or word-processing program.

   c. Open the file and display the code.

16.4

Steps for viewing the source code of a Web page.

click on MORE COOL STUFF, *Word* will open a document that provides a link to its Web site, where you can download more information and additional Web templates. If you click on WEB PAGE WIZARD, *Word* will walk you through the creation of a simple Web page using Web templates (see Figure 16.1).

Once you have created a Web page in *Word*, you can open that page in the *Explorer* browser to preview how it actually would look on the Internet. You must save the page first before previewing it; then, select WEB PAGE PREVIEW from the FILE menu or click on the WEB PAGE PREVIEW icon on the Web toolbar. *Word* will open the page in your default browser. You can alternate between working on your Web page in *Word* and previewing it using the Web browser. It is also possible for you to open any Web page that you have saved as a file directly in a Web browser. To do so, choose OPEN PAGE from the FILE menu of either *Explorer* or *Netscape*. A window will open that allows you to browse your disk drives and select the HTML file that you wish the browser to open. Once you have selected the appropriate file, the browser will display it in the window (see Figure 16.2).

Using *Netscape Composer* to Create Web Pages The *Netscape* Internet browser comes with an HTML editor called *Netscape Composer*. To begin creating Web pages in *Composer*, you first need to launch the *Netscape* browser. From the FILE menu, choose NEW and BLANK PAGE. This will put you in the *Composer* window. You should

16.5

Building Web pages with *Netscape Composer*.

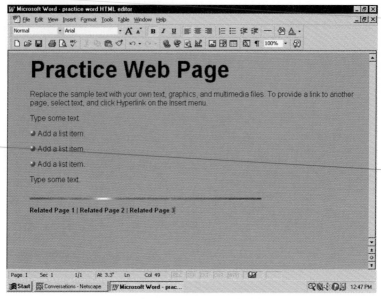

FIGURE 16.1 Practice Web Page Using *Word* Web Template

name and save the file by using the SAVE option from the FILE menu or clicking the DISK icon. Notice the toolbar at the top of the screen. You will use the tools on the toolbar to embed HTML code into your document (see Figure 16.3). However, the number of codes available from the toolbar is quite limited. To embed other HTML tags, choose HTML TAG from the INSERT menu. We will discuss the most commonly used tags in 16b-2. To find out what each of the tools on the toolbar is for, move your mouse over the icon without clicking and read the description provided. If you wish to preview your Web page, you can click on the PREVIEW icon or select BROWSE PAGE from the FILE menu. *Netscape* opens your page in a second window so that you can easily switch back and forth between the browser view and the *Composer* view as you work on your page. Remember to save and re-load your page so that you will see the newest version in your browser window.

Editing the HTML Source Code in *Word* and *Composer*
Oftentimes you will find it necessary to edit the HTML source code that the HTML editor has embedded into your Web page. To do so, you first need to go to the EDIT SOURCE option of your Web page. In *Word*, choose HTML SOURCE from the Web page VIEW menu. You may

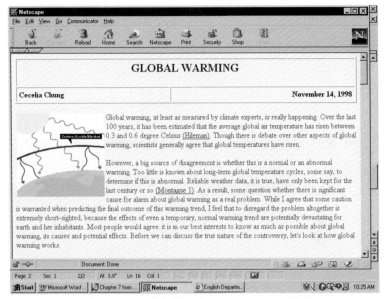

FIGURE 16.2 View of Cecelia's Web Page in Browser Window

be prompted to save your file, if you have not already done so. *Word* will provide you with a view of your HTML source code that you may edit. You can delete codes, insert additional codes, change existing codes, add text, and perform other functions. When you are finished editing, click on EXIT HTML SOURCE or close the source code window. You will once again be prompted to save your editing changes or refresh your screen upon returning to the Web document.

In *Composer*, you can also edit your source code as long as you select an external editor in which to do so. There are two ways in *Composer* to view the source code: one from the VIEW menu and one from the EDIT menu. When you click on PAGE SOURCE from the VIEW menu, you will be able to see the source code, but not edit it. However, when you click on HTML SOURCE from the EDIT menu of *Composer*, you will be prompted to select an editor for your use while editing. You can choose a shareware HTML editor, such as *HomeSite*, that you have downloaded from the Internet. Or, alternatively, you can simply choose a text editing or word-processing program, such as *Windows Notepad* or *Microsoft Word* as the program in which you wish to edit the HTML source code. If you change your mind about the editing program you wish to use, you can select PREFERENCES from the EDIT menu to change your *Composer* preferences.

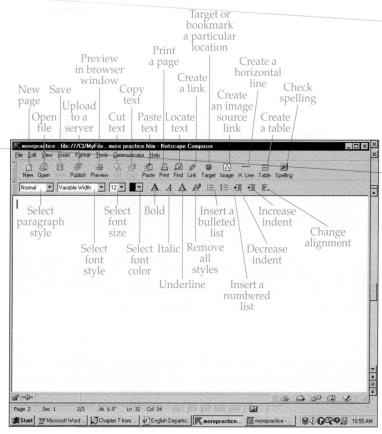

FIGURE 16.3 *Netscape Composer*—Blank Page

2 Using basic HTML codes

AUDIO

The basic principles of HTML.

As we mentioned in the previous section, there will be times when you will wish to edit the HTML codes in your Web page file by hand. To do so, you need a working knowledge of HTML. Most HTML codes, called **tags,** come in pairs: the first tag turns on the feature and the second turns it off. The second tag includes a slash, which the browser reads as signaling the end of that feature. All tags must be enclosed in angle brackets:

```
<B>Bold this sentence</B>
```

web

The pairs of HTML tags that surround the text they affect are called **containers**. Any text between the containers will be affected by the code. It does not matter whether the tag is in lowercase or uppercase letters, although it will be easier to locate the tags when you are reading the HTML source code if you type them in all caps.

Tags fall into two basic categories: **document tags,** which tell the browser how to handle major elements of the document such as the head and the body, and **appearance tags,** which tell the browser how to handle the appearance of the text. Some tags can take **attributes,** that is, codes that provide additional formatting information. For example, a header tag might include an alignment attribute, telling the browser how to place the header on the page:

```
<H1 ALIGN="center">My Title</H1>
```

Document Tags   The major document tags are HTML, head, title, and body. Your first task in composing a Web page is to enter the basic codes for these major document components. If you saved your word-processed document as an HTML file, or if you are using an HTML editor, these document tags will be entered for you.

1. *Creating the head and title.* All HTML documents begin with the tag <HTML> and end with the tag </HTML>. Within these containers, the information is divided into two major categories: head and body. Within the head of the document is included any descriptive information about the HTML document, such as date of origin, author of the page, version number, and so on. See for example the information included within the <HEAD> containers on the blank Web page in MS Word (Figure 16.4). Also included within the head is a document title, which may be different from the document's file name. It is important that you supply an accurate and descriptive title within the title containers because the title will help others to find your page when using search engines or bookmarks to navigate the Web. If you are working with a *Word Web* template or in *Netscape Composer,* you will only see the document tags when you view the HTML source code. Try opening a new Web page in *Word* or *Composer.* You will see a blank page with a toolbar at the top. Click the VIEW HTML SOURCE menu. You will now see the underlying document tags, as illustrated in Figure 16.4. To revise your title in *Composer,* select PAGE COLORS AND PROPERTIES from the FORMAT menu. In *Word,* select PROPERTIES from the FILE menu.

2. *Creating the body.* The body tag surrounds the rest of the Web file (after the head). The body tag can have a number of attributes that will specify how the body is to be interpreted by the browser. Such body attributes might include a background color or graphic,

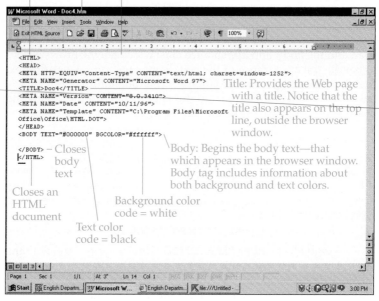

HTML: Head: Begins the header information
Begins an   (only the title will be displayed).
HTML   Title   Often includes information about the
document   Web file itself.

Title: Provides the Web page with a title. Notice that the title also appears on the top line, outside the browser window.

Closes body text

Body: Begins the body text—that which appears in the browser window. Body tag includes information about both background and text colors.

Closes an HTML document

Background color code = white

Text color code = black

FIGURE 16.4 View of HTML Document Tags for a Blank Web Page in *Microsoft Word*

text color, or link color. In Figure 16.4, notice that the body tag includes both a text color (TEXT="#000000") and a background color (BGCOLOR="#ffffff") attribute. Other attributes that might have been provided include the color of the links (LINK="green") or the color of visited links (VLINK="red"). To identify a color, your HTML editor will insert either a color code number or a color name. Either can be interpreted by the browser. In *Word*, you change the background color by selecting BACKGROUND from the FORMAT menu. In *Composer*, select PAGE COLORS AND PROPERTIES, also from the FORMAT menu. The code for the pale yellow color Cecelia selected for her on-screen background is

```
<BODY BGCOLOR="FFFFC0">
```

It is also possible to specify a graphics file as a background instead of a color. Using a background can greatly enhance the look of a page, provided it is light enough that the text shows through clearly. If Cecelia had wanted to include the graphics file name "sunpic.gif" as

a background instead of a color, the body tag attributes would have read as follows:

```
<BODY BACKGROUND="sunpic.gif">
```

3. *Creating a document comment.* Another frequently used but optional document tag is the comment tag, which always begins with an exclamation point and double dashes:

```
<!--Remember to add the link here-->
```

If you wish to insert a comment into your HTML document that will not show up as text, you can use the comment tag. As long as the appropriate code is included, the comments will not show up in the browser window. You may use comments to remind yourself of information you need to include or to provide instructions for future work on the document. Comment tags can be included anywhere within the body of the Web file.

Appearance Tags   HTML documents do not include embedded codes for typographical distinctions such as boldface, underlining, and highlighting in the same way that word processors do. To create these typographical distinctions, you must use formatting, or appearance, tags. The <H2> and </H2> appearance tags tell the browser to create a standard heading that is large and bold, and the <B> and </B> appearance tags tell the browser to boldface the words contained between the tags.

An appearance tag also must be inserted to begin a new line. The <br> tag instructs the browser to break, or begin a new line. Because the HTML system of coding assumes blocks of texts, blank lines (rather than indents) are typically used to distinguish one paragraph from the next. The <p> tag instructs the browser to insert a blank line to designate a new paragraph. Most HTML editors allow you to insert the major appearance tags (which tell the browser how to format text) with a click of your mouse (see Figure 16.5 on page 292).

3   Creating links

To provide readers with links to other documents on the World Wide Web, to other locations within the same document, or to related documents within the same Web site, you create a link. Your HTML editor will assist you in creating the link when you select the LINK icon from the toolbar. However, links can be tricky; they take a certain amount of practice and experimentation. If you know the

16.6
Details on how
to create links
on the Web.

underlying HTML code for various links, you will be able to troubleshoot by editing the HTML source code as needed.

Basic Hyperlink   Hyperlinks are coded with tags that refer to a specific Web site's URL. The basic format of a hyperlink is as follows:

```
<A HREF="http://www.webaddress.com">highlighted text</A>
```

| Anchor tag | Reference tag | URL | Hot text | Anchor tag |

The <A tag indicates the start of a hyperlink. HREF, which stands for Hypertext REFerence, refers to the address of the Web page with which you want to establish a link. In actual code, you would supply the Web address (URL) inside the quotation marks. The highlighted text becomes the **hot text,** linked to the referenced address. When the user clicks on the highlighted text, the browser will retrieve the document indicated in the hypertext reference. The </A> tag at the end closed the hyperlink.

Link to Another Web Document in the Same Web Site Often Web sites are made up of a series of documents that are linked

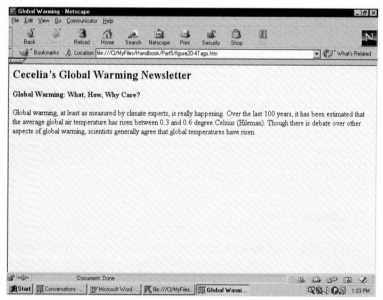

FIGURE 16.5 Browser Window After Appearance Tags Were Added

to each other. When the documents all reside at the same location (in the same directory or folder) within the Web server, the links are called relative links and you do not need to include the entire URL. Simply supply the appropriate file name inside the quotation marks and then, in your highlighted text, describe the page you want linked.

```
<A HREF="ceceliap2.html">next page</A>
```

Anchor   Reference File name   Hot   Anchor
tag   tag   text   tag

In Figure 16.6, hyperlinks connect Cecelia's homepage to her secondary Web page via relative links. When a reader points to the highlighted word using a mouse, a small hand appears, indicating a link, and the file name or URL for the link appears in the lower left-hand portion of the browser's screen. When the reader clicks on the highlighted word, the browser links to the Web file or URL indicated.

Link to a Specific Location on the Web Page   You can provide a link to a destination on the same Web page, allowing the reader to

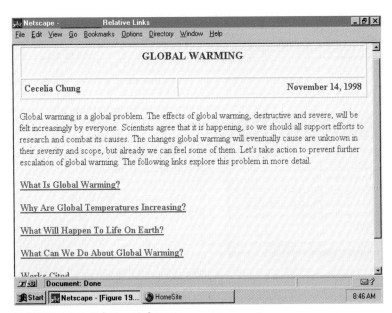

FIGURE 16.6 Relative Links

jump quickly from one part of the document to another. To jump within a single Web page, insert the name of a location that you have bookmarked or targeted instead of the URL inside the quotation marks:

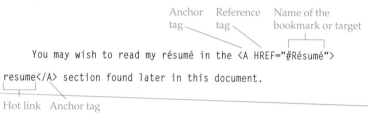

Anchor tag   Reference tag   Name of the bookmark or target

```
You may wish to read my résumé in the <A HREF="#Résumé">
resume</A> section found later in this document.
```

Hot link   Anchor tag

To show the browser where the linked text begins, you also need to name a destination tag (also called a bookmark or a target in some HTML editors). The destination tag indicates the point to which the browser should jump:

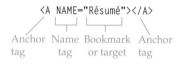

```
<A NAME="Résumé"></A>
```

Anchor tag   Name tag   Bookmark or target   Anchor tag

4 Locating images

Many wonderful images can be found on the Web. However, you need to be aware that all graphics, by virtue of their publication on the Web, are automatically copyrighted by the author. To use another person's graphics from a Web site, you must secure that person's permission. If an email address is included at a site, you can email the person and ask his or her permission to replicate the graphic on your site. Or, you may find a statement on the page permitting certain limited, noncommercial uses of the graphics. Remember: Using someone else's graphic on your own site without prior permission is a form of plagiarism (see 10a-3).

WEBLINK

http://www.snowcrest.net/kitty/hpages

The PageWorks homepage discusses fair use of graphics and has links to numerous image directories on the Web

Many sites on the Web were created specifically to make images available for use by others. A search engine will help you locate these images. For example, the InfoSeek search engine includes an Image-Seek directory. Or, you can search by name for the image you are looking for. For example, if you are looking for a picture of a tiger, you can instruct the search engine to search for "tiger image."

5 Inserting images

To include graphical images in a Web document, you need to insert a code, called an **image source tag,** in the body of the page telling the browser where to locate the image. Your HTML editor will assist you in creating the image source tag when you click the IMAGE or INSERT PICTURE icon on the Web tool bar. Image source tags allow you to incorporate into your document many kinds of graphical images, such as photographs, clip art, drawings, icons, charts and graphs, and animations. The basic format for the image source tag is as follows:

16.7
Instructions for
adding images
to a Web page.

```
<IMG SRC="gwarmpic.gif">
```
    Image   File name
  source tag

Include within the quotation marks the name of the image file you wish to use. The graphical image itself is not located within the HTML document; rather, it is linked to the document. The image source tag tells the browser to retrieve the appropriate graphics file (see Figure 16.7 for a browser window view). You must indicate the exact directory path in your image source tag so that the browser can locate the image's source.

AUDIO
Troubleshoot-
ing when
graphics do
not open.

Providing Text Alternatives to Images It is a courtesy to use the ALT tag as an attribute along with image source tags so that all users will receive a text explanation for what appears in a graphics box. Having an ALT tag is important for users who have turned off graphics to increase the speed of their browsers as well as for visually impaired users who have special browsers that "read" to them the information that appears on the screen. To allow all visitors to your site to see descriptive text of an image, add the following ALT tag within the image source tag itself:

```
<IMG SRC="sunpic.gif" ALT="Sun Graphic">
```
    Image   File name   ALT   Alternative text
  source tag   tag   description

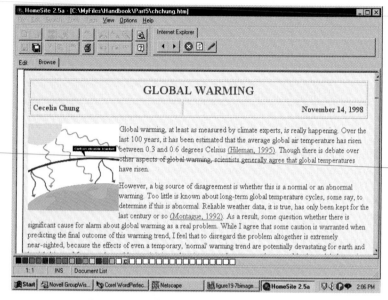

FIGURE 16.7 Browser Window After Image Source Tags Were Added

Aligning Images and Text When you insert an image into a document, the written text that follows the image tag will normally be aligned with the bottom of the graphic. If you want the text to appear somewhere else, you need to include the appropriate attribute in your image source tag:

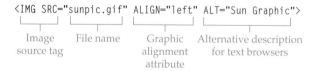

```
<IMG SRC="sunpic.gif" ALIGN="left" ALT="Sun Graphic">
```

| Image source tag | File name | Graphic alignment attribute | Alternative description for text browsers |

The ALIGN="left" code tells the browser to put the graphic to the left of the text. The text will wrap around the graphic. Other possible alignments include "right," which puts the graphic to the right of the text, and "center," which centers the graphic. If you do not want the words to wrap around the graphic, use the <BR CLEAR="left"> or the <BR CLEAR="right"> code. If you just want the text to drop down below the graphic before it resumes, include the break tag <br> as the next command following the image source tag. An HTML editor can make this alignment process easier. In *Word* or

HELP

How do I save an image from the Internet to my computer?

1. Locate an image on the Internet that is not protected by copyright.
2. Click on the image. (PC users should use the right mouse button.)
3. Select SAVE IMAGE AS on the menu that comes up.
4. The original file name will be displayed in the dialog box. Give the graphic a new name, if desired. (It will already be in a *gif* or *jpg* format, since these are the graphical formats that can be read by Internet browsers.)
5. Choose an appropriate directory or folder on your hard drive or disk for the graphics file.

You can now insert your graphics file into an HTML document by using the image source tag (see 16b-5).

NOTE: Some operating systems and browsers will not provide a menu in response to a mouse click.

16.8
Steps for saving an image from the Internet.

Composer you can simply click and drag the image to the appropriate location.

Sizing Your Images If you include images in your Web page, you will need to give the browser a size command that tells it how many pixels wide and high each picture should be when displayed on the screen. To avoid distorting the image, it is better to size the graphic before you save it rather than using the size codes in your image source tag. However, size code can be used to make minor adjustments to the width and height of the image after it has been saved as a file.

6 Scanning pictures

You may wish to scan your own photographs or graphics and save them as graphics files. To use a scanner, you will need basic instructions from your lab supervisor or instructor. Remember that graphics files should not exceed 30–50 K (kilobytes) in size. For advice on how to size your graphic appropriately, see the Help box on page 299.

7 Inserting your address

You should include your name, address, and the date of posting on any Web site you author (preferably at the bottom of every page). To do so, enclose your name, the dates on which the site was posted or last updated, your email address, plus any copyright or acknowledgment information within a pair of address tags, <address> and </address>. In order to link your email address, use the following code, entering the appropriate information within the address containers.

Address tag

```
<address>Cecelia Chung<br>

Established: 14 November 1998, Last Updated: 25 January
```

1999

Anchor   Reference   Mail tag   Hot   Close
tag   tag   and address   text   anchor tag

```
<A HREF=mailto:cecelia@cc.usu.edu>cecelia@cc.usu.edu</A>
```

```
</address>
```
Address tag

This coding follows the typical pattern of links: the first part after HREF tells the browser what email address should be linked, and the second part indicates the text to be highlighted on the page. When readers click on the highlighted text, they will be provided with an email screen that includes space to type an email message.

8 Using tables and frames

To place information appropriately on a page, you can use a table, which divides the page both vertically and horizontally into cells. The individual cells can vary in size, have borders of various types (either visible or invisible), and contain text or graphics. Tables allow Web authors to display information in vertical columns, for example. Most HTML editors will help you create a table. Or, you can create a table in your word-processing program; then the table will

HELP

How do I revise a graphic?

1. Launch your graphics program, such as *PhotoShop*, and open the graphics file you wish to revise.

2. Find the menu item that allows you to resize images. You may be able to use either pixels or inches to adjust width and height.

3. Change any other aspects of the graphic that need revising, such as shading, contrast, and sharpness.

4. Check the size of the graphics file to make sure that you have not made the file too large to load easily on the Web (30–50 K is a reasonable size; navigation graphics should be less than 10 K).

5. Resave the graphic. Be sure it is still in a *gif* or *jpg* format, since these are the graphical formats that can be read by Internet browsers. To be the most efficient, save multi-colored graphics as *jpg* files and graphics with few colors as *gifs*.

16.9

Steps for altering images with *PhotoShop.*

be converted into HTML code automatically when you save the document as an HTML file.

Another way Web authors divide information is by using frames to put the information into different windows on the page. It is beyond the scope of this handbook to describe writing in frames. However, most HTML editors provide such instruction, as do guidebooks on HTML authoring.

9 Using other media

In addition to using visual images to enhance your Web documents, you can also use other types of media, such as audio and video, to complement your discussion. However, it is important to remember that you should use only media elements that are integral to the meaning of your Web pages. Most Web users have experienced Web pages in which the multimedia applications overwhelm and obscure the message of the site: audio clips that automatically begin when you enter the page, visuals that take forever to load, and so on. When not used appropriately, multimedia components are distractions or irritations to your readers.

If audio or video media seem appropriate to your Web document, then be sure that you integrate such elements smoothly into the flow of your writing and explain them to your readers. For example, a student writing a Web document about singer Jimmy Buffet naturally wanted to incorporate into the site audio clips of some of Buffet's songs. The student found audio clips readily available on the Internet; he downloaded the files and saved them to his own computer. Then, he placed links to the sound files into his document at the appropriate places, along with icons that indicated the nature and size of each audio clip. By clicking on the audio link icon, the reader could hear the Buffet song. If you want to use sounds that are not readily available on the Internet, you can record your own sounds with the appropriate microphone and software, save the recordings as audio files, and add links to them in your Web document.

Whenever you add multimedia elements to your pages, be certain that you consider the "load time" of the clip. Video and audio files tend to be quite large—and hence take a long time to load into a browser. Waiting endlessly for a video clip to load can be extremely irritating to a reader. It is best to give readers a choice as to whether to load a file or not. Also, indicate somewhere the size of the file so that readers can anticipate how long it will take to load. To shorten load time, you can use excerpts of files or still shots from videos instead of the entire files. It just makes good rhetorical sense to consider your readers when incorporating multimedia elements into your Web documents.

10 Creating a template

Once you have created your homepage, you may want to design or customize your own template. It is easier for readers if all the pages at your site have the same look. The template should include elements such as background information, fonts, colors, headers, navigational buttons, author information, and your email address, if it will appear on all secondary pages at your site as well as your homepage. Save the template as a separate document, and title it template.htm. Then, each time you begin a new page for your site, you can open the template and use the SAVE AS option to save it under that page's designated file name.

Here is a sample template:

```
<html>

<head>

<title>Your site's name</title>
```

```
</head>

<BODY BGCOLOR="red">

<H2>The page's title as a number 2 heading</H2>

<!--Place the page's text here, including all relative and

remote links.-->

<p>

<A HREF="http:URL of your homepage">Home</A>

<!--This link will return to homepage-->

<Address>

Created by (Your Name)<br>

Established: (date), Last Updated: (date)<br>

<AHREF=mailto:yourlogin@yourschool.edu>yourlogin@yourschool.edu</A>

</address>

<!--This links to your email address-->

</body>

</html>
```

16c   Refine your Web site

Once you have created your homepage and secondary pages, review them carefully to ensure that the text is correct, the links are accurate, the graphics are well located, and the overall look of the site is pleasing. Refine your Web site, using the HTML editor of your choice. Preview your pages in the browser window from time to time to see how the site is shaping up. It would be a good idea to review the design principles in Chapters 14 and 15 at this time.

AUDIO
Revise areas of your site that need improvement.

1 Checking the text

Web texts should be written in simple, direct sentences that speak to all visitors to the site. You should typically use the second person "you" when addressing your readers. Since many readers may enter your site via secondary pages rather than the homepage, make certain that the text on each page is explanatory enough to stand on its own.

Be sure that the text of your page is absolutely correct—there should be no spelling or punctuation errors. Some HTML editors do not have spell checkers, so you should carefully spell-check the text through your word-processing program prior to saving it as an HTML file. Proofreading is more difficult on screen than on paper, so you might want to print out a copy of your Web site for proofreading. (See also the editing and proofreading advice in Chapter 4.) When you post your work to the Web, it will be published in a forum that can be read by anyone anyplace in the world. You want your site to reflect well on you and to highlight your abilities as a writer.

2 Checking the relative links

The relative links—to other Web pages on the same site and to other destinations on the same Web page—should all work in the browser window. If they do not, go back to the editing HTML source window and check your codes. Internet browsers are extremely literal—if a period or a quotation mark is missing in the code, the link will not work.

3 Checking the remote links

The remote links—to Web sites other than your own—should all be checked with the Internet browser. Open each page in the browser to ensure that all of the links connect you to the correct location on the Web. If they do not, you need to go back to the HTML editing window to check your codes. The URL for the link must be typed *exactly* as it is listed at the site or the link will not work. When you link to another person's Web site, as a courtesy, you should notify that person by email of your intention. Also be certain that you have given clear attribution to all information used from a remote site so as not to give a false impression that someone else's work is your own.

4 Checking the graphics

When you view your document in the HTML editor's browser window, the graphics that you have included should appear. If something is wrong, the browser will display an icon instead of the graphic. When an icon appears, first check the code for image source tags. Each graphics file name needs to be listed in the image source tag in exactly the same way as it is in your folder. Second, check the location of your graphics file. Either the graphics file must be in the same folder on your disk or hard drive as the HTML document file or you must provide the exact path, including all subfolders.

5 Checking the overall look

As a final check, open your Web site in your Internet browser (using the OPEN FILE IN BROWSER option from the FILE menu). Try to read the site as an objective reader might. Does the rhetorical stance you wish to portray (persona, purpose, audience) come across? Ask a friend, a classmate, or your instructor to view your site and give you feedback. Did he or she have any trouble with navigation? What impression did your site leave?

16d Transfer your site to an Internet server

Prior to sending the Web files to your Internet server, be certain that your site is exactly as you want it to be. Once the files are on the server, they will stay there until you send them again. You cannot edit your Web site from the server. Rather, you have to edit the files in the HTML editor and transfer them again, overwriting the original files. Use FTP (file transfer protocol) or PUBLISHER to send your Web files to the Internet server.

Web Site Checklist

Planning and Designing

Have I planned for my content to be useful and relevant?

Have I considered my rhetorical stance: audience, purpose, persona?

Have I considered a diversity of audiences and purposes?

Does my plan take advantage of the hypertext medium?

Have I designed a site that will use an appropriate number of secondary pages, so my site doesn't have "linkitis" from too many links?

Have I considered the 3 C's of design: clustering, contrasting, connecting?

Have I planned my navigation so that it will be user-friendly and intuitive?

(continued)

Web Site Checklist *(continued)*

Implementing

Have I created folders, directories, and subdirectories to store my Web pages appropriately?

Have I used file names and graphics files that the Web can recognize?

Have I used a template so my pages are consistent and have a coherent "look"?

Have I determined which graphics will enhance the meaning of my hypertext and not included any extraneous ones?

Have I used only those technologies that are appropriate and accessible to my intended audience?

Have I included "functional redundancy," that is, is repetition used effectively on different pages?

Have I obtained permissions for any copyrighted materials I have used on my Web pages?

Is the writing on all my pages clear, direct, and correct?

Do all my links work and are all my graphics appearing in the right place?

Does the overall "look" of my Web site show the principles of design (clustering, contrasting, connecting)?

Does the entire site seem coherent, readable, and user-friendly?

Special Purpose Writing

FAQs

6 Special Purpose Writing

CHAPTER 17

Using Electronic Communications

Using electronic mail, you can communicate with others around the world, much faster than through traditional "snail mail." Because it is fast, easy, and relatively inexpensive, email is enormously popular.

There may be several options available to you for accessing your email. Through its email program (called a mail client), your college may provide you with access to an email account on its Internet server. Or, you may use your Web browser's email program to read your mail. Finally, you may have access to a local mail client that resides on your own computer, such as *Eudora* or *Outlook*.

VIDEO
Levels of formality in email messages.

VIDEO
Participating in electronic conversations.

17a Locate email addresses

Email addresses have two parts: the user name and the domain name. These parts are separated by the @ sign, as in mparker@cc.mtu .edu. Collect frequently used email addresses just as you might phone numbers. Store these addresses in the address book on your mail client so that you do not have to retype them each time you want to send a message.

To find the address of someone on your own campus, go to your college's homepage on the Web and look for an email directory of students, faculty, and staff. To search for the address of someone on another campus, go to one of the Web search engines and type in the name of the college as the search term. For example, if you wanted to contact a friend at Washington University, you would type "Washington University" as the search term. Once you found and opened the university's homepage, you could look for your friend's address in the student email directory. Note, however, that not all schools allow outside access to their student directories.

Here are some other Internet sites that offer help in locating email addresses:

Bigfoot   *http://www.bigfoot.com*
WhoWhere   *http://www.whowhere.lycos.com*
Yahoo! People Search   *http://people.yahoo.com*
Internet Address Finder   *http://www.iaf.net*
Usenet Addresses Database   *http://usenet-addresses.mit.edu*
World Email Directory   *http://www.worldemail.com*

17.1

Step-by-step
instructions for
sending email.

HELP

How do I send an email message?

1. Open the email program (mail client) that you wish to use. Some common ones are *Outlook, Eudora,* or *Hotmail.*

2. Select NEW MESSAGE, and type the recipient's address in the "to" or "send" slot. (To reply to a message, click your mouse on the REPLY option rather than NEW MESSAGE. Your mail client will supply the address automatically.)

3. Type the subject on the "subject" line (for example, "Your question about our paper" or "Responding to Sara's point").

4. Type the full address of any other recipients on the "cc" line.

5. Type your email message, and then send it.

NOTE: If the program notifies you that the message has been returned, check the address in one of the directories listed on page 305.

Such email directories are not always comprehensive. If you cannot find someone's email address by using directories, contact that person directly via regular mail or telephone and ask for his or her email address.

17b Practice good email etiquette

17.2

Some guide-
lines for
electronic
etiquette.

WEBLINK

http://www.albion.com/netiquette/

A great netiquette homepage

Internet users have developed a set of rules to help keep the medium friendly and courteous. These rules have been nicknamed **netiquette.**

Behaviors that are not acceptable in other settings, such as verbal or sexual harassment, will not be tolerated on the Internet. Additionally, it is not appropriate to use your classmates' or employer's email addresses for chain letters, advertising, or other similar purposes. Nor is it appropriate to use those addresses to ask someone out on a date. Also, be sensitive about "flaming"—writing angry or abusive messages. If you are flamed, do not reply in kind. Either ignore the message or respond calmly.

Netiquette

- Always type a subject heading for your email that describes the message's content. Use the REPLY function to maintain continuity on a topic.
- Use an appropriate salutation. For informal messages, you can just begin with the person's name. For business messages, use the standard business salutation and form of address (for example, "Dear Ms. Smith:").
- Keep messages brief and to the point.
- End messages with your name and email address. Keep this information in your AUTOTEXT file or store it as a macro or the equivalent in your word processor. Alternatively, if your email program allows you to create and store a signature file, you can insert it at the end of your message with a click of the mouse. (Note: Some mail clients automatically attach the signature file, once it has been established.)
- Do not forward a message you received unless you have a compelling reason to do so. When people send you an email message, they are communicating with *you*, not with some undetermined person to whom you might forward the message.
- Do not quote from an email message unless the writer has given you explicit permission to do so.
- Be careful about punctuation and spelling—but also be tolerant of others' errors. Email is less formal than many other types of writing, and many people neglect to proofread their messages because of the conversational nature of the medium.
- Avoid using all capital letters in email messages because it is the electronic equivalent of shouting. Do not overuse punctuation—especially exclamation points.
- Carefully consider the potential effect of your message before you send it. If there is any chance that the message could be misinterpreted by the reader, take time to revise it.

AUDIO
The importance of netiquette.

17c Use file attachments

17.3

Tips for
using file
attachments.

Many email systems allow you to attach files or documents to your messages. Check your mailing system for an ATTACHMENT option. Using attachments is a convenient way to send your work to a classmate for peer review or to an employer if you are away from the office. One of the advantages of using attachments over the copy-and-paste method of incorporating text into an email message is that much of your word-processing format can be preserved. Instructors may ask that assignments be turned in as attachments so that they can see the exact formatting of your bibliography, for example, or the way in which you have formatted subheadings in your paper.

Sending attachments can pose problems, however. Compatibility between email systems is often an issue. For an attachment to be read by an email recipient, the sender's and the recipient's mailing systems must be compatible. Some experimenting may be needed before you can send attachments successfully. But it is worth the effort to investigate this feature because of the ease with which you can then share your writing.

17d Use instant messaging

Another feature of email communication is called instant messaging. This feature allows you to create a circle of email friends, classmates, or colleagues who are also users of the same network (e.g., *AOL* or *MSN*). The instant messaging service will notify you whenever someone on your email group list is also online so that you can begin a "chat" session with that person via the network, should you desire to do so. (You will not be added to someone's instant messaging circle without your prior approval.) With instant messaging, you can see when your friends are online and exchange instant messages with them. You can chat with them either individually or with up to four of them in the same conversation window. The automatic typing indicator lets you know when one of your friends is typing a response.

If you and a group of your peers are working together on a collaborative project, it might be worthwhile for all of you to set up email accounts on the same service. *MSN*, for example, allows anyone to set up a *Yahoo!* email account free of charge. Once everyone in your group has an email account on the same network, you can set up your instant messaging directory with everyone's email address in the group. Then, whenever anyone else from the group is online, your computer will send you a notice to inform you of that fact. Or, you can "call" a person's email to find out if that person is available for a chat. This is just another form of online communication that can instantly put you in touch with others who are also online.

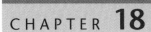

CHAPTER **18**

Writing about Literature

Readers of literary works ask interpretive or analytical questions: What sort of work is it? Does it have a powerful message? Much of the writing done in college literature courses is interpretive or analytical and seeks to answer such questions. Instructors generally expect students to make a claim about a literary work and then support that claim through reasoned arguments and evidence from the work itself and from other scholars (see Chapter 6). Your goal in writing interpretively or analytically is to shed light on an aspect of the work that the reader might not otherwise see.

WEBLINK

http://www.crayne.com/howcrit.html

"How to Critique Fiction"—an excellent introduction to literary analysis

18.1

A guide to the process of literary analysis.

18a   Read literature critically

Begin by reading the work critically. Using the following critical reading process when you read a piece of literature will start you on the way to writing an interpretive or analytical essay.

First, read the work straight through, with an eye toward understanding the text and noting its impressions on you as a reader. Does the work make you feel happy or sad? Is there a character, event, or scene that is particularly moving or striking? Does anything in the text confuse or puzzle you? Keep a journal (either on a computer disk or in a notebook) in which you jot down impressions as you read.

Once you have finished reading the work, skim it in its entirety to highlight important passages, such as scenes that are pivotal to the plot, revealing character descriptions, and vivid descriptive passages. Then try writing a brief plot outline for the work to be sure that you have a clear sense of the chronology. You might also list key characters and their relationships to each other.

Finally, review your marginal notes, outline, and lists to determine what aspects of the work interested you most. Try freewriting at your computer or in your journal for ten minutes (see 2b-2), recalling your overall impressions and any important points you may have overlooked earlier.

18b Determine purpose, persona, and audience

Once you have completed your critical reading, you should establish a rhetorical stance for your paper (see 2a-2). In determining your rhetorical stance, you will make decisions about your purpose for writing, your persona, and your intended audience. If you are writing to complete an assignment, begin by carefully studying the assignment itself.

To decide on your purpose for writing, look for key terms in the assignment, such as *analyze* or *discuss.* Both of these terms imply an interpretive or analytical purpose for writing (see 21a-3). Your instructor may have specified some aspect of the work that you should write about, or he or she may have left the topic open-ended. In most cases, your instructor will expect you to write a piece with an argumentative edge that makes a point about the work and supports that point with examples and illustrations from the text.

Next, think about your persona for the paper. How do you wish to come across as a writer? Will you be objective and fair or heated and passionate? Your persona is revealed in the paper through the words and sentence structures you choose.

Finally, ask yourself who the audience for the paper will be. Most often the audience, in addition to your teacher, will be intelligent readers who are interested in literature but who may not be acquainted with the particular text you are writing about. Your paper should provide your readers with background information about the text so that they will be able to follow your argument.

18c Develop a claim and write a thesis

How you interpret or analyze a work of literature will depend on what you have read, your interests, your prior knowledge, the information presented in class, and your general understanding of the work in question. If you have a choice, you should write about something that interests or intrigues you about the work. You will need to come up with your own critical interpretation or analysis of the work and then write a thesis statement that articulates your claim.

Literary works are typically analyzed with respect to some major aspect such as characters or plot. Aspects of Literary Works lists various questions you can use in arriving at a thesis related to one of the major aspects of literary works. The list does not cover every possible topic, but it should help you get started.

Aspects of Literary Works

Characters (Major Actors)

- How convincing are the characters?
- Does a particular character's behavior seem consistent throughout the work?
- Does the author reveal the thoughts of the narrator?

Plot (What Happens)

- How effective is the plot?
- Does it hold your interest and build to an effective climax?
- Does the plot line seem well connected or is it disjointed and hard to follow? What difference might this make to an interpretation of the work?

Theme (Major Idea or Main Message)

- What is the overall theme or point that the work is trying to make?
- Is the point one that you agree with?
- Does the author convince you that the point is well taken?
- Is the theme used consistently throughout the work, or are there contradictions?

Structure (Organization)

- What is the structure, or overall design, of the text itself?
- Does it skip around chronologically or geographically?

(continued)

Aspects of Literary Works *(continued)*

- Does one chapter lead logically to the next?
- What is the author trying to accomplish with the particular structure he or she has chosen?

Setting (Where and When the Events Take Place)

- How has the author used setting?
- Are descriptions of people and places particularly vivid?
- Did you feel as though you were in the place being described?
- How well did the author recreate a sense of place?

Point of View (Perspective of Whoever Presents the Ideas)

- What is the point of view adopted by the writer?
- Who is the narrator?
- Did the narrator color the way you reacted to the work?
- Does the point of view remain consistent?

Rhythm (Meter or Beat) and Rhyme (Correspondence in the Sounds of Words)

- Are there striking rhythmic patterns or rhyme schemes?
- What is the impact of the work's language?

Imagery (Visual Impressions Created) and Figures of Speech (Metaphors and Similes)

- Did the author use imagery and figures of speech effectively?
- Is a particular image repeated throughout the work?

Symbolism (Use of Familiar Ideas to Represent Something Else) and Archetypes (Traditional Models after Which Others Are Patterned)

- How have symbols and archetypes been used in the work?
- Does the author repeat a certain key symbol? To what purpose?
- Is there a mythical archetype at work? How effective is it?

(continued)

Aspects of Literary Works *(continued)*

Tone and Voice (Persona of the Author as Reflected Through Word Choice and Style)

- What tone or voice has the writer adopted?
- Is the tone appropriate to the theme? To the characters?
- How does the writer's tone affect you as a reader?

18d   Use the appropriate person and tense

In writing interpretively about literature, it is generally appropriate to use the first person (*I, we, our*) to express your own point of view: "*I* was greatly moved by the character's predicament." However, in academic papers, the third person (*he, she, it, they*) is typically used to discuss information found in sources.

Also, in writing about a work of literature, the commonly accepted practice is to use the present tense (sometimes called the *literary present*) when describing events that happened in the work: "Adam Trask *learns* about his wife's true character slowly." Similarly, use the present tense when discussing what an author has done in a specific literary work: "Steinbeck *uses* Cathy and Adam Trask to illustrate his point about the pure evil that *exists* in human nature."

18e   Write your literature paper

Once you have articulated a thesis, you can proceed to write your paper, following the advice in Part 1 of this handbook. In particular, it would be wise to review the Stages of the Writing Process. If your assignment specifies that you support your thesis through research, follow the advice in Part 2 of this handbook on researching your topic. For model student papers using MLA format, see pages 44 and 204 and the following paper that analyzes a poem by Elizabeth Bishop on pages 314–316.

18.2

Two model
literary analysis
papers.

Student and course number

Wayne Proffitt

Last name and page number in upper right-hand corner

English 1116-03

Double-spaced

May 15, 2002

Emotional Distance and Loss in a Poem

by Elizabeth Bishop

Thesis

Elizabeth Bishop (1911-1979) has only recently been recognized as one of the greatest poets of the 20th century (Burt). Bishop wrote one poem specifically about loss and accepting it. She offers her knowledge with humor and a casual air in "One Art." It seems that this poem may be autobiographical, as it describes not only things that people in general tend to lose but also specific items that the poet herself has lost during her lifetime. The reader is led through a list of lost objects that the speaker claims were

Words of the author in quotation marks

meant to be lost. "So many things seem filled with the intent" that when they finally do get lost it "is no disaster." The reader is advised--in a casual way--to get used to losing things and to practice getting better at letting go. The ironic encouragement of "the art of losing isn't hard to master" helps to make clear the speaker's real emotions and attitudes towards losing.

Proffitt 2

 The humorous and casual voice of the speaker becomes quite forced towards the end of the poem, however, and we suspect that the loss of her loved one was not really one that could be shrugged off. It is almost as if the speaker is trying to gear herself up for the final loss by convincing herself that there is nothing she cannot handle losing. With this armor in place, she attempts to deal with the grief of losing one well-loved, but finds that in the end she cannot hold her nonchalance and indifference steadily enough. At this point, perhaps both the speaker and the reader suddenly feel the art of losing for what it really is--an inevitable task--and that it can truly be "disaster" for the one who has lost. The remembered "joking voice, a gesture I love" bring a real beloved person into the poem and emphasize the enormity of the loss. The speaker has difficulty completing the closing sentence and must goad herself to "write it" and be done.

 The ability to create such distance between the speaker and the object being discussed increases the impact of the submerged emotion when it is finally allowed to surface. The very distance

Interpretation of the change in voice

Interpretation of the meaning of loss in the poem

Emotional impact of the poem

Proffitt 3

of this poem's opening stanzas is one of the
reasons that the emotional loss at the end of the
poem contains so much power. Personal suffering and
loss is not openly exposed in this poem, and
because of this, careful reading is necessary to
see past the distance crafted into the poem. The
effort of seeing more than is directly stated
contributes to the reader's eventual understanding
and even sharing of the sense of loss.

Proffitt 4

Works Cited

Source   Bishop, Elizabeth. "One Art." The Complete Poems
        1927-1979 by Elizabeth Bishop. New York:
        Farrar, 1983. 215.
        Burt, Steve. "Elizabeth Bishop's 'One Art': A
Internet   Review." Harvard Advocate 1998. 20 Apr. 1998
        <http://hcs.harvard.edu/ nadvocate/main.html>.

CHAPTER **19**

Business Writing

In business writing, you are often addressing multiple readers who may choose to only skim your writing, rather than read it thoroughly. Thus, when writing letters, memos, reports, proposals, and other forms of business correspondence, you must get to the point quickly and convey your message clearly and concisely.

19a Write concise and professional business letters

Business letters typically are addressed to a specific person, but they may be circulated to other readers as well. Thus, you should make the purpose of your letter clear at the outset, and you should anticipate the possibility that someone other than the addressee (an assistant, for example) might read it. Be sure to provide whatever background information these readers might need. Be clear and concise (see Chapter 31), and try to strike a friendly, courteous, and professional tone (see 36c).

The appropriate format and style depend on the medium. Letters that are mailed or faxed tend to be more formal and have a more traditional format than letters sent by email. (See Chapter 17 for a discussion of email.)

19.1

Samples and guidelines for professional writing.

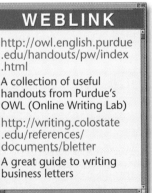

WEBLINK

http://owl.english.purdue.edu/handouts/pw/index.html

A collection of useful handouts from Purdue's OWL (Online Writing Lab)

http://writing.colostate.edu/references/documents/bletter

A great guide to writing business letters

The traditional business letter is printed on white or light-colored 8½" × 11" stationery, with every line starting at the left margin (this is known as the *full block* format). For the salutation, use *Dear Mr. ___* or *Dear Ms. ___* or an appropriate title. Avoid using either a first name (unless you know the recipient personally) or a generic

Guidelines for Email Business Letters

1. Use the subject line to orient the reader.
2. Provide any necessary background information in the first sentence; if appropriate, reference previous correspondence.
3. Quickly establish your purpose.
4. Focus on the main point, and repeat it at least once.
5. Use simple sentences and short paragraphs.
6. Use personal pronouns and active verbs.
7. Keep it short.
8. Use correct grammar and spelling.

phrase such as *Dear Sir.* If you are unsure of the recipient's gender, use the full name: *Dear Terry Norman.* If you do not know the recipient's name, use an institutional title or position: *Dear Service Department.* The body of the letter should be divided into block paragraphs, although you may want to use an indented list to draw the reader's attention to special information. Use a conventional closing such as *Sincerely, Sincerely yours,* or *Yours truly.* A sample business letter in the traditional format is shown in Figure 19.1.

19b Write specifically tailored letters of application

AUDIO
Proofread job letters and résumés.

WEBLINK

http://www.io.com/~hcexres/tcm1603/acchtml/lettov.html

All about business correspondence and résumés

A letter of application has the same general format as a business letter. It should be brief (no more than one page). The first paragraph should state clearly what position you are applying for. The next paragraph or two should describe your primary credentials for the position. The closing paragraph should express your desire for an interview and give the reader information about your availability. The tone of the letter should be polite, confident, and enthusiastic, but not pushy. A sample letter of application is shown in Figure 19.2.

2222 Stockton Street ⎤⎯ Return Address
Austin, TX 78701 ⎦

January 10, 2003 ⎤⎯ Date

Margaret Weston, Owner ⎤
Cliffside Climbing Gym
3345 S. Laurel Street ⎤⎯ Address
Waco, TX 76712 ⎦

Dear Ms. Weston: ⎤⎯ Salutation

I am a senior in Communication at the University of
Texas. For my class project in market research, I am
studying the recent proliferation of climbing gyms in
the United States. I would like to conduct several case
studies of climbing gyms and am writing to see if I may
include your gym among them.

To conduct my research, I would like to interview you,
your assistants, and several of your regular clients. Any
information I gather would be held in strict
confidentiality.

I sincerely hope you can help me with this research.
Unless I hear from you first, I will call next week to see
if you can accommodate my request.

Yours truly, ⎤⎯ Closing

Lorinda Brown
lorinda.brown@emx.cc.utexas.edu
Tel. (555) 580-5625

FIGURE 19.1 Sample Business Letter

2222 Stockton Street
Austin, TX 78701

February 4, 2003

Mr. Jeffrey Lee
Director of Marketing Training
Future Consumer, Inc.
4444 North Sycamore Avenue
Los Angeles, CA 90009

Dear Mr. Lee:

I am writing to apply for acceptance into your marketing training program. As a marketing student at the University of Texas, I believe I am ready to undertake this challenge and would welcome the opportunity to prove myself.

Marketing has been a major focus of my college and work experience. My studies have provided a strong foundation in communication and business. I have also had experience in product testing and merchandising through my jobs in market research and retailing. My ability to handle difficult customers earned me a promotion from direct sales to sales management.

My résumé is attached. I will be graduating in early June and would be available for training immediately thereafter. I look forward to hearing from you.

Sincerely yours,

Lorinda Brown
lorinda.brown@emx.cc.utexas.edu
Tel. (555) 580-5625

enclosure

FIGURE 19.2 Sample Letter of Application

19c   Write appropriately packed résumés

A **résumé** is a concise summary of an individual's accomplishments, skills, experience, and personal interests. It is more complete and inclusive than a letter of application.

(**ESL Note**) In some countries, a résumé may include an individual's age, marital status, religious affiliation, and other highly personal information. In the United States, such information is considered too personal and so should not be included.

A résumé should be densely packed with appropriate information. Most résumés use five standard categories of information: (1) Position Desired or Objective, (2) Education, (3) Experience or Employment, (4) Related Activities, and (5) References, in that order. If you think your experience or employment history is more impressive than your educational achievements, you may want to reverse the position of those two categories. The entries within any one category normally are listed in reverse chronological order (that is, the most recent achievement is listed first). For most students and other workers just starting out, a résumé should be no longer than a single full page.

1 Formatting a traditional résumé

A traditional résumé should be pleasing to the eye. Use suitable margins (about 1 inch all around), and use white space to set off the major categories and groupings. Use boldface type for your name and for major headings and subheadings. (See Chapter 14 for a more complete discussion of document design principles.) Using active-voice verbs will give you a dynamic image (see 24g). Always use white or light-colored paper. Avoid printing in color, as it will not reproduce on black-and-white copiers. A sample traditional résumé is shown in Figure 19.3.

19.2
Formatting a functional résumé.

2 Formatting a scannable résumé

Many companies are now using computer technology to create résumé databanks that can be computer-scanned for key words. Take advantage of this technology by putting keyword self-descriptors such as *retail sales* and *management experience* in a separate section at the beginning of your résumé.

Computer scanners are not always reliable when it comes to distinguishing letters, numbers, and other marks on paper, so avoid anything fancy. Start every line at the left margin; do not use

Lorinda Brown
2222 Stockton Street
Austin, TX 78701
(555) 580-5625

OBJECTIVE
Marketing/management trainee in the retail industry.
Am willing to relocate if necessary.

EDUCATION
Bachelor of Science, University of Texas at Austin,
June 2002 (present GPA: 3.4)

Major: Communication. Minor: Marketing. Completed
25 credit hours in marketing and management.

BUSINESS EXPERIENCE
Retail sales, Stevens Brown Sports, Austin, since
September 2000. Started with floor sales; promoted to
assistant manager of weekend operations. Designed
the company's Web site. Drew up new marketing plan
that increased sales by 15%.

Intern, Frito-Lay, Inc., Austin, June–August 2000.
Completed 10-week marketing internship, which
included product testing and merchandising. Handled
accounts during 6 weeks' absence of local
representative.

OTHER EXPERIENCE
Vice-President, University of Texas Black Student
Association, September 2000 to present.

Counselor-Tutor, Upward Bound, Austin, January–May
1999.

AWARDS
Employee of the Month, Stevens Brown, November 2001.

REFERENCES
Available upon request.

FIGURE 19.3 Sample Traditional Résumé

columns. Use light-colored, standard-size paper, a conventional typeface, and 10- to 14-point font sizes. Do not use italics, underlining, color, lines, graphics, or boxes. Print out the résumé on a high-quality printer. Do not fold or staple the résumé.

3 Formatting an electronic résumé

Many companies solicit résumés via email or the Internet. In such cases, you should format your résumé so that it conforms to the company's specifications. This usually means (1) using a simplified layout with a prominent keywords section, like that of the scannable résumé discussed above, and (2) putting the document in ASCII, Text Only, or Simple Text format. Rather than sending the résumé as an attached file, most companies prefer that you embed it in the email message you send in response to the company's solicitation, placing the résumé after the cover letter.

VIDEO

Tips for formatting electronic résumés.

19d Write focused memos

Memos (short for *memoranda*) are a common form of written communication in business and professional organizations. Memos serve

---

HELP

Where can I get online information about writing and posting a résumé?

Try these Web sites:

- Rebecca Smith's eRésumés and Resources
  http://www.eresumes.com
- CareerMosaic Résumé Writing Center
  http://www.careermosaic.com/cm/rwc/rwc1.htm
- JobWeb Guide to Résumé Writing
  http://www.jobweb.org/catapult/guenov/restips.html
- Taos Résumé Tips
  http://www.taos.com/resumetips.html
- The Damn Good Résumé
  http://www.damngood.com/jobseekers/tips.html

a variety of purposes: to inform, to summarize, to recommend, and to make a request, among other things. They are usually quite short (one or two pages), informal in tone, and focused on a single topic.

A memo typically has four parts: a *header*, an *introduction*, a *body*, and a *conclusion*. In addition, it may have *attachments*.

With most word-processing programs, you can create a document template, or preset form. If your department or company has a standard format for memos, you can create a template that conforms to this standard.

The sample memo in Figure 19.4 was written by two students to their writing instructor. The instructor, Professor Gilbert, had asked

Header containing basic information	To:	Prof. Gilbert
	From:	Mona Kitab and Fernando Marquez
	Date:	4 June 2002
	Subject:	Proposal for a service-learning project
Introduction, describing the problem and proposed solution	After telephoning five agencies, we have decided that the project we would most like to work on is an information brochure for the city's homeless shelter. The shelter is badly underfunded and needs more volunteers to help out. Miriam Hatcher, the shelter director, told us she thought that more university students would volunteer to help if they only knew more about it. She said that a well-written brochure answering students' questions about the shelter might be the answer.	
Body of memo giving details	We plan to create a six-panel, folded brochure that will answer the following questions: • What is the homeless shelter? • How many people does it serve, and in what way? • Why does it need volunteer help? • If I volunteered, what would I be doing? How much time would it take? • How do I sign up?	
Conclusion, summarizing the main point of the memo	The brochure will be well written, nicely illustrated, and elegantly formatted. We are enthusiastic about this project, as it seems to address an important need in our community, and we hope that it meets your approval.	

FIGURE 19.4 Sample Memo

all the students in the class to form two-person teams, call local non-profit agencies to find a suitable service-learning project, and then submit to her a one-page memo describing their proposed project.

CHAPTER 20

Oral Presentations Using *PowerPoint* and Other Tools

In many career occupations, the ability to communicate orally is just as important as the ability to write well. Simple conversations, interviews, phone calls, meetings—these are all staple forms of communication in the workplace. And so are oral presentations. This chapter offers advice on how to give good presentations.

VIDEO

Tips for delivering an oral presentation.

20a   Prepare thoroughly

The basic principle to keep in mind in preparing any kind of oral presentation is this: *all listeners have a limited attention span;* thus, you cannot expect them to follow closely everything you say. Their attention will probably wander from time to time, even if your presentation is only ten minutes long. So, if you want to make sure your listeners will come away from your talk with your main points clear in their minds, you must organize your presentation in such a way that these main points stand out. Here is how to do it:

WWW

20.1

Web resources for preparing oral presentations.

1. *Analyze your audience and limit your topic accordingly.* What do your listeners already know about the topic? What do they need or want to know about it? If you tell them what they already know, they'll be bored. If you give them too much new information too fast, they may not be able to keep up with you.

2. *Determine your primary purpose.* Is there some main point or idea you want to get across? If so, use it as the cornerstone on which to build your presentation.

3. *Select effective supporting information.* What kind of evidence will best support your main point? What kind of information will appeal to your listeners? These things will constitute the heart of your presentation, so put some thought into it.

4. *Choose an appropriate pattern of organization.* Do your subject matter and purpose lend themselves to a certain pattern of organization such as those described in Chapter 5 (problem-solution, narrative, classification, and so on)? If so, building your presentation around such a pattern will make it simpler for you to organize and present the talk and easier for your listeners to follow it.

5. *Prepare an outline.* Keep it brief: main points and main supporting points only. Arrange these points according to the pattern of development you chose in step 4.

6. *Select appropriate visual aids.* (See 20b, below.)

7. *Prepare a suitable introduction.* A good introduction should set up the topic so that your audience will be interested in what you have to say. You must convince them that it's an important subject, worthy of their attention. Are you addressing some problem? Make sure you define it so that your listeners know exactly what it is and can appreciate your proposed solution. Are you taking sides on an issue and arguing for your point of view? If so, make sure your listeners know exactly what the issue is.

8. *Prepare a closing summary.* Listeners are typically very attentive at the beginning of a presentation, less attentive as it wears on, and then suddenly more attentive again as it comes to an end. In other words, they perk up at the end, hoping to catch a summarizing comment or recommendation. You can take advantage of this fact by re-emphasizing your main points at the end.

20b Pick your visual aids carefully

Visual aids are of great help in giving an oral presentation. First, they serve as "cue cards," reminding you of all your important points and allowing you to stay on track without reading from a manuscript or from notes. Second, visual aids have tremendous power as attention-getters. Studies have shown that people remember the visual parts of speeches far better than they do the verbal parts. Finally, visual aids can help clarify your message.

Pick your visual aids carefully. Here are the basic options:

- *PowerPoint* projection
- Overhead transparencies

- Chalkboard
- Flip charts or posters
- Handouts
- 3-dimensional objects

Each of these technologies has its own strengths and weaknesses, and should be evaluated with the following questions in mind: Is it easy to prepare? Can it be altered easily during the presentation? Will it allow you to control the audience's attention—or will it distract attention from what you're saying? Will it let you present at an appropriate speed? How much information can it convey? How large an audience can you use it with? How reliable is it—does it depend on electronic equipment? Can the audience keep it for future reference? How well does it work as a "cue card"? Using these criteria, Table 20.1 compares the six types of visual aids listed above.

TABLE 20.1

Types of Visual Aids Evaluated for Use with Oral Presentations

	POWER-POINT	OVER-HEADS	CHALK-BOARD	FLIP-CHARTS OR POSTERS	HAND-OUTS	3-D OBJECTS
Ease of preparation	Excellent	Good	Excellent	Fair	Good	Good
Ease of alteration	Fair	Good	Excellent	Fair	Poor	Poor
Audience control	Excellent	Excellent	Excellent	Excellent	Poor	Varies
Speed	Excellent	Good	Poor	Good	Excellent	Excellent
Amount of information	Good	Good	Fair	Good	Excellent	Fair
Audience size	Excellent	Excellent	Fair	Fair	Excellent	Fair
Reliability	Fair	Good	Excellent	Excellent	Excellent	Excellent
Future reference	Good	Poor	Poor	Poor	Excellent	Poor
Cueing	Excellent	Excellent	Poor	Excellent	Excellent	Good

As can be seen, *PowerPoint* is probably the best overall visual aid for an oral presentation. It has more strengths and fewer weaknesses than any of the others. But each of the others has its own good uses for particular situations and should not be overlooked. (See sections 20e and 20f below for more information on using *PowerPoint* and overhead transparencies.)

20c Practice, practice, practice

Nothing is more helpful to the ultimate success of an oral presentation than practice. Not even the best of speakers can give a totally effective presentation without first practicing it. Practice allows you to spot the flaws in a presentation and correct them. It enables you to work on making smooth transitions instead of awkward stops and starts. And practice gives you an idea of how long your presentation will take, allowing you to make adjustments so that you can ultimately deliver it at a comfortable tempo. All of these benefits promote greater self-confidence, which will give you a more emphatic, convincing, and effective style of delivery.

The best way to practice a talk is by rounding up a few friends and trying it out on them. Ask them to hear you all the way through, taking notes but not interrupting you. Then ask them for an honest critique. In the absence of friends, you can use a video recorder or audiotape recorder and then critique yourself during playback.

Here are some specific things to work on while practicing an oral presentation:

1. *Devise ways of reiterating your important points without being too repetitive.* Since your important points should all contribute to a single cumulative effect, it's a good idea to reiterate these points occasionally as you go along—especially in summary form at the end of your talk. However, since exact repetition of a point can become annoyingly monotonous the third or fourth time around, try to vary your wording.

2. *Create smooth transitions between sections.* Take note of places where the flow of your presentation seems to break down, and see if you can't insert a phrase or two to act as a bridge. (If you can't, there may be a fundamental flaw in the overall structure of your presentation; in that case, try to reorganize it.)

3. *Familiarize yourself with the equipment you'll be using.* It's embarrassing—and annoying to the audience—to waste precious time by fumbling around with a computer, slide projector, or other equipment when you're supposed to be giving your presentation. If you

plan on using any equipment, check it out beforehand and become familiar with it. And have a backup plan if something goes wrong.

4. *Prepare yourself for questions.* Listeners may raise questions at any point in your presentation, and it is vitally important that you answer them satisfactorily. If you don't, your most precious asset as a speaker—your credibility—may be jeopardized. Be sure you know your topic *well.* One way to prepare yourself is by having some friends listen to you and deliberately throw tough questions at you; if they succeed in stumping you, do some more research.

5. *Develop your own speaking style.* Practice presenting as if you were telling friends a story. Be natural and expressive. Use animated gestures and vary your intonation and rate of speech. In short, let your enthusiasm show! At the same time, try to get rid of any distracting habits you might have, such as leaning against something, pacing back and forth, or fiddling with a pencil.

6. *If you are going to be reading from a manuscript, work on giving it a lively, expressive intonation.* There is a strong tendency when reading aloud to adopt a monotonous style of delivery that is very boring for an audience to listen to. So practice varying your intonation as you read aloud, just as you would if you were talking spontaneously. Mark up the manuscript, underlining those words that warrant special intonation and those places where you may want to pause. Give special emphasis to contrasting terms.

20d Speak with enthusiasm and focus

As the time draws near for delivering your oral presentation, you will experience what all speakers do—nervousness. One key to an effective delivery is to convert your nervousness into the kind of energy that injects liveliness, enthusiasm, and animation into your speech.

How can you control your nervousness? First of all, make sure you're properly prepared for your talk. This means getting all your visual aids and notes organized, and making sure you're properly dressed and groomed. Your personal appearance is one of the most powerful "visual aids" you have. If you know you're looking your best, it will give you a boost in confidence.

Second, as you are about to start your presentation, look for an opportunity to say something off the cuff. For example, you could acknowledge the occasion or you could share a spontaneous bit of humor. Don't feel you have to tell a prepared joke or story. If you're good at joketelling or storytelling, fine, but don't force it.

Finally, as you are actually giving your presentation, *concentrate your full attention on what you want to say.* Stick to your outline, and make sure you cover all your main supporting points. Convince your listeners that the topic is important and be enthusiastic about it. Show each of your visual aids long enough for the audience to understand and appreciate it, and then move on to the next one. Keep up the pace; don't dally.

Encourage questions from the audience, but don't let questions disrupt your presentation. Above all, do not show any antagonism toward a questioner. It will make your entire audience feel uncomfortable, and they may hold it against you even if the questioner is unfair or unpleasant.

20e Use overhead transparencies

Overhead transparencies provide good visual support for an oral presentation. They are relatively easy to prepare, and they can be written on (with a transparency marker) during the presentation itself. You can use them as "cue cards" to keep your thoughts on track without reading from a manuscript. At the same time, they allow you to control the attention of the audience while easily moving from one transparency to the next.

It's important to give your audience time to digest the information you have on your transparencies. Usually, that means putting relatively little information on each slide, so that you can keep moving along from one to the next. Figures 20.1 and 20.2 provide an ex-

---

20% of the students on this campus (=1500 students) are involved in community service projects. We can do even better.

Have served 72 nonprofit agencies in past year. Examples: YWCA, Family Literacy Center, Save Water Coalition, Peace Now.

Designed Web sites, wrote brochures, measured lead paint on old buildings, planted trees, distributed leaflets, helped elderly, etc.

Students usually work in teams, but there are also many individual volunteers.

FIGURE 20.1 Notes on an Index Card

Student Involvement in Community Service

- 1500 students on this campus participate, equal to 20% of the student population
- 31 courses have service learning projects
- The Bennion Center sponsors outreach programs
- Many more possibilities exist

FIGURE 20.2 Overhead Transparency Using the Same Notes

ample of how a student converted index card notes to an overhead transparency for a class presentation on service learning.

Notice how this student wisely used only some of her index card notes for the overhead transparency. Putting too much information on any one transparency may confuse an audience, distract attention from you the speaker, and slow down your presentation. It's better to split up the information and put it on two or more transparencies. Notice also the neat *design* of this transparency. It has a clear, thematic title, and its main points are cleanly set off as a bulleted list. It also has ample white space.

20f Use *PowerPoint*

Presentation software such as *PowerPoint* is becoming more and more common because it has almost all the benefits of overhead transparencies plus some special advantages: it projects color better than overhead transparencies; it can include animation, video, and sound; and it can be converted into HTML and put on a Web site for later reference. Also, it has a wizard and templates to guide you through the process of putting together a presentation. Although the templates are business-oriented, some of them can be adapted to academic presentations as well.

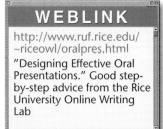

WEBLINK

http://www.ruf.rice.edu/
~riceowl/oralpres.html

"Designing Effective Oral Presentations." Good step-by-step advice from the Rice University Online Writing Lab

www

20.2

Step-by-step advice on how to give an oral presentation.

WWW

20.3

More tips
on oral
presentations.

WEBLINK

http://www.canberra.edu
.au/studyskills/oralpresX
.htm

Helpful tips for preparing
and delivering an oral
presentation; also has advice
on the use of *PowerPoint*

As with overhead transparencies, *PowerPoint* slides should be neatly formatted, easily readable, and not too cluttered with information. If the presentation is in a darkened room, the slides should have a light background; in a well-lit room, they should have a darker background. Any visual images or background sound should be relevant to the theme of the presentation.

Figures 20.3 and 20.4 illustrate "before" and "after" versions of a *PowerPoint* slide created from the index card notes in Figure 20.1.

Before

Have served 72 nonprofit agencies in past year. Examples: YWCA, Family Literacy Center, Save Water Coalition, Peace Now. Sample projects:
1. Designed Web sites,
2. wrote brochures,
3. measured lead paint on old buildings,
4. planted trees,
5. distributed leaflets,
6. helped elderly, etc.
    Students usually worked in teams but there are also many individual volunteers.

Format and type font too dull, should be more attention-getting.

No reason for numbered list. Bullets would do better.

Too much information on page. No clear theme.

FIGURE 20.3 Poor Example of a *PowerPoint* Slide

After

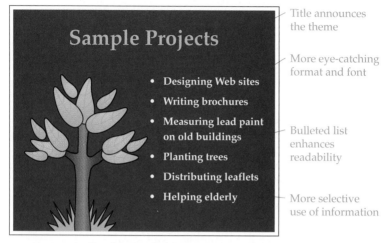

FIGURE 20.4 Good Example of a *PowerPoint* Slide

CHAPTER **21**

Essay Exams

In college and on the job, much of the writing you do will be "on demand"—that is, you will have a limited time in which to complete it. In college, such writing often takes the form of a timed essay exam or an in-class writing assignment. This chapter discusses some ways you can prepare for this type of writing.

AUDIO
Writing under time constraints for essay exams.

21a **Prepare for an essay exam**

You can use a number of strategies to prepare for on-demand writing in general and essay exams in particular. These strategies

VIDEO
Tips for taking essay exams.

include keeping up on your reading and notetaking, studying and reviewing your notes, and analyzing the exam question.

1 Keeping up on your reading and notetaking

Many instructors judge your success in a course by how well you are able to analyze and apply course material in a timed essay exam. In order to do a good job on such exams, you must be well prepared. Few essay exams are open-book, so you must learn the material well enough to be able to remember and write about it without access to your notes or textbooks.

WEBLINK

http://www.english.uiuc
.edu/cws/wworkshop/

Tips on writing essay exams

21.1

Access essay
exam advice
online.

You can prepare by keeping up with course assignments and discussions throughout the term. Attend every class and read your textbooks carefully, looking for key ideas and arguments. Pay close attention to chapter summaries, subheadings, and key terminology. Write the key ideas and terms down in a notebook for later review. When your instructor lectures, do not write down everything he or she says; rather, listen for and record main points and ideas that show relationships.

2 Studying and reviewing your notes

As the exam date approaches, you will want to study more systematically. Ask the instructor if he or she is willing to provide models of previous exam questions or some general guidelines about the kinds of questions that might be included on the exam. Organize a study group to discuss and review the course materials. If possible, the study group should meet regularly during the term, either in person or through an email discussion group. Practice responding to course readings by taking a stance opposite that of the authors or by questioning the authors' position. Review your class notes, paying particular attention to your lists of key ideas and terms. For each key idea, develop a practice thesis statement that you could explore and support in an essay.

Avoid the last-minute cram session. Cramming for several hours prior to the exam will not give you enough depth of knowledge to succeed on an essay exam. And if you stay up studying all night before an exam, you will be in no condition to take it the next day. Instead, pace your studying over several days and try to get a good night's sleep so that you will be fresh for the exam itself.

3 Analyzing the exam question

When you receive the exam question, the first step is to analyze it carefully. The question itself will guide the organization of your response. An essay question will ask you to focus on a specific issue, and you should address it rather than cataloging everything you learned from the course. Try to minimize your anxiety by taking a deep breath and focusing your thinking on the structure of your response. If the exam contains more than one question, determine how much time you have to devote to each question, so that you do not run out of time before you complete your writing. Table 21.1 shows appropriate responses to some of the organizational cue words that typically appear in essay questions.

21b Attend to the writing process

When you write an essay exam, you should briefly attend to each stage of the writing process.

1 Preparing an outline

When taking an essay exam, you will not have much time for prewriting, but you should take a few minutes to jot down in an informal outline (see 2d-5) some of the key concepts you want to cover in your answer. Begin your response with a thesis statement and a short introductory paragraph that captures the main thrust of your response. Then, in subsequent paragraphs, you can elaborate with examples and details until you run out of time.

2 Drafting your response

Try to remain focused as you draft your response. Your instructor will have many essays to read and will not want to plow through a lot of extraneous information. If you know a great deal about the question, resist the temptation to write down everything. Rather, stick to your thesis, and plan your writing so that your response is coherent and organized. The easier it is for the instructor to follow your line of argument, the better.

3 Analyzing and evaluating your response

Allow time to ensure that you have satisfied the demands of the assignment. When you read over your essay, you may find that you

TABLE 21.1
Cue Words in Essay Exam Questions

EXAMPLE QUESTION	CUE WORD	EXAMPLE QUESTION	CUE WORD
Analyze Shakespeare's use of dreams in *Macbeth*.	**Analyze:** Divide something into parts and discuss the parts in relationship to the whole.	Evaluate the effectiveness of the performance of Handel's *Water Music* by the San Francisco Symphony.	**Evaluate:** Give your opinion about something's value and provide the reasons on which your judgment is based.
Argue either for or against caps on political spending in presidential campaigns.	**Argue:** Take a position or stand and support it with reasoned arguments and evidence.	Explain why an object thrown up into the air falls to the ground.	**Explain:** Tell about something that is complex in a way that makes it clear.
Classify street people into types based on their sociological characteristics.	**Classify:** Divide some larger whole into groups on the basis of shared traits.	Illustrate the importance of color in Duchamp's *Nude Descending a Staircase*.	**Illustrate:** Provide examples and detail about something.
Describe the mechanism of the transmission of typhus.	**Describe:** Systematically explain something's features, sometimes visually or sequentially.	Summarize the major advantages of mainstreaming handicapped children in school.	**Summarize:** Repeat the main points in abbreviated form.
Discuss the structure of US society in terms of its economic relationships.	**Discuss:** Consider as many important elements related to an issue as you can.		

AUDIO
Cue words can guide your essay responses.

have overlooked the second part of a two-part question, for example, or that you have concentrated on defining terms when the question asked you to analyze information. Do not panic. If possible, write a new final paragraph that addresses the issues you missed.

Also, look carefully at your thesis statement. Does it reflect accurately the direction of your essay? If not, then revise it. Check your organization. Does your essay read smoothly and flow logically? If not, then perhaps you can insert transitional words or phrases that will help your instructor follow your argument. Have you included enough examples to support your thesis? If you need more, write a new paragraph and use an arrow to indicate where it should be inserted. Finally, does your conclusion provide your reader with a clear understanding of the main point of your essay? If not, then add a sentence or two to sum up your argument.

4 Proofreading and editing your response

Your instructor will not expect your writing to be grammatically and structurally perfect in a timed-writing situation. However, he or she will expect your exam response to be readable and clear. If possible, write your response in pencil so that you can easily erase and correct errors. Take a few minutes to proofread and also to check

Checklist for Writing Successful Essay Exam Responses

- Have I shown my understanding of the question by including a thesis statement at the beginning of my response?
- Have I organized my response so as to present my ideas in a logical progression that supports my thesis?
- Have I used the specific details, facts, or analyses called for in the question?
- Have I shown my own independent thoughts and insights in my response?
- Have I concluded with a brief sentence that sums up the gist of my response?
- Have I evaluated and edited my response as time allowed?

your penmanship. If your response is unreadable, your instructor cannot evaluate it fairly.

21c Review sample student responses to an essay exam question

To help you write better exam responses, we include here two student responses to the following essay exam question, which appeared on the midterm for a course in Twentieth-Century British Literature.

21.2
Sample student responses to essay questions.

EXAM QUESTION

Below you will find a quotation from a novel we read this term. Spend 15 minutes writing a short essay that performs a close reading of the passage. Pick out specific details from the quotation that illustrate some of the central themes or ideas of the novel. Your response should demonstrate both an ability to read closely and a general understanding of the novel.

AUDIO
ESL students and essay exams.

From Henry James's *The Turn of the Screw*: "I remember feeling with Miles in especial as if he had had, as it were, nothing to call even an infinitesimal history. We expect of a small child scant enough 'antecedents', but there was in this beautiful little boy something extraordinarily sensitive, yet extraordinarily happy, that, more than in any creature of his age I have seen, struck me as beginning anew each day. . . . I could reconstitute nothing at all, and he was therefore an angel."

GOOD STUDENT RESPONSE

This quotation expresses the governess' naivete regarding the innocence of the children she is looking after. She assumes that just because they are children, they have had little experience, and are, thus, pure "angels." Her perception of this, however, is erroneous and detrimental to Miles. Assuming that he is pure, she takes all measures to protect him from any horrors that may have happened in the past, not realizing that the past is part of Miles's history. His past takes the form of ghosts which haunt the governess, although they do not seem to frighten the children. In fact, the children are drawn to the ghosts and want the governess to go away. Her lack of experience and her innocence are actually greater than the children's, who no longer have parents and have experienced the death of two servants. Her inability to see this truth ends up killing Miles. Caught between the image of the governess and Peter Quint, Miles finally has to make evident to her what is so obvious to everyone else--Peter Quint exists, the past is a part of his present. Not willing to let Miles exist outside of her perceptions, the governess ironically reassures him, "I caught you." She strips him of his history, his identity, and he dies a young boy "dispossessed."

POOR STUDENT RESPONSE

The governess here is expressing how she feels about the child Miles vs. the Miles she knew once upon a time. The use of the run-on sentence is a radical change from the accepted format of the past. The form represents thought put on paper and not interpreted through writing. The affect that the child had on her doesn't seem realistic. It seems more mystic and of fantasy.

The instructor wanted the exam responses to demonstrate both an ability to read closely and a general understanding of the novel. In the first response, the student shows a clear understanding of the major themes of the novel, using specific details from the quotation to illustrate that understanding and connect the passage to the larger themes of innocence and history. In contrast, the second response does not draw any specific connections between the quotation and the major issues or themes of the novel. It appears from the second response that this student did not really understand the novel. Furthermore, the second response does not answer the question that was posed by the teacher. As reading these responses makes clear, you must understand both the subject and the examination question in order to answer well.

Correct Sentences

FAQs

▶ **Chapter 22**

What is the difference between a participle and a gerund? (22a-4)

What is an adverb? (22a-6)

What is a sentence subject? (22b-1)

What is a predicate? (22b-2)

▶ **Chapter 23**

Should I write "The jury took *its* time" or "The jury took *their* time"? (23a)

Is there anything wrong with "Tom invited Janice and he to lunch"? (23f)

Is it correct to write "Mark likes school more than me"? (23j)

▶ **Chapter 24**

What is wrong with the sentence "He believed that his thesis is credible"? (24e-2)

How can I decide when to use *sit* or *set?* (24f)

When I make an "if" statement, where should I put the *would?* (24h-1)

▶ **Chapter 25**

What is the difference between an adjective and an adverb? (25a, 25c)

Should I write "I feel bad" or "I feel badly"? (25d)

What is wrong with the phrase "most unique"? (25e)

CHAPTER **22**

Sentence Structure

Improving your grammar and writing style will allow you to express your thoughts more precisely and make your writing more readable and interesting. To improve your style, you will need to know the basic elements of sentence structure. This chapter provides that information.

AUDIO
Chapter
overview.

22a   Learn to identify parts of speech

In writing a sentence, you put words together in certain combinations. These combinations depend, in part, on the different kinds of words, or **parts of speech,** you use: nouns, pronouns, verbs, adjectives, adverbs, prepositions, conjunctions, and interjections.

1   Nouns

A **noun** (n) is the name of a person, place, thing, quality, idea, or action. Some examples of nouns are

HELP

How do I use a style/grammar checker?

1. Start the checker. (It may be on the TOOLS menu.)
2. Position your cursor on the IGNORE (or SKIP) command, and be prepared to click on it often.
3. Consider each suggestion the checker makes, but do not automatically follow its advice. In most cases, you will decide to click IGNORE.
4. If you are not sure whether to accept the checker's suggestion, use the EXPLANATION feature (if there is one).
5. If you are still in doubt, read the relevant discussions in this handbook (see 35a or the index). Use the book's advice to help you decide whether or not to revise.

| Picasso | Mexico | printer |
| honesty | democracy | stamp collecting |

Nouns are often preceded by *a, an,* or *the;* these words are known as **articles.** Use *a* before nouns beginning with consonant sounds; use *an* before nouns beginning with vowel sounds: *a* printer, *an* insult.

(**ESL Note**) The indefinite article (*a* or *an*) is used with a non-specific count noun (see below), whereas the definite article (*the*) is used with a count or noncount noun that refers to something specific. (See Chapter 43 for further discussion.)

Common nouns refer to general persons, places, things, concepts, or qualities: *city, generosity.*

Proper nouns, which are almost always capitalized, name particular persons, places, institutions, organizations, months, and days: *Buddhism, Monday.*

Concrete nouns specifically refer to things that can be sensed through sight, hearing, touch, taste, or smell: *bookshelf, thunder.*

Abstract nouns refer to ideas, emotions, qualities, or other intangible concepts: *sadness, truth.*

Count nouns name things that can be counted and thus can have a plural form: *violin(s), goose (geese).*

Noncount nouns, or **mass nouns,** name things that typically are not counted in English and thus cannot be made plural: *water, health.*

Collective nouns name groups; they are plural in sense but singular in form: *committee, crowd.*

2 Pronouns

Pronouns (pron), such as *she, they,* and *it,* are words that substitute for nouns. The noun a pronoun substitutes for is called the **antecedent** of the pronoun. The noun antecedent often precedes the pronoun in a sentence:

Lucinda said *she* was not feeling well.

Sometimes the noun antecedent follows the pronoun:

Saying *she* was not feeling well, *Lucinda* left the room.

Pronouns can be singular or plural, and their case form can vary depending on how they are used in a sentence. (See Chapter 23 for a discussion of pronoun case and pronoun-antecedent agreement.)

Types of Pronouns and Their Roles

Type	Role
Personal pronouns Singular: *I, you, he, she, it; me, you, him, her, it; mine, yours, his, hers, its* Plural: *we, you, they; us, you, them; ours, yours, theirs*	Refer to specific persons, places, or things: "I borrowed *his* book."
Demonstrative pronouns *this, that, these, those*	Point to their antecedent nouns: "*That* was an interesting idea!"
Indefinite pronouns *all, any, anybody, anyone, anything, both, everybody, everyone, everything, few, many, one, no one, nothing, somebody, someone, something, several, some*	Refer to nonspecific persons, places, or things and do not require an antecedent: "*Nothing* could be done."
Relative pronouns *that, what, which, who, whom, whose, whoever, whichever, whatever*	Introduce dependent clauses: "She is the teacher *who* runs marathons."
Interrogative pronouns *who, whom, which, what, whose*	Introduce questions: "*Whose* bike is this?"
Reflexive and **intensive pronouns** (consist of a personal pronoun plus *-self* or *-selves*) Singular: *myself, yourself, himself, herself, itself* Plural: *ourselves, yourselves, themselves*	A reflexive pronoun refers back to the subject to show that the subject itself is the object of an action: "She saw *herself* in the mirror." An intensive pronoun is used for emphasis: "They did it *themselves*."
Reciprocal pronouns *one another, each other*	Refer to the separate parts of a plural antecedent: "They gave presents to *each other*."

(continued)

Types of Pronouns and Their Roles *(continued)*	
Expletive pronouns *there, it*	Serve as introductory, "empty" words, occupying the position of grammatical subject: "*There* once was a pharaoh."

3 Verbs

A **verb** (v) is a word that expresses an action (*swim, read*) or a state of being (*is, seemed*). Main verbs are often accompanied by **auxiliary verbs** (also called **helping verbs**), which include forms of the verbs *be, have,* and *do,* and/or by **modal verbs,** such as *may, might, can, could, will, would, shall, should,* and *must.* Auxiliary and modal verbs are critical parts of special verb forms that express questions, future tenses, past tenses, and various degrees of doubt about or qualification of the main verb's action. (See Chapter 24 for more on verbs.)

Transitive verbs (vt) transfer action from an agent (usually the subject of the sentence) to an object or recipient (usually the direct object of the sentence): "Michael *fumbled* the ball" (see 22b-2, 22b-3). **Intransitive verbs** (vi) may express action, but they do not transfer it to an object or recipient: "The bridge *collapsed*." (See 24a, 24b for more on verb forms.)

Verbs also have an **active form,** called the **active voice** ("He *committed* the crime"), as well as a **passive form,** called the **passive voice,** consisting of a form of the verb *be* and a past participle ("The crime *was committed* by him"). Verbs may take alternative forms for different **moods.** In the **indicative mood,** they make assertions, state opinions, and ask questions. Past-tense forms express unreal conditions or wishes, in the **subjunctive mood:** "I wish I *were* in Hawaii." They appear in the base form to issue a command, in the **imperative mood:** "Don't *do* that again!" or, occasionally, "Don't you *do* that again!" (See 24h.)

4 Verbals

AUDIO
Comparing
gerunds and
participles.

A **verbal** is a verb form that functions in a sentence as a noun, an adverb, or an adjective. There are three types of verbals: participles, gerunds, and infinitives.

Participles are words such as *sweeping* and *swept,* the present and past participles of a verb (*sweep*) that function as adjectives and can modify nouns or pronouns: "Beware of *sweeping* generaliza-tions." "Keep floors *swept.*"

Gerunds are verb forms that end in *ing* and function as nouns: "*Sweeping* is something I do not enjoy."

An **infinitive** is the base form of a verb, often preceded by *to* (*to read, to fly*). Infinitives can function as nouns, adjectives, or adverbs: "To quit would be a mistake." "Her desire *to quit* is understandable."

5 Adjectives

An **adjective** (adj) is a word that modifies a noun or pronoun by qualifying or describing it. In English, the adjective usually precedes the noun it modifies (an *old* tree, the *other* day). In sentences such as "The program was *challenging,*" the adjective falls on the other side of a verb linking it to the noun it modifies. An adjective used in this way is called a **predicate adjective.**

Many adjectives have comparative and superlative forms cre-ated by the addition of *-er* and *-est* (*small, smaller, smallest*). (See Chap-ter 25.) Many other adjectives have the same form as the present or past participle of a verb (a *roaring* lion, a *deserted* island).

(ESL Note) If you use two or more adjectives before a noun, you often must put them in a certain order (see 52a).

Many pronoun-like adjectives are called **possessive adjectives** (*our* school), **demonstrative adjectives** (*this* page), **interrogative ad-jectives** (*Which* button do I push?), and **indefinite adjectives** (*some* money).

See Chapter 25 for a more detailed discussion of adjectives.

6 Adverbs

An **adverb** (adv) modifies a verb, an adjective, another adverb, or an entire clause or sentence. Adverbs usually answer one of the following questions: when? where? how? how often? to what extent?

The mayor lives *alone* in a downtown apartment. [*Alone* modifies the verb *lives.*]

She has a *very* busy schedule. [*Very* modifies the adjective *busy.*]

She *almost* never takes a vacation. [*Almost* modifies the adverb *never.*]

Apparently, she doesn't seem to need one. [*Apparently* modifies the entire sentence.]

(ESL Note) Adverbs must be positioned properly within a sentence (see 52c).

Conjunctive adverbs, such as *however, thus,* and *consequently,* modify an entire sentence or clause while linking it to the preceding sentence or clause. (See Chapter 32.) See Chapter 25 for a more detailed discussion of adverbs.

7 Prepositions

A **preposition** (prep) is a word such as *in, on, of, for,* or *by* that comes before a noun or pronoun and its modifiers to form a **prepositional phrase** (*in the water, off the deep end*). The noun or pronoun in such phrases (*water, end, them*) is called the **object of the preposition.** Here are some common prepositions used in English:

22.1
English on
"Who Wants
to Be a
Millionaire?"

about	below	in	over
above	beside	into	past
across	between	like	through
after	by	near	to
along	down	of	under
around	during	off	until
at	except	on	up
before	for	onto	with
behind	from	out	without

Prepositions also occur in multiword combinations: *according to, along with, because of,* and *with respect to.* Prepositions can be linked to certain verbs to form **phrasal verbs,** such as *do without, put up with,* and *look over.* In phrasal verbs, the preposition is called a **particle.**

(ESL Note) Phrasal verbs are common in idiomatic English. (See Chapters 51 and 53.)

8 Conjunctions

A **conjunction** (conj) joins two sentences, clauses, phrases, or words. The relationship between the two parts may be an equal, or coordinate, one; it may be an unequal, or subordinate, one.

Coordinating conjunctions (*and, but, or, nor, yet, so, for*) connect sentences, clauses, phrases, or words that are parallel in meaning and grammatical structure. **Correlative conjunctions** (*both/and, neither/nor, either/or, not/but, whether/or, not only/but also*) are pairs of conjunctions that give extra emphasis to the two parts of a coordinated construction. **Subordinating conjunctions** introduce dependent clauses and connect them to main clauses. Some common subordinating conjunctions are *although, because, if, since, unless,* and *while.*

See Chapter 32 for further discussion of conjunctions.

9 Interjections

An **interjection** is a short utterance such as *wow!* or *ouch!* that expresses an emotional response. Interjections usually stand alone and are punctuated with an exclamation mark.

22.2
Examples of commonly used interjections.

22b Learn to identify basic sentence patterns

Sentences are the basic units for expressing assertions, questions, commands, wishes, and exclamations. All grammatically complete sentences have a subject and a predicate. In a sentence fragment, one of these elements may be missing. (See Chapter 26 for more on fragments.)

EXERCISE
Sentence structure.

1 Sentence subjects

The **subject** (sub) of a sentence is a noun, a pronoun, or a noun phrase that identifies what the sentence is about. Usually it directly precedes the main verb.

You probably have a pointing device (PD) connected to your computer. *Many PDs* have a ball that rolls against wheels.

The rubber ball found inside most PDs oxidizes over time.

The **simple subject** is always a noun or pronoun. In the example sentences, the simple subjects are *you* and *ball.* The **complete subject** is the simple subject plus all its modifiers; the complete subjects are italicized in the example sentences. Some sentences have a **compound subject** including two or more simple subjects: "*Tips and techniques* can be found in the HELP menu." In im-

WEBLINK

http://owl.english.purdue
.edu/handouts/grammar/
index.html
Comprehensive coverage of parts of speech and sentence construction

perative sentences, which express a command or a request, the subject is understood to be *you,* even though it is not usually stated:

"[You] Wake up!" The subject of a sentence always agrees in number with the main verb. That is, a singular subject takes a singular verb, and a plural subject takes a plural verb: "The rubber ball . . . oxidizes," "Many PDs . . . have." Subject-verb agreement is discussed further in Chapter 28.

2 Predicates

The **predicate** is the part of a sentence that contains the verb and makes a statement about the subject. The **simple predicate** is the verb plus any auxiliary (helping) verbs: "With a Web browser, you *can locate* information efficiently." The **complete predicate** consists of the simple predicate plus any objects, complements, or adverbial modifiers: "The World Wide Web *offers information, media, and software.*" A **compound predicate** has two or more verbs that have the same subject: "A Web page *informs and entertains.*"

A **direct object** (DO) is a noun, a pronoun, or a noun phrase that completes the action of a transitive verb (see 22a-3)—one that is capable of transmitting action. In this sentence, *information* is the direct object of the verb *locate:*

Sub   V   DO
You can locate *information.*

An **indirect object** (IO) is a noun, a pronoun, or a noun phrase that is affected indirectly by the action of a verb. It usually refers to the recipient or beneficiary of the action described by the verb and the direct object.

      Sub   V   IO   DO
The teacher told *us* a story.

Most indirect objects can be presented instead as the object of the preposition *to* or *for.*

The teacher told *us* a story.   OR   The teacher told a story *to us.*

I bought *my mother* a plant.   OR   I bought a plant *for my mother.*

An **object complement** (OC) is a noun, a noun phrase, an adjective, or an adjective phrase that elaborates on or describes the direct object.

      Sub   V   DO   OC
The news made us *depressed.*

Sub   V   DO   OC

They appointed Laurie *head of the task force.*

A **subject complement** (SC) is a noun, a noun phrase, an adjective, or an adjective phrase that follows a linking verb (such as *is, was,* or *seems*) and elaborates on the subject.

Sub   LV   SC   Sub   LV   SC

Laurie is *happy.*   She is *the new head of the task force.*

3   Basic sentence patterns

The complete predicate is usually structured according to one of five basic sentence patterns:

Pattern 1: A sentence may have an intransitive verb and no object.

Pred

Sub   V

Time flies.

Pattern 2: A sentence may have a transitive verb with a direct object.

Pred

Sub   VT   DO

Time heals all wounds.

Pattern 3: A sentence may have a transitive verb with a direct object and an indirect object.

Pred

Sub   VT   IO   DO

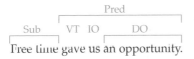

Free time gave us an opportunity.

Pattern 4: A sentence may have a transitive verb with a direct object and an object complement.

Pred

Sub   VT   DO   OC

Time pressures made us tense.

Pattern 5: A sentence may use a **linking verb,** which connects the subject to a subject complement, indicating a condition, quality, or state of being.

```
              Pred
          ┌──────────┐
    Sub  LV    SC
```
Time is precious.

22c Learn to expand sentences

The five basic sentence patterns can be expanded using words, phrases, or clauses to modify the subject or predicate.

1 Modifying with single words

Any simple sentence part can be modified, qualified, or described by appropriate single words. Verbs, adverbs, and adjectives can be modified by adverbs, and nouns can be modified by adjectives: "Time flies *quickly.*" "*Spare* time flies *very quickly.*" See Chapters 25 and 52 for more on placing adjectives and adverbs.

2 Modifying with phrases

22.3

An online guide to building sentences.

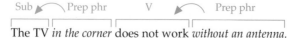

WEBLINK

http://www.uottawa.ca/academic/arts/writcent/hypergrammar/bldsent.html

All about sentence structure and options—even includes review exercises

Sentence parts can also be modified by phrases. A **phrase** is a group of words consisting of (1) a noun and its related words or (2) a verbal and its related words. Phrases add detail to any of the subjects, verbs, objects, or complements used in the five basic sentence patterns.

Adding Prepositional Phrases A preposition and its object (a noun or a pronoun) form a prepositional phrase: *in the dark, on time, outside Dallas.* Prepositional phrases can be used to modify nouns, verbs, or adjectives.

```
    Sub        Prep phr       V            Prep phr
   ┌───┐  ┌──────────────┐  ┌───┐  ┌──────────────────┐
The TV  in the corner  does not work  without an antenna.
```

```
Sub   V   Adj        Prep phr
```
Juan was jealous *beyond reason.*

Adding Verbal Phrases A verbal is a verb form that functions as a noun, an adverb, or an adjective (see 22a-4). The three kinds of verbals—infinitives, gerunds, and participles—can be combined with other words to form infinitive phrases, gerund phrases, and participial phrases.

An **infinitive phrase** consists of the base form of a verb (sometimes preceded by *to*) plus modifiers, objects, and/or complements. Such a phrase can function as a noun, an adjective, or an adverb.

We wanted *to plant the garden.*   [Infinitive phrase as a noun]

This gave us a chance *to reflect.*   [Infinitive phrase as an adjective]

The company was eager *to expand.*   [Infinitive phrase as an adverb]

A **gerund phrase** consists of the *-ing* form of a verb plus modifiers, objects, and/or complements. Gerund phrases function as nouns and thus can be used as sentence subjects, objects, or complements.

```
        Sub
```
Lifting boxes all day made Stan tired.

```
                    SC
```
Her favorite activity is *watching old movies.*

(**ESL Note**) Some English verbs can take only one kind of verbal as a complement—an infinitive ("I want *to go*") or a gerund ("I enjoy *biking*"); other verbs can take either ("Rebecca hates *cooking*" or "Rebecca hates *to cook*"). For further discussion, see Chapter 51.

A **participial phrase** consists of a present participle (the *-ing* form of a verb) or a past participle (the *-ed* or *-en* form of a verb) plus modifiers, objects, and/or complements. Participial phrases function as adjectives, modifying subjects and objects of sentences. (See Chapter 29.)

Having decided to quit his job, Roberto began looking for another one.   [The participial phrase modifies the sentence subject, *Roberto*.]

I caught someone *trying to break into my car.*   [The participial phrase modifies the object *someone*.]

Adding Appositive Phrases An **appositive phrase** is a noun phrase that describes or defines another noun. Appositive phrases directly follow or precede the nouns they modify and are usually set off by commas.

> The Ford Mustang, *a car originally designed by Lee Iacocca,* has been an enduring icon of the US automotive industry.

Adding Absolute Phrases An **absolute phrase** consists of a subject and an adjective phrase (most commonly a participial phrase). Unlike other kinds of phrases, which can modify single words, absolute phrases are used to modify entire clauses or sentences.

> *His curiosity fully satisfied,* Marco decided to move on to other topics.

3 | Modifying with clauses

A **clause** is a group of words that has a subject and a predicate. If a clause can stand alone as a sentence, it is an **independent clause** (or **main clause**); if it cannot, it is a **dependent clause** (or **subordinate clause**). There are three major types of dependent clauses: adjective, adverb, and noun.

Adjective clauses (also called **relative clauses**) modify nouns and pronouns. An adjective clause usually begins with a relative pronoun (*which, that, who, whose, whom*) or a subordinating conjunction (*where, when, how*) and immediately follows the noun or pronoun it modifies.

> The student *who is best prepared* is most likely to succeed.

> The place *where I work best* is in my basement.

Chapter 23 discusses the correct use of relative pronouns; Chapter 32 describes how to use adjective clauses to subordinate ideas.

Noun clauses function in a sentence the way simple nouns do—as subjects, objects, complements, or appositives (see 23g). A noun clause begins with a relative pronoun (*who, that, whom, whoever*) or a subordinate conjunction (*whatever, wherever, how, why*).

> Sub
> *Whoever leaked the news* should be punished.

> Ob
> No one seems to know *how the rumor got started.*

Adverb clauses modify verbs, adjectives, clauses, or other adverbs, answering questions such as the following: when? where?

why? how? An adverb clause begins with a subordinating conjunction (*if, although, because, whenever, while*).

If you cannot find the topic you want, double-click on the HELP button.

22d Learn how to classify sentences

Good writers vary the types of sentences they use in order to make their writing more interesting. The two main categories of sentence types are functional and structural.

1 Functional classifications

Sentences can be categorized functionally, or rhetorically, according to their role. A **declarative sentence,** for example, makes a direct assertion about something: "Our political system is heavily influenced by corporate interests." An **interrogative sentence** asks a question and ends with a question mark: "Have you ever traveled overseas?" An **imperative sentence** makes a request, gives a command, or offers advice. Although it is always addressed to *you,* the pronoun is usually omitted: "Use the TOOLBAR buttons to align or indent text." An **exclamatory sentence** expresses strong emotion and ends with an exclamation point: "We're finally connected!"

2 Structural classifications

Sentences can also be categorized structurally according to their overall grammatical construction. A **simple sentence** has a single independent clause and no dependent clauses. Although a simple sentence has only one clause, it may have many phrases and thus be quite long.

EXERCISE
Identifying
sentence
types.

I walk.

The high plateau of western Bolivia, called the *altiplano,* is one of the world's highest-elevation populated regions, with several towns at over 12,000 feet above sea level.

A **compound sentence** has two or more independent clauses and no dependent clauses. A compound sentence is created when two or more independent clauses are connected with a comma and a coordinating conjunction (*and, or, but, nor, for, so, yet*), with a semicolon and a conjunctive adverb (*therefore, however, otherwise, indeed*), with a semicolon alone, or with a correlative conjunction (*either/or,* *neither/nor, both/and, not only/but also*).

Ind cl   Ind cl
An eagle once flew past our house, *but* I got only a brief glimpse of it.

Ind cl
Personal computers are becoming more user-friendly; *therefore,*

Ind cl
more people are buying them.

A **complex sentence** contains one independent clause and one or more dependent clauses.

Dep cl   Ind cl
Although Alaska is a huge state, it has relatively few people.

A **compound-complex sentence,** as the name implies, consists of two or more independent clauses and one or more dependent clauses.

Dep cl
Millions upon millions of years before civilization had risen upon earth,

Ind cl
the central areas of this tremendous ocean were empty; *and*

Dep cl   Ind cl
where famous islands now exist, nothing rose above the rolling waves.

—James Michener, *Hawaii*

CHAPTER **23**

Pronoun Problems

Sometimes using pronouns in place of nouns can make writing more concise and readable. But pronouns can be confusing to readers if they are not used correctly.

AUDIO
Pronoun reference.

23a **Make pronouns agree in number and gender with their antecedents**

A **pronoun** substitutes for a noun (or noun equivalent), which is called the **antecedent** of the pronoun (see 22a-2). Pronouns and their antecedents must agree in number and gender.

AUDIO
Pronoun case.

Antecedent   Pronoun
Bad luck can happen to anyone, and *it* can happen at any time.

In this sentence, *bad luck* and *it* are both singular; therefore, they agree in **number.** They also agree in **gender** because *bad luck* is neuter (neither masculine nor feminine) and *it* can serve as a pronoun for neuter antecedents.

Be especially careful about agreement when the pronoun is far away from its antecedent:

Each of the graduating football players was asked to say a few

he
words about what ~~they~~ thought was the highlight of the season.

Here are some rules on pronoun-antecedent agreement.

EXERCISE
Maintaining agreement between pronouns and antecedents.

1. *A compound antecedent usually is plural and thus requires a plural pronoun.* A **compound antecedent** is a noun phrase containing two or more terms joined by *and.*

Mr. and Mrs. Kwan are here for *their* appointment.

WEBLINK

http://cctc2.commnet.edu/
grammar/pronouns.htm

A fun guide to pronoun agreement, with quizzes and exercises

2. *With disjunctive antecedents, the pronoun should agree in number and gender with the nearest part.* A **disjunctive antecedent** is a noun phrase consisting of two or more terms joined by *or* or *nor*. When a disjunctive antecedent contains both a singular and a plural part, this rule works well if the singular noun precedes the plural one.

> Either Tamara Wilson or *the Changs* will bring *their* barbeque set to the next picnic.

If the plural noun precedes the singular one, however, following the rule usually leads to an awkward-sounding sentence:

> Either the Changs or *Tamara Wilson* will bring *her* barbeque set to the next picnic.

In such cases, it is best to reword the sentence so as to either get rid of the pronoun or put the singular noun before the plural one.

EXERCISE
Pronoun antecedent agreement.

3. *As an antecedent, a collective noun can be either singular or plural, depending on its sense.* Both of these sentences are correct:

> *The jury* took only two hours to reach *its* verdict.

> *The jury* took only two hours to reach *their* verdict.

The first sentence emphasizes the singularity of the jury as a body, while the second puts more emphasis on the jury as a group of individuals.

4. *Pronouns must agree with antecedents that are indefinite pronouns.* Most indefinite pronouns (such as *everybody, anyone,* and *each*) are singular. When an indefinite pronoun serves as the antecedent for another pronoun, that pronoun should also be singular.

> *Everything* was in *its* place.

> *Each* of the women had *her* reasons for opposing the plan.

Some indefinite pronouns (*some, all, more*) can have either a singular or a plural sense. When one of these indefinite pronouns is used as the antecedent for another pronoun, the other pronoun can be either singular or plural, depending on the sense of the sentence.

> *Some* of the *news* was as bad as we thought *it* would be.

> *Some* of the team's *players* have lost *their* motivation.

5. *Sexist use of generic pronouns should be avoided.* In the past, the male pronouns *he, him,* and *his* were often used in generic statements referring to both sexes, as in this sentence: "A doctor should listen carefully to *his* patients." But this practice is clearly sexist, as it favors one gender over the other. Three ways to avoid such sexist pronoun usage are (1) making the pronoun and its antecedent plu-

> ## WEBLINK
>
> http://www.wisc.edu/
> writetest/Handbook/
> SubjectVerb.html
> Hypertext discussion of a
> variety of agreement issues,
> including subject-verb and
> pronoun agreement

ral, (2) rewording the sentence, and (3) using an occasional disjunctive pronoun such as *he or she.* (See 37a-2.)

23b   Refer to a specific noun antecedent

Pronouns (such as *she, it,* and *his*) work best when they refer back to a particular noun (the antecedent).

Only one of the new hockey players knew what *his* position would be.

23.1
Examples of
pronoun agree-
ment problems.

1   Avoiding generalized *they* or *you* or implied antecedents

In casual speech, people often use pronouns in vague ways, without explicit antecedents ("*They* say that television is dulling our brains"). In formal writing, however, such vagueness can sabotage meaning and must be avoided.

EXERCISE
Pronoun
reference.

VAGUE *THEY* REVISED

Some people
~~They~~ say that television is dulling our brains.

Similarly, avoid using the pronoun *you* unless you are addressing the reader directly.

VAGUE *YOU* REVISED

One never knows
~~You never know~~ when calamity will strike.

Pronouns should refer back to specific antecedents, not implied ones.

IMPLIED REFERENCE REVISED

the notes

Notetaking is very helpful in doing research, especially if ~~they~~ are well organized.

2 Clarifying references with more than one possible antecedent

Writers sometimes get into trouble by using a pronoun that could refer to more than one noun. Usually it is necessary to rewrite the sentence so that the antecedent is named, whether or not it has been mentioned previously in the sentence.

VAGUE REFERENCE REVISED

Fred

Neither Bill nor Fred knew what ~~he~~ should do.

OR

their friend

Neither Bill nor Fred knew what ~~he~~ should do.

If *he* refers either to Fred or to a mutual friend mentioned in a previous sentence, it is important to say so.

23c Avoid vague use of *this, that, which,* and *it*

The pronouns *this, that, which,* and *it* may be used with care to refer broadly to an entire statement:

> According to the linguistic school currently on top, human beings are all born with a genetic endowment for recognizing and formulating language. *This* must mean that we possess genes for all kinds of information, with strands of special, peculiarly human DNA for the discernment of meaning in syntax.
>
> —Lewis Thomas, *Lives of a Cell*

AUDIO

Using *this* without ambiguity.

In this excerpt, the word *this* leading off the second sentence refers clearly to the main clause of the first sentence ("human beings . . . language").

In many cases, though, using pronouns for broad reference may confuse the reader. What does *it* refer to in the following paragraph?

> Watching Monday Night Football on ABC has become a ritual for countless American sports lovers. *It* is symbolic of contemporary American life.

It could refer to (1) Monday Night Football, (2) watching Monday Night Football, or (3) watching Monday Night Football has become a

HELP

How do I identify possible pronoun reference problems?

1. Open the SEARCH feature of your word-processing program.
2. Enter *it* in the search field.
3. Run the search.
4. Whenever the program highlights an *it*, use the guidelines in this chapter to determine if you have used the word correctly.
5. Do a similar search for *this*, *that*, and *which*.

ritual for countless American sports lovers. One way to resolve this ambiguity is to replace the pronoun with a full noun phrase:

VAGUE REFERENCE REVISED

> Watching Monday Night Football on ABC has become a ritual for
> countless American sports lovers. *Monday Night Football* ~~It~~ is symbolic of contemporary
> American life.

23d   Be consistent with use of *that* and *which*

The relative pronoun *that* is used only with essential (restrictive) relative clauses—clauses that are essential to identify the nouns they modify:

ESSENTIAL CLAUSE

> First prize went to the long-haired collie *that came all the way from Hartford.*   [There were other longhaired collies in the competition.]

Although many people prefer using *which* only for nonessential relative clauses, it can be used either with essential relative clauses or with nonessential (nonrestric-tive) relative clauses—clauses that merely add extra information (see 40e, 40j):

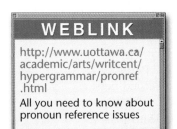

WEBLINK

http://www.uottawa.ca/academic/arts/writcent/hypergrammar/pronref.html

All you need to know about pronoun reference issues

23.2

An online guide to pronoun reference.

NONESSENTIAL CLAUSE

> First prize went to the longhaired collie, *which came all the way from Hartford.* [It was the only longhaired collie in the competition.]

ESSENTIAL CLAUSE

> First prize went to the longhaired collie *which came all the way from Hartford.* [There were other longhaired collies in the competition.]

23.3
More essential
and nonessen-
tial clauses.

The style/grammar checker on your computer will probably suggest that you use *that* for essential clauses, but this is not a strict rule. Many expert writers use either *that* or *which* for essential relative clauses, depending on how formal they want to sound. (*Which* is slightly more formal than *that*.)

23e Use the subjective case when a pronoun functions as a sentence subject, clause subject, or subject complement

Case refers to the form a pronoun takes to indicate its grammatical relation to other words in a sentence. See Pronouns According to Case.

23.4
A brief history
of English
pronouns.

Pronouns According to Case

	Subjective Case	Objective Case	Possessive Case
First-person singular	I	me	my, mine
Second-person singular	you	you	your, yours
Third-person singular	he, she, it	him, her, it	his, her, hers, its
First-person plural	we	us	our, ours
Second-person plural	you	you	your, yours
Third-person plural	they	them	their, theirs
Relative and interrogative	who, whoever	whom, whomever	whose

The **subjective case** (*I, you, he, she, it, we, they, who, whoever*) is required for all pronouns used as subjects, including pronouns that are paired with a noun to form a compound subject or to rename the noun (see 23g).

She and Octavio are good friends.   [Sentence subject]

It seems that only Harrison and *I* were not invited.   [Clause subject]

In predicate nominative constructions, the verb *be* is used to set up an "equation" between a noun subject or a pronoun subject such as *it, that, this* and a personal pronoun such as *he, she, it,* or *they*.

"Hello, is Carol there?" "Yes, this is ~~her~~ she."
Who will be the lead actor—~~him~~ he or ~~me~~ I?

23f Use the objective case when a pronoun functions as an object

The **objective case** (*me, you, him, her, it, us, them, whom, whomever*) is required for all pronouns used as objects, indirect objects, and objects of prepositions, including any pronoun paired with a noun or another pronoun to form a compound object.

EXERCISE
Pronoun case.

The boss invited Janice and *him* to lunch.   [Pronoun as indirect object]

Just between *you* and *me,* don't you think Marty's been a little out of line lately?   [Pronoun as object of a preposition]

23g Test for pronoun case in compound constructions by using the pronoun alone

Most problems with pronoun case arise in compound constructions, when a pronoun is paired with a noun:

The instructor gave Natasha and [*me, I*] an extra project to do.

In such sentences, the case of the pronoun—subjective or objective—depends on its function in the sentence. If you are unsure about which

WEBLINK

http://www.uottawa.ca/ academic/arts/writcent/ hypergrammar/pronouns .html

All about pronouns and their proper uses

case to use, the best way to find out is to try the sentence without the noun:

The instructor gave [*me, I*] an extra project to do.

Seeing it in this form makes it easier to decide what the correct form is:

The instructor gave Natasha and *me* an extra project to do.

A special type of pronoun-noun pairing, called an **appositive,** occurs when a pronoun is conjoined with a noun.

~~*We Americans* tend to be patriotic.~~

Sometimes people from other countries complain about *us Americans*.

Again, if you are unsure about which case to use in such situations, just omit the noun and see which pronoun form is correct.

We tend to be patriotic.

Sometimes people from other countries complain about *us*.

HELP

How do I customize a style/grammar checker to search for pronoun case problems?

1. Open the style/grammar checker.
2. Click on the OPTIONS feature.
3. Instead of one of the standard rule sets (such as FORMAL or CASUAL), select a CUSTOM file.
4. Open the customization feature.
5. Deselect all the grammar and style features except the one for pronoun case problems, which should be called something like PRONOUN ERRORS.
6. Run the program on your document. *Remember:* It may not catch all your errors!

NOTE: You can use the customization feature for many similar purposes. For example, if you want to check for run-on sentences (Chapter 27), turn off PRONOUN ERRORS and select CLAUSE ERRORS instead.

23h   Choose the form for an interrogative or relative pronoun based on how it functions in its clause

The pronouns *who, whom, whoever, whomever,* and *whose* are used in questions and relative clauses (see 22c-3). In questions, they are called **interrogative pronouns;** in clauses, they are called **relative pronouns.**

Who reserved this book?   [Interrogative pronoun]

I'd like to find the person *who* reserved this book.   [Relative pronoun]

AUDIO
That versus *who.*

When you ask a question and reverse normal sentence word order, choosing the correct interrogative pronoun can be puzzling:

[*Who, Whom*] are you going to invite to the wedding?

In conversational English, many speakers would use *Who* in this sentence. But, in formal usage the correct form is *Whom.* To understand why, rearrange the question into a statement, using a personal pronoun: "You are going to invite [*he, him*] to the wedding." After rewording, you will have no trouble recognizing the correct personal pronoun—in this case, *him.* The rewording clearly points to the objective case and the choice of the objective form *whom.*

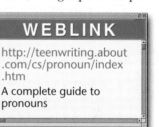

WEBLINK

http://teenwriting.about
.com/cs/pronoun/index
.htm

A complete guide to
pronouns

WWW
23.5
Visit a complete guide to pronouns online.

As a writer, you must decide whether the *wh-* pronoun functions as a subject or an object in the clause in which it is used. Because independent and dependent clauses are often tightly linked, the choice can be unclear. If you are uncertain about which form to use, try this test: (1) isolate and, if necessary, transpose the clause in which the *wh-* pronoun occurs, (2) substitute different personal pronouns (such as *she, her, he,* or *him*) for the *wh-* pronoun and see which case sounds best, and then (3) select the corresponding *wh-* pronoun.

EXERCISE
Deciding when to use *who* and *whom.*

23i   Use possessive pronouns to show ownership

There are two types of possessive pronouns. **Attributive possessive pronouns** (*my, your, her, his, its, our, their*) are used directly before a noun, while **nominal possessive pronouns** (*mine, yours, hers, his, its, ours, theirs*) are used with a linking verb (*is, was*).

> This is *my* car.

> This car is *mine.*

Note that the possessive forms ending in *s* (*yours, hers, ours, its, theirs*) do not take an apostrophe (see 43a).

> Gerunds require an attributive possessive pronoun:

> *His* wanting to do extra work was what impressed me.

In this sentence, *wanting to do extra work* is a gerund phrase. Since gerunds act as nouns, the possessive pronoun modifying this phrase should be an adjectival one (*his*). Be sure not to make the mistake of using the objective case pronoun (*him*) in this kind of construction.

> *His*
> ~~Him~~ wanting to do extra work was what impressed me.

23j Choose the case for a pronoun in a comparison based on how it would function in its own clause

What is the meaning of this sentence?

> Mark likes school more than me.

Technically, it means that Mark has a greater liking for school than he does for the speaker of the sentence. It does not mean that Mark has a greater liking for school than the speaker does. The latter meaning is correctly expressed with this construction:

> Mark likes school more than I.

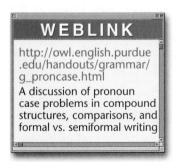

WEBLINK

http://owl.english.purdue
.edu/handouts/grammar/
g_proncase.html
A discussion of pronoun
case problems in compound
structures, comparisons, and
formal vs. semiformal writing

You can avoid this problem by recognizing that the second part of the comparison (the part after *than*) is an incomplete clause. The complete versions of the two sentences make the distinction clear:

> Mark likes school more than
> [he likes] me.

> Mark likes school more than I
> [like school].

A similar procedure can be used with *as . . . as* constructions.

CHAPTER **24**

Verbs

Using verbs correctly can help make writing lively and precise. This chapter explains some of the major aspects of verb usage: form, tense, voice, and mood. (Two other aspects, gender and number, are discussed in 23a.)

AUDIO
Chapter overview.

24a Learn the regular verb forms

All verbs in English, except *be*, have five basic forms or **principal parts.**

Base Form	Present Tense (-s form)	Past Tense	Past Participle	Present Participle
jump	jumps	jumped	jumped	jumping
erase	erases	erased	erased	erasing
veto	vetoes	vetoed	vetoed	vetoing

Most English verbs are **regular verbs.** Their forms follow the pattern of the preceding examples: adding *s* (or *es*) to the base form to make the third-person singular present tense, adding *d* (or *ed*) to make the past tense and past participle, and adding *ing* to the base form (and sometimes dropping the final *e*) to make the present participle.

The **base form,** or **simple form,** of a verb is the form listed in a dictionary, the form normally used with plural nouns or the pronouns *I, you, we,* or *they* in the present tense: "Hummingbirds *migrate* south in winter." "I *walk* two miles every day."

When the subject of a sentence is *he, she, it,* or some other third-person singular subject, the **present tense** of the verb has an *s* added to it: "She *visits* New York every month." "My neighbor *walks* laps around our block." Sometimes a slight change is required in the spelling of the base form (*fly/flies, veto/vetoes*).

The **past tense** of a verb is used to describe action that occurred in the past. For a regular verb, add *d* or *ed* to the base form to get the past tense: "Fox TV *televised* Super Bowl XXXI." "We *wanted* to see the game."

The **past participle** of a regular verb is similar in form to the past tense. The past participle can be used (1) with *has* or *have* in the present perfect tense, (2) with *had* in the past perfect tense, (3) with some form of *be* to create a passive-voice construction, and (4) by itself, as an adjective, to modify a noun.

We *have petitioned* the school board for a new crosswalk.
[Present perfect]

Before last night's meeting, we *had talked* about going directly to the mayor. [Past perfect]

Last year, two students *were injured* trying to cross this street.
[Passive voice]

The parents of the *injured* students are supporting our cause.
[Adjective]

The **present participle** is created by adding *ing* to the base form of a verb. It is used (1) with some form of *be* to indicate ongoing action (the progressive tense), (2) as a gerund, and (3) as an adjective.

Joaquin *is working* on a new project. [Progressive tense]

He enjoys *working*. [Gerund]

This is a *working* draft of my paper. [Adjective]

24b Learn common irregular verb forms

VIDEO

Using irregular verbs.

An **irregular verb** is one whose past tense and past participle do not follow the standard pattern of being created by adding *d* or *ed* to the base form. Following is a list of some of the most common irregular verbs and their past tense and past participle forms.

Base Form	Past Tense	Past Participle
be	was, were	been
beat	beat	beaten
become	became	become
begin	began	begun
bite	bit	bit, bitten
blow	blew	blown
break	broke	broken
bring	brought	brought
build	built	built
burn	burned, burnt	burned, burnt

Base Form	Past Tense	Past Participle
buy	bought	bought
catch	caught	caught
choose	chose	chosen
come	came	come
cost	cost	cost
dig	dug	dug
do	did	done
draw	drew	drawn
drink	drank	drunk
drive	drove	driven
eat	ate	eaten
fall	fell	fallen
fight	fought	fought
fly	flew	flown
forget	forgot	forgotten, forgot
get	got	gotten, got
give	gave	given
go	went	gone
grow	grew	grown
hang	hung	hung
hide	hid	hidden
keep	kept	kept
know	knew	known
lay	laid	laid
lead	led	led
leave	left	left
lie	lay	lain
lose	lost	lost
mean	meant	meant
pay	paid	paid
ride	rode	ridden
run	ran	run
see	saw	seen
set	set	set
shake	shook	shaken
show	showed	shown, showed
shrink	shrank	shrunk
sing	sang	sung
sink	sank	sunk
sit	sat	sat
speak	spoke	spoken
steal	stole	stolen
stick	stuck	stuck

Base Form	Past Tense	Past Participle
strike	struck	struck, stricken
swear	swore	sworn
swim	swam	swum
take	took	taken
teach	taught	taught
tear	tore	torn
think	thought	thought
throw	threw	thrown
wake	woke, waked	woken, waked
wear	wore	worn
write	wrote	written

24c Know how to use auxiliary verbs

An **auxiliary verb** (or **helping verb**) is one that is used with a main verb to indicate tense (see 24d), mood (see 24h), or voice (see 24g). The most common auxiliary verbs are *be, have,* and *do.*

She *is finishing* her paper.   [Progressive tense, indicating ongoing action]

The college *has adopted* a new honor code.   [Present perfect tense, indicating past action with ongoing effects]

We *do need* to get going.   [Emphasis]

My roommate *has been asked* to run for the student senate.   [Passive voice, present perfect tense]

Does he *know* what's involved?   [Question]

Other important helping verbs are the **modal auxiliary verbs** (*may/might, can/could, will/would, shall/should, must, ought to,* and *have to*). These verbs communicate degrees of probability, necessity, or obligation. A modal auxiliary verb is used only with the base form of another verb:

The concert *might be* sold out.

We *should get* tickets before it is too late.

Modal auxiliaries can be used with forms of *be, have,* or *do,* but not with other modal auxiliaries.

NONSTANDARD   We might *could* do that.

REVISED   We might *be able to* do that.   [Verb phrase substituted]

In some cases, you can simply eliminate one of the modal auxiliaries:

NONSTANDARD	Sally *should ought to* cancel her appointment.
REVISED	Sally *should* cancel her appointment.
	OR
	Sally *ought to* cancel her appointment.

24d Learn the verb tenses

Verb tense expresses the time of the action or the state of being indicated by a verb. English has three basic tenses: past, present, and future. Each tense can also take on a **verbal aspect,** indicating duration or completion of the verb's action or state of being. The three verbal aspects in English are progressive, perfect, and perfect progressive. With all possible combinations of tenses and aspects, English has twelve verb tenses.

WWW

24.1
Examples of twelve verb tenses.

1 Present tenses

The **simple present tense** is used to express a general truth, to make an observation, or to describe an habitual activity: "A rolling stone *gathers* no moss." "Oates's stories *depress* me." With an appropriate time expression, the simple present can be used to refer to a scheduled future event: "The show *begins* in five minutes." The simple present is used in stage directions and in critical discussions of literary works: "In *The Tempest,* all the action *occurs* in one place during one day." The simple present also is used to express a scientific fact or law: "Water *boils* at 100° Celsius."

The **present progressive tense** is formed with the auxiliary verb *am, are,* or *is* and the present participle (*-ing* form) of a main verb. The present progressive is used to indicate action occurring at the present time: "Jennifer *is preparing* for the MCAT exam." With an appropriate time expression, the present progressive can be used to announce future events: "A new supermarket *is opening* next week."

ESL Note Certain verbs, called **verbs of state,** do not have any progressive tenses. These verbs include *know, believe, need, consist,* and *exist.* Thus, it is incorrect to say "I am needing a new computer" (see 51f).

The **present perfect tense** is formed with the auxiliary verb *have* or *has* and the past participle of a main verb. The present perfect is used to indicate action that began in the past and either is continuing or has continuing effects in the present: "Many people *have expressed* alarm about environmental degradation."

The **present perfect progressive tense** is formed by combining *have been* or *has been* with the present participle of a main verb. The present perfect progressive is used similarly to the present perfect but emphasizes the ongoing nature of the activity: Eric *has been studying* German for two years.

2 Past tenses

The **simple past tense** is used to describe actions or conditions that occurred or applied entirely in the past: "In 1950, the United States *consisted* of only forty-eight states."

The **past progressive tense** is formed by combining the auxiliary verb *was* or *were* with the present participle of a main verb. The past progressive describes action continuing over a period of time in the past. It is often used to set the stage for another action of shorter duration: "He *was cleaning* the living room when the phone rang."

The **past perfect tense** is created by combining the auxiliary verb *had* with the past participle of a main verb. The past perfect is used to describe a past action that preceded another past action: "Before her accident, Amanda *had thought* of taking the job."

The **past perfect progressive tense** functions like the past perfect tense but puts more emphasis on the continuing or repetitive nature of the past action. The past perfect progressive is formed by combining *had been* with the present participle of a main verb: "Before her accident, Amanda *had been thinking* of taking the job."

3 Future tenses

The **simple future tense,** as its name implies, expresses actions or conditions that will occur in the future. The simple future consists of the modal auxiliary verb *will* and the base form of a main verb: "Ames *will be* a half hour late."

(**ESL Note**) In casual English, future conditions are often expressed using the modal auxiliary *is going to* instead of *will,* as in "Ames *is going to* be a half hour late." It is best to avoid this usage in formal English.

The **future progressive tense** is formed by combining *will be* with the present participle of a main verb. The future progressive expresses action that will be continuing or repeated in the future: "Next year my son *will be going* to college."

The **future perfect tense** consists of *will have* and the past participle of a main verb. The future perfect is used to describe an action that will occur in the future but before some specified time: "By the end of this year, gun-related violence *will have doubled*."

The **future perfect progressive tense** is similar to the future perfect but emphasizes the continuous or repetitive nature of the action. The future perfect progressive consists of *will have been* plus the present participle of a main verb: "By next year, I *will have been working* for fifteen years."

24e Observe sequence of tenses

Good writing presents a coherent framework of time. Since time is indicated in part by verb tense, it is important to select verb tenses carefully and logically. The relationship between two or more verbs in the same sentence or in adjacent sentences is called the **sequence of tenses.**

1 Sequence of verb tenses in compound or adjacent sentences

Two or more independent clauses about closely related events or situations may be connected by a coordinating conjunction (*and, or, but*) to form a compound sentence. Alternatively, two related independent clauses may be presented as consecutive sentences. Typically, the main verbs in each clause or sentence have the same tense: "Joe *wants* to go to the game, but Lori *does* not."

2 Sequence of verb tenses in complex sentences

A complex sentence has one independent clause and one or more dependent clauses (see 22d-2). Each clause has its own main verb. The appropriate tense for each main verb depends on the context and the intended meaning. If the actions expressed by these verbs occur at approximately the same time, the verbs should be in the same tense: "Before you *sit* down, *adjust* the height of your chair."

When you need to make it clear that one past action or event preceded another, use the past perfect or past perfect progressive tense in one clause and the simple past tense in the other clause: "Amanda *had thought* of taking the job, but now she *said* no." When you need to show that a past action or event preceded a present or future one, use the present perfect or present perfect progressive tense to express the past action or event: "Since the Pope *has been* to Mexico already, he probably *will* not *go* again."

3 Sequence of verb tenses with infinitives

There are two kinds of **infinitives:** the **present infinitive** (the base form of a verb, often preceded by *to*) and the **perfect infinitive** (*to have* plus the past participle of a verb) (see 22a-4). Use the present infinitive for an action that occurs at the same time as or later than the action expressed by the main verb: "Samantha *wants* me *to pick up* the car." Use the perfect infinitive for an action that occurs prior to the action expressed by the main verb: "Samantha *wants* me *to have picked up* the car."

4 Sequence of verb tenses with participles

The **present participle** (the *-ing* form of a verb) can be used to represent an action that occurs at the same time as that expressed by the main verb: "*Walking* into the house, Jim sensed danger."

The **past participle** is used to indicate that an action occurs before or during the action expressed by the main verb: "*Stung* by criticism of his latest film, Costner is working hard on a new one."

The **present perfect participle** (*having* plus the past participle) expresses an action occurring prior to the action of the main verb: "*Having signed* a contract, Deanna was left with no options."

24f Use transitive and intransitive verbs correctly: *sit/set, lie/lay, rise/raise*

A **transitive verb** is a verb that takes a direct object (see 22a-3). In other words, a transitive verb transfers an action from a subject to an object. The sentence "A virus damaged my hard drive" has a transitive verb (*damaged*) that transfers the action to the direct object (*hard drive*). Some typical transitive verbs are *see, hear, consult, kick, recognize,* and *mix.* Transitive verbs are usually marked in dictionaries with the abbreviation *vt* or *tr.*

An **intransitive verb** is one that does not take a direct object. Some typical intransitive verbs are *sleep, relax, die, go, fall, come,* and *walk.* Intransitive verbs are usually identified in dictionaries by the abbreviation *vi* or *intr.*

Many English verbs can be used either transitively or intransitively. For example, the verb *jump* is transitive in the sentence "Mike jumped the fence" but intransitive in the sentence "Mike jumped for joy." Some other common "two-way" verbs are *run, dream, write, eat, grow,* and *develop.*

Many speakers of English confuse *sit* and *set, lie* and *lay,* and *rise* and *raise.* The two verbs in each of these pairs sound somewhat alike and have related meanings, but they differ as to whether they can take an object (see 22b-3). The first member of each pair is intransitive and cannot take an object; the second member is transitive and does take an object.

INTRANSITIVE	Jorge *will sit* over there. [The verb has no object.]
TRANSITIVE	Jorge *will set* the *flowers* over there. [The verb has an object, *flowers.*]
INTRANSITIVE	I think I *will lie* down. [The verb has no object.]
TRANSITIVE	We *will lay* the *groundwork* for the project. [The verb has an object, *groundwork.*]
INTRANSITIVE	The sun *rises* in the east. [The verb has no object.]
TRANSITIVE	The senator always *raises* a lot of *money* for his re-election campaigns. [The verb has an object, *money.*]

EXERCISE
Editing troublesome verbs.

24g Favor active over passive voice

Voice is the characteristic of a verb that indicates whether the subject of a sentence is acting or being acted upon. In the **active voice,** the subject of the sentence performs an action on a direct object (see 22b). In the **passive voice,** the subject of the sentence is acted upon. Only transitive verbs can be cast in active and passive voice (see 24f).

Subject/actor   DO
ACTIVE   My friend Julie *handcrafted* this pin.   [The subject acts on an object.]

Subject   DO/actor
PASSIVE   This pin *was handcrafted* by my friend Julie.   [The subject is acted upon by the object following the verb.]

The passive voice consists of an appropriate form of the auxiliary verb *be* and the past participle of a main verb (see 24a). A passive-voice sentence may refer to the performer of the action in a *by* phrase following the verb. In practice, though, the *by* phrase is often omitted, which has the effect of concealing or de-emphasizing the performer of the action: "This pin *was handcrafted.*"

In general, good writers favor the active voice over the passive voice. The active voice is more concise and more direct—and thus

VIDEO
Using the passive voice.

more vigorous—than the passive. In some cases, however, the passive voice works better than the active voice. For example, when identifying the performer of an action is unimportant or difficult, using the passive voice allows you to write a grammatical sentence without mentioning the actor (see 31d): "Bacterial infections are usually treated with antibiotics."

(Style/Grammar Checker Alert)   Your style/grammar checker may highlight most of the passive verbs in your writing and make a comment like "This main clause may contain a verb in the passive voice."

WEBLINK

http://cctc2.commnet
.edu/grammar/verbs.htm
A superb resource on verbs, including quizzes and lots of cool graphics

24.2
A fun online review of verbs and verbals.

If you decide to change some of the passive verbs to the active voice, you can do so by simply making the actor (whether stated or concealed) the subject of the sentence and changing the predicate. Note, however, that some passive-voice sentences are perfectly fine and should be left unchanged (see 31d).

24h Make sure verbs are in the proper mood

The **mood** of a verb indicates the type of statement being made by the sentence—an assertion, a question, a command, a wish, or a hypothetical condition. English verbs have three moods: indicative, imperative, and subjunctive.

WEBLINK

http://owl.english.purdue
.edu/handouts/grammar/
g_vmood.html
Discussion and examples of verb mood and voice

The **indicative mood** is used to make assertions, state opinions, and ask questions. It is the most commonly used mood in English.

Washington *was* the first president of the United States.   [Assertion]

Citizens *should take* more interest in local government.   [Opinion]

Do you *want* to vote?   [Question]

24.3
Examples of formulaic uses of the subjunctive.

The **imperative mood** is used to express commands and give instructions. Commands are always addressed to a second person, although the explicit *you* is normally omitted. Instructions are often cast in the imperative mood (see 22a-3, 22d-1): "*Insert* Setup Disk 1 in the drive. Then *run* the program."

The **subjunctive mood** is used for hypothetical conditions, polite requests, wishes, and other uncertain statements. A verb in the subjunctive mood often appears in dependent clauses beginning with *if* or *that*. The present subjunctive is the same as the base form of the verb. The past subjunctive is identical to the past tense of the verb. The only exception is *were*, which is used for all subjunctive uses of *be* except after verbs of requesting, requiring, or recommending, where *be* is used: "I wish I *were* an A student!" "She asked that her client *be* given probation." The past perfect subjunctive has the same form as the ordinary past perfect.

EXERCISE
Subjunctive
mood.

1   Hypothetical *if* constructions

When an *if* clause expresses a contrary-to-fact or unreal condition, the verb of the clause should be in the past subjunctive or past perfect subjunctive mood. The main clause verb should include the modal auxiliary *would, could,* or *might.*

> If I *were* you, I *would* make up my Incompletes as soon as possible.
> [Expresses a hypothetical future condition]

> If John *had been* there, he *might* have been able to help.   [Expresses a hypothetical past condition]

Do not use *would, could,* or *might* in a hypothetical *if* clause. In contrary-to-fact sentences, modal auxiliaries such as *would* and *could* belong in the main clause, not in the conditional (subordinate) clause. Use the subjunctive in the conditional clause.

SUBJUNCTIVE FORM REVISED

>   *lived*
> If we ~~would live~~ closer to San Francisco, we would go there more often.

2   Dependent clauses expressing a wish

In a dependent clause following the verb *wish*, use the past subjunctive for present contrary-to-fact conditions and the past perfect subjunctive for past contrary-to-fact conditions: "I wish [that] he *were* here." "I wish [that] he *had stayed.*"

AUDIO
Correct use of
the subjunctive.

3   Dependent clauses expressing a request, suggestion, or demand

Verbs such as *require, demand, suggest,* and *insist* are usually followed by a dependent clause beginning with *that*. The verb in the *that* clause should be in the subjunctive mood: "The police require that all pets *be* kept on a leash." Sometimes *that* is omitted.

CHAPTER **25**

Adjectives and Adverbs

AUDIO
Chapter
overview.

Using adjective and adverbs allows writers to add details to their work, making it more precise and colorful. But adjectives and adverbs have their proper uses, and it is important not to confuse them or use them incorrectly.

25a Use adjectives to modify nouns

An **adjective** is a word that modifies a noun (see 22a-5). Typically, adjectives answer one of the following questions: which? what kind? how many? Sometimes an adjective is placed next to the noun it modifies, either directly before the noun (an *ancient* building, the *first* page) or directly after (a dream *forsaken*, his curiosity *satisfied*). Other times an adjective is separated from the noun it modifies, as in the sentence "The movie was *exciting*." In these cases, a linking verb (such as *is, was,* or *seemed*) connects the noun and its modifier to form a predicate adjective and a subject complement.

WEBLINK

http://www.uottawa.ca/
academic/arts/writcent/
hypergrammar/adjectve
.html

A complete discussion of
adjectives

Many adjectives have the same form as the present and past participles of verbs (a *roaring* lion, a *deserted* island). There also are many pronoun-like adjectives: **possessive adjectives** (*her* guitar), **demonstrative adjectives** (*this/that* tree), **interrogative adjectives** (*Which* way do I go?), and **indefinite adjectives** (*some* ideas). Note that demonstrative adjectives must be either singular or plural, to agree with the nouns they modify: "I like *this* kind of tree, but *those* kinds are hardier."

25b Avoid overuse of nouns as modifiers

A noun can modify another noun to form a **noun compound** that functions as an adjective. Some examples are *park* bench, *soda* pop, *letter* opener, *telephone* book, *fender* bender, *tape* player, and *movie* theater.

Noun compounding can help you save a few words—*windshield* is more concise than *shield against the wind*—but it can be confusing for readers, especially if you use more than three nouns in a row. To avoid long noun strings such as *the picnic table cross brace*, use a prepositional phrase: *the cross brace under the picnic table*. Such phrasing may take a few more words, but the meaning will be clearer.

25c Use adverbs to modify verbs, adjectives, other adverbs, and clauses

An **adverb** is a word that modifies a verb, an adjective, another adverb, or a clause (see 22a-6). Adverbs modify verbs by answering such questions as these: when? how? how often? where? to what degree?

VIDEO
Recognizing adjectives and adverbs.

Linda *often* goes to the gym to work out.   [Modifies the verb *goes*]

They made a *very* bad mistake.   [Modifies the adjective *bad*]

The car was turned *almost* upside down.   [Modifies the adverb *upside down*]

Luckily, I was able to find a backup disk.   [Modifies the entire clause]

25d Be aware of some commonly confused adjectives and adverbs

The pairs of words *good/well* and *bad/badly* are misused by many writers who fail to recognize that *good* and *bad* are adjectives, whereas *well* and *badly* are adverbs. The sentence "Fielder runs *good* for a man his size" is ungrammatical. The correct version is

> **WEBLINK**
>
> http://www.uottawa.ca/
> academic/arts/writcent/
> hypergrammar/adverbs
> .html#adverb
>
> A complete discussion of adverbs

www
25.1
A comprehensive guide to adverbs.

Fielder runs *well* for a man his size.   [The adverb *well* modifies the verb *runs*.]

The adjective *good* is appropriate when the word being modified is a noun.

He has a *good*, long stride.   [The adjective *good* modifies the noun *stride*.]

AUDIO
Well as an adjective or adverb.

When the main verb expresses a feeling or a perception (such verbs include *look, appear, feel, seem, taste,* and *smell*), the correct modifier is an adjective complement.

I feel *bad* about what I did. [Not *badly;* the adjective *bad* modifies the noun *I.*]

This gazpacho tastes *good.* [Not *well;* the adjective *good* modifies the noun *gazpacho.*]

25e Use comparative and superlative forms of adjectives and adverbs correctly

Most adjectives and a few adverbs can be used to make comparisons.

WEBLINK
http://cctc2.commnet.edu/
grammar/adjectives.htm
An excellent review of
adjectives, with exercises

Ted works *hard.* He is *determined* to get ahead. [Positive form]

Ted works *harder* than I do. He is *more determined* than I am. [Comparative forms]

Ted works the *hardest* of anybody I know. He is the *most determined* person I have ever met. [Superlative forms]

Using both *more* and a comparative form of an adjective or adverb (with the *-er* ending) is incorrect:

Ted works ~~more~~ harder than I do.

Likewise, using both *most* and a superlative form of an adjective (with the *-est* ending) is incorrect:

Ted is the ~~most~~ hardest working person I know.

Adjectives of one or two syllables usually add *-er* and *-est* in their comparative and superlative forms. For adjectives with more than two syllables, the comparative and superlative forms typically consist of the positive form with *more* and *most.*

	Comparative	*Superlative*
tasty	tastier	tastiest
beautiful	more beautiful	most beautiful

Some common adjectives have irregular comparative and superlative forms:

good	better	best
bad	worse	worst
far	farther/further	farthest/furthest

Only a few adverbs—those that are similar in form to adjectives—have regular comparative and superlative forms. Some of these regular adverbs are

early	earlier	earliest
fast	faster	fastest
hard	harder	hardest
late	later	latest
long	longer	longest

Several other adverbs have irregular forms:

badly	worse	worst
far	farther/further	farthest/furthest
little	less	least
much	more	most
well	better	best

When making comparisons, be accurate, complete, and logical. When comparing two items, use the comparative form. When comparing three or more items, use the superlative form.

Of the two candidates, I like Johnson *better.*

Of the three candidates, I like Johnson *best.*

Use *few, fewer,* or *fewest* with count nouns (such as *books, calories, flowers,* and *dollars*). Use *little, less,* or *least* with noncount nouns (such as *water, understanding,* and *progress*).

The team has *fewer* fans than it used to have.

The new package contains *less* rice.

Make sure the terms of a comparison are complete. Do not write a sentence such as "This headache remedy works better." Many readers will wonder, "Better than what?" Including a *than* phrase as part of the comparison makes it clear:

This headache remedy works better *than any other.*

WEBLINK

http://cctc2.commnet.edu/grammar/adverbs.htm
An excellent review of adverbs, with exercises

Certain adjectives, by definition, express an absolute condition or quality and thus logically cannot have different degrees. Words such as *unique, dead, pregnant, final,* and *incomparable* belong in this category. It makes no sense to say that something or someone is *more unique* or *less dead.*

Michael Jordan is the most ~~unique~~ *talented* basketball player in the world.

25f   Avoid double negatives

A **double negative** is a sentence or phrase containing two negative modifiers (typically adverbs such as *never, no, not, hardly, barely,* and *scarcely*) that carry the same meaning. Double negatives are considered nonstandard in modern English and should be avoided in formal writing and speaking.

The city buses do not have n̶o̶ *any* lifts for disabled passengers.

The passengers c̶a̶n̶'̶t̶ *can* hardly get on board.

Common Grammar Problems

FAQs

CHAPTER 26

Sentence Fragments

A **fragment** is a grammatically incomplete sentence such as

The one in the corner.

Runs like the wind.

Because we had no choice.

AUDIO
Chapter
overview.

Complete sentences (1) have a complete predicate, (2) have a grammatical subject, and (3) do not begin with a subordinating conjunction or relative pronoun unless they are connected to a main clause (see 22c-3). In the three examples of fragments, the first has no predicate, the second has no subject, and the third begins with an unattached subordinating conjunction (*Because*).

26a Make sentences grammatically complete

If you have a good style/grammar checker in your computer, it should identify most of the sentence fragments in your writing. But it will not be able to tell you how to fix them. So, you will need to solve these problems on your own.

1 Does the sentence have a complete predicate?

In standard English, all sentences must have a complete predicate—that is, a main verb plus any necessary helping verbs and complements. The main verb must be a *finite* verb, not an infinitive (*to* form) or a gerund (*-ing* form).

The second part of the following example has been incorrectly set off as a separate sentence; it does not have a finite verb and so cannot be a full sentence:

Seven is a very symbolic number in Judeo-Christian culture.
Appearing often in the Bible and other sacred texts.

Simply replacing the period with a comma will correct the problem:

Seven is a very symbolic number in Judeo-Christian culture, appearing often in the Bible and other sacred texts.

2 Does the sentence have a subject?

In standard English, all sentences (except commands) must have a grammatical subject (see 22b-1).

Sometimes, a fragment can be corrected by simply inserting an appropriate subject and making other related changes:

> Most of today's sitcoms are not about families in suburbia. ~~But~~
> *Rather, they are*
> ~~rather~~ about young adults in the big city.

Sometimes, simply changing the punctuation and making the fragment part of the previous sentence will correct the error:

> *but*
> Most of today's sitcoms are not about families in suburbia. ~~But~~
>
> rather about young adults in the big city.

By removing the period after *suburbia*, you enable *most of today's sitcoms* to serve as the subject for the rest of the sentence, thereby eliminating the fragment.

3 Are the subordinating phrases or clauses connected to a main clause?

EXERCISE

Fragments.

Check to be sure that word clusters beginning with a subordinating conjunction (such as *because, although,* or *if*) or a relative pronoun (such as *which, who,* or *that*) are connected or subordinated to a main subject and predicate (see 26b).

HELP

How do I locate sentence fragments?

1. Open the SEARCH function of your word-processing program.
2. Launch a search to locate each period in your document.
3. Look carefully at the group of words preceding each period located. Determine whether each group is indeed a complete sentence, using the questions raised in 26a.

26b Connect dependent clauses

Dependent clauses have a subject and a predicate but are linked to a main clause with a subordinating conjunction (such as *because, although,* or *if*) or a relative pronoun (such as *which, who,* or *that*). Because dependent clauses depend for their meaning on their connection to a main clause, they cannot stand alone. Therefore, if you begin a clause with a subordinating conjunction or relative pronoun and then end it with a period or semicolon before connecting it to a main

WEBLINK

http://owl.english.purdue
.edu/handouts/grammar/
g_frag.html
A basic discussion of
fragments, with exercises

WWW

26.1
A guide to revising fragments, plus exercises.

clause, you have produced a fragment, not a sentence. In the following sentence, changing the period to a comma allows the *Before* clause to serve as a dependent clause linked to *I must first discuss . . . ,* the main clause.

> Before I delve into critically analyzing the characters,/I must first
>
> discuss the opening sequence.

Likewise, relative clauses also need to be connected to a main clause. In the following sentence, the solution is simply to eliminate the period and join the two clauses:

AUDIO
How poor punctuation causes fragments.

> What seems annoying to me. ~~May~~ ^{may} not bother you at all.

26c Connect phrases

Phrases are similar to clauses except that they lack full verbs (see 22c-2). Phrases can be used as modifiers, subjects, objects, or complements—but never as sentences. Make sure that all of your phrases are connected to main clauses.

> Many nations began to process their own food, minerals, and other
>
> raw materials. ~~Using~~ ^{using} foreign aid and investments to back their efforts.

Often you can turn the fragment into an independent sentence.

EXERCISE
Combining sentences.

FRAGMENT   Some of the problems facing African nations can be traced to colonialism. *Some European nations doing little to prepare their colonies for independence.*

REVISED   Some of the problems facing African nations can be
               traced to colonialism. Some European nations did little
               to prepare their colonies for independence.   [Changing
               the verb of the fragment into a full verb turns the fragment
               into an independent sentence.]

26d Use sentence fragments only for special effect

Occasionally sentence fragments can be used for special effect, such as to add emphasis or to make writing sound conversational. Here is an example from the writing of Molly Ivins:

> Shrub's proposal to cut property taxes, on which our public schools depend, by $1 billion merely shifts the tax burden even more dramatically to the folks with the least money. *Nice work, Shrub.*
>
> —Molly Ivins, "Truly Happy News"

WEBLINK

http://www.english.uiuc
.edu/cws/wworkshop/
grammar/sentence_
fragments.htm
A full review of sentence
fragments, with exercises

WWW

26.2
A model paper
uses fragments
for special
effect.

In the last sentence, Ivins uses a common conversational expression, in the form of a fragment, to make a sarcastic comment.

Be cautious about using fragments in any kind of formal writing you do, since readers might see them only as grammatical mistakes, not as "special effects."

CHAPTER **27**

Comma Splices and Run-on Sentences

Joining two independent clauses with a comma creates a **comma splice**:

> The best keyboard for one-handed users is the Dvorak keyboard, it has a more convenient layout than the standard Qwerty keyboard.

WEBLINK

http://cctc2.commnet.edu/grammar/runons.htm
All you need to know about comma splices and run-on sentences, with exercises

27.1
Guidelines for revising run-on sentences.

Although comma splices are found in casual English, they are *not* acceptable in formal written English (see 40j).

Putting two independent clauses together without a conjunction or any punctuation creates a **run-on sentence** (or **fused sentence**):

> Dvorak keyboards put the most frequently typed characters within easy reach they are often used in speed-typing competitions.

AUDIO
Chapter overview.

(**Grammar Checker Alert**)   When looking for comma splices and run-on sentences with a style/grammar checker, remember that style/grammar checkers are not always reliable. You should look carefully at each case the checker identifies to see if it is really a comma splice or a run-on sentence.

77 2
Sample misdiagnoses from a grammar checker.

Run on sentences are incorrect in standard English and are often confusing to readers. There are four main ways to correct comma splices and run-on sentences:

- Turn one clause into a subordinate clause.
- Add a comma and a coordinating conjunction.
- Separate the clauses with a semicolon.
- Separate the clauses with a period.

EXERCISE
Comma splices and fused sentences.

VIDEO

Recognizing comma splices.

HELP

How do I identify comma splices and run-on sentences?

1. Open your style/grammar checker.
2. Click on the OPTIONS feature.
3. Select a CUSTOM file.
4. Open the customization feature.
5. Deselect all the grammar and style features except the one called something like CLAUSE ERRORS or COMMA SPLICE or FUSED SENTENCE.
6. For extra speed, turn off the spell checker.
7. Run the program on your document.

27a Turn one clause into a subordinate clause

Often the best way to correct a comma splice or run-on sentence is to convert one of the two clauses into a subordinate clause. This can be done by using either a subordinating conjunction (such as *while, although, because,* or *if*) or a relative pronoun (such as *which, that,* or *who*).

> *which*
> The best keyboard for one-handed users is the Dvorak keyboard, it
>
> has a more convenient layout than the standard Qwerty keyboard.

Sometimes this technique may require switching the two clauses around:

> *Because* it has a more convenient layout than the standard Qwerty keyboard, the best keyboard for one-handed users is the Dvorak keyboard.

27b Separate clauses with a comma and a coordinating conjunction

If the two parts of a comma splice or run-on sentence are of equal importance, you can put a comma and a coordinating conjunction (such as *and, or, but, nor,* or *yet*) between them:

An eagle once flew past our house ⌃ ; but ⌃ I only got a brief glimpse of it.

Simply inserting a comma in a run-on sentence is not enough, for that only produces another error (a comma splice); you must also insert a conjunction.

27c Separate independent clauses with a semicolon

If the two parts of a comma splice or run-on sentence are of equal importance, you can insert a semicolon between them.

Desktop computers usually have bigger screens than laptops do ⌃ ; ⌃

laptops are easier to carry around.

If you use a conjunctive adverb such as *however, therefore,* or *for example,* be sure to place the semicolon before it:

Laptops are coming down in price ⌃ ; ⌃ *therefore,* more people are

buying them.

27d Separate independent clauses with a period

Often the easiest way to correct a comma splice or run-on sentence is by inserting a period between the two independent clauses:

Dvorak keyboards put most frequently typed characters within

easy reach ⌃ . *They* ⌃ are often used in speed-typing competitions.

Although adding a period is the easiest way to correct these errors, it is not usually the best way. Inserting a period between the two clauses turns them into two separate sentences, thereby making it more difficult for the reader to see the relationship between them. As a general rule, try to use one of the other three methods before settling on this one.

WEBLINK

http://www.wisc.edu/ writetest/Handbook/ CommonErrors.html

An essential checklist that covers all sorts of common writing problems, including comma splices

CHAPTER **28**

Subject-Verb Agreement

Subjects and verbs should agree in number; that is, they must both be either singular or plural. "He go to work at nine o'clock" is ungrammatical because *he* is singular and *go* is plural. Here are some rules on subject-verb **agreement.**

28a Use plural verbs with plural subjects; singular verbs with singular subjects

He goes to work at nine o'clock.

We see each other later in the day.

With a modified subject, be sure to make the verb agree with the simple subject (see 22b-1).

Meg's circle of friends gives her a lot of support.   [*Circle* is the

simple subject of the phrase *Meg's circle of friends.*]

When a singular subject is followed by a phrase beginning with *as well as, along with, in addition to,* or *together with,* the verb should be in the singular.

Meg, as well as her friends, usually votes for the more liberal

candidate.

If this seems awkward to you, you can restructure the sentence to create a compound subject (which takes a plural verb):

Meg and her friends usually vote for the more liberal candidate.

(ESL Note) Speakers of languages that do not mark nouns and verbs for number (for example, Chinese and Japanese) often have trouble with subject-verb agreement in English.

28b   Use plural verbs with most compound subjects

Compound subjects refer to two or more people, places, or things and are formed with the conjunction *and*. In most cases, compound subjects have a plural sense and thus require plural verbs.

WEBLINK

http://cctc2.commnet.edu/ grammar/sv_agr.htm

A great guide to subject/verb agreement, complete with quizzes and exercises

28.1

An online guide to pronouns.

Geography and history are my

favorite subjects.

In some cases, a compound subject has a singular sense and requires a singular verb.

Rock 'n' roll has remained popular for decades.

28c   Make the verb agree with the closest part of a disjunctive subject

A **disjunctive subject** consists of two nouns or pronouns joined by *or* or *nor*. The verb in a sentence with such a subject agrees with the second part of the subject.

Either my sister or my parents are coming.

Neither my parents nor my sister is coming.

If the singular verb sounds awkward to you with such a mixed subject, you can switch the two parts of the subject and use the plural form of the verb:

Neither my sister nor my parents are coming.

28d   Make the verb agree in number with the sense of the indefinite pronoun

Indefinite pronouns include *anybody, everyone, nothing, each,* and *much.* Unlike regular pronouns, they do not necessarily refer to any particular person or thing. Most indefinite pronouns are grammatically singular. Therefore, when used as subjects, they should have singular verbs.

No one is here.

Something needs to be done about this.

Each of the candidates is giving a short speech.

28.2

Agreement
errors made by
President G. W.
Bush.

A few indefinite pronouns, including *both* and *others,* are plural and therefore require plural verbs. Other indefinite pronouns, such as *some, all, any, more,* and *none,* can be used with either singular or plural verb forms, depending on what they refer to.

All of the members were at the meeting.   [*All* refers to plural *members.*]

All of their attention was directed at her.   [*All* refers to singular *attention.*]

28e Use singular verbs with most collective nouns

Collective nouns are words such as *team, faculty, jury,* and *committee,* which can have either a singular or a plural sense depending on whether they refer to the group or to the individuals within the group (see 22a-1). These nouns usually take singular verbs.

The team is doing better than expected.

The band seems to be road-weary.

To emphasize the plural sense of collective nouns, simply insert an appropriate plural noun.

The band members seem to be road-weary.

OR

The members of the band seem to be road-weary.

28f Use singular verbs with nouns that are plural in form but singular in sense

Words such as *mathematics, athletics, politics, economics, physics,* and *news* look like plural nouns because of the *-s* ending. However, these nouns are usually singular in meaning and thus require singular verbs.

EXERCISE

Subject-verb
agreement.

Economics is my favorite subject.

The news from Lake Wobegon always interests me.

Likewise, titles of creative works and names of companies that look plural in form but actually refer to a singular entity take a singular verb.

The Brothers Karamazov was probably Dostoevsky's best novel.

Barnes & Noble has a Web site that is easy to navigate.

28g Be sure a linking verb agrees with its subject

Sometimes you may find yourself faced with a sentence of the form "X is Y," in which the subject X is singular and the subject complement Y is plural, or vice versa. In such cases, the linking verb should agree in number with the subject, not with the subject complement (see 22b-3).

Her main interest is boys.

Boys are her main interest.

28h Make the verb agree with its true subject, not the expletive *here* or *there*

In a sentence beginning with *here* or *there* and some form of the verb *be*, the true (grammatical) subject is usually the noun that immediately follows the *be* verb form.

There are some people at the door.

Here is the address you were looking for.

EXERCISE
More subject-
verb agree-
ment.

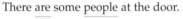

CHAPTER **29**

Misplaced and Dangling Modifiers

Modifiers are words, phrases, or clauses that qualify other words, phrases, or clauses. Used properly, modifiers can make writing richer and more precise.

29a Position modifiers close to the words they modify

AUDIO
Placing modifiers next to what they modify.

For maximum clarity, modifiers should be placed as close as possible to (ideally, right next to) the words they modify.

Unlike George,
Kramer does not need the approval of anyone, ~~unlike George~~.

frequently
Businesses publish the URLs for their Web sites ~~frequently~~ in advertisements.

Take special care with limiting modifiers such as *only, just, even, not,* and *almost,* which are often used imprecisely in ordinary speech. In formal writing, they should generally be positioned directly before the word or phrase they modify.

only
The yucca plant ~~only~~ grows well in full sunlight.

won   not
England ~~did not win~~ the battle because of superior firepower but because of better tactics.

29b Avoid ambiguity

WWW

29.1
A guide for avoiding misplaced modifiers.

WEBLINK

http://www.uottawa.ca/academic/arts/writcent/hypergrammar/msplmod.html

How not to use misplaced and dangling modifiers in your writing

A modifier that is not carefully positioned may present the reader with two or more possible interpretations.

Bound, gagged, and trussed up nude in a denim bag with plugs in her ears and tape over her eyes, Cleveland teacher Brenda P. Noonan told yesterday how she was kidnapped and taken to Florida without knowing where she was going or why.

—Quoted in Richard Lederer, *Anguished English*

It must have been quite a trick to describe these things while being bound and gagged! The following version of the sentence is clearer:

Cleveland teacher Brenda P. Noonan told yesterday how she was kidnapped and taken to Florida bound, gagged, and trussed up nude in a denim bag with plugs in her ears and tape over her eyes, without knowing where she was going or why.

Adverbs like *happily, quickly,* and *easily* are often ambiguous if they are positioned between two verb phrases.

Most people who responded to the ad *quickly* decided not to look at the car.

In this sentence, does *quickly* modify *responded* or *decided?* The ambiguity can be resolved by repositioning the modifier:

Most people who *quickly* responded to the ad decided not to look at the car.

OR

Most people who responded to the ad decided *quickly* not to look at the car.

29c Try to put lengthy modifiers at the beginning or end

When a lengthy modifier is placed in the middle of a sentence, it tends to disrupt the basic structure (subject–verb–complement) of the sentence. By moving such modifiers to the beginning or end of the sentence, you preserve the basic structure and make the sentence more readable.

29.2
Examples of embedded transitional words.

MODIFIER IN THE MIDDLE OF THE SENTENCE
A television network usually, *after it airs a documentary,* makes the film available to groups for a nominal rental fee.

REVISED
After it airs a documentary, a television network usually makes the film available to groups for a nominal rental fee.

29d Avoid disruptive modifiers

English sentences are made up of subgroupings of words, such as the verb and its object or the word *to* and the rest of the infinitive construction. When modifiers are inserted into these subgroupings, there is a risk of interrupting and obscuring the vital connections between key words.

1 Modifiers between the verb and its object

Readers like to be able to move easily through the main predicate of a sentence, going from verb to object without interruption. For this reason, it is best to avoid inserting any interrupting modifiers between the verb and its object.

The magician ⌃shuffled *quickly* the cards.
 quickly

2 Split infinitives

EXERCISE
Modifiers.

Some readers prefer to see both parts of an infinitive construction (*to escape*) together, as in "He hoped *to escape* easily." Other readers will accept a one-word interruption between parts, or **split infinitive,** as in "He hoped *to* easily *escape*." Almost all readers have difficulty comprehending an infinitive construction when its parts are split with a longer phrase, as in "He hoped *to* easily and quickly *escape*."

SPLIT INFINITIVES REVISED

 go
Star Trekkers hope to ⌃*boldly, loyally, and optimistically go* where none

have gone before.   [With all due respect for the original motto, too many modifiers splitting the infinitive here interrupt the sense of the sentence.]

(**Style/Grammar Checker Alert**)   Many style/grammar checkers allow a range of choices regarding split infinitives.

29e Avoid dangling modifiers

EXERCISE
Misplaced and dangling modifiers.

WEBLINK

http://owl.english.purdue
.edu/handouts/grammar/
g_dangmod.html
Another site on using
modifiers correctly

A mistake that plagues many writers is the use of the **dangling modifier,** an introductory verbal phrase that does not have a clear referent.

> *Breaking in through the window of the girls' dormitory,* the dean of men surprised ten members of the football team.
> —Quoted in Richard Lederer, *Anguished English*

Did the dean break into the girls' dormitory? To prevent this misinterpretation, the writer should have put the real culprits in the subject position of the main clause.

> Breaking in through the window of the girls' dormitory, ten members of the football team were surprised by the dean of men.

It will not do simply to mention the missing agent somewhere in the main clause; the referent must be in the subject position.

29.3
Examples of dangling and misplaced modifiers.

CHAPTER **30**

Faulty Shifts

Readers expect writers to use a consistent focus, time frame, and tone. Writers should try to satisfy this expectation by avoiding unnecessary shifts.

AUDIO
Chapter overview.

30a Avoid shifts in focus

The *focus* of a piece of writing is what or whom the writing is about. It is indicated usually by the choice of point of view, as expressed by a singular or plural subject pronoun: first person (*I, we*), second person (*you*), or third person (*he, she, it, they*). A first-person focus is an appropriate point of view for personal narratives and informal correspondence; a second-person focus is appropriate for instructions; a third-person focus is appropriate for most academic, professional, and other types of formal writing. Shifting from one focus to another can be confusing to readers.

AUDIO
Mixing spoken and written English.

> You should start writing a paper well before the deadline;
> *you*
> otherwise, ~~one~~ may end up doing it at the last minute, with no
> chance to revise it.

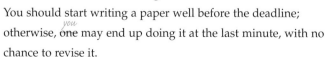

We were hoping to get tickets to the Smashing Pumpkins' concert.
But the line was so long ~~you~~ *we* had no chance.

If you use two or more words to refer to the same thing, make sure that they are consistently singular or consistently plural (see Chapter 28).

Anyone who weaves in and out of traffic is endangering ~~their~~ *his or her* fellow drivers.

OR

People
~~Anyone~~ who weaves in and out of traffic ~~is~~ *are* endangering their fellow drivers.

30b Avoid unnecessary shifts in verb tense and mood

30.1
A guide for controlling shifts in verb tense.

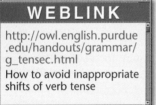

WEBLINK
http://owl.english.purdue.edu/handouts/grammar/g_tensec.html
How to avoid inappropriate shifts of verb tense

Verb tense indicates the time frame of an action (see 24e). Unless you are describing a situation where there is a natural or logical difference in time frames, it is best to use the same verb tense throughout.

In 1995, the median pay for full-time female workers in the United States was $22,497, while the median pay for males was $31,496. In other words, women ~~make~~ *made* 71 cents to a man's dollar.

Accounts of literary narratives are usually written consistently in the present tense:

Huxley's *Brave New World* depicts a nightmare utopia in which there ~~was~~ *is* no passion, no frustration, and no deviation from normalcy.

There are three **moods** in English: indicative, imperative, and subjunctive. The **indicative mood** is used for facts and assertions, the **imperative mood** for commands, and the **subjunctive mood** for conditions that are contrary to fact (see 24h). If you mix moods in the same sentence, you may confuse your readers:

INCONSISTENT MOOD

> If China were a democracy, it will have elections at periodic intervals.

REVISED

> If China *is* a democracy, it *will have* elections at periodic intervals. [Both verbs are in the indicative, suggesting a factual assertion.]

> If China *were* a democracy, it *would have* elections at periodic intervals. [Both verbs are in the subjunctive, indicating a contrary-to-fact condition.]

EXERCISE
Shifts in tense.

30c Avoid shifts in tone

Tone refers to the writer's attitude toward the subject matter or the audience (see 36c). It can be formal or informal, ironic or direct, friendly or hostile, and so on. Since readers need to get a clear sense of what the writer's attitude is, a writer should strive to maintain a consistent authorial tone.

INCONSISTENT TONE

> The world of folklore and fairy tales is one that attracts adults and children alike. As adults, we look back fondly on childhood cartoons and still get a kick out of 'em.

REVISED FROM COLLOQUIAL TO FORMAL

> The world of folklore and fairy tales is one that attracts adults and children alike. As adults, we look back fondly on childhood cartoons and find them as enjoyable as ever.

30.2
Examples of shifts used for effect.

30d Avoid mixed constructions

Mixed constructions are those that result when a writer starts a sentence in a certain way but then changes track and finishes it differently. The two parts of the sentence end up being incompatible—and confusing to the reader.

MIXED

> In the world created by movies and television makes fiction seem like reality.

WEBLINK

http://ccc.commnet.edu/
grammar/confusion
.htm#mixed_constructions

Upbeat advice on maintaining consistency—even includes a quiz

REVISED

> The world created by movies and television makes fiction seem like reality.

OR

> In the world created by movies and television, fiction seems like reality.

30e Create consistency between subjects and predicates

Subjects and predicates should always harmonize, both logically and grammatically. When they do not, the result is **faulty predication.**

FAULTY   Writer's block is when you cannot get started writing.

In this sentence, a noun (*writer's block*) is compared to an adverb of time (*when . . .*).

                     N   N

REVISED   *Writer's block* is *a condition* in which you cannot get started writing.

Similar errors are sometimes made with *is where* or *the reason is because.*

30f Avoid unmarked shifts between direct and indirect discourse

Direct discourse is language that is taken word for word from another source and thus is enclosed in quotation marks. **Indirect discourse** is language that is paraphrased and therefore is *not* enclosed in quotation marks. If you shift from one mode to the other, you may have to alter not only punctuation but also pronouns and verb tenses so as not to confuse your readers.

CONFUSING   Agassiz, the legendary Swiss scientist and teacher, once said I cannot afford to waste my time making money. [Without quotation marks, this statement seems to refer to two different people: Agassiz and the writer.]

REVISED   Agassiz, the legendary Swiss scientist and teacher, once said that *he could not* afford to waste his time making money. [By signaling indirect discourse, the change of pronouns and verb tense makes it clear that Agassiz is referring only to himself.]

Effective Sentences and Words

FAQs

▶ **Chapter 31**

What is a passive sentence? (31d)

How can I tighten up my writing and avoid wordiness? (31e)

▶ **Chapter 32**

What is the best way to avoid "choppy" writing? (32a)

▶ **Chapter 33**

How do I write sentences with two or more parallel parts?
(33a)

▶ **Chapter 34**

How can I improve my writing style? (34a–34c)

▶ **Chapter 35**

Should I use the résumé template in my computer to create
my résumé? (35b)

Are there any Internet sites that can help me with my
writing? (35d)

▶ **Chapter 36**

What is the difference between "denotation" and
"connotation"? (36a, 36b)

Should I try using figures of speech? (36f-2)

▶ **Chapter 37**

What is sexist about the sentence "Everyone should pay
attention to his spelling"? (37a-2)

How can I avoid stereotyping? (37a–37c)

▶ **Chapter 38**

If a dictionary gives several different meanings for a word,
how can I tell which to use? (38b-3)

CHAPTER 31

Clarity and Conciseness

Readers today often are under time pressure and are not willing to spend valuable minutes trying to decode a piece of writing. Writers should accommodate their readers by making their writing as clear and concise as possible.

31a   Avoid excessively long sentences

Sentences that are more than about twenty-five words long sometimes can be difficult for a reader, especially if the sentences are complicated.

> Despite their significance in contemporary society, social movements seldom solve social problems, because in order to mobilize resources a movement must appeal to a broad constituency, which means that the group must focus on large-scale issues which are deeply embedded in society.

This sentence is forty-two words long. The following three shorter sentences say the same thing and are much easier for the reader to understand:

> Despite their significance in contemporary society, social movements seldom solve social problems. To mobilize resources, a movement must appeal to a broad constituency. This means that the group must focus on large-scale issues which are deeply embedded in society.

31b   Avoid unnecessary repetition and redundancy

A certain amount of repetition is necessary, both for emphasis and to maintain focus. Repetition is especially useful for linking one sentence to another (see 5c). However, unnecessary repetition will only clutter your writing and irritate readers.

HELP

How do I guard against using long sentences?

1. Open your style/grammar checker.
2. Select the CUSTOMIZE SETTINGS feature. (It may be under OPTIONS.)
3. If there is a sentence length entry, use it to set a maximum word limit of twenty-five words.
4. Thereafter, whenever you write, use your style/grammar checker to flag all sentences longer than twenty-five words.

Life offers many lessons ~~about life~~.

People seem to learn things best when they ~~learn~~ *experience* them firsthand.

31.1
More examples of wordy sentences.

Redundancy is the use of words that could be left out without changing the meaning of the sentence. Saying that something is *blue in color* is redundant, because readers already know that blue *is* a color. Some other redundant phrases are *repeat again, combine together, end result, true fact,* and *basic essentials.* Such phrases should always be pruned.

I was caught ~~unexpectedly~~ off guard by the boss's telling me I had ~~successfully~~ made the grade in my new job.

31c Use expletives only where appropriate

An **expletive pronoun** is an "empty" word, such as *there* or *it,* that occupies the subject position in a sentence but is not its grammatical subject (see 22a-2). Because expletives can be overused, look for opportunities to convert expletive constructions into more direct expressions.

My computer has many new features.
~~There are many new features that can be found in my computer~~.

should
~~It is recommended that~~ all candidates be on time for their interviews.

31d   Use passive voice only where appropriate

In passive-voice constructions, the subject position is occupied not by the agent of the verb's action but by the recipient (see 24g). Since passive-voice constructions tend to be wordier and less direct than active-voice constructions, try to write most of your sentences in the active voice.

WEBLINK

http://ccc.commnet.edu/
grammar/concise.htm
A helpful guide to concise
writing

31.2
A guide to writing concise
sentences.

PASSIVE   Flexible songs, containing a variety of motifs arranged to its liking, are sung by the robin.

ACTIVE   The robin sings flexible songs, containing a variety of motifs arranged to its liking.

Passive sentences are appropriate when the recipient of the verb action is the topic of discussion or when the agent can be omitted without loss of clarity.

Over the past ten years, more than three million white-collar jobs have been eliminated in the United States.

31e   Eliminate wordy phrases

Many commonly used phrases are unnecessarily long. If you can replace them with no loss of meaning, you should do so.

~~In a very real sense,~~ trickle-down economics ~~exhibits a tendency~~ *tends* to trickle up, benefiting only the rich.

EXERCISE
Editing for
wordiness
and redundancy

Wordy Phrases	*Concise Phrases*
as a matter of fact	in fact
at the present time	today, presently
at this point in time	now
due to the fact that	because
in the event that	if
until such time as	until

31f   Avoid a noun-heavy style

A noun-heavy style is characterized by many more nouns than verbs. It tends to make excessive use of the verb *be* (*am, are, is, was, were*) and have strings of prepositional phrases.

NOUN-HEAVY   Thomas Jefferson was not a believer in the divinity of Jesus Christ and indeed was the author of a version of the Four Gospels that included the removal of all references to "miraculous" events.

MORE VERBAL   Thomas Jefferson did not believe in the divinity of Jesus Christ and indeed wrote a version of the Four Gospels from which he removed all references to "miraculous" events.

Noun-heavy writing also is created through the use of phrasal expressions such as *perform an examination* instead of simple verbs like *examine*.

                 purchasing

Before ~~making the purchase of~~ a used car, one should always
           examine
~~perform an examination on~~ it.

31g Choose words that express your meaning precisely

WEBLINK

http://www.wisc.edu/
writetest/Handbook/
ClearConciseSentences
.html

A resource for writing clear and concise sentences

Good writing conveys its meaning efficiently, with precision. Such precision is achieved largely through the careful selection of words. Minimize your use of vague nouns such as *area, aspect, factor, kind, nature, situation, sort, thing,* and *type,* as well as your use of vague adjectives such as *bad, good, interesting, nice,* and *weird* and vague adverbs such as *basically, completely, definitely, really,* and *very.*

Democracy   *an*

~~A democratic type of government basically~~ requires ~~a pretty~~

informed citizenry.

31h Use *that* to clarify sentence structure

Clear sentence structure helps the reader see how the pieces of a sentence fit together. In sentences with a main clause–*that* clause structure, it usually helps to include the *that.*

            that

It is important ⌄we understand the instructions before we proceed.

Sometimes, failure to include *that* can cause the reader to initially misinterpret the sentence.

> Some people are claiming their rights have been violated by the government.

By beginning with a string of words that looks like a sentence in itself ("Some people are claiming their rights . . ."), the writer of this sentence risks misleading the reader. Inserting *that* after *claiming* helps to clarify the sentence structure.

> Some people are claiming *that* their rights have been violated by the government.

31i   Make comparisons complete and clear

Comparative constructions inherently involve two terms: "*A* is _____er than *B*." In formal writing, you should make both terms of the comparison explicit.

INCOMPLETE   Talk radio has become a popular form of entertainment because it gets people more involved.   [More involved than what?]

COMPLETE   Talk radio has become a popular form of entertainment because it gets people more involved than most other media do.

Comparative constructions sometimes are open to two possible interpretations. In such cases, add a few words to help the reader know which interpretation is meant.

AMBIGUOUS   Abstract expressionism was more influenced by cubism than surrealism.

CLEAR   Abstract expressionism was more influenced by cubism than *it was by* surrealism.

EXERCISE
Conciseness,
clarity, and
directness.

(See 25e on comparative and superlative forms.)

CHAPTER **32**

Coordination and Subordination

AUDIO
Chapter overview.

In any piece of writing, readers will instinctively look for the most important points. By emphasizing these points and de-emphasizing others, writers make their main points easier to locate in the text and thereby make their writing more readable.

Two important ways to create emphasis are through coordination and subordination of sentence elements. Remember, *form should reflect content*. If two related ideas are equally important, *coordinate* them by putting them on the same grammatical level. If they are not equally important, put the less important idea in a grammatically *subordinate* form.

32a Look for a way to combine closely related sentences

Writing that contains one short sentence after another not only is unpleasantly choppy but also fails to emphasize some sentences more than others.

www

32.1
Advice on combining sentences.

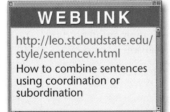

WEBLINK

http://leo.stcloudstate.edu/style/sentencev.html
How to combine sentences using coordination or subordination

TOO CHOPPY

I was born and raised in a small midwestern town. It was easy to make friends. I got to know a lot of people. I was able to achieve almost all of my goals. I could do almost anything I wanted to. School and sports were a challenge. But I could always make my way to where I wanted to be.

VIDEO
Practice sentence combining.

This paragraph is so choppy that it is hard to get a sense of what the writer's main point is. You can solve this problem by noticing that several pairs of sentences are closely related and combining these sentences.

REVISED VERSION

I was born and raised in a small midwestern town. It was easy to make friends, *and so* I got to know a lot of people. *Since* I could do almost anything I wanted to, I was able to achieve almost all of my goals. School and sports were a challenge, *but* I could always make my way to where I wanted to be.

32b   Coordinate related sentences of equal value

Coordination is the pairing of sentences or sentence elements by putting them in the same grammatical form and linking them via a coordinating conjunction, conjunctive adverb, or semicolon. The coordinating conjunctions include *and, but, or, nor, for, so,* and *yet.*

USE OF A COORDINATING CONJUNCTION

A high-fiber diet appears to lower the risk of certain cancers, *so* the National Cancer Institute recommends consuming 25–35 grams of fiber a day.

Conjunctive adverbs provide another way of giving equal emphasis to two conjoined sentences. The conjunctive adverbs include *however, consequently, therefore, thus, hence, furthermore, moreover, afterward, indeed,* and *otherwise.* They often are preceded by a semicolon.

WWW

32.2
Examples of conjunctive adverbs.

USE OF A CONJUNCTIVE ADVERB

The 1928 Pact of Paris offended nobody, since it included no compulsory machinery of enforcement; *hence,* the European nations rushed to sign it.

A coordinate relationship also can be created between two sentences simply by using a semicolon.

USE OF A SEMICOLON

People are affected by social forces sometimes far removed from their immediate perceptions; they perceive only a relatively small portion of the influences that play upon them.

EXERCISE
Coordination.

For further discussion of semicolon use, see Chapter 41.

32c   Subordinate less important ideas

To combine two closely related but unequal ideas, use **subordination;** put the more important idea in a main clause and the lesser one in a subordinate clause. Subordinate clauses are typically set off by subordinating conjunctions (such as *although, because, if, since,* *though, unless, until,* and *while*) or by relative pronouns (such as *that, which, who, whom,* and *whose*).

USE OF A SUBORDINATING CONJUNCTION

> *Even though* we know that advertisers are "out to get us," we do not make much of an attempt to refute their messages.

> Using hands-on experience is one of the best ways of learning, *as* it helps the student learn on a more interactive level.

USE OF A RELATIVE PRONOUN

> The Great Lakes cool the hot winds of summer and warm the cold winds of winter, *which* gives the state of Michigan a milder climate than some of the other north central states.

EXERCISE
Subordina-
tion.

Sometimes a relative clause can be reduced to an **appositive phrase** (see 22c-2).

USE OF AN APPOSITIVE

> Julia Cameron, *a British photographer,* is considered one of the most important portraitists of the 19th century.

CHAPTER **33**

Parallelism

AUDIO
Chapter
overview.

Whenever a writer links two or more words or phrases that have similar roles in a sentence, readers expect to see them in the same grammatical form. When the linked similar words or phrases are balanced and in the same form, the result is called **parallelism** (or *parallel structure* or *parallel form*). When Benjamin Franklin wrote "A penny saved is a penny earned," he was using parallelism. The adjective *saved* parallels in content and form the adjective *earned.*

VIDEO
Achieving
parallelism.

Parallelism not only can make writing more elegant; it also can direct the reader's attention to important structural relationships among ideas within sentences. Putting two elements in parallel form makes it easy for the reader to compare them.

33a Put parallel content in parallel form

Words and phrases that are linked by the coordinating conjunctions *and, but, or,* or *nor* often are parallel in content. In such cases, they also should be parallel in form, using the same grammatical structure.

> *cease* and *desist*   [Both verbs]
>
> *hook, line,* and *sinker*   [All nouns]
>
> *of the people, by the people,* [and] *for the people*   [All prepositional phrases]

Sometimes sentences that link comparable content can drift away from parallel grammatical form. Such sentences need to be revised to correct faulty parallelism.

To make sure that you use parallelism appropriately, follow this three-step procedure:

1. Whenever you write a sentence that has words or phrases joined by *and, but, or,* or *nor,* ask yourself if there is comparable content somewhere on each side of the conjunction. If so, identify exactly what that comparable content is.

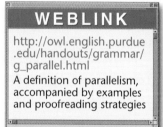

WEBLINK

http://owl.english.purdue .edu/handouts/grammar/ g_parallel.html

A definition of parallelism, accompanied by examples and proofreading strategies

2. Check to see if the comparable parts are in the same grammatical form.

3. If the comparable parts are not in the same grammatical form—but should be—use the elements in one part of the sentence as a model and put the elements in the other parts in the same grammatical form.

EXERCISE
Parallelism.

Consider the parallel content in this sentence. Notice that the active voice in the first clause is not parallel with the passive voice in the second. The revision uses the active voice.

> Good therapists will assess a client's general problems fairly early, and *they will set* ^ provisional goals ~~will be set~~ for the client.

33b Make all items in a list or series parallel

Whenever you present any kind of listing in formal or academic writing, whether it is a formatted list such as an outline or just a

HELP

How do I find places where I should be using parallelism?

1. Open the SEARCH (or FIND) feature of your word-processing program.
2. Enter the word *and* in the search field, and run the program.
3. Whenever the program highlights an *and*, examine the phrases linked by it to see if they represent comparable or equivalent content. If they do, they should be in parallel form.
4. Follow the same procedure with *but*, *or*, and *nor*.

series of items in a sentence, all of the items should be in the same grammatical form.

NONPARALLEL SERIES REVISED

The last decades of the 19th century through the early decades

of our present century marked a period when Americans

confronted rapid industrialization, a communications revolution,

the growth of big business.

and ~~big business was growing~~.   [A third noun phrase is put into the series to replace the distracting clause.]

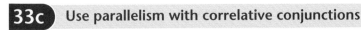

33c   Use parallelism with correlative conjunctions

Whenever you use correlative conjunctions such as *both/and, either/or, neither/nor,* or *not only/but,* you are lining up two sentence elements for comparison. Thus, those elements require parallel grammatical form.

Either *we go full speed ahead* or *we stop right here.*

33d   Use parallelism for comparisons or contrasts

A comparison or contrast involves two statements or terms that are seen as somehow equivalent; indeed, it is this equivalence that allows them to be compared. These two statements or terms therefore should be parallel. A good example of contrasting parallelism occurs in Shakespeare's *Julius Caesar*, where Brutus tries to justify, before the citizens of Rome, his assassination of Caesar:

> Not that I loved Caesar less, but that I loved Rome more. Had you rather Caesar were living, and die all slaves, than that Caesar were dead, to live all free men?
>
> —*Julius Caesar*, 3.2.21–24

33e Make parallel constructions complete and clear

In addition to similar grammatical form, parallelism generally involves one or more words that appear in both parts of the construction. Usually only a few matching words are needed to complete the parallelism and clarify the connection for the reader.

WEBLINK

http://ccc.commnet.edu/grammar/parallelism.htm
Full coverage of parallelism, with good examples and quizzes

www

33.2
This guide to parallelism includes two quizzes.

INCOMPLETE PARALLELISM REVISED

It seems apparent to even the casual observer that all people crave some form of recognition, ⟨that⟩ no one lives in total isolation, and ⟨that⟩ any healthy society will find some way to meet this human imperative.
[Inserting *that* makes it clearer that there are three things "that seem apparent."]

CHAPTER **34**

Variety

Good writers always try to make their writing interesting, not only in content but also in style. This is where variety comes in. By varying your style, you change the rhythm of your writing and keep your readers interested. If you write the same kind of sentence over and over again, you are likely to put your readers to sleep.

AUDIO
Chapter overview.

34a Vary sentence length

One of the easiest and most effective ways to alter the rhythm of your writing is to vary the length of your sentences. You do not have to change length with every sentence, but you certainly should do so from time to time. Note how Barbara Kingsolver does it in the opening paragraph of *The Bean Trees:*

AUDIO

How a lack of sentence variety creates monotony.

> I have been afraid of putting air in a tire ever since I saw a tractor tire blow up and throw Newt Hardbine's father over the top of the Standard Oil sign. I'm not lying. He got stuck up there. About nineteen people congregated during the time it took for Norman Strick to walk up to the Courthouse and blow the whistle for the volunteer fire department. They eventually did come with the ladder and haul him down, and he wasn't dead but lost his hearing and in many other ways was never the same afterward. They said he overfilled the tire.
> —Barbara Kingsolver, *The Bean Trees*

34b Vary sentence structure

Another way to alter the rhythm and cadence of your writing is by varying the structure of your sentences. Based on clause structure (see 22c-3), sentences can be divided into four basic types (see 22d-2):

A **simple sentence** contains one independent clause and no other clauses.

A **compound sentence** contains two independent clauses.

A **complex sentence** contains one independent clause and one or more subordinate clauses.

A **compound-complex sentence** contains two independent clauses and at least one subordinate clause.

All four sentence types are found in the following paragraph.

Complex	One of the great paradoxes in history is that the truest expression of Christianity is to be found not in the
Complex	West but in the East. In India countless millions of people are living out the ideas of Christ, though they do not call themselves Christians and are unfamiliar with Christian
Simple	theology. They are the poor, the meek, the merciful, and
Compound	the pure in heart. They regard life as sacred and they will
Simple	not harm it in any of its forms. They practice renuncia-
Compound-complex	tion. They believe in nonviolence and they worship the memory of a human being who perhaps has come closer

Simple

to enacting Christianity than anyone in modern history. Interestingly enough, Gandhi's struggle was directed against a Western Christian nation.

—Norman Cousins, *Human Options*

34c Avoid excessive repetition

Repetition always draws attention. If you use it deliberately to create parallelism (see Chapter 33) or emphasis, that is fine. But if you use it for no particular reason, you will only draw attention to your repetitiveness—not a good way to liven up your style! Following are some typical sources of excessive repetition:

> **WEBLINK**
>
> http://owl.english.purdue.edu/handouts/general/gl_sentvar.html
>
> How to create variety by combining, restructuring, or varying the length of sentences

34.1
A guide to sentence variety.

1. Continual use of sentences of the same length
2. Continual use of the same sentence type
3. Overuse of a particular grammatical form (for example, passive voice, *there is,* or *it is*)
4. Continual use of the same grammatical subject

Strategies for Increasing Sentence Variety

1. Revise for clarity and conciseness (see Chapter 31).
2. If sentences sound short and choppy, try forming an occasional long sentence by combining two shorter ones.
3. If sentences are so long that you would have to take a deep breath after each one if you were reading aloud, create some shorter sentences by dividing a few of the long ones.
4. Move some transitional expressions; they do not always have to be at the beginning of the sentence.
5. Move some modifiers. They often can either precede or follow what they are modifying.
6. Restructure some sentences.
7. Eliminate excessive repetition of words and phrases.

VIDEO
Achieving variety.

34.2
Practice revising for repetition.

5. Frequent use of the same kind of sentence opener (for example, a subordinate clause, transitional phrase, or adverbial phrase)
6. Frequent use of the same word

CHAPTER **35**

Word-Processing Tools and Online Resources for Improving Sentences

Among the conveniences of using a computer for writing is the ready access to editing and formatting tools, which are found in any standard word-processing program. But these tools must be used with care. This chapter discusses such word-processing tools as style/grammar checkers and style templates. (Thesauruses and dictionaries are discussed in Chapter 38.) The chapter concludes with a brief discussion of the kinds of Internet sites that can be helpful in sentence revision.

35a Use a style/grammar checker only with caution

VIDEO
Options for using style/ grammar checkers.

WEBLINK

http://www.writepage.com/ writing/gramchek.htm

"Grammar Checkers, Reading Ease and Other Faery Tales"

A typical style/grammar checker will scan your document and apply whatever rules it has been programmed to observe. Since the rules reflected in the programs are taken from traditional grammar and style books, computerized style/grammar checkers are similar in the kinds of things they flag, such as long sentences, archaic words, sexist expressions, double negatives, sentence fragments, and passive verbs.

You may be able to get a full listing of the rules observed by your style/grammar checker, along with an explanation of each, by clicking on the customization feature. You can then select which rules you want to apply to your writing. Some word processors allow you to choose a particular set of rules appropriate to a particular style—formal or informal, for example.

1 Problems overlooked by style/grammar checkers

Style/grammar checkers can be useful in pointing out potential trouble spots, but they have serious shortcomings. First, they overlook many potential problems. Of all the stylistic and grammatical problems illustrated in the examples in Part 8 of this book, for example, our style/grammar checker could identify only a third. It was unable to identify any of the pronoun reference problems in Chapter 23, or any of the modifier problems in Chapter 29, or any of the consistency problems in Chapter 30.

2 Nonconstructive suggestions made by style/grammar checkers

Style/grammar checkers flag many things that are not problematic. In some cases, the computer misreads the sentence. In other cases, it applies a rule too simplistically. For example, if your style/grammar checker flags a passive-voice verb, you may decide that you should change it to active voice. But using the passive voice is not always wrong; indeed, sometimes it is the best choice (see 31d). Many stylistic choices depend on things that a computer cannot assess—such as purpose, tone, coherence, ambiguity, pronoun reference, consistency, emphasis, and variety. When we ran our style/grammar checker on this paragraph, we received eight suggestions, none of which were constructive and all of which we chose to ignore.

35b Use style templates

Style **templates** are preset formats for common types of documents, such as business letters, memos, résumés, and reports. Whenever you need to write these types of documents, you can get off to a quick start by just opening the template (usually in the FILE menu).

Style templates are handy tools, especially if you frequently write the same kind of document. But do not hesitate to modify any

Typical Rules Found in Style/Grammar Checkers

Cross-references to sections in this book appear in parentheses.

1. Correct ungrammatical expressions. (Parts 7 and 8)
2. Use correct pronoun case. (Chapter 23)
3. Make subjects and verbs agree in number. (28a)
4. Use proper agreement with *here* and *there*. (28h)
5. Use complete sentences. (26a)
6. Avoid run-on sentences. (Chapter 27)
7. Avoid excessively long sentences. (31a)
8. Avoid redundant expressions. (31b)
9. Use passive verbs sparingly. (31d)
10. Avoid wordy expressions. (31e)
11. Avoid strings of three or more nouns. (31f)
12. Avoid multiple negatives. (25f)
13. Avoid excessive repetition. (34c)
14. Avoid split infinitives. (29d-2)
15. Do not misuse words. (Chapter 36)
16. Avoid common word confusions. (36a)
17. Avoid informal expressions in formal writing. (36c)
18. Use contractions only in informal writing. (36c-2, 43b)
19. Avoid jargon. (36d)
20. Avoid pretentious words. (36e)
21. Avoid overused phrases and clichés. (36f)
22. Avoid sexist expressions. (37a)
23. Avoid misspellings. (Chapter 49)
24. Use homophones correctly. (49b)
25. Avoid punctuation errors. (Part 10)
26. Use noncount and count nouns correctly. (50a)
27. Use appropriate prepositions, especially with phrasal verbs. (51a)

template that is preset in your computer. Most word-processing programs do not offer much variety in the way of templates, and the templates they do provide are not always the best. As noted in Chapter 19, even standard types of documents such as business letters, résumés, memos, and reports have variable formats. Learn how to create and modify the templates on your word processor so that you can tailor them to your tastes and needs.

35c Use other applications for sentence revision

In addition to style/grammar checkers and style templates, word processors offer a number of special functions that can be used in revising sentences or paragraphs. For example, a revisions program allows you to insert changes in a draft and then compare what the draft looks like with and without the changes. There are a variety of options with such a program. For example, the revisions can appear on the screen and/or on the printed document; the changes can be marked by underlining, boldface, or italics in the left or the right margin; and the deletions can be marked by different-colored strikethroughs.

WEBLINK

http://ccc.commnet.edu/ grammar/index.htm
A fabulous guide to grammar and writing

WWW

35.1
Online guide to grammar and writing.

VIDEO

Tracking changes in documents.

There are also window display options, including split-screen windows that allow you to modify one section of a document while keeping another in view.

One of the most useful word-processing features is the SEARCH, or FIND, feature (often located in the EDIT menu). With this feature you can specify the context in which you want to find a specific word or letter combination. For example, if you want to track each instance of *the* in your text (but not *them, theater,* or *there*), you might simply type SPACE-*t-h-e*-SPACE in the SEARCH box. To replace all instances of a certain form, just use the SEARCH and REPLACE features. For instance, if you have made a mistake repeatedly throughout a paper—for example, writing *it's* when you meant *its*—just enter *it's* in the SEARCH box and *its* in the REPLACE box and then run the procedure; the problem will be taken care of in a flash. Of course, if you correctly used the contraction *it's* anywhere to stand for *it is,* it too will be replaced by *its,* creating an error. In general, it is a good idea to learn what you can about the SEARCH function on your computer. The Help boxes in Parts 7–12 offer many suggestions for using this function to locate key items likely to need revision.

Help Boxes in Parts 7–12

- How do I identify possible pronoun reference problems? (pages 359, 362)
- How do I locate sentence fragments? (page 382)
- How do I identify comma splices and run-on sentences? (page 386)
- How do I guard against using long sentences? (page 400)
- How do I find places where I should be using parallelism? (page 408)
- How do I identify punctuation errors in my writing? (page 438)
- How can I spot places where I need a semicolon with a conjunctive adverb? (page 446)
- How do I identify possible apostrophe problems? (page 449)
- How do I find out whether I have a "parenthesis habit"? (page 457)
- How can I speed up spell checking? (page 478)
- How do I check my placement of adverbs? (page 501)

35d Consult Internet resources for writing help

Chapters 8 and 17 describe how to use the Internet and networking resources for research and for peer exchanges or collaborative work associated with the composition process. In addition, the Internet can provide you with help in writing and revising sentences and in developing stronger word usage. Some of this help can come from useful and entertaining Web sites that offer advice on all kinds of grammar, usage, and vocabulary topics (see the Weblink boxes found throughout this book). Some of these sites will answer questions put to the Webmaster by email.

WEBLINK

http://www.tc.cc.va.us/writcent/gh/hotlinol.htm
A state-by-state directory of grammar hotlines

http://web.uvic.ca/wguide/Pages/StartHere.html
The most complete online writing guide around

www

35.2
Discover grammar hotlines across the country.

Other links can be set up through Usenet so that you can post bulletin board questions. Finally, a number of colleges and universities and some college publishers have set up Web pages on sentence writing and word choice, providing instructional material—and sometimes even feedback—to supplement what you get from textbooks or classes. From some of the university Web sites, you can gain access to extensive samples of student writing, which may spark ideas or give you a model or point of comparison for writing projects of your own.

CHAPTER **36**

Choosing the Right Words

Since meaning is conveyed through words, a writer's choice of words, or **diction,** is crucial. Choose your words carefully, and you will make your writing clearer and more interesting; choose your words carelessly, and you may leave your readers frustrated.

AUDIO
Chapter
overview.

36a Choose the right denotation

The **denotation** of a word is its basic dictionary meaning. The verbs *walk, stroll, hobble, saunter, promenade, hike, march,* and *tramp* all have the same basic meaning, or denotation—"to move by alternately putting one foot in front of the other, always having at least one foot on the ground." Unlike these

WEBLINK

http://ccc.commnet.edu/
grammar/notorious.htm
An extensive list of
commonly confused words

words, the verbs *run, walk,* and *crawl* differ in denotation:

Immediately after the accident, Julie *ran* to the nearest house.

Immediately after the accident, Julie *walked* to the nearest house.

Immediately after the accident, Julie *crawled* to the nearest house.

Your first obligation in choosing words is to select ones that accurately denote whatever idea you are trying to convey. If Julie *crawled* to the nearest house, it would be a misrepresentation to say that she either *walked* or *ran*.

1 General statements vs. specific details

As noted in Chapter 6, all good writing involves a mixture of general statements and specific details. General statements establish main points, while specific details make these points precise, vivid, and memorable. Good writers thus continually make choices among words whose denotations range from general to specific. For example, instead of deciding whether Julie *ran*, *walked*, or *crawled*, the writer could have chosen to use a verb with a more general meaning, such as *go:*

Immediately after the accident, Julie *went* to the nearest house.

2 Abstract vs. concrete nouns

Abstract nouns are those that have broad, often vague denotations, such as *power, romance,* and *democracy*. Such words refer to concepts rather than to tangible objects. **Concrete nouns** refer to things that are available to the senses—things that we can see, touch, hear, smell, or taste. For example, *raccoon, Statue of Liberty,* and *radishes* all bring to mind tangible, concrete objects. As with general statements and specific details, you should aim for a mixture of the abstract and the concrete. Abstractions state ideas, while concrete expressions make those ideas more vivid and real.

In the following example, Norman Cousins defines and describes an abstract concept (despair) by means of a series of vivid concrete images: *calling out to one another, frozen faces, clouds racing across the sky*. He even talks about the "breaking up" of words!

> Human despair or default can reach a point where even the most stirring visions lose their regenerating and radiating powers. It will be reached only when human beings are no longer capable of calling out to one another, when words in their poetry break up before their eyes, when their faces become frozen toward their young, and when they fail to make pictures out of clouds racing across the sky.
>
> —Norman Cousins, *Human Options*

36b Choose the right connotation

Connotations are the extra nuances of meaning that distinguish otherwise synonymous words. *Walk, stroll, hobble, saunter, promenade, hike, march,* and *tramp* all are considered synonyms, yet each brings to mind a somewhat different image. Make sure that you are aware of a word's connotations before you use the word; otherwise, the message you convey to your readers may be very

WEBLINK

http://www.uottawa.ca/ academic/arts/writcent/ hypergrammar/diction .html

A hyperlinked discussion of denotation, connotation, catch phrases, and clichés

36.1
Some basics about diction.

different from the one you intended, as in this excerpt from an annual Christmas letter to family and friends.

MISLEADING   It was another interesting year on the social scene.
                    People say we have the most *contrived* parties in town.

The writer meant to say that their parties reflect ingenuity and cleverness. But *contrived* connotes a phoniness and artificiality that the author did not mean to convey.

36c Find the right level of formality

Words vary in their level of formality, or **register,** from very formal to colloquial. Always listen to what you are writing, to make sure that you consistently use words in the appropriate register.

1 Formal, academic vocabulary

Virtually all writing you do for school and college assignments (except for special cases such as creative writing or personal narratives) should be in a fairly formal register, as is this handbook. Formal, academic vocabulary consists largely of words derived from Latin and Greek—words like *inevitable, hypothesis, perception, theory,* and *superfluous*—which is why you are tested on such words when you take the SAT or ACT exam.

2 Informal vocabulary

Informal words are those you might use in ordinary, everyday contexts such as talking with friends and sending email messages.

The informal register consists mainly of words derived from the Germanic roots of English—words like *keep, laugh, throw, kitchen,* and *hassle.* Such words tend to be shorter than their Latinate equivalents, but they are often used with prepositions to form longer **idiomatic expressions.** For example, the formal Latinate words *inspect* and *examine* have as their equivalent the informal idiomatic phrase *take a close look at.* The informal register also contains many **contractions,** such as *can't, she's,* and *they'll.*

(**ESL Note**) The difficulties for non-English speakers caused by idiomatic phrases are discussed in 53c.

Although informal vocabulary is sometimes acceptable in formal writing, you should generally try to use the more formal equivalents where possible.

Informal	*Formal*	*Informal*	*Formal*
friendly	amicable	do again	repeat
worn out	exhausted	go faster	accelerate
hard-working	industrious	take apart	dismantle
funny	amusing	get hold of	seize

36d Avoid jargon, slang, or dialect

AUDIO

Using jargon, slang, and dialect appropriately.

There are many versions of English, only one of which—Standard Edited English—is represented in this book. Standard Edited English is the version most widely used in academic and professional contexts and most widely understood around the world. Other versions, including jargon, slang, and dialect, are valuable in their own right. However, they are less widely understood, and thus you should refrain from using them except with audiences composed of fellow "insiders."

Jargon is any technical language used by professionals, sports enthusiasts, hobbyists, or other special interest groups. By naming objects and concepts that are unique to a group's special interests, jargon facilitates communication among members of the group. (Imagine computer engineers trying to get by without terms like *buffer, cache, serial port, CPU,* and *configuration.*) But it has the opposite effect when used with outsiders.

VIDEO

Exploring appropriate language.

Used by teenagers and other subcultures, **slang** is a deliberately colorful form of speech, whose appeal depends on novelty and freshness. For this reason, slang terms tend to be short-lived, quickly giving way to newer, fresher replacements. At the time this book was written, student slang included terms like *bro', dweeb, ditsy, tweak,* and *rad,* and hacker slang included *nastygram, fritterware, hungus, frob,* and *cruft* (all of which are now probably outdated). Like jargon, slang is understood and appreciated only by insiders.

(**ESL Note**) A good Web site for learning American slang and idiomatic expressions is Dave's ESL Cafe at *http://www.eslcafe.com/ slang/list.html.*

A **dialect** is the type of speech used by a specific social, ethnic, or regional group. Dialects typically have a distinctive accent, many unique words and expressions, and even some grammatical patterns that differ from those of Standard Edited English. For example, in some dialects you might hear a sentence like "She be working hard" or "They might could of done it." While perfectly logical and correct within that dialect, such sentences are likely to confuse outsiders— that is, people who do not speak that dialect. If you are addressing a broad audience, avoid using dialect in your writing.

WWW

36.2
A brief linguistic discussion of Ebonics.

36e Avoid pretentiousness

College students are continually exposed to the discourse of academics—professors, scholars, textbook writers—who have spent most of their adult lives developing a large vocabulary and an embellished style of writing. If you find yourself tempted to imitate this style of discourse, do so with great caution. You are at risk of sounding pretentious.

VIDEO
Avoiding pretentiousness in academic writing.

PRETENTIOUS   By virtue of their immersion in a heterogeneity of subcultures, the majority of individuals have internalized an extensive repository of collective aphorisms about a multitude of quotidian concerns.

The following rewritten version says essentially the same thing but in clearer, simpler language:

BETTER   Because of their participation in a variety of subcultures, most people know a large number of common sayings about many everyday issues.

36f Use figurative language

Figurative language uses words in nonliteral, creative ways to enhance the reader's understanding. Two of the most common figures of speech are simile and metaphor, both of which attempt to explain the unfamiliar by comparing it to the familiar.

EXERCISE
Choosing your words.

1 Similes

A **simile** is the explicit use of one thing (called the *vehicle*) to describe another (the *tenor*). In the following example, scientist Carl Sagan uses similes to explain how the two hemispheres of the brain work:

> The left hemisphere processes information sequentially; the right hemisphere simultaneously, accessing several inputs at once. The left hemisphere works in series; the right in parallel. *The left hemisphere is something like a digital computer; the right like an analog computer.*

—Carl Sagan, *The Dragons of Eden*

Assuming that readers are more familiar with computer technology than with neuroscience, Sagan uses the former to explain the latter.

Similes are created in the space of a single sentence, normally using the word *like* or *as* to make a simple, straightforward comparison. When a simile extends beyond one sentence, it is called an **analogy.**

2 Metaphors

A **metaphor** is an implicit simile. It draws the reader's attention to a surprising similarity between otherwise dissimilar things, but it does so without using *like*, *as*, or other explicit markers. When you say "Her ideas *cast some light* on the subject" or "I *fell* into a deep depression," you are speaking metaphorically. Feel free to use metaphors in your writing, as Gretel Ehrlich does in this passage describing springtime in the Wyoming plains:

> Spring weather is capricious and mean. It snows, then blisters with heat. There have been tornadoes. They lay their elephant trunks out in the sage until they find houses, then slurp everything up and leave. I've noticed that melting snowbanks hiss and rot, viperous, then drip into calm pools where ducklings hatch and livestock, being trailed to summer range, drink. With the ice cover gone, rivers churn a milkshake brown, taking culverts and small bridges with them. . . .

—Gretel Ehrlich, *The Solace of Open Spaces*

Ehrlich's use of metaphor gives us a vivid picture of Wyoming spring weather. She describes tornadoes in terms of elephants, melting snowbanks in terms of snakes (*viperous*), and rivers in terms of milkshakes. In using words like *capricious* and *mean*, she gives the weather a distinct human personality. This is an example of the use of **personification,** in which inanimate objects or abstractions are described as having human traits.

You can use different metaphors in a single piece of writing, as Ehrlich does, so long as you do not put them too close together. Otherwise, you will have what is called a **mixed metaphor.**

MIXED METAPHOR   The idea was hatched two years ago, but it didn't
                 catch fire until last month, when the school
                 principal decided to jump on board.
                                         —Adapted from Richard Lederer, *Anguished English*

This sentence mixes three incompatible metaphors: newborn chicks, fires, and boats.

3 Clichés

When they are still fresh, metaphors add sparkle to writing. But over time, if they are used heavily, they become worn out and lose their charm. An overused metaphor is called a **cliché.** Some examples of clichés are *white as a sheet, barking up the wrong tree,* and *climbing the ladder of success.* Good writers avoid clichés in formal writing, partly because such overused figures of speech detract from an original idea and also because they can create confusing or ridiculous mixed images:

36.3
Examples of
catchy head-
lines and ads.

WEBLINK
http://quotations.about
.com/cs/cliches/
Links to good sites on
clichés

EXERCISE
Editing clichés.

                              getting worse
CLICHÉ REVISED   The slowdown is ~~accelerating~~.

CHAPTER **37**

Avoiding Biased Language

AUDIO

Chapter overview.

Writers sometimes use the power of language negatively to express bias, the one-sided (usually negative) characterization of an entire group. Writers should try at all times to avoid bias in their writing.

37a Avoid biased gender references

In the past, men and women had distinctly different roles in society. Language developed accordingly. A doctor was presumed to be male; in the relatively few cases where a doctor happened to be a woman, she was referred to as a *woman doctor*. A nurse, on the other hand, was presumed to be female; gender was indicated only in those relatively few cases involving a *male nurse*.

WWW

37.1

An online guide to avoiding sexist language.

> **WEBLINK**
>
> http://www.wmich.edu/mus-theo/nsl.html
> Guidelines for nonsexist language from the Society for Music Theory
>
> http://www.ncte.org/positions/gender.shtml
> Guidelines from the National Council of Teachers of English on avoiding sexist language

Today, women are pursuing career paths long dominated by men, participating in what were once considered male sports, and challenging old stereotypes. To acknowledge and encourage this trend, we all need to rethink our use of gender references.

Stereotyping can arise unwittingly through the careless use of examples and illustrations. Try to vary the roles of men and women in your examples, thereby broadening the spectrum of possibilities for both sexes.

1 Gender-specific nouns

In general, do not use gender-marked terms in situations where a person's gender should not be of any relevance.

Sexist	Gender-Neutral
businessmen	businesspersons
foremen	supervisors
mankind	humanity, humankind
manpower	personnel, staff
policemen	police officers
salesmen	salesclerks, salespersons
stewardess	flight attendant
workmen	workers

EXERCISE
Avoiding gender stereotyping.

2 Generic pronouns

Traditionally, *he, him,* and *his* were used as **generic pronouns** to refer to all members of a group, regardless of sex. A sentence such as "Everyone should pay attention to his spelling" would supposedly apply to both males and females. But using only masculine words as generic pronouns has been found to be discriminatory in its psychological effects. How to Avoid the Generic Pronoun Problem lists four ways around this problem.

How to Avoid the Generic Pronoun Problem

1. *Pluralize the antecedent and use* they/their: "All writers should pay attention to their spelling."
2. *Restructure the entire sentence to get rid of the pronoun:* "Spelling deserves careful attention." This often works, although it lacks the vividness of the personal pronoun.
3. *Keep the singular antecedent and use* he or she (*or* his or her, *or* him or her): "Everyone should pay attention to his or her spelling." This is a cumbersome solution and should be used sparingly.
4. *Use the passive voice to get rid of an antecedent subject:* "Spelling should be paid close attention to." This solution produces an indirect statement that is less forceful than an active-voice statement; it too should be used sparingly.

AUDIO
Strategies to avoid generic pronoun problems.

37b Avoid biased language about race and ethnicity

37.2

Tips for avoiding racial and ethnic biases.

Language that either intentionally or unintentionally discriminates against people because of their race or ethnicity is a form of verbal aggression. Unbiased writers reject the sort of disparaging stereotyping evident in ethnic jokes and in sweeping statements about ethnic groups.

Terms such as *inner-city residents* and *illegal immigrants* also can be discriminatory if they are consistently linked to a specific ethnic or racial group. Although such terms do have legitimate uses, they are often used as indirect labels or "code words," to refer only to certain kinds of inner-city residents or illegal immigrants. Do not let yourself be drawn into this kind of stereotyping.

37c Avoid biased language about age and other differences

EXERCISE

Avoiding biased language.

In our youth-oriented culture, it is not uncommon to hear demeaning references to age. Indeed, the adjective *old* often is used gratuitously as a way of denigrating others, as in "When the first President Bush lost the election, people said that was the end of the line for old George." (This is the same man who, five years later, took up skydiving!) Avoid focusing on the negative aspects of aging and assuming that anyone beyond a certain age is unworthy of respect. Avoid age-related stereotypes and expressions in examples and jokes.

Occupational, religious, political, regional, socioeconomic, and disability-related groups are among the many other groupings in our society that are subject to stereotyping. As with ethnic groups, it is generally best to refer to such groups in ways that they themselves prefer. For example, most people with physical disabilities prefer to be called *physically disabled* rather than *handicapped,* and most people who clean buildings prefer the title of *custodian* rather than that of *janitor.* Such preferences should be respected.

CHAPTER **38**

Using a Thesaurus and Dictionary

A writer needs tools, and two of the best are a good thesaurus and a good dictionary.

AUDIO
Chapter overview.

(ESL Note) If you are a non-English speaker, consider getting one of the specialized dictionaries that contain information about count and noncount nouns (see 50a), phrasal verbs (see 51a), verb complements (see 51b), and collocations (see 53b) and offer many sample sentences. (See Chapter 53 for specific references.)

38a Use a thesaurus to find the exact word

Part of being a good writer is choosing words that accurately express your thoughts (see Chapter 36). A **thesaurus** is a listing of synonyms and antonyms that allows you to zero in on the exact word you are looking for.

A word of advice: Do not use a thesaurus just to find fancy words with which to dress up your writing. As synonyms often have special conditions of use and are not freely interchangeable (see 36b), substituting fancy synonyms for more common words just to impress your readers is likely to have the opposite effect.

WEBLINK

http://www.m-w.com/thesaurus.htm

The free, online WWWebster Thesaurus

WWW

38.1
Access the Merriam-Webster Thesaurus online.

AUDIO
Getting maximal use out of a thesaurus.

1 Electronic thesaurus

Today, most word-processing programs have a built-in thesaurus, which you can use as you write. (It is usually on the same menu as the spell checker.) You can also find thesauruses on the Internet. Or, you can buy a thesaurus on a CD-ROM, either by itself or as a supplement to a dictionary.

With an electronic thesaurus, you have a great writing tool that is quick and easy to use. If you notice that a word you have written is not quite the word you want to use, all you have to do is select the word and then click on THESAURUS. You will get a listing of synonyms and, in some cases, antonyms and related words.

2 Traditional thesaurus

WWW

38.2

Benefits of using a traditional thesaurus.

You should also feel comfortable using a thesaurus in traditional book form. The pocket-size versions are handy for carrying around; larger, desk-size thesauruses are found in all libraries and many offices. In many pocket-size thesauruses, the words are arranged alphabetically, as in a dictionary. With most desk-size thesauruses, you first look up the word in an index at the back of the book and then turn to the most relevant sections indicated.

38b Use a dictionary to learn about words

Traditional, printed dictionaries come in two types: pocket size and desk size. The pocket size is handy, but the desk size contains more complete information. Electronic dictionaries usually have as much information as desk-size types and can be found in CD-ROM format or on the Internet.

WEBLINK

http://www.m-w.com/
dictionary.htm
The free, online WWWebster
Dictionary

A typical entry from a comprehensive dictionary, whether printed or electronic, will look something like the one in Figure 38.1, from *The American Heritage College Dictionary*, 3rd ed.

1 Spelling, word division, and pronunciation

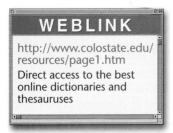

WEBLINK

http://www.colostate.edu/
resources/page1.htm
Direct access to the best
online dictionaries and
thesauruses

A typical dictionary entry begins with the main word, correctly spelled and divided into syllables: *ha•rass.* Knowing where to divide a word is helpful for typing if you do not use automatic hyphenation on your computer (see 48a). If a word has two correct spellings, they are both listed, with the preferred

Spelling and word division

Pronunciation   Part of speech   Word endings

ha•rass (hăr′əs, hə-răs′) *tr.v.* **ha•rassed, ha•rass•ing, ha•rass•es. 1.** To irritate or torment persistently. **2.** To wea: out; exhaust. **3.** To impede and exhaust (an enemy) by repeated attacks or raids. [French *harasser,* possibly from Old French *harer,* to set a dog on, from *hare,* interjection used to set a dog on, of Germanic origin.] —**ha•rass′ er** *n.* —**ha•rass′ ment** *n.*

Word senses (definitions)

Etymology

Related words

VIDEO
Using pronun-
ciation guides.

Words having similar meanings, with examples

SYNONYMS: harass, harry, hound, badger, pester, plague, bait These verbs are compared as they mean to trouble persistently or incessantly. *Harass* and *harry* imply systematic persecution by besieging with repeated annoyances, threats, demands, o: misfortunes: *The landlord harassed tenants who were behind in their rent.* "*Of all the griefs that harass the distress'd*" (Samuel John son). *A gang of delinquents harried the storekeeper. Hound* suggest: unrelenting pursuit to gain a desired end: *Reporters hounded the celebrity for an interview.* To *badger* is to nag or tease persistently *The child badgered his parents to buy him a new bicycle.* To *pester i:* to inflict a succession of petty annoyances: "*How she would have pursued and pestered me with questions and surmises*" (Charlotte Brontë). *Plague* refers to the infliction of tribulations, such a: worry or vexation, likened to an epidemic disease: "*As I have no estate, I am plagued with no tenants or stewards*" (Henry Field ing). To *bait* is to torment by or as if by taunting, insulting, o: ridiculing: *Hecklers baited the speaker mercilessly.*

Authoritative opinions about correct usage

USAGE NOTE: Educated usage appears to be evenly divided on the pronunciation of *harass.* In a recent survey 50 percent o the Usage Panel preferred a pronunciation with stress on the first syllable, while 50 percent preferred stress on the second syllable. Curiously, the Panelists' comments appear to indicate that each side regards itself as an embattled minority.

EXERCISE
Using a the-
saurus and
dictionary.

FIGURE 38.1 Entry from *The American Heritage College Dictionary* Copyright © 2000 by Houghton Mifflin Company. Reproduced by permission from *The American Heritage College Dictionary, Third Edition.*

spelling first. The word's pronunciation is indicated next, in parentheses: (hăr′əs, hə-răs′), with the preferred form first. Most modern dictionaries have a pronunciation key at the bottom of the page to help you decipher the pronunciation. For words of more than one syllable, a heavy accent mark (′) indicates which syllable should receive primary stress; some words have a secondary accent (′) as well. Some electronic dictionaries allow you to click on a button and get a voice recording of the correct pronunciation of the word.

2 Parts of speech, word endings, and word senses

Next come symbols describing some aspect of the word—for example, what part of speech it is (such as a noun, verb, or adjective) or whether it is singular or plural. The most common abbreviations are these:

adj.	adjective	*intr.*	intransitive	*pron.*	pronoun
adv.	adverb	*n.*	noun	*sing.*	singular
aux.	auxiliary	*pl.*	plural	*suff.*	suffix
conj.	conjunction	*pref.*	prefix	*tr.*	transitive
interj.	interjection	*prep.*	preposition	*v.*	verb

Often an entry will include variants of the main word, showing different word endings. For verbs, for example, a comprehensive dictionary will give the principal tenses (see 24a). For adjectives, usually the comparative and superlative forms are listed. For nouns, irregular plural forms will be listed.

Many words have more than one meaning, or **sense.** Each sense has a separate listing, generally preceded by a boldfaced number. In some dictionaries, these senses are arranged historically, according to when they entered the language; in other dictionaries, senses are listed according to current popularity, with the most commonly used sense appearing first. (It is a good idea to consult the front of your dictionary to see which system it uses.)

3 Etymology, related words, synonyms, and usage

Information about a word's origin, or **etymology,** is given in square brackets. This information can help you to learn the word and use it accurately. Sometimes, **related words**—words derived from the same root—are given as well.

Some dictionaries list **synonyms** for certain words, along with explanations of the differences among them and examples. Also, some dictionaries provide **usage notes,** which typically represent the judgments of a panel of authorities about "correct" usage. In many dictionaries, particular senses of a word may be given **usage labels** such as *Informal, Colloquial, Non-Standard, Slang, Vulgar, Obscene, Offensive, Archaic,* or *Obsolete.* You may want to check the front of your dictionary to see how the different kinds of usage are defined.

EXERCISE
Synonyms.

Punctuation

FAQs

▶ **Chapter 39**

Which is correct: *FBI* or *F.B.I.*? (39c)

▶ **Chapter 40**

Should I use a comma before *and* and *but*? (40b)

▶ **Chapter 41**

Do semicolons go inside or outside of quotation marks? (41d)

▶ **Chapter 42**

How does the colon differ from the semicolon? (42b)

▶ **Chapter 43**

Should I write *1990's* or *1990s*? (43c-2)

▶ **Chapter 44**

How do I introduce a quotation? (44e)

▶ **Chapter 45**

When should I use dashes instead of parentheses? (45d, 45e)

CHAPTER **39**

End Punctuation

There are three ways to punctuate the end of a sentence: with a period, a question mark, or an exclamation point.

AUDIO
Chapter overview.

THE PERIOD

The period is used to indicate the end of a statement, to punctuate initials and abbreviations, and to mark basic divisions in units and computer names.

39a Use a period to mark the end of a statement

Sometimes called a "full stop," the period is most commonly used to mark the end of a sentence. Just make sure before you place the period that the words form a *complete grammatical sentence,* or else you will be creating a sentence fragment (see Chapter 26).

If the sentence ends with a quotation mark, place the period *inside* the quotation mark (see also 44e). If the sentence ends with a parenthesis, place the period *outside* the parenthesis unless the entire sentence is a parenthetical comment (see also 45a, 45b, 45c).

39b Use periods to punctuate initials, abbreviations, unit divisions, and computer names

Initials that stand for middle names or first names take periods.

Mary W. Shelley   O. J. Simpson   F. Scott Fitzgerald

WWW

39.1
Examples of European punctuation conventions.

Leave one space after each period when punctuating initials in names. Most abbreviations ending in lowercase letters take periods.

Ms.   a. m.   St.   Jan.

Dr.   e. g.   apt.   Inc.

For further discussion of abbreviations, see Chapter 47.

Use periods with initials, abbreviations, units, computer names

431

Basic divisions in money, measurements, email addresses, and file names all take periods:

$99.50   3.2 meters   13.5 gallons
English.paper.doc   michael.okiwara@u.cc.utah.edu

39c Avoid common misuses of periods

WEBLINK

http://stipo.larc.nasa.gov/
sp7084/sp7084ch3.html
A description of all uses of
the period and the question
mark

1. *Do not use a period to mark just any pause.* If you insert a period whenever you want readers to pause, you run the risk of creating sentence fragments. Consider this example:

> Attempts to challenge reactionary political views are often branded as "politically correct" by those same reactionaries. *Who support only their own versions of "free speech."* [The second sentence is a fragment.]

2. *Do not use periods with acronyms and other all uppercase abbreviations.*

CA	NJ	USA	UN	FBI
NOW	NAACP	MS-DOS	CD-ROM	COBOL

3. *Do not use periods at the end of stand-alone titles or headings.* The title of this chapter and its numbered headings are examples of stand-alone titles and headings, respectively.

4. *Do not use periods at the end of sentences within sentences.*

The famous statement "I think, therefore I am" originated in an essay by the French philosopher Descartes.

5. *Do not use periods after items in a formatted list (except for full sentences).* The table of contents for this handbook is an example of a formatted list. Only when the items in the list are full sentences is it acceptable to have periods after the individual items.

WWW

39.2
Online help for
using question
marks.

THE QUESTION MARK

Question marks are placed after direct questions, whereas periods follow indirect questions. Do not use a comma or a period after a question mark.

39d · Use a question mark after a direct request

REQUESTING
INFORMATION

Who wrote *Jesus Christ, Superstar*?

ASKING FOR
CONFIRMATION

It's a complicated situation, isn't it?

MAKING A
POLITE REQUEST

Could you please be a little quieter?

1 Using question marks with direct and indirect quotations

If the direct quotation is a question and it is at the end of the sentence, put the question mark inside the quotation marks.

The police officer asked me, "Do you live here?"

Do not use a question mark after an indirect question. An indirect question is the writer's rewording of a question posed by someone else.

A tourist asked me where the Lincoln Memorial was.

(See 44e for more on question marks used with quotation marks.)

AUDIO
Punctuating
indirect ques-
tions.

2 Using question marks in a series

It is acceptable to put a question mark after each independent item in a series, even if it is not a full sentence.

Will our homeless population continue to grow? Stay about the same? Get smaller?

If the question is an either/or type, put a question mark only at the end of the sentence.

Are you coming with us or staying here?

THE EXCLAMATION POINT

Exclamation points are used to show strong emotion, including amazement and sarcasm. Do not use a comma or a period after an exclamation point.

39e Use an exclamation point to signal a strong statement

VIDEO
Exploring end punctuation.

The statement marked with an exclamation point does not have to be a full sentence.

AN OUTCRY OR COMMAND	Oh! Watch out!
STRONG EMPHASIS	People before profits!
ASTONISHMENT	Imagine reading this news report and not getting upset!
SARCASM	And the cigarette companies claim that smoking is not addictive!

WEBLINK

http://www.uottawa.ca/academic/arts/writcent/hypergrammar/endpunct.html

All about end punctuation

(See 44e for use of exclamation marks in quotations.)

Avoid overuse of exclamation points. Exclamation points are rarely used in college papers, essays, and other kinds of formal writing. Try not to use them except in highly unusual circumstances. Any kind of writing—even informal writing—that has too many exclamations sounds juvenile. There are better ways to express your enthusiasm.

EXERCISE
End punctuation.

CHAPTER **40**

The Comma

The comma is the most common and most useful punctuation mark in the English language—and also perhaps the most difficult to master. Commas are used essentially to interrupt the flow of a sentence, to set off certain parts of it and thereby enhance the sentence's readability. This chapter provides some *guidelines* (not rules) for the use of commas. In most cases, these guidelines will help you clarify meaning and follow conventions for separating confusing elements.

AUDIO
Chapter overview.

40a **Use a comma to set off an introductory phrase or clause**

When readers start to read a sentence, one of the first things they do (unconsciously) is try to locate the grammatical subject. Help them do this by setting off with a comma any potentially distracting words that *precede* the subject. In the following excerpt, note how the commas allow the reader to identify easily the sentence subjects that follow them: *cultural relativism, most US citizens,* and *bullfighting.*

WEBLINK

http://owl.english.purdue
.edu/handouts/grammar/
g_comma.html
A discussion of the main uses of the comma, accompanied by good proofreading strategies and exercises

WWW
40.1
A guide to the use and abuse of commas.

> *Because we tend to use our own culture to judge others,* cultural relativism presents a challenge to ordinary thinking. *For example,* most US citizens appear to have strong feelings against raising bulls for the sole purpose of stabbing them to death in front of crowds shouting "Olé!" *According to cultural relativism, however,* bullfighting must be viewed strictly within the context of the culture in which it takes place—its history, its folklore, its ideas of bravery, and its ideas of sex roles.

—James M. Henslin, *Sociology*

Using a comma after an introductory element is especially important in cases where it is needed to prevent possible confusion.

CONFUSING   Soon after starting the car began making funny noises.

CLEAR   Soon after starting, the car began making funny noises.

Exception: If the introductory element is short and unemphatic, you do not need to insert a comma.

Today I have class from 9:00 a.m. to 1:00 p.m.

Sometimes the mail does not get here until late afternoon.

40b   Use a comma before a coordinating conjunction to separate independent clauses

The combination of a comma and a coordinating conjunction (*and, but, or, nor, for, so, yet*) is one of the most common ways of connecting independent clauses.

Members of a mainstream culture often feel threatened by a counterculture, *and* they sometimes move against it in the attempt to affirm their own values.

Conflict theorists acknowledge that social institutions were originally designed to meet basic survival needs *but* they do not see social institutions as working harmoniously for the common good.

When the two clauses are closely linked, however, you may want to omit the comma, as in this example from a short story.

It was very hot *and* the men had marched a long way. They slumped under the weight of their packs *and* the curiously black faces were glistening with sweat.

—George Orwell, "Marrakech"

When you are using a coordinating conjunction to link phrases rather than clauses, you generally do not insert a comma.

Acupuncture has proved effective for treating chronic pain, and for

blocking acute pain briefly. [The simple parallel phrases need no separation; a revision removes the unnecessary comma.]

40.2

Using the comma for rhetorical effect.

However, writers sometimes insert a comma to create more separation between the two parts.

Acupressure is similar to acupuncture, but does not use needles.

[The contrastive phrase is separated with a comma.]

Here the writer has put a comma between the two verb phrases in order to emphasize the contrast in meaning between them. (See 22d, 26b, and Chapter 27 for more on using phrases and clauses in sentences.)

40c Use commas between items in a series

A series of three or more items should have commas after all but the last item.

My super-patriotic neighbor says *red, white, and blue* are his favorite colors.

Each day, cigarettes contribute to over 1,000 deaths from *cancer, heart disease, and respiratory diseases.*

Occasionally in journalistic writing or in company names composed of three or more personal names, the last comma in the series—called the **serial comma**—is omitted.

My uncle used to work for *Pierce, Fenner and Smith.*

40d Use commas to separate coordinate adjectives

When the adjectives in a series could be arranged in any order or could be (but are not) strung together with the use of *and,* they are termed **coordinate adjectives.** To show their loose relationship and also to avoid confusion with adjectives that cumulate in a particular order to modify each other, separate coordinate adjectives with commas (see 40j).

A *rusty, dented, broken-down* car was left behind.

In this example, each adjective modifies the word *car,* and the string of adjectives could be rearranged:

A *broken-down, dented, rusty* car . . .

(See Chapter 52 for more on word order.)

40e Use commas to set off nonessential phrases or clauses

A **nonessential element,** or **nonrestrictive element,** provides an extra piece of information that can be left out without changing the basic meaning of the sentence. Always use punctuation to set off nonessential, or nonrestrictive, elements from the rest of the sentence. (By contrast, elements that are essential, or restrictive, are always integrated into the sentence without separating punctuation; see 40j.) Nonessential elements are most commonly set off with commas; however, parentheses (45a) or dashes (45d) may also be used.

Lung cancer, *the leading cause of cancer deaths in the United States,* kills more than 153,000 Americans each year. [A nonessential appositive is set off with commas.]

Universal health care, *which guarantees every citizen at least basic medical benefits,* is found in every industrialized country in the world except the United States and South Africa. [A nonessential clause is set off with commas.]

Unless the nonessential element ends the sentence, be sure to use *two* commas to set it off, not just one.

FAULTY SINGLE COMMA REVISED

Alzheimer's disease, *a progressive impairment of the brain* strikes over 4 million older Americans every year.

40f Use commas to set off conjunctive adverbs

Conjunctive adverbs include the words and phrases *however, therefore, consequently, thus, furthermore, on the other hand, in general,*

HELP

How do I identify punctuation errors in my writing?

1. Open the style/grammar checker.
2. Click on the OPTIONS feature.
3. Select the CUSTOM setting.
4. Open the customization feature.
5. Deselect all grammar and style features except the one called something like PUNCTUATION ERRORS.
6. Run the procedure on your document. For extra speed, turn off the spell checker.

NOTE: The computer will identify only *possible* punctuation errors. You need to check these "errors" against the guidelines in this book.

and *in other words* (see 32b). They serve as useful transitional devices, helping the reader to follow the flow of the writer's thinking. By enclosing conjunctive adverbs in commas, you give them more prominence, clearly marking a shift in thinking.

> Over eighty million people in the United States suffer from chronic health conditions. Their access to health care, *however,* is largely determined by whether or not they have health insurance.

> Resistance training exercises cause microscopic damage to muscle fibers, which take twenty-four to forty-eight hours to heal; *therefore,* resistance training programs require at least one day of rest between workouts.

40g Use commas with dates, place names and addresses, titles and degrees, and numbers

1 Using commas with dates

When writing a date in the traditional American format of month, day, and year, set off the year by placing a comma after the day.

> John F. Kennedy died on November 22, 1963.

Do not use a comma if only the month and year are given.

> John F. Kennedy died in November 1963.

Do not use a comma when writing the date in inverse order (day, month, year).

> John F. Kennedy died on 22 November 1963.

2 Using commas in place names and addresses

Use commas after all major elements in a place name or address. However, do not put a comma before a zip code.

> Aretha Franklin was born in Memphis, Tennessee, on March 25, 1942.

> Alfredo's new address is 112 Ivy Lane, Englewood, NJ 07631.

3 Using commas with titles and degrees

Use commas to set off a title or degree following a person's name (see 47a).

Stella Martinez, MD, was the attending physician.

Ken Griffey, Jr., is one of the best power hitters in baseball.

4 Using commas in numbers

Use a comma in numbers of five digits or more, to form three-digit groups. In a number of four digits, the comma is optional.

2,400 OR 2400

56,397

1,000,000

Exceptions: Do not use commas in street numbers, zip codes, telephone numbers, account numbers, model numbers, or years.

40h Use commas with speaker tags

If you are quoting someone and using a speaker tag (such as *he said, according to Freud,* or *notes Laurel Stuart*), put a comma between the tag and the quotation.

Thomas Edison said, "Genius is 1 percent inspiration and 99 percent perspiration."

"The only thing about the fishing industry that has not changed much," *she writes,* "is the fishermen themselves."

Note that if a quote ends in a comma, the comma goes *inside* the quotation mark (see 44e).

A comma is not used if the quote ends in another punctuation mark.

"What a marvelous performance!" exclaimed the Queen.

A comma is not used if the quotation is introduced with *that.*

A well-known talk-show host claimed that "the poorest people in America are better off than the mainstream families in Europe."

40i Use commas with markers of direct address

Put commas around words that indicate that you are talking directly to the reader: words such as *yes* or *no,* the reader's name (*Bob*), question tags (*don't you agree?*), or mild initiators (*Well, Oh*).

Yes, the stock market is likely to turn around.

Do you really think, *Grace,* that Professor Wilson will postpone the test?

Intelligence is impossible to measure with just one type of test, *don't you think?*

Some people say we should all have guns to protect ourselves. *Well,* I do not agree.

40j Avoid misuse of commas

1. *Never use a single comma between the subject and predicate.* When a complex subject begins a sentence, writers sometimes feel inclined to add an inappropriate comma that splits the subject and predicate.

WEBLINK

http://www.grammarbook
.com/punctuation/
commas.html
An excellent illustrated
guide to commas, with
quizzes

FAULTY COMMA REVISED

Numerous psychological and

social factors, have a strong

influence on how people age.

This mistake arises only if you insert a *single* comma between subject and predicate. A nonrestrictive element between the subject and the predicate may be set off by two commas.

Police discretion, the decision as to whether to arrest someone or even to ignore a matter, is a routine part of police work.

2. *Never use commas with restrictive elements.* **Restrictive elements** are phrases or clauses that are essential to defining the meaning of the sentence. They should not be set off with commas.

Consumers, who are considering using a hospital or clinic,

should scrutinize the facility's accreditation. [In this sentence, the writer is referring not to all consumers but only to those who are considering using a hospital or clinic.]

3. *Avoid using commas with cumulative adjectives.* Adjectives that accumulate before a noun, each one modifying those that follow, are called **cumulative adjectives.** Their modifying relationships, which depend on their order, are likely to be confused by the separating commas that are common with adjectives in a coordinate series (see 40d).

CONFUSING COMMAS REVISED

The suspect was seen driving a *small, new, Italian, luxury* car.

4. *Avoid putting a comma before* than. Resist the urge to heighten a comparison or contrast by using commas to separate the *than* clause from the rest of the sentence.

FAULTY COMMA REVISED

Beating our arch-rival was more important, than getting to the

state playoffs.

5. *Avoid using a comma after a subordinating conjunction.* A comma should not be used to separate a subordinating conjunction from its own clause; it should be used before the conjunction to separate the entire clause from the rest of the sentence.

FAULTY COMMA REVISED

Although, the car is fifteen years old, it seems to be in good

shape.

ALTERNATIVE REVISED SENTENCE

The car seems to be in good shape, although it is fifteen years old.

6. *Never use a comma before parentheses or after a question mark or exclamation point.* A comma is superfluous with an opening parenthesis, question mark, or exclamation point.

UNNECESSARY COMMAS REVISED

Muhammad was born in Mecca, (now in Saudi Arabia) and

founded the religion of Islam around AD 610.

"Where are you going?," he asked.

7. *Do not insert a comma before a list.* Resist the urge to punctuate before a listed series. (For cases where a colon is appropriate, see 42a.)

UNNECESSARY COMMAS REVISED

Some countries, such as, Holland, Sweden, and Denmark, have

very compassionate welfare systems.

My toughest subjects are, math, biology, and physics.

8. *Do not use a comma in a two-item series.* While commas are needed to separate three or more items in series, separating two items with a comma is unnecessary and distracting.

UNNECESSARY COMMA REVISED

Her outfit used strong contrasts between red, and blue.

CHAPTER **41**

The Semicolon

There are three ways to show a close relationship between independent clauses: with a *comma* and coordinating conjunction (see 40b), a *colon* (see 42b), or a *semicolon*. A semicolon is used when the two clauses have a coordinate relationship—that is, when they convey equally important ideas (see 32b)—but do not have a coordinating conjunction (*and, but, or, nor, for, so, yet*) between them.

AUDIO
Chapter overview.

> **WEBLINK**
> http://stipo.larc.nasa.gov/ sp7084/sp7084ch3.html
> A thorough description of all uses of the semicolon

41a Use a semicolon to separate independent clauses not linked by a coordinating conjunction

When there is no coordinating conjunction, related independent clauses should be connected with a semicolon rather than a comma.

The first panacea for a mismanaged nation is inflation of the currency; the second is war. Both bring a temporary prosperity; both bring a permanent ruin

—Ernest Hemingway, *Notes on the Next War*

WWW
41.1
Six guidelines for using semicolons.

> **WEBLINK**
> http://www.wisc.edu/ writetest/Handbook/ Semicolons.html
> A complete guide to semicolons

41b Use a semicolon to separate independent clauses linked by a conjunctive adverb

If you separate two independent clauses with a conjunctive adverb such as *however, therefore,* or *nevertheless,* you must use a semicolon (see 27c):

More than 185 countries belong to the United Nations; *however,* only five of them have veto power.

Japan and Germany are now among the five most powerful nations in the world; *therefore,* they would like to have veto power, too.

41c Use semicolons in a series with internal punctuation

A **complex series** is one that has internal punctuation. Normally, commas are used to separate items in a series (see 40c); however, if the individual items contain commas, it can be difficult for readers to determine which commas are internal to the items and which commas separate the items. In these cases, semicolons are used to separate the items.

I have lived in Boulder, Colorado; Corpus Christi, Texas; and Vero Beach, Florida.

AUDIO

Using a semi-colon between balanced clauses.

41d Place semicolons outside quotation marks

Semicolons are always positioned outside quotation marks.

Those who feel abortion is not a woman's prerogative say they are "pro-life"; those who feel it is say they are "pro-choice."

HELP

How can I spot places where I need a semicolon with a conjunctive adverb?

1. Open the SEARCH (or FIND) program in your computer.
2. Enter *however* in the SEARCH field, and run the search.
3. Wherever your computer flags the word *however,* see whether there are independent clauses on both sides of the word.
4. If there are, insert a semicolon before *however* and a comma after it (see 27c).
5. Do the same with *therefore, for example, nevertheless,* and other conjunctive adverbs.

41e   Avoid common semicolon errors

1. *Do not use a semicolon between an independent clause and a dependent clause or phrase.* Dependent clauses or phrases are linked to independent clauses most often by commas, not semicolons (see Chapter 40).

When we say that a country is

"underdeveloped"; we imply

that it is backward in some way.
[The introductory clause should be linked by a comma, not a semicolon (see 40a).]

WEBLINK

http://www.uottawa.ca/
academic/arts/writcent/
hypergrammar/semicoln
.html
Abbreviated help with use
of semicolons

www

41.2
Online help
for using
semicolons.

2. *Do not use a semicolon to introduce a list.* Use a colon instead (see 42a).

Utah has five national parks; Arches, Bryce, Canyonlands, Capitol Reef, and Zion.

EXERCISE
The semi-
colon.

CHAPTER **42**

The Colon

In formal writing, the colon is used mainly after a general statement to announce details related in some way to the statement. These details may be a list of items, a quotation, an appositive, or an explanatory statement.

AUDIO
Chapter
overview.

42a   Use a colon to introduce a list or appositive

In using a colon to introduce a list or appositive, be sure that the introductory part of the sentence is a grammatically complete clause.

In creating a macro, you can
assign it to any one of three
places: the toolbar, the
keyboard, or a menu.

One principle should
govern your choice: which
one is most convenient?

FAULTY COLON USE

The four main parts of a
memo are: header, introduction, summary, and details.

AUDIO
When to use a
colon to intro-
duce a list.

FAULTY COLON USE REVISED

A memo has four main parts: header, introduction, summary, and
details.

In academic writing, the phrase *as follows* is often used. It directly
precedes the colon.

There are four main parts to a memo, as follows: header,
introduction, summary, and details.

42b Use a colon to set off a second independent clause that explains the first

Rock climbing is like vertical chess: in making each move up the
wall, you should have a broad strategy in mind.

WWW

42.1
Instructions for
how to avoid
overusing
colons.

(Note) You may begin the clause after the colon with either an
uppercase letter or a lowercase letter.

Although both the colon and the semicolon can be used to separate independent clauses, they cannot be used interchangeably. A
semicolon is used when the two clauses are balanced (see 41a); a
colon is used when the second clause is a specification of the first.

COLON   Blessed are the pure in heart: for they shall see God.

SEMICOLON   And the earth was without form and void; and darkness
             was upon the face of the deep.

42c Use a colon to introduce a quotation

When a colon is used to introduce a quotation, the part of the
sentence that precedes the colon should be grammatically independent (see 42a).

In *Against Empire,* Michael Parenti states his concern about American foreign policy**:** "We should pay less attention to what US policymakers profess as their motives—for anyone can avouch dedication to noble causes—and give more attention to what they actually do."

If the part introducing the quotation is not an independent clause, use a comma instead of a colon.

In *Against Empire,* Michael Parenti states**,** "We should pay less attention . . . ."

42d   Use colons in titles

Colons are often used in the titles of academic papers and reports. The part of the title that follows the colon is called the subtitle. It usually provides a more explicit description of the topic than does the title.

Nature and the Poetic Imagination**:** Death and Rebirth in "Ode to the West Wind"

42e   Use colons in business letters and memos

In business letters and memos, colons are used in salutations (*Dear Ms. Townsend***:**), to separate the writer's initials from the typist's initials (*TH***:***ab*), and in memo headings (*To***:**, *From***:**, *Date***:**, *Subject***:**, *Dist***:**). (See Chapter 19 for more on business writing.)

EXERCISE
The colon.

42f   Use colons in numbers and addresses

Colons are used in Biblical citations to distinguish chapter from verse (*Matthew 4***:***11, Genesis 3***:***9*), in clock times to separate hours from minutes and minutes from seconds (*5***:***44 p.m.*), in ratios (*3***:***1*), and in Web site addresses (*http***:***//www.fray.com*).

WEBLINK

http://leo.stcloudstate
.edu/punct/colon.html
A comprehensive discussion
of all uses of the colon

42.2
A guide to
punctuating
with colons.

CHAPTER **43**

The Apostrophe

AUDIO
Chapter overview.

The apostrophe is used to indicate possession, to alert the reader to contractions and omitted letters, and to form certain plurals.

43a Use apostrophes with nouns to indicate possession

In its grammatical sense, *possession* refers to ownership, amounts, or some other special relationship between two nouns. With singular nouns, possession is usually indicated by attaching *'s* to the end of the noun.

Sue Ellen's jacket   yesterday's bad weather

There are two exceptions to this rule:

WEBLINK

http://www.grammarbook
.com/punctuation/apostro
.html

An excellent guide to apostrophes, including exercises

43.1
A guide to the apostrophe, with exercises.

1. If the rule would lead to awkward pronunciation, the extra *s* may be omitted: *Euripides' plays, Moses' laws, Mister Rogers' Neighborhood.*

2. In names of places, companies, and institutions, the apostrophe is often omitted: *Robbers Roost, Kings County, Starbucks, Peoples Republic.*

For plural nouns ending in *s*, form the possessive by just adding an apostrophe at the end:

the Browns' car   the Yankees' star pitcher   my parents' friends

For plural nouns not ending in *s*, form the possessive by adding *'s:*

women's rights   children's section   sheep's wool

1 Avoiding apostrophes with possessive pronouns

Pronouns never take apostrophes to indicate possession. They have their own possessive forms: *its, his, her/hers, your/yours, their/theirs, our/ours, my/mine* (see 23i).

Be careful not to confuse *its* and *it's*. The former is possessive; the latter is a contraction for *it is*.

FAULTY CONTRACTED POSSESSIVE REVISED

> *its*
> The university has revised it̶'̶s̶ policy on hate speech.

FAULTY CONTRACTION REVISED

> *it's*
> If you fall way behind in your studies, i̶t̶s̶ hard to catch up.

2 Showing possession with multiple nouns

With multiple nouns, use apostrophes according to your intended meaning. If you want to indicate joint possession, add an apostrophe only to the last of the nouns:

Bush and Cheney's campaign

If you want to show *separate* possession, put an apostrophe after each of the nouns:

Omar's, Gretchen's, and Mike's birthdays

EXERCISE
Apostrophes mark possession.

HELP

How do I identify possible apostrophe problems?

1. Open the SEARCH (or FIND) feature of your word-processing program.
2. Enter an apostrophe (') in the SEARCH field.
3. Run the search.
4. Whenever the program flags an apostrophe, use the guidelines discussed in this chapter to determine whether you have used it correctly.

43b Use apostrophes to indicate contractions and omitted letters

WWW

43.2
Basics on apostrophe use.

WEBLINK

http://owl.english.purdue
.edu/handouts/grammar/
g_apost.html

A discussion of all uses of the apostrophe, accompanied by proofreading strategies and exercises

In casual speech, syllables are sometimes omitted from common word combinations. For example, *cannot* becomes *can't*. In formal writing, such contractions are generally inappropriate. In much informal writing, however, such as email messages and personal letters, contractions are quite common. Just be sure to punctuate them correctly with an apostrophe.

EXERCISE

Apostrophes mark contractions and omissions.

will not → won't	should not → shouldn't	it is → it's
I am → I'm	you have → you've	they are → they're

The apostrophe also can be used for less common contractions, especially if you are trying to create a colloquial, slangy tone.

the 1990s → the '90s	magazine → 'zine
underneath → 'neath	neighborhood → 'hood

43c Use apostrophes to mark certain plural forms

When a letter or symbol is used as a noun, the usual way of pluralizing nouns (adding an *s* or *es*) does not work well: "There are four *ss* in *sassafras*." In such cases, an apostrophe can help out.

1 Forming the plurals of letters, symbols, and words referred to as words

Adding *'s* instead of *s* clarifies the plural forms of unusual nouns.

There are four *s*'s in *sassafras*.

How can she have two @'s in her email address?

2 Forming the plurals of numbers and abbreviations

Both the Modern Language Association and the American Psychological Association recommend omitting the apostrophe in forming plurals like the following:

the 1990s   several IOUs   a shipment of PCs

43d Avoid misusing the apostrophe

Be careful not to use apostrophes where they do not belong. The following box lists some of the most common apostrophe errors.

Common Apostrophe Errors

1. Do not use an apostrophe for the possessive form of *it*.

   NO   Her dog lost *it's* collar.

   YES   Her dog lost *its* collar.

2. Do not use an apostrophe with nonpossessive nouns.

   NO   This report discusses four major *features'* of modern mass media.

   NO   This report discusses four major *feature's* of modern mass media.

   YES   This report discusses four major *features* of modern mass media.

3. Do not use an apostrophe with present-tense verbs.

   NO   TV news reporting *seem's* like yet another form of entertainment.

   YES   TV news reporting *seems* like yet another form of entertainment.

AUDIO
It's versus *its*.

CHAPTER **44**

Quotation Marks

The primary use of quotation marks is to acknowledge other people's words and statements. Using quotation marks is especially important in academic writing, which puts a premium on the ownership of ideas.

AUDIO
Chapter overview.

44a Use quotation marks for exact direct quotations

Quotation marks should be placed around any words, phrases, or sentences that you have borrowed from someone else (unless the quotations are so lengthy that you prefer to set them off as an indented block).

> In *The End of Work,* Jeremy Rifkin said, "In the years ahead, more than 90 million jobs in a labor force of 124 million are potentially vulnerable to replacement by machines."
>
> One reviewer called it "a very readable and timely book."

1 Paraphrasing or quoting indirectly

A summarization, restatement, or paraphrase of a statement made by someone else is a form of **indirect discourse,** and quotation marks are not used. Putting quotation marks around words that were not those of the speaker or writer would be extremely misleading.

MISLEADING QUOTATION MARKS REVISED
> Rifkin argues that "in the future more than two-thirds of the
> American workforce could be displaced by automation."

2 Setting off long quotations in block form

A long quotation (more than about four lines) should be set off as a block (indented one inch or ten typewriter spaces) without quotation marks.

> Rifkin sees this reduction of the workforce as having profound social effects:
>
> > The wholesale substitution of machines for workers is going to force every nation to rethink the role of human beings in the social process. Redefining opportunities and responsibilities for millions of people in a society absent of mass formal employment is likely to be the single most pressing social issue of the coming century.

44b Use quotation marks to suggest skepticism about a term

Sometimes you may find yourself writing about a concept that you think does not deserve the respect other people are giving it. In such cases, you can convey your skepticism by putting the name of the concept in quotation marks.

> Although many people consider the family the foundation of American society and talk about a return to "family values" as a desirable objective, it is clear that the modern American family looks quite different from families of previous generations.

This application of quotation marks should be reserved for cases where you believe that a term is being misused by others. In a sense, you are quoting others (see 44a), although not directly. Only on rare occasions should you use quotation marks simply to make ironic or sarcastic comments.

MISUSED QUOTATION MARKS
> Action films are very "intellectual," aren't they?

MISUSED QUOTATION MARKS REVISED
> Action films are not very intellectual, are they?

44c Use quotation marks to indicate shifts of register

Quotation marks can be used occasionally to set off a colloquial term from the more formal discourse surrounding it.

> One should always try to avoid an inflexible, "cookie-cutter" approach to rhetorical criticism.

(Note) Colloquialisms should be used sparingly in formal writing, even when punctuated with quotation marks.

44d Use quotation marks when citing titles of short works

When referring by title to short stories, book chapters, poems, essays, songs, and other brief works, enclose the titles in quotation marks.

> "Smells Like Teen Spirit" is a '90s classic.

> Chapter 14, "Design Principles and Graphics," talks about the functionality and aesthetics of formatting.

Titles of longer or more encompassing works are italicized or underlined (see 46e).

44e Follow standard practice in using other punctuation with quotations

1. *Put commas and periods inside the end quotation mark.* Standard American editorial practice calls for commas and periods to be placed as shown in the following passage:

WEBLINK

http://ccc.commnet.edu/
grammar/marks/quotation
.htm

A description of all uses of quotation marks, with links to exercises and related topics

44.1

A guide to using quotation marks.

"The definition of community implicit in the market model," argues Patricia Hill Collins, "sees community as arbitrary and fragile, structured fundamentally by competition and domination. In contrast, Afrocentric models of community stress connections, caring, and personal accountability."

2. *Put colons and semicolons outside the end quotation mark.*

One critic called 1990 "the year in which rock & roll was reborn": the fusing of metal and rap by groups like Living Colour and Faith No More broke down racial barriers in a way reminiscent of early rock & roll.

One of the things that distinguishes Snoop Doggy Dogg from other rappers is his style, which has been described in the *New York Times* as "gentle"; "where many rappers scream," said *Times* reporter Touré, "he speaks softly."

3. *Put other punctuation marks inside the end quotation mark if they are part of the quotation; otherwise, put them outside the end quotation mark.* Question marks, exclamation points, dashes, parentheses, and other punctuation marks should be positioned according to meaning.

AUDIO

Using quotation marks with question marks.

PART OF QUOTED TITLE

Whitney Houston's "How Will I Know?" entered the pop charts at number one.

PART OF SENTENCE

What do you think of controversial songs like "Deep Cover" and "Cop Killer"?

4. *Use single quotation marks (' ') for quotation marks within quotation marks.*

Garofalo notes that "on cuts like 'JC' and 'Swimsuit Issue,' Sonic Youth combined an overt sexuality with uncompromisingly feminist lyrics about women's issues."

Common Quotation Mark Errors

1. Do not use quotation marks just to call attention to something.

   NO   Pete Sampras has won the Wimbledon championship "six" times.

   YES   Pete Sampras has won the Wimbledon championship six times.

2. Do not use quotation marks for indirect discourse (see 30f).

   NO   President Clinton said "he was sorry about the Monica Lewinsky affair."

   YES   President Clinton said he was sorry about the Monica Lewinsky affair.

3. When presenting the title of your paper on a title page or at the head of the paper, do not put quotation marks around it. If your title contains within it the title of *another* short work, that work's title should be enclosed in quotation marks. (See 14a-1 for an example.)

44.2
Entertaining examples of misused quotation marks.

5. *Introduce quotations with the punctuation standard grammar calls for.* The sentence or phrase you use to introduce a quotation should be punctuated according to the grammatical relationship between the introduction and the quotation. If the introduction is not a grammatically complete sentence, do not use any punctuation.

> The conservative Parents Music Resource Center maintained that heavy metal was "the most disturbing element in contemporary music."

EXERCISE
Using quotation marks.

If the introduction is a quotation tag such as *she said* or *he notes,* use a comma.

> As *Rolling Stone* noted, "Beneath the 'save the children' rhetoric is an attempt by a politically powerful minority to impose its morality on the rest of us."

EXERCISE
More on using quotation marks.

If the introduction is a grammatically independent clause, use a colon.

> Nelson Mandela indicated his understanding of the power of mega-concerts when he thanked the performing artists backstage for their efforts: "Over the years in prison I have tried to follow the

developments in progressive music. . . . Your contribution has
given us tremendous inspiration. . . . Your message can reach
quarters not necessarily interested in politics, so that the message
can go further than we politicians can push it."

CHAPTER **45**

Other Punctuation Marks

VIDEO
Exploring other
punctuation
marks.

Parentheses, dashes, brackets, ellipses, and slashes can all be
used, in moderation and in proper contexts, to clarify meaning and
add interest to writing.

PARENTHESES

Parentheses are indispensable to formal writing. Be sure,
though, not to overuse them.

45a Use parentheses to insert parenthetical comments

WEBLINK

http://stipo.larc.nasa.gov/
sp7084/sp7084ch3.html
A full discussion of
parentheses, dashes,
brackets, ellipses, and
slashes

Usually, parenthetical comments—clarifications, asides, examples, or other extra pieces of information—are embedded within
sentences. They can be as short as a
single word or as long as an entire
sentence.

For most right-handed people,
the left hemisphere of the brain
controls manual skills and
language (and vice versa for most left-handed people). . . . The
fact that manual skill (i.e., the skill associated with tool-making

How do I find out whether I have a "parenthesis habit"?

1. Select several pages of your writing.
2. Open the SEARCH (or FIND) feature of your word-processing program.
3. Enter a left parenthesis in the SEARCH field, and have the program search your document.
4. Record how many times you have to click FIND NEXT.
5. Using your style/grammar checker, determine how many sentences are in your document.
6. If you have more than one parenthesis for every four or five sentences, you may have a parenthesis habit.

and tool-using) is usually localized in the same hemisphere as speech has led some anthropologists to speculate that tool-making either necessarily preceded or developed concurrently with language.

Another common use of parentheses is in documentation. The scientific reference style calls for inserting reference citations in parentheses within sentences (see Chapters 12 and 13). This parenthetical style is the preferred method of the MLA, APA, and CBE.

45b Do not overuse parentheses

Parentheses are so handy that you may be tempted to overuse them. Resist the temptation. Too many parentheses can make it difficult for readers to follow the main train of thought. If you find yourself developing a "parenthesis habit" (see the Help box), look for ways to rewrite some of the parenthetical comments as modifiers (see 22c) or as subordinate clauses (see 32c).

45c Use parentheses around letters or numbers to set off embedded lists

Listed phrases or clauses embedded in a longer sentence may be itemized with numbers or letters placed within parentheses.

EXERCISE
Practice with
parentheses.

Socialism has three essential components: (1) the public ownership of the means of production, (2) central planning, and (3) distribution of goods without a profit motive.

DASHES

Dashes are an informal kind of punctuation, with several uses and some misuses. You can create a dash either by typing two hyphens, which some word processors will then convert into a solid dash, or by opening the special character or symbol feature on your word-processing program and selecting the full-length dash (called the "em dash").

45d   Use dashes to highlight extra informational comments

Dashes set off internal, informational comments in a more emphatic way than parentheses do.

Public decision makers have a tendency to focus mostly on the more obvious and immediate environmental problems—usually described as "pollution"—rather than on the deterioration of natural ecosystems upon whose continued functioning global civilization depends.

Dashes are particularly useful for setting off an internal list:

As costs have climbed, resistance to increased pollution controls by some business and industry groups has also risen, contributing to the environmental backlash. Particularly hard hit have been small businesses in California—paint dealers, gas stations, and dry-cleaning establishments—which the state began regulating in 1990.

45e   Use dashes to set off important or surprising points

If not overused, dashes can be a dramatic way to set off an inserted comment.

While the Marshall Islanders continue to wrestle with the consequences of nuclear testing, a new proposal is on the table that will make the islands a dumping ground for American garbage— literally. An American waste disposal company, Admiralty Pacific, proposes to ship household waste from the west coast of the US to the Pacific islands—an estimated 34 billion pounds of waste in the first five years of the program alone.

45f   Confine yourself to one pair of dashes per sentence

Dashes, like parentheses, can be overused. If you need to add more than one informational comment to a sentence, use commas (see 40e) or parentheses around the other comments. Too many dashes in a paragraph are a sign of poorly integrated ideas.

45.1
Three ways to punctuate asides.

(**Style/Grammar Checker Alert**)   If you suspect that you have a "dash habit," check your writing for dashes, using the SEARCH process described for parentheses (page 457).

BRACKETS

Brackets are an important editorial device for providing proper context for the quoted or cited material used in research writing.

45g   Use brackets to insert editorial comments or clarifications into quotations

Quotations represent someone's exact words. If you choose to alter those words (because of a misspelling in the original quotation or to add explanatory information, for example), you must indicate that you have done so by putting brackets around the alterations.

WEBLINK

http://ccc.commnet.edu/grammar/marks/marks.htm

Excellent coverage of a range of punctuation marks, from the common to the rarely used, with illustrations and exercises

45.2
Review punctuation with the "Punctuation Tree."

"One of the things that will produce a stalemate in Rio [*the site of the 1992 UN conference on the environment*] is the failure of the chief negotiators, from both the north and the south, to recognize the contradictions between the free market and environmental protection."

The reference to "Rio" in this quotation might not be understood out of context, so the author has inserted a brief clarification between brackets.

The Latin word *sic* (meaning "so" or "thus") indicates a mechanical error—for example, an error of grammar, usage, or spelling—in a quotation. Enclose it in brackets.

"Any government that wants to more and more restrict freedoms will do it by financial means, by creating financial vacums [*sic*]."

45h Use brackets to acknowledge editorial emphasis within a quotation

When you quote a passage, you may want to emphasize a certain part of it that is not emphasized in the original. You can do so by underlining or italicizing that part and then, at the end of the passage, acknowledging the change by writing *emphasis added* or *italics mine* between brackets.

Brown states,

Whereas in the past the world has relied primarily on fishers and farmers to achieve a balance between food and people, it now depends more on family planners to achieve this goal. *In a world where both the seafood catch and the grain harvest per person are declining, it may be time to reassess population policy.* [Emphasis added.]

45i Use brackets for parenthetical comments within parentheses

If one parenthetical comment is nested within another, punctuate the inner one with brackets to distinguish it from the outer one.

The spectacular palace that King Louis XIV built at Versailles (which is located 19 kilometers [12 miles] west of Paris) required 35,000 workers and 27 years to construct.

ELLIPSES

An **ellipsis** (plural: **ellipses**) is a series of three periods, used to indicate a deletion from a quotation or a pause in a sentence. An ellipsis consists of three *spaced* periods (. . .), not three bunched ones (...). If you end a quoted sentence with an ellipsis, use a fourth period to indicate the end of the sentence.

"The notion of literature as a secular scripture extends roughly from Matthew Arnold to Northrop Frye. . . ."

The *MLA Handbook for Writers of Research Papers*, 6th edition, notes that some instructors advocate placing brackets around any ellipses points you insert in a quoted passage. However, it prefers using brackets only to distinguish your own omissions from those of the quoted author.

45j Use an ellipsis to indicate a deletion from a quotation

The sentence with an ellipsis should not be significantly different in meaning from the original sentence, nor should it be ungrammatical.

"Practically any region on earth will harbor some insect

species—native or exotic—that are functioning near the limits
          ^
of their temperature or moisture tolerance."

An ellipsis can be used to mark a deletion from either the middle or the end of a sentence, but not the beginning of a sentence.

45k Use an ellipsis to indicate a pause in a sentence

To mark a pause for dramatic emphasis in your own writing, use an ellipsis.

I was ready to trash the whole thing ... but then I thought better of it.

Beware, however, of overusing ellipses to indicate pauses.

SLASHES

Slashes serve a variety of purposes in both formal and informal writing.

45l Use slashes to separate lines of poetry quoted within a sentence

If you are quoting lines of poetry without setting them off in separate lines as they appear in the poem, put a slash (surrounded by spaces) between the lines.

Gerard Manley Hopkins's poetry features what he called "sprung rhythms," as can be heard in these lines from "The Windhover": "No wonder of it: sheer plod makes plow down sillion / Shine, and blue-bleak embers, ah my dear / Fall, gall themselves, and gash gold-vermilion."

45m Use a slash to show alternatives and to indicate a fraction

Slashes are used in expressions such as *either/or*, *pass/fail*, *on/off*, *win/win*, and *writer/editor*. Readers may object, though, if you overuse them. The expressions *he/she*, *his/her*, and *s/he* are admirable attempts at gender neutrality, but many people dislike their phonetic clumsiness. We suggest you use *he or she* and *his or her* or find other ways of avoiding sexist pronouns (see 37a-2).

Fractions that would be set in formal mathematics on separate lines also can be shown on one line, with a slash dividing the numerator from the denominator:

1/3   3/8   2-2/5

Your word-processing program may automatically convert fractions into more elegant versions like ½ and ¼, but first you have to type them with slashes. (Check under AUTOFORMAT to see whether your program will format fractions for you.)

45n Use slashes in Internet addresses and informal dates

Slashes are indispensable components of URLs (Web site addresses) as in *http://www.ablongman.com/compsite/*. Include the last slash if it brackets a directory, but not if it brackets an actual HTML file. (Tip: If your browser automatically adds a final slash to the address, that tells you the final term names a directory, not a file.)

EXERCISE
Other punctuation
marks.

Note that some lines of computer code require a backward slash (\), which needs to be reproduced exactly when lines of code are quoted.

Instead of writing out a date like June 16, 2003, you can write the date informally, with slashes: 6/16/03. (*Note:* In many other countries, this date would be written 16/06/03.)

Mechanics and Spelling

FAQs

▶ **Chapter 46**

Should I capitalize the first word of a sentence in
   parentheses? (46a)
Should I capitalize directions like *east* and *northwest?* (46b)
Do I need to capitalize email addresses? (46d)
If I cite a URL, should I put it in italics? (46f)
Should all foreign words be italicized? (46h)

▶ **Chapter 47**

Is it okay to use abbreviations in formal writing? (47e)
When should I spell out numbers? (47f–47j)

▶ **Chapter 48**

Should I hyphenate a term like *third grader?* (48a)
What are the rules for hyphenating a word at the end of a
   line? (48e)

▶ **Chapter 49**

My spell checker is too slow. Can I make it go faster? (49a)
Are there certain times when I should not depend on a spell
   checker for help? (49b)
What are the most helpful spelling rules? (49d)

11 Mechanics and Spelling

Capital Letters and Italics

CAPITAL LETTERS

AUDIO
Chapter
overview.

Capital (uppercase) letters are used to indicate the start of a new sentence. They also are used for proper names, proper adjectives, and some abbreviations.

46a **Capitalize the first word of all free-standing sentences**

WEBLINK

http://stipo.larc.nasa.gov/
sp7084/sp7084ch4.html
A discussion of almost all
uses of capital letters

Sentences like the one you are now reading should always start with a capital letter. Sentences that are embedded in other sentences, however, may or may not start with a capital letter, depending on the situation.

If a sentence follows a colon or dash, capitalization is optional:

Some employees have strong objections to mandatory drug testing in the workplace: They believe that their civil liberties are being violated.

OR

Some employees have strong objections to mandatory drug testing in the workplace: they believe that their civil liberties are being violated.

If a sentence occurs in parentheses within another sentence, the first word of the parenthetical sentence should not be capitalized:

Major league baseball no longer seems to enjoy the civic loyalty it used to (For example, several teams have threatened to leave their cities if new facilities are not built).

If, however, the parenthesized sentence is set off as a separate sentence, the first word should be capitalized:

Major league baseball no longer seems to enjoy the civic loyalty it used to. (For example, several teams have threatened to leave their cities if new facilities are not built.)

If a sentence occurs as a quotation within another sentence and is set off by a colon, comma, or dash, the first word should be capitalized:

Rush Limbaugh once said, "~~vegetarians~~ *Vegetarians* are a bunch of weaklings who wouldn't be able to bench press 50 pounds after one of their meals."

However, if the quotation is not set off by a colon, comma, or dash, the first word should be lowercase:

Rush Limbaugh once said that "~~Vegetarians~~ *vegetarians* are a bunch of weaklings who wouldn't be able to bench press 50 pounds after one of their meals."

Question fragments can also be capitalized.

Will the stock market start booming? Level off? Take a dive?

If you are quoting a poem, capitalize the first letter of each line (if the original did so).

> Long as the heart beats life within her breast
> Thy child will bless thee, guardian mother mild,
> And far away thy memory will be blest
> By children of the children of thy child.
> —Alfred, Lord Tennyson, 1864

46b Capitalize all names, associated titles, and proper adjectives

Capitalize the first letter of any name, title, or proper adjective referring to a particular person, place, or thing.

1. *Capitalize names and associated titles of people.*

Ruth Bader Ginsburg	Dr. Harris
Professor Mixco	Dale Earnhardt, Jr.

(Note) Professional titles and family relationships are not capitalized if they are not used as part of the person's name:

My aunt is a doctor specializing in internal medicine.

2. *Capitalize place names.*

San Diego, California	the Rockies
Lake Michigan	Maple Street
the Mississippi River	Apartment 34

Note Compass points (north, southwest) are capitalized only when they are incorporated into a name (North Carolina) or when they function as nouns denoting a particular region (the Southwest).

3. *Capitalize the names of historic events.*

World War II	the Middle Ages
Reconstruction	the My Lai Massacre

4. *Capitalize the names of days, months, holidays, and eras.*

Monday	the Reagan Era
April	Thanksgiving

Note Seasons of the year usually are not capitalized:

last fall   winter sports   spring semester

5. *Capitalize the names of organizations, companies, and institutions.*

Common Cause	Intel Corporation
the United Nations	Alameda Community College

6. *Capitalize the names of products and unique objects.* In most cases, only the first letter of each word in an object or product name is capitalized:

the Hope Diamond	the North Star
the *Titanic*	the Boeing 767

Some manufacturers, however, especially in the computer industry, use intercaps (internal caps):

WordPerfect	QuarkXPress
HotJava	GlobalFax

Many objects and products have abbreviated names in all upper-case letters: *MS-DOS, AOL, RISC* (see 47d).

www

46.1
Rules for internal capitalization.

7. *Capitalize religious, national, and ethnic names.*

Catholicism	Chicano
the Koran	Passover
Buddha	the Ten Commandments
Korean	African American

8. *Capitalize adjectives based on proper nouns.*

American football	Jewish literature
French history	Southern hospitality
Newtonian physics	Islamic tradition

46c Capitalize all significant words in titles

46.2
Online help
with capitaliza-
tion.

WEBLINK

http://www.grammarbook
.com/punctuation/caps
.html

A brief guide to
capitalization

In titles of books, poems, articles, plays, films, and other cultural
works, every word except articles
(*a, an, the*), conjunctions, and short
prepositions should be capitalized.
The first word of the title and of the
subtitle should be capitalized, even
if it is an article, conjunction, or
short preposition.

EXERCISE
Practice with
capitals.

The Joy Luck Club
Death of a Salesman
Pulp Fiction

"Ode to the West Wind"
"Learning in Context:
    A Qualitative Study"

(Note) The APA reference style calls for capitalizing only the first
word of the title and of the subtitle and any proper nouns (see 13d).

46d Follow the owner's preferences in capitalizing email addresses and URLs

Although most of the Internet is not case-sensitive, there are two
important reasons for writing email and Internet addresses exactly as
the owners do. First, some parts of Net addresses, such as the URL
pathnames that follow the first single slash, *are* case-sensitive. Second, some Netizens use uppercase and lowercase letters to make important distinctions in their addresses. For example, Joe Opiela at
Allyn & Bacon uses uppercase and lowercase letters to help users
make sense out of his email name: Instead of *jopielaab*, he writes
JOpielaAB.

ITALICS

In published documents, *italic* typeface is used for a number of
purposes. (*Note:* Although most word processors permit the selection of an italic typeface, many instructors—and MLA guidelines—
prefer that students use underlining instead of italics in their papers,
as underlined letters and words stand out more than italicized ones.
If you prefer to use italics, check first with your instructor.)

46e Italicize titles of independent creative works

Titles of books, magazines, digital magazines ("e-zines"), newspapers, and other creative products that are independently packaged and distributed to a public audience should be written with italics or underlining (see Chapters 12 and 13). Here are some examples:

WEBLINK

http://ccc.commnet.edu/grammar/italics.htm
A brief guide to using italics and underlining

BOOKS	*The Scarlet Letter* or The Scarlet Letter
MAGAZINES	*National Geographic* or National Geographic
E-ZINES	*Salon* or Salon
NEWSPAPERS	*Los Angeles Times* or Los Angeles Times
LONG POEMS	*Paradise Lost* or Paradise Lost
MOVIES	*Dead Man Walking* or Dead Man Walking
PLAYS	*The Iceman Cometh* or The Iceman Cometh
TV PROGRAMS	*The X-Files* or The X-Files
PAINTINGS	*Nude Descending a Staircase* or Nude Descending a Staircase
SCULPTURES	Rodin's *The Kiss* or Rodin's The Kiss
CDS	*Cracked Rear View* or Cracked Rear View
MUSIC VIDEOS	*Binge & Purge* or Binge & Purge
COMPUTER GAMES	*Mortal Kombat* or Mortal Kombat
ONLINE WORKS	*Encarta* or Encarta

(Note) The names of personal or commercial homepages should not be underlined or italicized.

46f Italicize URLs and email addresses

When writing an Internet or email address in the body of a text, use underlining or italics.

Helpful information about current Congressional legislation can be found at *http://thomas.loc.gov/*. The email address is *thomas@loc.gov*.

46g Italicize names of vehicles

Names of particular vehicles, not types of vehicles, should be underlined or italicized. These include the names of spacecraft, airplanes, ships, and trains.

Voyager 2 or Voyager 2

Spirit of St. Louis or Spirit of St. Louis

46h Italicize foreign words and phrases

In general, it is best to avoid using foreign words and phrases when writing in English. However, if you need to use a foreign expression (for example, because there is no good English equivalent), write it with underlining or italics and, if possible, provide a brief English explanation.

My Dutch friends say they like being in a *gezellig* environment, one that has a lot of human warmth.

Latin names for plants, animals, and diseases should be underlined or italicized.

The sandwich tern (*Sterna sandvicensis*) is slightly larger than the common tern.

Foreign words that have become common English words should *not* be italicized or underlined. Here are some examples:

machete (Spanish)   judo (Japanese)
sauerkraut (German)   coffee (Arabic)
pasta (Italian)   data (Latin)

46i Italicize words, letters, and numbers referred to as such

When you write a word, letter, or number so as to talk about it as a word, letter, or number, use underlining or italics.

Many people misspell the word *misspell;* they write it with only one *s.*

The witness said the license plate had two *5*'s in it.

Underlining or italics is also appropriate for a word you are about to define. (Alternatively, boldface type can be used.)

Before starting up a cliff, rock climbers sometimes like to get *beta*—advice from someone who has already done the climb.

46j   Italicize words for emphasis

You can use underlining or italics to emphasize a certain word or phrase.

WEBLINK

http://webster.commnet
.edu/grammar/italics.htm
A thorough description of
the different uses of italics

EXERCISE
Practice with
capital letters.

> According to a US Senate hearing, $13 billion the Pentagon handed out to weapons contractors between 1985 and 1995 was simply "lost." Another $15 billion remains unaccounted for because of "financial management troubles." That's *$28 billion*—right off the top—that has simply *disappeared.*
>
> —Mark Zepezauer and Arthur Naiman, *Take the Rich off Welfare*

EXERCISE
More on capital letters
and underlining/italics.

Be sure, however, not to overdo it.

CHAPTER **47**

Abbreviations and Numbers

In certain kinds of writing—for example, writing about technical or scientific topics—you may find it necessary to use either abbreviations or numbers or both. Your instructor may ask you to use a specific style for abbreviations or numbers (perhaps that outlined by the APA or the CBE). If your instructor does not specify a particular style, however, you can follow the general guidelines given in this chapter.

AUDIO
Chapter
overview.

ABBREVIATIONS

Abbreviations include shortened versions of words (*Mr., Rev., fig.*), initialisms formed from the first letters of a series of words (*FBI, NBC, IBM*), and acronyms, or initialisms that are pronounced as

VIDEO
Exploring abbreviations.

words (*OPEC, NASA, RAM*). In formal writing, abbreviations should be used sparingly. If you are not sure that readers will know what a certain abbreviation stands for, spell out the word the first time it is used and put the abbreviation in parentheses right after it:

> The Internet uses a domain name system (DNS) for all its servers worldwide.

47a Abbreviate titles, ranks, and degrees only before or after full names

Title before full name	Degree or rank after full name
Dr. Teresa Rivera	Derek Rudick, CPA
Prof. Jamie Smith-Weber	Young-Sook Kim, PhD
Gen. Colin L. Powell	Chris L. Miller, DSW

When titles or ranks are followed by only a surname, they should be spelled out:

> General Powell   Senator Wellstone   Professor Davis

47b Use abbreviations after numerical dates and times

The following abbreviations are commonly used in writing dates and times:

124 BC ("before Christ") OR 124 BCE ("before the common era")

AD 567 (*anno Domini,* or "year of our Lord") OR 567 CE ("common era")

9:40 a.m. (*ante meridiem*) OR 0940 hrs (military or international twenty-four-hour time)

4:23 p.m. (*post meridiem*) OR 1623 hrs

Avoid using *a.m.* or *p.m.* unless it is adjoined to a specific number:

The package arrived late in the a.m. *morning.*

Avoid abbreviating the names of months, days, and holidays in formal writing:

This year Xmas fell on a Thurs. *Christmas* *Thursday.*

47c Use Latin abbreviations sparingly

The following abbreviations, derived from Latin, are appropriate in academic writing. Be careful, however, not to overuse them.

Abbreviation	Latin term	English meaning
cf.	*confer*	compare
e.g.	*exempli gratia*	for example
et al.	*et alii*	and others
etc.	*et cetera*	and so forth
i.e.	*id est*	that is
N.B.	*nota bene*	note well

WWW

47.1

More examples of scholarly abbreviations.

47d Use acronyms and initialisms only if their meaning is clear

An **initialism** is an abbreviation formed from the first letters of a name—for example, *FBI* (for *Federal Bureau of Investigation*). Usually the letters are all capitalized. An **acronym** is an initialism that is pronounced as a word—for example, *ASCII, PAC, AIDS.* Some abbreviations, such as *JPEG, MS-DOS,* and *DRAM,* are *semi-acronyms:* part of the term is pronounced as one or more letters, the rest as a word (for example, "jay-peg"). As long as your audience knows what they mean and as long as you do not overdo it, there is nothing wrong with using such abbreviations where appropriate.

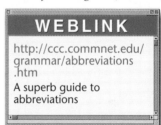

WEBLINK

http://ccc.commnet.edu/
grammar/abbreviations
.htm

A superb guide to abbreviations

AUDIO

Acronyms and periods.

47e Avoid most other abbreviations in formal writing

Place names, including the names of states, countries, provinces, continents, and other localities, should not be abbreviated except in addresses and occasionally when used as adjectives (for example, in *US government*). Organization and company names should not be abbreviated unless they are extremely familiar (*UNESCO, IBM, UCLA*) or the full name has first been given. Fields of study should not be abbreviated. Write *political science* (not *poli sci*) and *psychology* (not *psych*).

EXERCISE

Abbreviations.

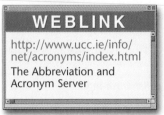

WEBLINK

http://www.ucc.ie/info/net/acronyms/index.html

The Abbreviation and Acronym Server

In formal, nontechnical writing, most units of measure should be spelled out: *inches, yards, meters, square feet, gallons.* In technical and scientific writing, abbreviations are standard: *m, kg, bps, dpi, mips, GB, rpm.* Symbols such as @, #, &, +, and = should not be used in the body of a paper. They can be used, though, in graphs, tables, and email addresses and for other similar purposes.

NUMBERS

When you are writing text and need to cite a number, keep in mind the following guidelines.

47f Use figures with abbreviations and conventionally numerical references

Time

7:00 a.m.	0700 hrs	seven o'clock in the morning
2:45 p.m.	1445 hrs	two forty-five in the afternoon

Dates

65 BC (or BCE)	AD 126 (or 126 CE)	the 1890s
May 15, 1996	from 1996 to 1998	1996–1998
1996–98		

Money

$23.4 billion $12,566 $7.99   45¢   forty-five cents   one dollar

WEBLINK

http://owl.english.purdue.edu/handouts/esl/eslnumber.html

An excellent guide to the use of numbers

Rates of speed

55 mph	33.6 bps
200 MHz	3000 rpm

Decimals and percentages

.05   5 percent (or 5%)

Telephone numbers

617-555-1284 [US]
+1 (617) 555 1284 [International]

Addresses

233 East 19th Street   PO Box 45   Route 66
New York, NY 10011

Divisions of books and plays

volume 2, chapter 11, pages 346–55
King Lear, act II, scene i, lines 5–7 OR *King Lear* II.i.5–7
The Alchemist, act 2, scene 1, lines 5–7 OR *The Alchemist* 2.1.5–7

47g Write out other numbers that can be expressed in one or two words

One to ninety-nine

fifteen   twenty-two   eighty-four

Fractions

two-thirds   one-fourth   five-sixteenths

Large round numbers

thirteen hundred   four thousand   thirty million

Decades and centuries

the eighties (or the '80s)

the twenty-first century (or the 21st century)

VIDEO
Exploring numbers.

47h Write out numbers that begin sentences

FAULTY   18% of Americans believe that career preparation should begin in elementary school.

REVISED   Eighteen percent of Americans believe that career preparation should begin in elementary school.

When a number is too large to write out (more than two words), keep the numerical form but rearrange the sentence so as to avoid beginning with a number.

FAULTY   240,183 people could be fed for one year with the food we Americans waste in one day.

REVISED   We Americans waste enough food in one day to feed 240,183 people for one year.

EXERCISE
Using numbers at the beginning of sentences.

47i Write one number as a figure and the other as a word when one number modifies another

EXERCISE
Abbreviations
and numbers.

We bought fourteen $25 tickets.

There were 75 twelfth-graders at the dance.

47j Write related numbers in the same way

EXERCISE
More abbre-
viations and
numbers.

When comparing two or more numbers in the same sentence or paragraph, make the comparison easy to see by putting the numbers in the same form, as either words or figures.

It takes ~~nine hundred~~ 900 hours of training to become a licensed hair

braider in New York City but only 117 hours to become an

emergency medical technician.

CHAPTER **48**

The Hyphen

AUDIO
Chapter
overview.

The hyphen (-) is typed as a single keystroke, with no space before or after. It differs from a dash, which is typed as two consecutive hyphens (--) and then usually converted by the computer into what looks like a long hyphen (—). The hyphen has two main functions: punctuating certain compound words and names (*self-destruct, fifty-fifty, Coca-Cola*) and dividing a word at the end of a line.

48a Consult your dictionary on hyphenating compounds

A **compound** is a word made up of two smaller words. Sometimes these smaller words are connected by a hyphen (*screen-test*), sometimes they are separated by a space (*screen pass*), and sometimes they are fused (*screensaver*). There are no firm rules for determining how to write a particular compound, so it is best to check your dictionary.

48b Hyphenate compounds acting as adjectives before nouns

When a compound is placed in front of a noun to act as a modifier, it is usually hyphenated.

I teach *seventh-grade* algebra.

Notice that the same compound, when *not* put before a noun, is *not* hyphenated.

I teach algebra to the *seventh grade*.

Exceptions to this rule include everyday compounds like *science fiction, long distance,* and *zip code,* which can be used as modifiers without hyphens.

Do you have a *zip code directory*?

Complex compounds are compounds made up of three or more words, like *cut-and-paste, ultra-high-density,* and *up-to-date*. When you hyphenate a complex compound, be sure to hyphenate all its parts—put hyphens between all the terms.

WEBLINK

http://www.grammarbook.com/punctuation/hypens.html

All about hyphens

www

48.1

Fifteen rules for using hyphens, plus examples.

I do a lot of *cut-and-paste* revising.

48c Hyphenate spelled-out fractions and numbers from twenty-one through ninety-nine

one-half	three-eighths	forty-four
two-fifths	twenty-six	seventy-nine

48d Hyphenate to avoid ambiguity and awkward spellings

Some words, especially those with the prefix *re-*, *pre-*, or *anti-*, require hyphens to prevent misreadings, mispronunciations, and awkward-looking spellings:

Now that Professor Muller has complicated the problem, we will
have to ~~resolve~~ it.   [Without the hyphen, *re-solve*, "to solve again,"
would be read as *resolve*, "to deal with successfully."]

re-solve

Hyphens can be used in series to indicate the omission of repeated words.

My neighbor has both first- and second-generation satellite dishes
for his TV.   [The hyphen after *first* helps the reader understand that
the writer is referring to *first-generation*.]

48e   Use hyphens for end-of-line word division

In general, it is best to avoid dividing a word at the end of a line.
But there are situations where word division is desirable. For example, if you are trying to arrange text in columns (in a brochure or
résumé, for instance), end-of-line hyphenation may provide valuable
extra space.

1. *Divide words only between syllables.* End-of-line hyphenation
should occur only at syllable breaks. If you are using a computer, you
can have the hyphenation program divide words for you. Otherwise,

VIDEO
Understanding
word division
problems.

Checklist for Using Automatic Hyphenation

1. Can the document have a ragged right margin?
   a. If so, you can disable your word-processing pro-
      gram's automatic end-of-line hyphenation without
      running the risk of having large gaps, or "rivers," in
      the middle of lines. Rivers reduce readability (see
      14b-4).
   b. If the document is a brochure or newsletter, for ex-
      ample, and requires block-justified text, activate the
      hyphenation program so as to avoid internal rivers.
2. Does the justified text have too many hyphenated
   lines? If so, further steps are needed, as excessive hyphenation can interfere with readability.
   a. You may want to adjust some of the hyphenated
      lines manually.
   b. You might consider changing the width of your
      columns.

consult a dictionary to find out where the syllable breaks are. In most dictionaries, a dot indicates a syllable break. For example, the entry **den • si • ty** means that the word can be hyphenated as either *density* or *densi-ty*.

48.2
Examples of special cases for using hyphens.

2. *Avoid a second hyphen in a hyphenated word.* Words with prefixes like *self-, ex-,* and *all-* and complex compounds should not be hyphenated anywhere else.

Jimmy Carter has set a new standard for civic activism by ex-~~Presi-~~
Presidents.
~~dents~~.

3. *Leave at least two letters on a line.* Do not divide a word so that a single letter is left hanging either on the first line or on the second line.

emo-
Stress management requires an examination of one's ~~e-~~
tional
~~motional~~ responses to others.

If you have to divide a name that includes two or more initials, keep the initials together.

W. E. B.
In the movement for racial equality, few stand taller than ~~W. E.~~

~~B.~~ Dubois.

4. *Avoid consecutive lines ending in hyphens.* Ending three or more lines in a row with hyphens draws attention and looks ungainly.

Admitting to your feelings and allowing them to be expressed through either communication or action is a stress-
management technique that can help you through many difficult situations.

When using a word processor, you can prevent such situations by clicking on the LIMIT CONSECUTIVE HYPHENS feature in the hyphenation program and setting the maximum number of hyphens in a row at two. Alternatively, you can widen the hyphenation zone (which determines the range in the width of the characters on the line).

EXERCISE
The hyphen.

CHAPTER **49**

Spelling

AUDIO
Chapter overview.

Modern English is a product of many other languages, including German, French, Latin, Greek, Scandinavian, and Spanish. One unfortunate result of this hybridization is an irregular system of spelling that causes problems for many users of the language. If you are one of those people, be assured that you are not alone. However, it is important that you work on your spelling and keep trying to improve it. Many readers have little tolerance for bad spelling.

49a Use a spell checker

VIDEO
Recognizing spelling problems.

A computerized spell checker makes it easy to review for spelling errors. If you are not already doing so, you should routinely run a final spell check on any important document you write. Some word processors allow you to set the spell checker so that it will identify possible misspellings either while you are typing or after you have finished. Although spell checking can be frustratingly slow, there are things you can do to speed it up (see the Help box).

HELP

How can I speed up spell checking?

1. If you have already checked part of your document for spelling errors, you can set the spell checker so that it skips that part the next time you run it. (See the HELP menu in your word-processing program.)

2. If you are using a lot of specialized terms, consider customizing the spell checker by installing one or more specialized dictionaries. (The HELP menu in your word-processing program will explain how.)

Spell checkers are far from perfect. Sometimes they flag words that are spelled correctly (especially names), and sometimes they fail to flag words that are spelled incorrectly. The first problem is particularly annoying, but it can be resolved. For example, suppose you are writing a paper on Hemingway and your spell checker keeps flagging the name *Hemingway*. Instead of clicking IGNORE every time, you can customize the spell checker so that it will recognize the name. With most spell checkers, you can customize as you write. You also can add special dictionaries from the Web to the one on your word-processing program.

WEBLINK

http://www.asu.edu/duas/wcenter/spelling.html

Spelling rules and advice

49.1

View "Ten Rules for Better Spelling" online.

Identifying misspellings that the spell checker missed is a more difficult problem. Spell checkers will accept any word that happens to match a word in its dictionary, even if the word is misused. For example, if you write *golf coarse,* the spell checker will not recognize the misspelling of *course* because the word *coarse* is in its dictionary. Thus, even with a spell checker, you must have the knowledge to prevent or correct misspellings. The most effective ways to gain such knowledge are by (1) mastering troublesome homophones, (2) guarding against common spelling errors, and (3) learning some general spelling rules and patterns. The remainder of this chapter is devoted to these topics.

49b   Master troublesome homophones

Homophones are words that sound alike but are spelled differently and have different meanings. They are one of the most common causes of misspelling in English and cannot be detected by a spell checker. For this reason, you should study them and learn their differences, especially those listed here:

AUDIO

Use pronunciation differences to learn homophones.

its	possessive pronoun
it's	contraction of *it is*
loose	adjective: "free, not tightly secured"
lose	verb: "to fail to keep"
their	possessive form of *they*
there	adverb: "in that place"
they're	contraction of *they are*

to	preposition
too	adverb: "also"
two	adjective and noun: "2"

| who's | contraction of *who is* |
| whose | possessive form of *who* |

| your | possessive form of *you* |
| you're | contraction of *you are* |

Some other frequently confused homophones and near homophones are identified in this book's Glossary of Usage, which you should consult whenever you are unsure of a sound-alike word.

49c Guard against common spelling errors

Although a spell checker can flag many spelling errors for you, it is still worth learning the correct spelling of the most commonly misspelled words. Some of these words follow.

Commonly Misspelled Words

accidentally	develops	occasionally
accommodate	environment	occurred
achieved	exaggerate	parallel
address	exceed	quantity
apparent	February	receive
appropriate	government	recommend
argument	heroes	seize
basically	lose	separate
beneficial	maintenance	success
calendar	manageable	therefore
committee	misspell	truly
definitely	necessary	until
dependent	noticeable	without

49.2
A guide to
British/Ameri-
can spelling
differences.

If you find your spell checker flagging the same misspelled words over and over, create a "Personal Spelling Demons" document on your word processor. Add words you repeatedly misspell to the document, and study them from time to time.

Many words include letters or syllables that are not pronounced in casual speech (or even, in some cases, in careful speech). Here are examples of such words; try to "see" the silent letters or syllables as you visualize these words.

address	dumb	foreign
candidate	environment	government
different	February	interest

library	probably	surprise
parallel	quantity	therefore
pneumonia	recognize	tomatoes
privilege	restaurant	Wednesday

49d Learn general spelling rules and patterns

Although English is not the simplest language in the world to learn when it comes to spelling, it does have a number of general rules and patterns that make things easier.

1 Prefixes

Prefixes are small word parts, like *re-*, *anti-*, and *pre-*, placed at the beginnings of words. Prefixes do not change the spelling of the root word: *anti-* added to *-freeze* becomes *antifreeze*. In some cases, though, a hyphen is required: *anti-* plus *-intellectual* is spelled *anti-intellectual* (see 48d).

WEBLINK

http://ccc.commnet.edu/grammar/spelling.htm
Rules and advice about spelling, along with many quizzes

mis + spell = misspell

un + necessary = unnecessary

re + entry = reentry

dis + service = disservice

2 Suffixes

Suffixes are small word parts, like *-age*, *-ence*, *-ing*, and *-tion*, placed at the ends of words. By adding suffixes to a root word such as *sense-*, you can create different meanings: *sensitive*, *sensual*, *sensory*, *senseless*. In doing so, however, you must observe the following spelling rules.

1. If the word ends in a silent *e* and the suffix starts with a vowel, drop the *e*.

imagine + ation = imagination

debate + able = debatable

There are some exceptions. Some words need to retain the *e* in order to be distinguished from similar words (*dyeing/dying*), to prevent mispronunciation (*mileage, being*), or to keep a soft *c* or *g* sound (*noticeable, courageous*).

2. If the word ends in a silent *e* and the suffix starts with a consonant, do not drop the *e*.

require + ment = requirement

spine + less = spineless

Some exceptions are *argument, awful, ninth, truly,* and *wholly*.

3. When adding a suffix to a word that ends in *y*, change the *y* to *i* if the letter preceding the *y* is a consonant.

study + ous = studious

comply + ance = compliance

pay + ment = payment

Exceptions are words with the suffix *-ing*, which keep the *y* in all cases: *studying, carrying, drying, paying*.

4. In creating adverbs from adjectives, add *-ly* to the adjective unless the adjective ends in *-ic*, in which case use *-ally*.

silent + ly = silently

vile + ly = vilely

basic + ally = basically

An exception is *publicly*.

5. In choosing between *-able* and *-ible*, use *-able* if the root word can stand alone; otherwise, use *-ible*.

understand + able = understandable

change + able = changeable

vis + ible = visible

Some exceptions are *resistible, probable,* and *culpable*.

6. Double the final consonant of the root word if (a) the root word ends with a single accented vowel and a single consonant and (b) the suffix begins with a vowel.

drop + ed = dropped

slim + er = slimmer

sleep + ing = sleeping   [Root word has two vowels.]

commit + ment = commitment   [Suffix does not start with a vowel.]

happen + ing = happening   [Root word does not end with an accented vowel.]

3 Plurals

English has several different ways of forming plurals from singular nouns. Following are some rules for forming plurals.

1. For most words, add *s.*

   tool, tools   minute, minutes

2. For words ending with *s, sh, ch, x,* or *z,* add *es.*

   bus, buses   sandwich, sandwiches

   quiz, quizzes   [Note the doubled final consonant.]

3. For words ending with a consonant followed by *y,* change the *y* to *i* and add *es.*

   enemy, enemies   strawberry, strawberries

4. For some words ending with *f* or *fe,* change the *f* or *fe* to *v* and add *es.*

   half, halves   thief, thieves

   Some exceptions are *belief, beliefs; chief, chiefs; proof, proofs;* and *motif, motifs.*

5. For compound nouns written as single words, add the plural ending as you would to an ordinary noun.

   laptop, laptops   database, databases

6. For compound nouns written as two or more words or hyphenated, add the plural ending to the noun being modified.

   video game, video games   [The noun being modified is *game.*]

   word processor, word processors   [The noun being modified is *processor.*]

   sister-in-law, sisters-in-law   [The noun being modified is *sister.*]

Irregular plurals must be learned individually. Sometimes, an internal vowel must be changed to make a noun plural:

   woman, women   mouse, mice

With some nouns derived from Latin or Greek, a final *us, um,* or *on* must be changed to *i* or *a:*

   syllabus, syllabi   medium, media   criterion, criteria

Some nouns have the same form for both singular and plural:

   deer, deer   species, species

4 The "*i* before *e*" rule

The rule you had to memorize in elementary school is worth keeping in mind: "*i* before *e* except after *c* or when sounded like *ay*, as in *neighbor* or *weigh*."

I BEFORE *E*

achieve   field

EXCEPT AFTER *C*

ceiling   receive

OR WHEN SOUNDED LIKE *AY*

eight   vein

Some exceptions are *ancient, caffeine, conscience, counterfeit, either, foreign, height, leisure, neither, seize, science,* and *weird.*

ESL Issues

FAQs

▶ Chapter 50

Why is it necessary to use articles?
How do I know whether to use *a* or *the?* (50a–50d)
When is it okay to use no article at all? (50e)

▶ Chapter 51

I have trouble with verbs like *look out for* and *look over.* Do I need to learn them? (51a)
If it is correct to write "I like to read," why is it incorrect to write "I dislike to read"? (51b, 51c)
What is wrong with the sentence "The program is consisting of four parts"? (51f)
What are the correct verb tenses for *if* sentences? (51i–51k)

▶ Chapter 52

If I have several adjectives in a row, how should I order them? (52a)
How can I create new terms by stringing nouns together? (52b)
Where should adverbs be placed? (52c–52f)

▶ Chapter 53

How can I best learn common word combinations? (53b)
Can I use idiomatic expressions in academic writing? (53c)

CHAPTER 50

Tips on Nouns and Articles

Articles (*a, an, the*) are important in the English language because they clarify what nouns refer to. There is a significant difference in meaning between "I found *a* new Web site" and "I found *the* new Web site." The first sentence introduces new information, while the second sentence implies that the new Web site is something the reader or listener already knew about. Articles can be used to mark other subtleties as well. Because many other languages do not use articles in this way, though, many nonnative speakers of English have trouble with articles.

AUDIO
Chapter
overview.

50a Use the plural only with count nouns

To use articles correctly, you first need a clear understanding of the difference between count nouns and noncount nouns. **Count nouns** refer to things that have a distinct physical or mental form and thus can be counted, such as *book, apple, diskette, scientist,* and *idea.* Count nouns can be enumerated and pluralized—for example, *eight books, three apples, several diskettes, two scientists,* and *many ideas.*

Common Examples of Two-Way Nouns

As a count noun	As a noncount noun
a wine (a type of wine)	*wine* (the fermented juice of grapes)
a cloth (a piece of cloth)	*cloth* (fabric made by weaving or knitting)
a thought (an idea)	*thought* (mental activity, cogitation)
a beauty (a lovely person or thing)	*beauty* (loveliness)
a hair (a single strand of hair)	*hair* (filamentous mass growing out of the skin)

Noncount (or **mass**) **nouns** are words such as *air, rice, electricity, excitement,* and *coverage* that do not have a distinct form as a whole. (Even though each grain of rice may have a distinct form, rice as a

WEBLINK

http://leo.stcloudstate
.edu/grammar/countnon
.html

Help with count and
noncount nouns

mass quantity is variable in form.) Noncount nouns are neither enumerated nor pluralized. No one would say *eight airs, three rices, several electricities, two excitements,* or *many coverages.* Noncount nouns are quantified with expressions like *a lot of, much, some,* and *a cup of*—for example, *some air, a cup of rice, much excitement,* and *a lot of coverage.*

Some nouns can be used as either count or noncount nouns. In such cases, the countable sense is more specific than the uncountable sense. See the Common Examples of Two-Way Nouns. (See also 22a-1 for more on count and noncount nouns.)

50b Use *the* for specific references

In deciding whether to use *the, a, an,* or no article at all, keep in mind the concept of specificity. Does the noun refer to some particular thing or set of things, or does it refer to something general? As

WWW

50.1
Situations re-
quiring the use
of *the.*

WEBLINK

http://owl.english.purdue
.edu/handouts/esl/
eslcount.html

A discussion of the use of
articles, with links to count
vs. noncount nouns and
exercises

mentioned in the introduction to this chapter, "*the* Web site" refers to a specific, unique Web site, whereas "*a* Web site" refers to any Web site.

There are many different types of situations in which nouns refer to specific things and must be preceded by *the.* In all these cases, the writer assumes that the reader knows *which* thing or set of things is being referred to. If you are using a

noun that names something unique and specific, use the definite article *the* with the noun, whether or not the noun is countable. (*Note:* This guideline applies to common nouns only, not to most proper nouns.)

1 Using *the* with superlative adjectives

Adjectives like *best, worst,* and *most interesting* single out one particular thing among many.

Mount Everest is *the tallest mountain* in the world.

2 Using *the* with unique things

The past, the present, the sun, and *the solar system* all have unique identities. There is only one past, only one present, only one sun (in our solar system anyway).

Thirty minutes after boarding, the plane was still on *the ground.*

3 Using *the* with nouns followed by a modifier

Many nouns are followed by a phrase or clause that restricts the noun's identity.

The theory <u>of relativity</u> was developed by Einstein.

The girl <u>in the corner</u> is in my physics class.

4 Using *the* to refer to something previously mentioned

Once something has been mentioned, it becomes part of the reader's knowledge. When you refer to it again, use *the* so that the reader knows that you are talking about the same thing.

I went shopping today and bought some beans, rice, and *chicken.* We can cook *the chicken* for dinner.

(Note) For clarity or emphasis, the demonstrative adjective *this, that, those,* or *these* may sometimes be used instead of *the.*

5 Using *the* to draw on shared knowledge

If you and your reader can draw on shared experience to identify something in particular, use *the* to mark it.

Please shut down *the computer* when you are done with it.

6 Using *the* for contextual specificity

Sometimes the context of a situation allows you and your reader to identify something as unique. Consider, for example, the word *printer.* There are many printers in the world, but if you are writing about a computer and you want to mention the printer attached to it, use *the* to indicate that it is the only printer in this particular context.

I was using my friend's computer and could not get *the printer* to work.

7 Using *the* to denote an entire class of things

The can be used with a singular count noun to denote an entire class or genre of things.

The earthworm is one of nature's most valuable creatures.

(Note) This generic use of *the* to refer to an entire class of things applies only to singular count nouns, not to plural count nouns or noncount nouns.

50c Use *the* with most proper nouns derived from common nouns

Proper nouns are names of things such as persons, places, holidays, religions, companies, and organizations. Most proper nouns, even though they uniquely identify somebody or something, do not take the definite article:

Muhammad Ali   Mother Theresa   New York   Microsoft

Many proper nouns, though, do take the definite article:

the Rolling Stones   the United States

the Panama Canal   the International Red Cross

Those that take the definite article have a head noun derived from a common English noun: *stones, states, canal, cross.*

There are many exceptions, however, to this pattern: *Elm Street, Salt Lake City, Carleton College, Princeton University, Lookout Mountain.* We suggest that you pay close attention to each proper name you encounter and note whether it is used with *the.*

50d Use *a* or *an* in nonspecific references to singular count nouns

Nonspecific nouns refer to *types* of things rather than to specific things. With nonspecific singular count nouns, such as *shirt, jacket, belt,* and *hat,* you must use an indefinite article (either *a* or, if the next sound is a vowel sound, *an*) or some other determiner (for example, *my, your, this,* or *each*).

I bought *a shirt* and *an overcoat.*

50e   Use no article in nonspecific references to plural count nouns or noncount nouns

With nonspecific plural count nouns, such as *shirts, jackets, belts,* and *hats,* no article is used. You may use, however, determiners like *our, some, these,* and *no.*

WEBLINK

http://www.aitech.ac.jp/
~iteslj/ESL.html

A great collection of self-study quizzes for ESL students

www

50.2

A thorough guide to determiners, with quizzes.

There were *socks* and *shorts* on sale, but *no belts.*

Nonspecific noncount nouns, such as *clothing, apparel,* and *merchandise,* do not take articles either. They can, however, take determiners like *some, much, enough, your, their, this,* and *no.*

People were buying *lots of clothing,* but I did not have *enough money* to get everything I needed.

Figure 50.1 summarizes the guidelines contained in sections 50b–e.

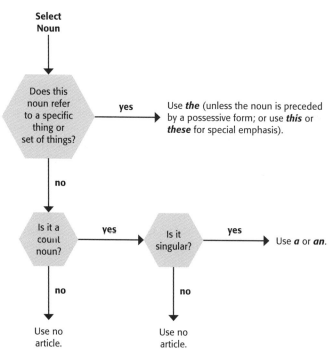

Select Noun

Does this noun refer to a specific thing or set of things? — **yes** → Use **the** (unless the noun is preceded by a possessive form; or use **this** or **these** for special emphasis).

no ↓

Is it a count noun? — **yes** → Is it singular? — **yes** → Use **a** or **an**.

no ↓ Use no article.

no ↓ Use no article.

FIGURE 50.1 Deciding Which Article to Use, If Any

CHAPTER **51**

Tips on Verbs

The main features of the English verb system are discussed in Chapter 24, subject-verb agreement in 28a, and tense and mood in 30b. This chapter addresses aspects of the verb system that may give nonnative speakers of English special difficulties: phrasal verbs, verb complements, verbs of state, modal auxiliary verbs, and conditional sentences.

PHRASAL VERBS

Phrasal verbs are made up of a verb and one or two **particles** (prepositions or adverbs)—for example, *pick over, look into, get away with.* They are sometimes called **two-word verbs** or **three-word verbs.** Phrasal verbs are common in English, especially in informal speech. Some phrasal verbs mean something quite different from their associated simple verbs. For example, if a friend of yours says, "I just *ran into* Nguyen in the library," the encounter probably had nothing to do with running. *To run into* means "to encounter unintentionally." Other phrasal verbs are used merely to intensify the meaning of the simple verb. For example, *fill up* is a more emphatic version of *fill.*

> **WEBLINK**
>
> http://www.gsu.edu/ ~wwwesl/egw/three.htm
>
> Three rules for distinguishing phrasal verbs from verb-plus-preposition combinations

Some phrasal verbs are **transitive** (that is, they have direct objects), while others are **intransitive.** For example, *dig up* (meaning "find") is transitive ("I *dig up* some information for my paper"), but *speak up* (meaning "speak louder") is intransitive ("Please *speak up*").

WWW

51.1

A list of phrasal verbs and their meanings.

Some phrasal verbs have both transitive and intransitive meanings. For example, *show up* can mean either "expose or embarrass (someone)" or "arrive," depending on whether it is used transitively or intransitively: "He tried to *show up* the teacher" (transitive) versus "He never *shows up* on time" (intransitive). (See 22a-3 and 24f for more on transitive and intransitive verbs.)

Some transitive phrasal verbs are **separable,** meaning that the particle may be placed after the object of the verb: "I quickly *looked over* my paper" or "I quickly *looked* my paper *over*." Other transitive phrasal verbs are **inseparable,** meaning that the verb and the particle must be kept together: "I quickly *went over* my paper," not "I quickly *went* my paper *over*."

51a Note phrasal verbs as you listen and read

The list of Some Common Phrasal Verbs represents only a small fraction of all the phrasal verbs in the English language. To master idiomatic English, you must learn hundreds of such verbs. The best way to do so is by listening to and reading as much informal English as you can and noting the phrasal verbs. Also consult a good pocket dictionary of phrasal verbs, such as *Handbook of Commonly Used American Idioms,* 3rd ed., by A. Makkai, M.

WEBLINK

http://www.aitech.ac.jp/
~iteslj/ESL.html
Fun quizzes on idioms,
phrasal verbs, and slang

WWW

51.2
Quizzes on
idioms, phrasal
verbs, and
slang.

Boatner, and J. Gates (New York: Barron's, 1995). A good Web site to visit is Dave Sperling's Phrasal Verb Page (*http://www.eslcafe.com/pv/*).

Some Common Phrasal Verbs

Phrasal verb	Formal equivalent	Example
bring up	raise	He *brought up* the issue of salaries.
brush up on	refresh one's knowledge of	I need to *brush up on* my German.
check up on	investigate	The police are *checking up on* him.
check with	consult	You should *check with* your advisor.

(continued)

Some Common Phrasal Verbs (continued)

Phrasal verb	Formal equivalent	Example
come across	discover, encounter	I *came across* a new bug in the program.
come through	satisfy a need	My family *came through* with the money.
come up with	develop, find	He *came up with* a solution to the problem.
fall back on	have recourse to	We can always *fall back on* our original plan.
fall through	not happen, fail	I hope the car deal does not *fall through*.
go over	review, examine	We should *go over* our notes before the exam.
hang on	persist	If you *hang on,* I am sure things will work out.
keep on	continue	It is important to *keep on* trying.
look for	seek	She went to *look for* her sweater.
look over	review, examine	Do you want to *look over* the practice test?
pick out	identify, choose	He finally *picked out* the flowers he wanted.
put off	postpone	We should *put off* our meeting until tomorrow.
put up with	tolerate	No teacher should *put up with* cheating.
run out of	exhaust, deplete	My printer seems to be *running out of* ink.

VERB COMPLEMENTS

Verb complements include gerunds (*swimming*), *to* infinitives (*to swim*), and unmarked infinitives (*swim*). English verbs differ in the kinds of verb complements they can take.

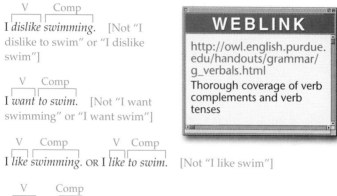

I *dislike swimming.* [Not "I dislike to swim" or "I dislike swim"]

I *want to swim.* [Not "I want swimming" or "I want swim"]

I *like swimming.* OR I *like to swim.* [Not "I like swim"]

I *made* her *swim.* [Not "I made her swimming" or "I made her to swim"]

> **WEBLINK**
>
> http://owl.english.purdue.edu/handouts/grammar/g_verbals.html
> Thorough coverage of verb complements and verb tenses

51b Learn which verbs take gerunds as complements

The following verbs take gerunds (verbals ending in *ing*), but not infinitives, as complements, as in "Maria *acknowledged skipping* class."

acknowledge	deny	give up	put off
admit	depend on	have trouble	quit
advise	detest	imagine	recommend
anticipate	discuss	insist on	regret
appreciate	dislike	keep	resist
avoid	dream about	miss	result in
cannot (can't) help	enjoy	object to	risk
consider	escape	plan on	succeed in
consist of	evade	postpone	suggest
delay	finish	practice	talk about

51c Learn which verbs take *to* infinitives as complements

The following verbs take *to* infinitives, but not participles, as complements, as in "Kim cannot *afford to buy* a car."

afford	decide	intend	offer	seem
agree	demand	learn	plan	struggle
ask	expect	like	prepare	tend
attempt	fail	manage	pretend	threaten
claim	hesitate	mean	promise	wait
consent	hope	need	refuse	want

51d Learn which verbs take either gerunds or *to* infinitives as complements

The following verbs can take either a gerund or a *to* infinitive as a complement: "He *began learning* English as a small child" or "He *began to learn* English as a small child."

begin	dread	like	stop*
cannot (can't) stand	forget*	love	try
continue	hate	remember*	

For those verbs marked with an asterisk, the meaning of the sentence depends on the type of complement: "He *forgot to go* to the store" means that he did not go to the store, while "He *forgot going* to the store" means that he did go to the store but then did not remember going there.

51e Learn which verbs take only unmarked infinitives as complements

Some verbs, when followed by a noun or pronoun, take an infinitive without *to* (an "unmarked" infinitive), as in "She *let him pay* for dinner." Such verbs include

have   help   let   make

(Note that *help* can also take a *to* infinitive as a complement.)

VERBS OF STATE

Many English verbs depict states or conditions rather than events or actions. These verbs are called **verbs of state.**

51f — Do not use the progressive aspect with verbs of state

Verbs of state generally do not take on the progressive aspect. For example, *consist of* is a verb of state and therefore cannot occur in the progressive (see 24d).

> *consists*
> The program is consisting of four parts.

The following verbs do not take on the progressive aspect:

appear	contain	know	result in
believe	correspond	mean	seem
belong	differ from	need	suppose
consist of	exist	possess	understand
constitute	involve	represent	want

MODAL AUXILIARY VERBS

The **modal auxiliary verbs** include *can, could, may, might, must, will, would,* and *should* (see 22a-3, 24c). They are used to express a variety of conditions including possibility, necessity, ability, permission, and obligation. Each modal auxiliary has at least two principal meanings, one relating to social interaction and the other to logical probability. For example, the word *may* in a sentence like "*May* I sit down?" requests permission, an aspect of social interaction, while the word *may* in a sentence like "It *may* rain today" denotes logical possibility. Within these two general categories, the modal auxiliaries carry different degrees of strength, as shown in the box. Modal auxiliary verbs have certain distinct grammatical features that can cause problems for nonnative speakers.

51g — Use only a base verb form immediately after a modal auxiliary

Any verb immediately following a modal auxiliary must be in the base, or simple, form (for example, *teach, have, go, run*), not in the *to* infinitive or gerund form.

NO   History *can to teach* us many good lessons.

YES   History *can teach* us many good lessons.

Modal Auxiliaries Ranked by Strength

Modal verb	Social interaction meaning	Logical probability meaning	Strength
will	intention	certainty	**Strong**
must	obligation	logical necessity	↑
would	conditionality	conditional certainty	
should	advisability	probability	
may	permission, possibility	possibility	
can	permission	possibility	↓
might/could	very polite permission, possibility	low possibility	**Weak**

51h Do not use more than one modal at a time

NO   If I study hard, I *might could* get an A.

YES   If I study hard, I *might* get an A.

YES   If I study hard, I *could* get an A.

If you want to combine a modal auxiliary verb with some other modal meaning, use a modal phrase such as *be able to, be allowed to,* or *have to.*

YES   If I study hard, I *might be able to* get an A.

CONDITIONAL SENTENCES

Conditional sentences have two parts: a subordinate clause beginning with *if* (or *when* or *unless*) that sets a condition and a main clause that expresses a result. The tense and mood of the verb in the subordinate clause depend on the tense and mood of the verb in the main clause. There are three main types of conditional sentences: factual, predictive, and hypothetical.

51i   In factual conditionals, use the same verb tense in both parts

Factual conditional sentences depict factual relationships. The conditional clause begins with *if, when, whenever,* or some other condition-setting expression; the conditional clause verb is cast in the same tense as the result clause verb.

If you don't *get* enough rest, you *get* tired.

When we *had* a day off, we *went* hiking in the mountains.

51j   In predictive conditionals, use a present-tense verb in the *if* clause and an appropriate modal in the result clause

Predictive conditional sentences express future possible conditions and results. The conditional clause starts with *if* or *unless* and has a present-tense verb; the result clause verb is formed with a modal (*will, can, should, may,* or *might*) and the base form of the verb.

If we *leave* now, we *can be* there by 5 o'clock.

She *will lose* her place in class unless she *registers* today.

51k   In hypothetical conditionals, use a past-tense verb in the *if* clause and *would, could,* or *might* in the result clause

Hypothetical conditional sentences depict situations that are unlikely to happen or are contrary to fact (see 24h-1). For hypothetical past situations, the verb in the conditional clause should be in the past perfect tense and the verb in the main clause should be formed from *would have, could have,* or *might have* and the past participle.

If we *had invested* our money in stocks instead of bonds, we *would have gained* a lot more.

For hypothetical present or future situations, the verb in the conditional clause should be in the past tense and the verb in the main clause should be formed from *would, could,* or *might* and the base form.

If we *invested* our money in stocks instead of bonds, we *would gain* a lot more.

CHAPTER **52**

Tips on Word Order

Unlike many other languages, English depends on word order to convey meaning. A change in word order often produces a different meaning. For example, "Kevin likes Maria" means something quite different from "Maria likes Kevin." This chapter discusses word-order patterns involving strings of adjectives, compound nouns, and adverb placement.

52a String adjectives in the order preferred in English

52.1
All about ordering adjectives.

WEBLINK

http://webster.commnet
.edu/grammar/adjective
_order.htm
Good stuff on ordering
adjectives, with exercises

If you string two or more adjectives together, you have to put them in the appropriate order.

FAULTY   The *wood broken* fence will be repaired.

REVISED   The *broken wood* fence will be repaired.

The following list shows the preferred ordering of adjectives in English:

1. Article or determiner: *the, a, an, my, our, Carla's, this, that, those*
2. Ordinal expression: *first, second, last, next, final*
3. Quantity: *one, two, few, many, some*
4. Evaluation: *beautiful, delicious, interesting, unfortunate, ugly*
5. Size: *tiny, small, short, tall, large, big*
6. Shape: *square, oval, cylindrical, round*
7. Condition: *shiny, clean, dirty, broken*
8. Age: *new, young, old, ancient*
9. Color: *black, red, yellow, green, white*

10. Nationality: *Mexican, Chinese, Vietnamese, Japanese*
11. Religion: *Catholic, Confucian, Buddhist, Muslim*
12. Material: *cotton, stone, plastic, gold*
13. Special use or purpose (may be a noun used as an adjective): *carving, carrying, sports, medical, computer*
14. The noun being modified

Here are some expressions created by following the preferred ordering:

1	2	3	4	5	6	7	8	9	10	11	12	13	14
The	first			small		shiny	new		Japanese			sports	car
A	few						young			Buddhist			monks
Her		favorite		long				yellow			silk		flowers

52b   String nouns for easiest recognition

Stringing nouns together to form **noun compounds** is common in English (see 25b). Terms like *bike lock, keyboard, houseboat, picnic table,* and *bookmark* were formed by putting two ordinary nouns together. And it is easy to add a third noun to make them more descriptive: *combination bike lock, keyboard cover, houseboat community, picnic table leg,* and *bookmark program.*

In all noun compounds, the rightmost noun is the **head noun** and the nouns preceding it serve as modifiers. These modifier nouns can modify either the head noun or another modifier noun.

Modifier	Head		Modifier	Head
noun	noun		noun	noun

  combination bike lock   mountain bike lock

AUDIO
Hyphenating a three-noun compound.

Nouns used as modifiers typically lose any plural endings they might have. Someone who loves movies is a *movie lover,* not a *movies lover;* the juice from cranberries is *cranberry juice,* not *cranberries juice.* (Exceptions to this pattern include *claims adjuster* and *weapons manufacturer.*)

52c   Use meaning to place adverbs that modify verbs

Adverbs can modify verbs, adjectives, other adverbs, or entire sentences (see 25c). Adverbs that modify verbs can be placed at either the beginning, the middle, or the end of a clause, depending on their meaning.

1 Placing adverbs of frequency

Adverbs of frequency (*usually, seldom, always, never*) are usually placed directly before the main verb (and after the auxiliary verb, if there is one).

52.2
All about English adverbs.

WEBLINK

http://cctc2.commnet.edu/ grammar/adverbs.htm
Fun discussion of adverb placement, with exercises

Tim says he *usually* writes his papers on time, yet he is *always* turning them in late.

Some adverbs of frequency (*often, twice, many times*) can also be placed at the end of the clause.

He has missed class *quite often.*

2 Placing adverbs of time when

Adverbs of time when (*yesterday, at eight o'clock, last year*) are normally placed at the end of the clause.

The exhibit will open *next month.*

Will they be there *after dinner*?

3 Placing adverbs of place

Adverbs of place (*upstairs, in the park, under a tree*) usually follow the verb. However, they should not intervene between the verb and an object.

Mike went *inside* to escape the heat.

She took her dog for a walk *in the park.*

52d Place adverbs directly before adjectives or adverbs that they modify

An adverb that modifies an adjective or another adverb should be placed directly before the word it modifies.

Jose is an *unusually quick* learner. He concentrates *very intensely* on his studies.

52e Place adverbs before sentences or clauses that they modify

An adverb that modifies a whole sentence or clause is usually placed at the beginning of the sentence or clause.

Unfortunately, his younger brother Ramon does not follow his example.

Less commonly, it is placed after the grammatical subject or at the end of the sentence.

His younger brother Ramon, *unfortunately,* does not follow his example.

His younger brother Ramon does not follow his example, *unfortunately.*

52f Do not put an adverb between a verb and its object

Nonnative speakers sometimes make the mistake of positioning an adverb between the verb and its object or objects.

FAULTY   Javier writes *often* letters to his family.

REVISED   Javier *often* writes letters to his family.

◼HELP

How do I check my placement of adverbs?

Using the fact that most adverbs end in *-ly,* you can often have your word-processing program flag the majority of the adverbs in a passage.

1. Open the SEARCH (or FIND) feature of your word-processing program.

2. Type *ly* in the SEARCH FOR (or FIND WHAT) field, and then have your program do the search.

3. Inspect each word. If it is an adverb, use the guidelines given in this chapter to determine whether it has been properly placed.

CHAPTER **53**

Tips on Vocabulary

AUDIO

Chapter
overview.

Many nonnative speakers of English feel that they just do not know enough words to express their thoughts as fully as they would like. This chapter covers some of the most common vocabulary problems for nonnative speakers—those related to cognates, collocations, and idioms.

53a Look for cognates, but watch out for "false friends"

Cognates are words that have a formal relation to similar words in another language. They are usually quite recognizable. For example, the English *telephone* and Spanish *teléfono* are cognates, and it is easy for speakers of either language to recognize this word when learning the other language.

If your native language is closely related to English, cognate recognition is a good strategy for learning new words. In most cases, you can trust a cognate to carry more or less the same meaning in your second language as it has in your first language. Of course, there are often subtle differences that you should pay attention to. For example, although the word *collar* is used in both English and Spanish to refer to the band around the neck of an animal, in Spanish it is also used to mean "necklace."

Sometimes, however, words that look similar in two different languages have entirely different meanings. These words are called **false cognates** or **false friends**. An example of a false cognate is the English *jubilation* and Spanish *jubilación*. The English word means "happiness," while the Spanish one means "retirement, pension (money)." You should always be on the alert for false cognates. Never assume that two words mean the same thing just because they look similar.

Some Spanish/English False Cognates

Spanish	Meaning	English	Meaning
bonanza	fair weather	bonanza	a treasure
coraje	anger, rage	courage	bravery, valor
desgracia	misfortune	disgrace	dishonor
eventual	possible	eventual	final, ultimate
falacia	deceit, fraud	fallacy	false reasoning
informal	unreliable	informal	casual
lunático	temperamental	lunatic	insane
particular	private, personal	particular	specific
sensible	sensitive	sensible	reasonable
voluble	moody, fickle	voluble	talkative

53.1
Some false cognates from other languages.

53b Try to get a feel for collocations

Collocations are words that commonly occur together. For example, the word *advice* commonly occurs with the verbs *give, get,* and *receive* and with the adjectives *good, bad,* and *sound.* This is why the sentence "She gave me some good advice" sounds like normal American English, while the sentence "She presented me some nice advice" does not.

WEBLINK

http://www.better-english .com/strongcollocation/ collocations.htm
The Better English quiz on collocations

53.2
Take a quiz on collocations.

A steep ~~upshoot~~ *rise* in grain prices could topple many governments in the Third World.

Lazy thinkers tend to make ~~wide~~ *broad* generalizations about things.

The best way to develop your knowledge of collocations is to pay attention to them in the English you see and hear around you. In this way, you will develop a feel for which words go with which.

You can also get help with collocations through a specialized English learner's dictionary that provides plenty of example sentences. Good choices include the *Longman Dictionary of Contemporary English*, 3rd ed. (London: Longman, 1996), the *Longman Dictionary of American English*, 2nd ed. (London: Pearson, 2002), and the *Oxford Advanced Learner's Dictionary*, 6th ed. (New York: Oxford University Press, 2000). On the Internet, try OneLook Dictionaries at *http://www.onelook.com* and CSEN Global List of Special Dictionaries at *http://www.csen.com/special-dictionaries*.

53c   Learn idioms in their entirety

AUDIO

Using idiomatic expressions.

A special type of collocation, an **idiomatic expression,** or **idiom,** is a fixed phrase whose meaning cannot be deduced from the meanings of its parts. For example, even if you know the words *kick* and *bucket*, you may not know what the idiom *kick the bucket* means (it means "die"). The same holds true for other idioms like *beat around the bush, have a screw loose,* or *lip service.* Because of their unpredictability, you have to learn idioms in their entirety, one at a time. And you have to use them in exactly the right form. If you said *kick a bucket* or *kick the pail,* many listeners would not understand what you meant. Many idioms involve phrasal verbs (see 51a).

> **WEBLINK**
>
> http://www.eslcafe.com/idioms/
> An interactive site for learning colloquial idioms
>
> http://www.aitech.ac.jp/~iteslj/ESL.html
> A great collection of self-study quizzes for ESL students

The best way to learn a language's idioms is by listening to native speakers. Some good Web sites can also be of help: Dave Sperling's Idiom Page at *http://www.pacificnet.net/~sperling/idioms.cgi*, The Weekly Idiom at *http://www.comenius.com/idiom/index.html*, and Vocabulary on the Internet at *http://www.hku.hk/engctr/vec/vocint.html*.

Because most idioms are colloquial, you should generally avoid them in formal written English (see 36c). They are most often used for casual communication, as in ordinary conversation, email correspondence, or chat groups. Some idioms, though, are quite acceptable in more formal uses.

Some Idioms That Can Be Used in Academic Writing

Idiom	Meaning	Example
allow for	take into consideration	My calculations failed to *allow for* random errors.
by and large	more often than not	*By and large,* women can bear pain better than men.
catch up on	do what was postponed earlier	Now that exams are over, I want to *catch up on* my sleep.
dwell on	be overly concerned with	Why *dwell on* problems that we cannot control?
enlarge upon	explain in more detail	The instructor said I should *enlarge upon* this idea.
keep abreast of	be up to date with	It is important to *keep abreast of* the latest developments in the field.
out of the question	impossible	Getting new funding for this project is *out of the question.*
play on	influence	Many television shows *play on* the viewer's emotions.
to the letter	precisely	He followed the professor's instructions *to the letter.*

Glossary of Grammatical and Rhetorical Terms

absolute phrase A subject and an adjective phrase (often a participial phrase) used to modify an entire clause—for example, *"Her curiosity satisfied,* she left the meeting." (22c-2)

abstract noun A word that names an idea, emotion, quality, or other intangible concept—for example, *beauty, passion, despair.* (22a-1, 36a-2)

acronym A pronounceable word that is formed from the first letters of a multiword name and is usually written in uppercase letters—for example, *UNESCO, ASCII, RAM.* (47d)

active voice The form a transitive verb takes to indicate that the subject is performing the action on the direct object. Also called the *active form.* (22a-3, 24g)

adjective A word that modifies a noun by qualifying or describing it—for example, *new, interesting.* (22a-5, Chapter 25). *See also specific types of adjectives.*

adjective clause A dependent clause, usually introduced by a relative pronoun, that modifies a noun or pronoun. Also called a *relative clause.* (22c-3)

adverb A word that modifies a verb, adjective, clause, sentence, or other adverb—for example, *quickly, well.* (22a-6, Chapter 25, 52c–52f). *See also specific types of adverbs.*

adverb clause A dependent clause that begins with a subordinating conjunction and answers the question when, where, how, or why. (22c-3)

agreement The grammatical requirement that a verb and its subject have the same number (either plural or singular) and that a pronoun and its antecedent have the same number and gender. (Chapter 28)

analogy A simile that extends beyond one sentence. (36f-1)

annotating Making summary notes in the margin, as well as underlining or highlighting important words and passages. (1b-3)

antecedent The noun that precedes and is replaced by a pronoun. For example, in the sentence "David is proud of himself," *David* is the antecedent of *himself.* A pronoun should agree in number and gender with its antecedent. (22a-2, 23a, 23b)

appositive A special type of pronoun-noun pairing in which a pronoun is conjoined with a noun—for example, *we students.* Also, a noun that is placed next to the subject to give it extra characterization. *See also* appositive phrase. (23g)

appositive phrase A noun phrase, placed next to another noun, that describes or defines the other noun and is usually set off by commas—for example, "Ken Griffey, Jr., *my favorite baseball player,* may someday break the home run record." Also called an *appositive.* (22c-2, 32c)

article A word that precedes a noun and indicates definiteness or indefiniteness. Standard Edited English has three articles: *a, an, the.* (22a-1, Chapter 50)

aspect *See* verbal aspect.

attributive possessive pronoun A possessive pronoun used directly before a noun. (23i)

auxiliary verb A verb, such as *has, be,* or *do,* that combines with a main verb to form a simple predicate—for example, "The guests *have* left." Also called a *helping verb.* (22a-3, 24c)

base form The main form of a verb, given as the headword in the dictionary—for example, *run, ask, consider.* Also called *simple form.* (24a)

brainstorming Generating random ideas or fragments of thought about a topic. (2b-1)

case The form a pronoun takes to indicate its grammatical relation to other words in the sentence. (23e). *See also* objective case, subjective case.

clause A group of words that has a subject and a predicate. Compare with *phrase.* (22c-3). *See also specific types of clauses.*

cliché An overused expression—for example, *sick and tired, climbing the ladder of success.* (36f-3)

clustering A prewriting technique that helps a writer to see relationships among ideas. (2b-4)

cognates Two words, from different languages, that are similar in form and meaning—for example, the English *disaster* and the Spanish *desastre.* (53a)

coherence The characteristic of writing that makes it "stick together" from sentence to sentence and paragraph to paragraph. (4b-2)

collective noun A singular word that names a group—for example, *team, band, trio.* (22a-1)

collocations Two or more words that frequently occur together—for example, *write* and *check.* (53b)

comma splice Two independent clauses joined only by a comma. Comma splices are not acceptable in formal English. (Chapter 27)

common noun A word that names one or more persons, places, things, concepts, or qualities as a general category—for example, *flowers, telephone, determination.* Common nouns are lowercased. (22a-1)

complement *See* object complement, subject complement, verb complement.

complete predicate The simple predicate plus any objects, complements, or adverbial modifiers. (22b-2, 22b-3)

complete subject The simple subject of a sentence, plus all modifiers. (22b-1)

complex compound A word made up of three or more words. (48b)

complex sentence A sentence that has a single independent clause and one or more dependent clauses. (22d-2, 34b)

complex series   A series in which individual items contain internal commas, necessitating the use of semicolons to separate the items. (41c)

compound   A word made up of two smaller words. (48a)

compound antecedent   A noun phrase consisting of two or more terms joined by *and*—for example, *Kim and her brother*. It is usually considered plural; therefore, if it is referred to later by a pronoun, the pronoun should be plural. (23a)

compound-complex sentence   A sentence that has two or more independent clauses and one or more dependent clauses. (22d-2, 34b)

compound predicate   A predicate containing two or more verbs with the same subject. (22b-2)

compound sentence   A sentence that has two or more independent clauses and no dependent clauses. (22d-2, 33b)

compound subject   A sentence subject consisting of two or more simple subjects. (22b-1)

concrete noun   A word that names something that can be touched, seen, heard, smelled, or tasted—for example, *automobile, music, cloud*. (22a-1, 36a-2)

conjunction   A word that joins two sentences, clauses, phrases, or words—for example, *and, or, but*. (22a-8). *See also specific types of conjunctions.*

conjunctive adverb   An adverb that modifies an entire sentence or clause while linking it to the preceding sentence or clause—for example, *however, therefore*. (22a-6, 32b, 40f)

connotation   Extra nuances of meaning that a word has, beyond its basic meaning. Compare with *denotation*. (36b)

contraction   A reduced form of a word or pair of words—for example, *can't* for *cannot*, *I'll* for *I will*. (36c-2)

coordinate adjectives   A series of adjectives, separated by commas, that could be arranged in any order—for example, a *rusty, dented, broken-down* car. (40d)

coordinating conjunction   A conjunction used to connect sentences, clauses, phrases, or words that are parallel in meaning—for example, *and, but, or, nor, yet*. (22a-8, 32b)

coordination   The pairing of equivalent sentences or sentence elements by putting them in the same grammatical form and linking them via a coordinating conjunction, conjunctive adverb, or semicolon. (32b)

correlative conjunctions   Conjunctions that are used in pairs—for example, *both/and, either/or, neither/nor*. The two elements connected by such conjunctions should be in parallel grammatical form. (22a-8, 33c)

count noun   A word that names something that can be counted and pluralized—for example, a *book*, some *friends*, three *dollars*. (22a-1, 50a)

cumulative adjectives   A series of adjectives, each one modifying those following it—for example, *a small new Italian luxury* car. These adjectives must follow a certain order, and commas are not used to separate them. (40j)

dangling modifier   An introductory verbal phrase that does not refer to the subject of the sentence. Dangling modifiers are unacceptable in formal English. (29e)

debating   A prewriting technique that helps writers to examine arguments for and against a controversial issue. (2b-5)

declarative sentence   A sentence that makes a statement about something. In most writing, declarative sentences predominate. (22d-1)

deductive reasoning   Argumentation that starts with some general rule or assumption and then applies it to a specific fact to arrive at a logical conclusion. (6a-2)

demonstrative adjective   An adjective that singles out a specific noun—for example, *this* book, *those* promises. (22a-5, 25a)

demonstrative pronoun   A pronoun that points to its antecedent noun—for example, *this*, *those*. (22a-2)

denotation   The basic dictionary meaning of a word. Compare with *connotation*. (36a)

dependent clause   A clause that cannot stand alone as a sentence but must be attached to a main clause. A dependent clause typically begins with a subordinating conjunction or relative pronoun. The three types of dependent clauses are adjective, adverb, and noun clauses. Also called a *subordinate clause*. (22c-2, 26b, 32c)

development   The depth of coverage given to particular topics in a piece of writing reveals its development. (4a)

dialect   Speech that is identified with a particular social, ethnic, or regional group. (36d)

diction   A writer's choice of words. (Chapter 36)

direct discourse   Language that is taken word for word from another source and is enclosed in quotation marks. (30f)

direct object   A noun, pronoun, or noun phrase that completes the action of the verb in an active sentence—for example, "Our neighbor plays *the piano.*" (22b-2)

disjunctive antecedent   A noun phrase consisting of two or more terms joined by *or* or *nor*—for example, *the wife or the husband*. If the disjunctive antecedent is referred to later by a pronoun, the pronoun should agree in number with the last term in the phrase. (23a)

disjunctive subject   A sentence subject consisting of two nouns or pronouns joined by *or* or *nor*. (28c)

double negative   Sentence or phrase containing two negative modifiers that carry the same meaning. (25f)

ellipsis   Three spaced periods marking the omission of a word or phrase. (10d-2, 45j, 45k)

enthymeme   A syllogism with one of the premises unstated. (6a-2)

etymology   Information about a word's origin and historical development. (38b-3)

exclamatory sentence   A sentence that expresses strong emotion and is punctuated with an exclamation point. (22d-1)

exemplification   The use of examples to make difficult concepts understandable. (5b-8)

expletive pronoun   An introductory word (*it*, *there*) that opens a sentence but carries little meaning. Expletives are sometimes overused. (22a-2, 31c)

false cognates Two words, from different languages, that resemble each other but have different meanings—for example, the Spanish *compromiso* and the English *compromise*. Also called *false friends*. (53a)

false friends *See* false cognates.

faulty predication An ungrammatical construction in a sentence in which the subject and the predicate are not consistent with each other. (30e)

focus Refers to how well a piece adheres to its topic and purpose. (4a)

format (*n*) The way a piece of writing delineates its subtopics and parts through headings, typeface, typestyle, and so forth. (*v*) To set up a piece of writing's visual style. (4a)

fragment *See* sentence fragment.

freewriting Writing down thoughts in connected sentences as they come to mind. (2b-2)

fused sentence *See* run-on sentence.

future perfect progressive tense A verb tense formed by combining *will have been* and the *-ing* form of the main verb. It emphasizes the continuous or repetitive nature of an action—for example, "Next month, my father *will have been teaching* for 30 years." (24d-3)

future perfect tense A verb tense formed by combining *will have* and the past participle of the main verb. It describes an action that will occur in the future but before some specified time—for example, "Soon I *will have completed* all the requirements." (24d-3)

future progressive tense A verb tense formed by combining *will be* and the *-ing* form of the main verb. It expresses action that will be continuing or repeated in the future—for example, "My daughter is on vacation now, but she *will be going* back to school in the fall." (24d-3)

future tense A verb tense formed by combining the modal auxiliary *will* and the base form of the main verb. It expresses actions or conditions that will occur in the future—for example, "The final exam *will be* hard." Also called *simple future tense*. (24d-3)

gender Classification of a noun or pronoun as masculine, feminine, or neuter. (23a)

generic pronoun A pronoun used to refer to all people regardless of gender. (37a-2)

gerund A verb form that ends in *-ing* and functions as a noun—for example, "My favorite sports are *skiing* and tennis." (22a-4)

gerund phrase A phrase consisting of a gerund and any modifiers, objects, and/or complements: "*Running a business* can be difficult." (22c-2)

head noun The rightmost noun in a noun compound. (52b)

helping verb *See* auxiliary verb.

homophones Words that sound alike but are spelled differently and have different meanings—for example, *brake* and *break*. (49b)

idiom *See* idiomatic expression.

idiomatic expression A phrase whose meaning cannot be deduced from the meanings of its individual words—for example, *kick the bucket*. Also called an *idiom*. (36c-2, 53c)

imperative mood A grammatical form of a verb used to express a command or a strong request and give instructions. Imperative sentences are always addressed to an understood subject *you*, which is usually omitted. (22a-3, 24h, 30b)

imperative sentence A sentence that expresses a command, a request, or a suggestion, usually with an understood subject *you*—for example, "Don't fret!" "Try using the toolbar buttons." (22d-1)

indefinite adjective A nonspecific adjective—for example, *some* people. (22a-5, 25a)

indefinite pronoun A pronoun that refers to one or more nonspecific persons, places, or things and does not require an antecedent—for example, *anybody, anything*. (22a-2, 23a)

independent clause A group of words that includes a subject and predicate and can stand alone as a sentence. Also called a *main clause*. (22c-3)

indicative mood A grammatical form of a verb used to make assertions, state opinions, and ask questions. (22a-3, 24h, 30b)

indirect discourse A summarization, restatement, or paraphrase of a statement made by someone else. (30f, 44a-1)

indirect object A noun, pronoun, or noun phrase that is indirectly affected by the action of the verb—for example, "My boyfriend gave *me* a present." (22b-2)

inductive reasoning A pattern in which the writer states the main claim for an argument late in the work, in order to first present a skeptical audience with supporting evidence. (6a-2)

infinitive The base form of a verb usually preceded by *to*. It can function as a noun, adjective, or adverb. (22a-4, 24e-3). *See also* perfect infinitive, present infinitive.

infinitive phrase A phrase consisting of an infinitive and any modifiers, objects, and/or complements—for example, "Kevin said he wanted *to make his own way*." (22c-2)

initialism An unpronounceable abbreviation formed from the first letters of a multiword name and usually written in uppercase letters—for example, *FBI, CPU*. (47d) Compare with *acronym*.

inseparable verb A transitive phrasal verb whose particle must be kept together with the verb—for example, "I quickly *went over* my paper." Compare with *separable verb*. (Chapter 51)

intensive pronoun A pronoun that consists of a personal pronoun plus -*self* or -*selves* and is used for emphasis—for example, "They did it *themselves*." (22a-2)

interjection A short utterance that expresses an emotional response. (22a-9)

interrogative adjective An adjective that raises a question about a noun—for example, "*Which* way do I go?" "*Whose* hat is this?" (22a-5, 25a)

interrogative pronoun A pronoun that introduces a question—for example, *who, what, whose*. (22a-2, 23h)

interrogative sentence A sentence that raises a question and is punctuated with a question mark. (22d-1)

intransitive verb A verb that does not take a direct object—for example, "My driver's license *has expired.*" (22a-3, 24f, Chapter 51)

irregular verb A verb whose past tense and past participle are not formed through the standard pattern of adding *d* or *ed* to the base form—for example, *run (ran, run); know (knew, known).* (24b)

jargon Specialized, technical language used by a professional or special interest group. (36d)

linking verb A verb that joins a sentence subject to a subject complement, indicating a condition, quality, or state of being—for example, "They *will be* late." (22b-3)

main clause *See* independent clause.

mass noun *See* noncount noun.

metaphor A figure of speech in which the writer describes something in a way normally reserved for something else, thus presenting it in a new light. (36f-2)

mixed construction An ungrammatical sentence that starts out one way but finishes in another. (30d)

mixed metaphors Two different metaphors put close together in a piece of writing—for example, "Milwaukee is the golden egg that the rest of the state wants to milk." Mixed metaphors should be avoided. (36f-2)

modal auxiliary verb A special type of verb that indicates necessity, probability, or permission—for example, *may, might, should, can.* Also called a *modal verb.* (22a-3, 24c, 51g, 51h). *See also* auxiliary verb.

modal verb *See* modal auxiliary verb.

modifier A word, phrase, or clause that adds detail to another word, phrase, or clause. (22c, Chapter 29). *See also* dangling modifier, split infinitive.

mood The form of a verb that indicates the type of statement made—indicative, imperative, or subjunctive. (22a-3, 24h, 30b)

narrative A type of writing that tells a story in a time-ordered sequence. (5b-7)

nominal possessive pronoun A possessive pronoun that is used with a linking verb—for example, "This book is *yours.*" (23i)

noncount noun A word that names something that typically is not counted or pluralized—for example, *milk, generosity, rain.* Also called a *mass noun.* (22a-1, 50a)

nonessential element *See* nonrestrictive element.

nonrestrictive element A phrase or clause that provides extra information in a sentence. A nonrestrictive element can be omitted without changing the basic meaning of the sentence; it is set off with commas, dashes, or parentheses. Also called a *nonessential element.* (40e)

noun A word that names a person, place, thing, quality, idea, or action. (22a-1). *See also specific types of nouns.*

noun clause A dependent clause that begins with a relative pronoun and functions as a sentence subject, object, complement, or appositive. (22c-3)

noun compound A sequence of two or more nouns, with the rightmost noun being the head noun and the other noun(s) serving to modify it—for example, *income tax form.* (25b, 52b)

number   Classification of a noun, pronoun, or verb as singular or plural. (23a)

object   *See* direct object, indirect object, object of the preposition.

object complement   A noun, noun phrase, adjective, or adjective phrase that elaborates on or describes the direct object of a sentence—for example, "The film made me *angry.*" (22b-2)

object of the preposition   A noun or pronoun in a prepositional phrase—for example, "He was on the *boat.*" (22a-7)

objective case   The form a pronoun takes when it is used as a grammatical object. (23f)

organization   The plan that a piece of writing follows, typically based on the thesis and opening paragraphs. (4a)

paragraph   A sentence or group of sentences, presented in a text as a unit, that develops a main idea. (Chapter 5)

parallel form   *See* parallelism.

parallel structure   *See* parallelism.

parallelism   The use of similar grammatical form for words or phrases that have a coordinate relationship. Also called *parallel structure* or *parallel form.* (5e, Chapter 33)

participial phrase   A phrase consisting of a present or past participle plus any objects, modifiers, and/or complements—for example, "I saw someone *running down the street.*" (22c-2)

participle   A verb form that can serve as an adjective—for example, *earned* income or *earning* power. (22a-4). *See also* past participle, present participle, present perfect participle.

particle   A preposition or adverb that, when attached to a verb, creates a phrasal verb—for example, look *into,* see *through,* knock *out.* (22a-7)

parts of speech   The different categories in which words can be classified according to their grammatical function: nouns, pronouns, verbs, adjectives, adverbs, prepositions, conjunctions, and interjections.(22a)

passive voice   The form a transitive verb takes to indicate that the subject is being acted on. Also called the *passive form.* (22a-3, 24g)

past participle   A verb form that can be used by itself as an adjective or can be combined with some form of the auxiliary *have* to form perfect tenses or with some form of the verb *be* to create passive-voice sentences. With regular verbs, it is similar in form to the past tense—for example, *picked,* *opened.* (24a, 24e-4)

past perfect progressive tense   A verb tense formed by combining *had been* and the present participle of the main verb. It puts emphasis on the continuing or repetitive nature of a past action—for example, "By the time he crossed the bridge, Roy *had been running* for two hours." (24d-2)

past perfect tense   A verb tense created by combining *had* and the past participle of the main verb. It is used to describe a past action that preceded another past activity—for example, "Before she injured her knee, Beth *had hoped* to become a top ski racer." (24d-2)

past progressive tense   A verb tense formed by combining the auxiliary verb *was* or *were* and the present participle of the main verb—for example, "I *was* just *starting* to cook when our guest arrived." (24d-2)

past tense   A verb tense that indicates past action—for example, "World War I *started* in 1914." With regular verbs, the past tense is formed by adding *d* or *ed* to the base form. Also called *simple past tense.* (24a, 24d-2)

perfect infinitive   A verb form consisting of *to have* plus the past participle of the verb—for example, *to have changed, to have stopped.* It is used for an action that occurs prior to the action expressed by the main verb. (24e-3)

persona   A writer's presentation of himself or herself through a piece of writing. (2a-2, 15b-2)

personal pronoun   A pronoun that refers to one or more specific persons, places, or things—for example, *she, it, they.* (22a-2)

personification   A type of metaphor in which an inanimate object or abstraction is described as having human traits. (36f-2)

phrasal verb   A verb consisting of a verb and one or two particles—for example, *pick over, look into, get away with.* Also called a *two-word verb* or *three-word verb.* (22a-7, Chapter 51)

phrase   A group of related words that does not have both a subject and a complete predicate (compare with *clause*). Phrases can function as nouns, verbs, or modifiers. (22c-2). *See also specific types of phrases.*

plagiarism   Unauthorized or misleading use of the language and thoughts of another author. (10a)

possessive adjective   An adjective that indicates possession—for example, *my* coat, *their* country. (22a-5, 25a)

predicate   The part of a sentence that contains the verb and makes a statement about the subject. (22b-2)

predicate adjective   An adjective that follows a linking verb and refers back to the noun subject. (22a-5)

prefix   A word part, such as *anti-, re-,* or *dis-,* that is attached to the beginning of a word—for example, *anti*freeze, *re*new, *dis*cover. (49d-1)

preposition   A word that indicates a relationship between a noun or pronoun and some other part of the sentence—for example, *to, in, at, from, on.* Also called a *particle* in phrasal verbs. (22a-7)

prepositional phrase   A group of words consisting of a preposition plus a noun or pronoun and its modifiers. (22a-7, 22c-2)

present infinitive   A verb form consisting of *to* plus the base form of the verb—for example, *to go, to hesitate.* It is used for an action that occurs at the same time as or later than the action expressed by the main verb. (24e-3)

present participle   A verb form created by adding *ing* to the base form—for example, *sewing, writing.* It can be used by itself as an adjective or noun or can be combined with some form of the verb *be* to form the progressive tenses. (24a, 24e-4)

present perfect participle   A verb form consisting of *having* plus the past participle of the verb. It is used to express an action occurring prior to the action of the main verb—for example, "*Having changed* my PIN number, I cannot remember it." (24e-4)

present perfect progressive tense   A verb tense formed by combining *have been* or *has been* and the present participle of the main verb. It typically emphasizes the ongoing nature of an activity—for example, "People *have been complaining* about the working conditions for years." (24d-1)

present perfect tense A verb tense formed by combining the auxiliary verb *have* or *has* and the past participle of the main verb. It is used to indicate action that began in the past and either is continuing or has continuing effects in the present—for example, "The United Nations *has served* many purposes." (24d-1)

present progressive tense A verb tense formed by combining the auxiliary verb *am, is,* or *are* and the *-ing* form of a main verb. It is typically used to indicate present action—for example, "Mike *is taking* a heavy load of classes this term." (24d-1)

present tense The verb tense used to express a general statement, make an observation, or describe an habitual activity—for example, "Geese *fly* south in autumn." Also called *simple present tense*. (24a, 24d-1)

primary research Generating information or data through processes such as interviewing, administering questionnaires, and observing. (7a-1, 7f-6)

principal parts The major forms of a verb: base form, present tense, past tense, past participle, and present participle. (24a)

process description A type of writing that depicts a step-by-step procedure. (5b-7)

pronoun A word that substitutes for a noun or noun phrase. (22a-2, 23a). *See also specific types of pronouns.*

proper noun A word that names a particular person, place, institution, organization, month, or day—for example, *Anne, New York City, Monday*. Proper nouns are almost always capitalized. (22a-1)

reciprocal pronoun A pronoun that refers to the separate parts of a plural antecedent—for example, "They made promises to *one another*." (22a-2)

redundancy The use of words that could be left out without changing the meaning of a sentence. (31b)

reflexive pronoun A pronoun that consists of a personal pronoun plus *-self* or *-selves*. It refers back to the subject to show that the subject is the object of an action—for example, "Katy cut *herself*." (22a-2)

register The overall degree of formality of a piece of writing, including its identification with a particular field or community of users. (36c)

regular verb A verb that forms the third-person singular present tense by adding *s* or *es* to the base form, forms the present participle by adding *ing* to the base form, and forms the past tense and past participle by adding *d* or *ed* to the base form. (24a)

related words Words derived from the same root. (38b-3)

relative clause *See* adjective clause.

relative pronoun A pronoun that introduces a dependent clause—for example, *that, which, whom.* (22a-2, 23h)

restrictive element Information essential to the meaning of a sentence and thus not set off with commas. Compare with *nonrestrictive element*. (40j)

résumé A concise summary of an individual's accomplishments, skills, experience, and personal interests. (19c)

rhetorical stance A writer's approach to his or her topic, encompassing purpose, persona, and audience. (2a-2)

run-on sentence   Two independent clauses fused together without any intervening conjunction or punctuation. Run-on sentences are not acceptable in formal English. Also called a *fused sentence*. (Chapter 27)

secondary research   Finding information in secondary, or previously published, sources. (7a-1)

sense   The meaning of a word. (38b-2)

sentence   The basic unit of written language for expressing a thought. All sentences except commands have a stated grammatical subject and a predicate. (22b). *See also specific types of sentences.*

sentence fragment   A grammatically incomplete sentence. (Chapter 26)

sentence subject   *See* subject.

separable verb   A transitive phrasal verb whose particle may be placed after the object of the verb—for example, "I quickly *looked* my paper *over.*" Compare with *inseparable verb*. (Chapter 51)

sequence of tenses   The time relationship among verbs in a block of text, expressed by verb tenses. (24e)

serial comma   In a series of items, the comma that separates the last two items. (40c)

simile   A figure of speech in which the writer uses one thing to describe another. Similes typically employ the word *like* or *as*—for example, "The brain is somewhat like a computer." (36f-1)

simple form   *See* base form.

simple future tense   *See* future tense.

simple past tense   *See* past tense.

simple predicate   A main verb plus any auxiliary verbs. Also called a *verb phrase*. (22b-2). *See also* predicate.

simple present tense   *See* present tense.

simple sentence   A sentence that has a single independent clause and no dependent clauses. (22d-2, 34b)

simple subject   The noun or pronoun that constitutes the heart of a sentence subject. (22b-1)

slang   Nonstandard language characterized by short-lived, colorful expressions. It is most commonly used by teenagers and members of tight-knit subcultures. (36d)

split infinitive   A *to* infinitive with one or more words between *to* and the verb—for example, *to quickly retreat.* (29d-2)

stative verb   *See* verb of state.

subject   A noun, pronoun, or noun phrase that indicates what a sentence is about and typically precedes the main verb of the sentence. (22b-1, 26a-2, Chapter 28). *See also specific types of subjects.*

subject complement   A noun, noun phrase, adjective, or adjective phrase that elaborates on the subject of a sentence and usually follows a linking verb—for example, "Joanne was elected *student body president.*" (22b-2)

subjective case   The form a pronoun takes when it is used as a grammatical subject. (23e)

subjunctive mood   A grammatical form of a verb used to express hypothetical conditions, wishes, and other uncertain statements. Verbs in subjunctive mood often appear in dependent clauses beginning with *if* or *that*. (22a-3, 24h, 30b)

subordinate clause   *See* dependent clause.

subordinating conjunction   A conjunction that is used to introduce a dependent clause and connect it to an independent clause—for example, *although, because, if, since*. (22a-8)

subordination   In a sentence containing two ideas that are not equal in importance, making the lesser idea into a subordinate, or dependent, clause. (32c)

suffix   A word part, such as *-ful, -ship*, or *-ness*, that is attached to the end of a word—for example, boast*ful*, fellow*ship*, kind*ness*. (49d-2)

syllogism   A form of deductive logic consisting of a major premise, a minor premise, and a conclusion. (6a-2)

synonyms   Words that are similar in meaning—for example, *desire* and *want*. (38b-3)

tense   *See* verb tense.

thesaurus   A collection of synonyms and antonyms. (38a)

thesis statement   A sentence or two that concisely identifies the topic and main point of a piece of writing. (2d-2)

three-word verb   *See* phrasal verb.

tone   The tone of a piece of writing, including the attitude a writer conveys toward the subject through language choices. (4a)

topic sentence   A sentence, usually at the beginning of a paragraph, that gives readers an overview of the paragraph. (5a-1)

transitive verb   A verb that acts on an object—for example, *carry, show*. In the active voice, a transitive verb acts on the direct object of the sentence. In the passive voice, it acts on the subject. (22a-3, 24f, Chapter 51)

two-word verb   *See* phrasal verb.

unified paragraph   A paragraph that focuses on and develops a single main idea. (5a)

usage label   In dictionaries, a notation indicating a particular sense of a word—for example, *Informal, Archaic*. (38b-3)

usage note   In dictionaries, an expert judgment about the "correct" use of a word. (38b-3)

verb   A word that expresses action, occurrence, or existence. (22a-3, Chapter 24). *See also specific types of verbs.*

verb complement   A participial or infinitive phrase attached to a verb—for example, in the sentence "I like to swim," *to swim* is the complement of the verb *like*. (51b–51e)

verb of state   A verb that expresses a condition or state, rather than an action or event—for example, *involve, need, consist of*. Verbs of state do not have progressive tense forms. Also called a *stative verb*. (24d-1, 51f)

verb phrase   *See* simple predicate.

verb tense   The form a verb takes to indicate the time of the action or the state of being. (24d, 30b)

verbal   A verb form that functions in a sentence as a noun, adverb, or adjective. There are three types of verbals: participles, gerunds, and infinitives. (22a-4, 22c-2)

verbal aspect   The particular form a verb takes, within its tense, to indicate duration or completion of the verb's action or state of being. Standard Edited English has three verbal aspects: perfect, progressive, and perfect progressive. Also called *aspect.* (24d)

voice   The form a transitive verb takes to indicate whether the subject is acting (*active voice*) or being acted on (*passive voice*). (24g)

warrant   An assumption in the form of a general statement or rule (often unstated) that logically connects the evidence or data a writer is using to the point he or she is making. (6d-2)

Glossary of Usage

a, an   Use *a* before words beginning with a consonant sound: *a* program, *a* uniform. Use *an* before words beginning with a vowel sound: *an* open book, *an* uncle.

accept, except   *Accept* is a verb meaning "to receive gladly." *Except* is usually a preposition meaning "with the exclusion of." "The restaurant *accepts* any form of payment *except* credit cards."

advice, advise   *Advice* is a noun meaning "guidance." *Advise* is a verb meaning "to guide." "I *advised* her to take my *advice.*"

affect, effect   Most commonly, *affect* is used as a verb meaning "to influence": "Bad weather seems to *affect* my mood." *Effect* is generally used as a noun meaning "result." As a verb, *effect* means "to bring about": "The new policy will *effect* important changes."

ain't   Nonstandard. *Am not, is not, are not,* and *have not* are preferred in Standard Edited English; the contractions *isn't, aren't,* and *haven't* are acceptable in casual discourse.

all ready, already   *All ready* is an adjective phrase meaning "all prepared": "They were *all ready* to go." *Already* is an adverb meaning "by this time": "They have *already* left."

allusion, illusion   An *allusion* is an indirect reference. An *illusion* is a false perception of reality.

amongst   British equivalent of *among.*

an   See *a.*

as   See *like.*

awful, awfully   Avoid using these terms to mean "very," except in informal communication.

bad, badly   *Bad* is an adjective: "I feel *bad.*" *Badly* is an adverb: "He plays *badly.*"

because of, due to   Use *because of* when a clause describes the situation to which you are attributing a cause: "She had a headache *because of* stress." Use *due to* when a noun describes the situation to which you are attributing a cause: "Her headache was *due to* stress."

can't hardly, can't scarcely   Nonstandard for *can hardly* or *can scarcely.* "Even accountants *can hardly* make sense of the tax code."

center around   In formal writing, *center on* is preferred. "My paper will *center on* hate speech."

cite, site   *Cite* is a verb meaning "to quote." *Site* is a noun meaning "place."

complement, compliment   To *complement* is to complete so as to make a whole: "The flowers beautifully *complemented* the table setting." To *compliment* is to express praise: "She *complimented* me on my dancing."

conscience, conscious   *Conscience* is a noun meaning "a sense of right and wrong." *Conscious* is an adjective meaning "aware" or "intentional." "Todd made a *conscious* decision to clear his guilty *conscience.*"

could of   Nonstandard for *could have.* "He *could have* tried harder."

criterion, criteria   *Criterion* is a singular noun, meaning "standard of judgment." *Criteria* is the plural form.

data   Traditionally, *data* was used only as the plural form of *datum.* However, it is now commonly used as a singular form to mean "numerical information."

different from, different than   In formal writing, use *different from* when the comparison is between two persons or things: "My opinion is *different from* hers." Use *different than* when the object of comparison is a full clause: "The party turned out *different than* I wanted it to be."

discreet, discrete   *Discreet* mean "tactful" or "modest." *Discrete* means "distinct" or "separate."

due to   See *because of.*

effect   See *affect.*

elicit, illicit   *Elicit* is a verb meaning "to call forth." *Illicit* is an adjective meaning "illegal."

emigrate, immigrate, migrate   *Emigrate* means "to move permanently away from." *Immigrate* means "to move permanently to." *Migrate* means "to move temporarily from one place to another."

eminent, immanent, imminent   *Eminent* means "distinguished": "She is an *eminent* scholar." *Immanent* means "inherent": "God's spirit is *immanent* in nature." *Imminent* means "about to occur": "A stock market crash is *imminent.*"

except   See *accept.*

farther, further   *Farther* refers to distance: "She hit the ball *farther* than anyone else." *Further* refers to time or degree: "Should we go *further* with our research?"

fewer, less   Use *fewer* with items that can be counted. Use *less* with general amounts associated with noncount nouns. "He had *fewer* problems and *less* anxiety than I did."

firstly, secondly, thirdly   Common in British English. In American English, *first, second,* and *third* are preferred.

further   See *farther.*

good, well   *Good* is an adjective. *Well* is an adverb. "When I feel *good,* I write *well.*"

gorilla, guerrilla   A *gorilla* is a large ape. A *guerrilla* is a member of a rebel army.

he/she, him/her, his/her   Although these forms can be used to avoid the sexism of the generic *he, him,* or *his,* use them sparingly (see 37a-2).

heard, herd   *Heard* is the past tense of the verb *to hear. Herd* is a group of animals.

hisself   Nonstandard for *himself.* "He shot *himself* in the foot."

hole, whole   *Hole* is a noun meaning "gap" or "cavity." *Whole* is an adjective meaning "complete" or "entire."

hopefully   Technically, *hopefully* may be used as a sentence adverb: "*Hopefully,* the war will soon be over." However, some critics object to this usage because there is no subject to be full of hope. You can replace *hopefully* with *I hope that.*

illicit   See *elicit.*

illusion   See *allusion.*

immanent   See *eminent.*

immigrate   See *emigrate.*

imminent   See *eminent.*

imply, infer   *Imply* means "to suggest indirectly." *Infer* means "to draw a conclusion from what someone else has said." "The owner *implied* that I did not have enough experience; I *inferred* that she would not offer me the job."

incredible, incredulous   *Incredible* means "unbelievable": "His performance was *incredible.*" *Incredulous* means "disbelieving": "He was *incredulous* when he heard the news."

infer   See *imply.*

irregardless   Nonstandard for *regardless.*

its, it's   *Its* is the possessive form of *it. It's* is the contracted form of *it is.* "*It's* important that a company give *its* employees a sense of security."

lay, lie   *Lay* takes a direct object and means "to place": "They want to *lay* a wreath at his grave." *Lie* does not take a direct object and means "to recline": "I think I'll *lie* down for a while." (Note, however, that *lay* is also the past tense of *lie.*)

lead, led   *Led* is the past tense of the verb *to lead:* "Our efforts have *led* to nothing." *Lead,* pronounced the same way as *led,* is a noun referring to a certain type of metal.

leave, let   *Leave* means "to go away": "She plans to *leave* tomorrow." *Let* means "to allow": "*Let* me pay for this."

lend, loan   Both verbs mean "to give something temporarily." But *loan* is used only for physical transactions, such as *loaning money,* while *lend* can be used more figuratively as in *lending someone a hand.*

less   See *fewer.*

lie   See *lay.*

like, as   In formal writing, use *like* as a preposition before a noun phrase: "She looked *like* her mother." Use *as* as a conjunction before a clause: "She looked *as* I thought she would."

loan   See *lend*.

lose, loose   *Lose* is a verb meaning "to fail to keep." *Loose* is an adjective meaning "not fastened."

man, mankind   Avoid these terms in situations where gender-inclusive terms, such as *people, humanity, humans, humankind,* or *men and women,* can be used instead.

migrate   See *emigrate*.

moral, morale   A *moral* is a lesson taught in a story. *Morale* is a state of mind reflecting levels of confidence and cheerfulness.

must of   Nonstandard for *must have*. "They *must have* lost their way."

okay, OK, O.K.   Informal. In formal writing, use more precise terms like *enjoyable, acceptable,* or *pleasing* (if an adjective is needed), *approve* or *authorize* (if a verb is needed), or *approval* or *authorization* (if a noun is needed).

patience, patients   *Patience* is the quality of being tolerant and steadfast. *Patients* are people who receive medical treatment.

peace, piece   *Peace* is the opposite of war. A *piece* is a segment or part.

personal, personnel   *Personal* is an adjective meaning "private" or "individual." *Personnel* is a noun meaning "the people employed by an organization."

piece   See *peace*.

plain, plane   *Plain* is a noun meaning "flat area of land" or an adjective meaning "obvious," "clear," or "ordinary in appearance." *Plane* is the short form of the noun *airplane* or a geometrical surface.

presence, presents   *Presence* is the opposite of absence. *Presents* are gifts.

pretty   In formal writing, avoid using *pretty* as an adverb. "JFK was a rather good writer."

principal, principle   *Principal* is an adjective meaning "foremost." *Principle* is a noun meaning "rule" or "standard." "Our *principal* concern is to maintain our high *principles*."

raise, rise   *Raise* is a transitive verb meaning "to lift" or "to build": "He *raises* his hand." *Rise* is an intransitive verb meaning "to stand up" or "to ascend": "She *rises* from her chair."

real, really   *Real* is an adjective; *really* is an adverb. In most cases, both of these terms should be avoided in formal writing. "The economy is doing extremely well."

respectfully, respectively   *Respectfully* means "with respect." *Respectively* means "in the order given": "The teacher called on Bart and Juana, *respectively*."

rise   See *raise*.

secondly   See *firstly*.

set, sit   *Set* is used most often as a transitive verb meaning "to place" or "to arrange": "*Set* the table." *Sit* is an intransitive verb meaning "to take a seat": "*Sit* down over here."

shall, will   Use *shall* for polite questions in the first person: "*Shall* we sit down?" Otherwise, use *will*.

should of   Nonstandard for *should have*.

sit   See *set*.

site See *cite*.

stationary, stationery *Stationary* is an adjective meaning "not moving." *Stationery* is a noun meaning "writing materials."

than, then *Than* is a conjunction used to introduce the second part of a comparison: "Donna is taller *than* Jo." *Then* is an adverb meaning "at that time."

that, which As a relative pronoun, *that* is used only in restrictive clauses: "The storm *that* [or *which*] everyone talks about occurred ten years ago." *Which* can be used with either restrictive or nonrestrictive clauses: "The storm of 1989, *which* I will never forget, destroyed part of our roof."

their, there, they're *Their* is the possessive form of *they*: "They retrieved *their* car." *There* is an adverb of place; it is also used in expletive constructions: "*There* is someone at the door." *They're* is a contraction for *they are*: "*They're* too young to drive."

theirselves Nonstandard for *themselves*.

then See *than*.

thirdly See *firstly*.

threw, through/thru *Threw* is the past tense of the verb *to throw*. *Through* is a preposition: "Walk *through* the house." Do not use *thru* in formal writing.

till, until, 'til *Till* and *until* are both acceptable in formal writing; *'til* is informal.

use, utilize In most cases, *use* is the better choice. *Utilize* should be used specifically to mean "to make practical use of."

weak, week *Weak* is the opposite of strong. *Week* is a period of seven days.

weather, whether *Weather* is a noun meaning "atmospheric conditions." *Whether* is a conjunction meaning "if" or "either."

well See *good*.

which See *that*.

who, whom *Who* and *whom* are used as interrogative or relative pronouns (see 22h). *Who* stands for a grammatical subject: "*Who* is calling?" *Whom* stands for a grammatical object: "*Whom* are you calling?"

whole See *hole*.

who's, whose *Who's* is a contraction for *who is*. *Whose* is the possessive form of *who*.

will See *shall*.

would of Nonstandard for *would have*.

your, you're *Your* is the possessive form of *you*. *You're* is a contraction for *you are*. "*You're* loyal to *your* friends."

Credits

Allyn & Bacon Compsite. 14 Feb. 2003 <http://abacon.com/compsite>
American Heritage College Dictionary, The. 3rd ed. Boston: Houghton, 2000.
  Copyright © 2000. Copyright © 2000 by Houghton Mifflin Company.
  Reproduced by permission from The American Heritage College Dic-
  tionary, Third Edition.
Barlow, John Perry. "Crime and Puzzlement." *CyberReader.* Ed. Victor Vitanza.
  Boston: Allyn, 1996. 92–115.
Beebe, Steven A., and Susan J. Beebe. *Public Speaking: An Audience-Centered
  Approach.* 4th ed. Boston: Allyn, 2002.
Corel® WordPerfect Suite 8.
Cousins, Norman. *Human Options.* New York: Berkley, 1981. 41–42, 63, 90.
Donatelle, Rebecca J., and Lorraine G. Davis. *Access to Health.* 4th ed. Boston:
  Allyn, 1996. Copyright © 1996 by Allyn & Bacon. Reprinted by permission.
Ehrlich, Gretel. *The Solace of Open Spaces.* New York: Viking, 1985. 7.
Environmental Periodicals Bibliography. Citation taken from *Environmental
  Periodicals Bibliography* database (copyright, International Academy at
  Santa Barbara). This database is available on CD-ROM and on the Inter-
  net. Subscription information is available on the Academy's Website at
  <http://www.iasb.org>.
Farb, Peter. *Living Earth.* New York: Harper & Row, 1959.
Garofalo, Reebee. *Rockin' Out: Popular Music in the USA.* Boston: Allyn, 1997.
  Copyright © 1997 by Allyn & Bacon. Reprinted by permission.
Hemingway, Ernest. "Notes on the Next War: A Serious Topical Letter."
  By-Line: Ernest Hemingway. Ed. William White. New York: Scribner's,
  1967. 206.
The Henry James Review_ [Online]. <http://muse.jhu.edu/demo/
  henry_james_review/v022/22.1cohn.html>. © 2001 The Johns Hopkins
  University Press. All rights reserved.
Henslin, James M. *Sociology: A Down-to-Earth Approach.* 6th ed. Boston: Allyn,
  2003. Copyright © 2003 by Allyn & Bacon. Reprinted by permission.
Homesite, Vers. 2.5a. Allaire Corporation. 10 March 1998
  <http://www.allaire.com/homesite>.
Hopper, Vincent F., and Bernard D. N. Grebanier. *Essentials of European Liter-
  ature.* Vol. 2. Great Neck, NY: Barron's, 1952.
HotBot [Online]. <http://www.hotbot.com>. 2003. Lycos Network, Inc.
  Lycos® is a registered trademark of Carnegie Mellon University. All
  rights reserved.
Ivins, Molly. "Truly Happy News to Look For: Better 'Doug Jones' Average,"
  syndicated column, published by Creators Syndicate; appeared in *Salt
  Lake Tribune,* 2/20/97.
Kantrowitz, Barbara. "Men, Women, Computers." *Newsweek,* May 16, 1994.
Kingsolver, Barbara. *The Bean Trees.* New York: Harper, 1988. 1.

Lederer, Richard. *Anguished English.* New York: Wyrick, 1987. 115, 150–153. Excerpts from *Anguished English,* copyright 1987 by Richard Lederer. Published by Wyrick & Company.

Lycos [Online]. 5 Feb. 2001 <http://www.lycos.com>. © 2001 Lycos, Inc. Lycos® is a registered trademark of Carnegie Mellon University. All rights reserved.

Meyer, Michael, with Anne Underwood. "Crimes of the 'Net.'" *CyberReader.* Ed. Victor Vitanza. Boston: Allyn, 1996. 63–65.

Microsoft Corporation. Screen shots from Microsoft Windows Explorer®, Internet Explorer®, Windows ftp, and Microsoft Word 2000® reprinted by permission from Microsoft Corporation.

Netscape. Copyright Netscape Communications Corporation, 1997. All Rights Reserved. Netscape, Netscape Navigator and the Netscape N logo are registered trademarks of Netscape in the United States and other countries.

New Book of Knowledge, The. New York: Grolier, 1998.

Orwell, George. "Marrakech." *A Collection of Essays.* Garden City, NY: Doubleday, 1957. 186–192.

Riflin, Jeremy. *The End of Work.* New York: Putnam, 1995.

Sagan, Carl. *The Dragons of Eden.* New York: Ballantine, 1977. 177.

Terkel, Studs. *Working.* New York: Avon, 1972. xix.

Thomas, Lewis. *Lives of a Cell.* New York: Viking, 1974. 107.

Utah State University Library [Online]. <http://www.library.usu.edu>. 2003. USU Library Online Catalog. Used by permission.

Voice of the Shuttle [Online]. <http://vos.ucsb.edu/index.asp> Ed. Alan Liu. 2003. University of California, Santa Barbara, English Department.

Woolfolk, Anita E. *Educational Psychology.* 9th ed. Boston: Allyn, 2004.

Yahoo! [Online] 5 Feb. 2001 <http://www.yahoo.com>. Text and artwork copyright © 2001 by Yahoo! Inc. All rights reserved. YAHOO! And the YAHOO! logo are trademarks of YAHOO! Inc.

Zepezauer, Mark, and Arthur Naiman. *Take the Rich Off Welfare.* Monroe, ME: Odonian, 1966.

Index

Revision Symbols

Boldface numbers and letters refer to chapters or sections in the handbook.

ab	abbreviation	**47a–e**	ref	unclear pronoun	
ad	form of adjective/			reference	**23**
	adverb	**25**	rep	unnecessary	
agr	agreement	**28**		repetition	**31b**
awk	awkward diction				
	or construction	**29, 36**	search	check research or	
				citation	**9, 10, 12, 13**
ca	case form	**23e–g**	sp	spelling error	**49**
cap	capitalization	**46**	shift	inconsistent, shifted	
coh	coherence	**5c**		construction	**30**
coord	coordination	**32b**	sub	sentence	
cs	comma splice	**27**		subordination	**32c**
d	diction, word		t	verb tense	
	choice	**36, 38**		error	**24d–h**
dev	development		trans	transition	
	needed	**2, 3, 4, 5f**		needed	**4, 5c**
dm	dangling modifier	**29**			
doc	check		var	sentence variety	**34**
	documentation	**12, 13**	vb	verb form error	**24**
frag	sentence fragment	**26**	w	wordy	**31b, 31e**
fs	fused sentence	**27**	ww/wc	wrong word;	
				word choice	**36, 37**
hyph	hyphen	**48**			
			//	faulty parallelism	**33**
inc	incomplete		.?!	end punctuation	**39**
	construction	**22b, 30**	:	colon	**42**
ital	italics	**46e–j**	$\check{v}$	apostrophe	**43**
			—	dash	**45d–f**
lc	lowercase letter	**46a–d**	( )	parentheses	**45a–c**
log	logic	**6g**	[ ]	brackets	**45g–i**
			. . .	ellipses	**45j–k**
mm	misplaced modifier	**29**	/	slash	**45l–n**
mix	mixed		;	semicolon	**41**
	construction	**30d**	$\check{v}\check{v}$	quotation marks	**44**
			comma	**40**	
no ¶	no paragraph needed	**4**	close up		
num	number	**47f–j**	∧	insert a missing	
				element	
¶	paragraph	**5**	delete		
¶ dev	paragraph development		transpose order		
	needed	**5**			